Flute in the
Marching Band

Flute in the Marching Band

(A White Woman's Non-Fiction Memoir Of The 1965 Selma March For Voting Rights)

Gwen Simon Gain

Library of Congress Control Number:		2010909629
ISBN:	Softcover	978-1-4535-3031-3
	Ebook	978-1-4535-3032-0

This book was printed in the United States of America.

To order additional copies of this book, contact:
Xlibris Corporation
1-888-795-4274
www.Xlibris.com
Orders@Xlibris.com
80546

CONTENTS

*   Names with asterisks mean fictitious name.

Dedicated
To My Children,
Wendi, Ken, Scott and Julie
Who Someday, I Presume,
Will Want To Know
The Details

ACKNOWLEDGMENTS

The author wishes to thank Mary Hill and Estelle Drill who, black and white friends of mine typing together, helped me to set my adventure down in book form back in 1976. Using copious notes taken at the time and place of the 1965 Selma March on Montgomery, many in Gregg shorthand, I attest that every bit of my book is true to the best of my abilities.

Thanks are due also to my husband Robert Smith and my friend Beverley Brown, who gave me moral support throughout the writing, and of course to Rabbi Albert Friedlander, my march companion, and to Mrs. Adelaide Sims, my hostess in Selma, both of whom were key to many of my personal memories.

Several of my children and grandchildren have helped me in the regeneration of my book in 2006. Now that we are well into the computer age forty-five years later, they have helped me with the scanning, the editing, the paging, and the burning onto a CD of the finished manuscript. I can never thank them enough for their support and encouragement. Special thanks are due also, to my grandson Derek Gain who, in 2007, linked my chapters together on my computer and numbered the pages.

And last but not least, my gratitude goes to my mother, Helen Alberty Simon, who not only sent me to Selma, but who was always and forever my biggest fan.

Gwen Simon Gain
June 2010

"Sometimes history and fate meet at a single time, in a single place, to shape a turning point in man's unending search for freedom. So it was at Lexington and Concord. So it was a century ago at Appomatox. So it was last week in Selma, Alabama."

—President Lyndon Johnson, on March 15, 1965 in an address to the Congress of the United States, requesting voting rights legislation that would help Negroes in nine Southern states to register and vote.

BACKGROUND

The time was the mid 1960's: March of 1965, to be exact. The Second World War had been over for twenty years, the Korean "Police Action" for eleven, and once again a nebulous tension was rising in the United States of America. President Kennedy had been assassinated in November of 1963, and the entire country was still recovering from the shock. Young people by the millions were challenging their elders' standards and mores. Young men were being drafted into the military service and sent over to the unending quagmire that was the war in Vietnam, thirty-three thousand of them to die there. Young women's hearts were breaking over the sight on the evening news of many body bags. Pop singers were warbling songs like "Blowin' In The Wind," and "Where Have All The Flowers Gone."

Rioting in black neighborhoods in protest against unfair, discriminatory economic practices had broken out during the long, hot summer of 1964 in several inner cities across the land. Newark. Detroit. Houses and shops and cars were ransacked and burned. Dozens of American citizens, some white, most black, were killed during the melees.

Using techniques from organizing economic boycotts to integrating interstate buses and department store lunch counters, Southern Negroes had since the nineteen fifties been protesting the Jim Crow laws in the South that kept them segregated from the larger society as second-class citizens. Their leader was a young black minister from Georgia, Dr. Martin Luther King, Jr., who advocated and practiced the principles of "non-violence direct action." By that summer of 1964, young white college students from the North, male and female, were heading south in droves to assist their "black brothers and sisters" in demanding civil rights for Negroes. The main issue had become the denial to them of the right to register and vote.

As for me, a white woman of thirty-five with a husband and four children, all of us living in a nice, safe house in Southern New Jersey, a tension had begun rising inside of me, as well. I had been aware since childhood of the denigration and mistreatment of America's Negro population. A practical but committed idealist, I had long appreciated the wisdom of Great Men in regard to the compassionate conduct of one's life; the need to demand justice for all in one's society along with freedom for oneself. And over the years I had fallen more and more in love with the splendid concept of American democracy, and yearned to help bring it at last to full fruition.

For the past few years my husband and I had been volunteers in fair housing efforts in our South Jersey county of Gloucester, which meant accompanying professional black couples in their nearly always unsuccessful efforts to buy or rent housing of their choice in the suburbs. Already sensitized to racial discrimination practices, my disgust and indignation came close to a boiling point over the events occurring in Selma, Alabama, in March of 1965. Several hundred of the city's Negro citizens, many of them women and children and old men, announced their intention to march the fifty-four miles to their state capital of Montgomery, there to hand to the governor a petition. They intended to claim the right of Alabama's adult Negroes to register and vote in city, state and national elections, something that had been denied to them since Reconstruction in the 1870's.

Once across the Edmond Pettus bridge onto Route 80, however, the marchers had been confronted by the Dallas Country sheriff, and ordered to turn around and go back. But before they had a chance to comply, they had been attacked by state troopers on horseback, beaten by bullwhips and sprayed with tear gas. Many had been sickened and injured. The television stations across the nation had shown the entire brutal business in truth-telling black-and-white.

A few days later, this time led by Dr. King himself, as well as by his colleagues in the Southern Christian Leadership Conference, the marchers had been stopped in a street in the so-called Negro Compound of Selma, ordered to go no further, and had been allowed to peacefully retreat. That Saturday a young white Unitarian minister had been attacked and killed on one of Selma's downtown streets. It was then that Dr. King had sent out over the news media a televised plea for help from white Americans. Come march with us this coming Sunday, had been the gist of his message, as we walk out of Selma and head for Montgomery.

And President Lyndon Johnson had made to the nation on TV his famous speech about the historical significance of what was happening in Selma. He had said he was sending to Congress a Civil Rights Bill that, if passed, would end Jim Crow forever.

He had ended his words with the stirring mantra of the Civil Rights Movement, "And we *shall* overcome."

What follows is the story of my participation in that historic event, as well as an explanation of the influences that impelled me, at the time a 35-year-old wife and mother of four young children, to go on a bus from New Jersey to Alabama to march out of town with Martin Luther King.

Gwen Simon Gain   Winter Garden, Florida   June 19, 2010

PART ONE

A NEW DAY

1.

"What men believe is a function of what they are. And what they are is, in part, what has happened to them."
—William Golding, British author,
and writer for Holiday magazine
(from Gwen Gain's "Words To Live By")

"You the white lady that likes to sleep with niggers?"
—Anonymous male phone caller
(Post-Selma comment from one of the folks back home)

March 20, 1965. A new day had dawned bright and clear, almost without me. I opened my eyes just past sunrise to my first Alabama morning and remembered with a rush of astonishment that I was far from home.

Still slumbering peacefully next to me lay the same brown-skinned stranger I had seen asleep on the far side of the double bed when I had crawled in only hours before, well past midnight. Fat pink rollers were stationed in orderly rows about the girl's head, each cylinder silently shaping into one large curl a captured cluster of the girl's jet black hair. Even in the faint light from behind drawn window shades, the carefully smoothed-out sections of hair stood out starkly against the pink plastic of the curlers. Fantastic job, I told myself admiringly. Getting all the strands rolled in like that. I could never have done it on my own hair, I well knew, even if I'd wanted to.

Entranced by the sight, I lay staring at the blissful expression under the pink plastic bonnet. I marveled that a human being of any age or race could sleep so soundly on those self-applied instruments of torture. And then I reflected that my own young Wendi, back in our home in Merchantville, New Jersey, and probably also asleep at this very moment, would be lying on identical hollow cylinders, just as skillfully rolled. She had been positioning them in her shoulder-length blond hair the night before last when I'd bade her goodbye. She did that with such practiced fingers, as if she'd been doing it all her life instead of a mere three years. She wound her hair up nearly every evening at bed time, and slept on identical plastic rollers too.

Strange, I hadn't noticed this trend among Negro females in my country before now. (In that racially and politically ingenuous year of 1965, the large population of American Negroes had not as yet been willing to be labeled "black." And they were years away from accepting "African-American.") I had not noticed that they were striving to achieve the same sleekly flipped-up coiffures as were fashionable with girls and young women in white society. But now that I thought about it as I lay there cozily analyzing—of course! There was Edna, my reliable part-time housekeeper, before she'd found Allah and become a Black Muslim and had to start pulling her hair back from her face in the severe bun her ascetic new lifestyle demanded.

Briefly I pictured in my mind's eye a pre-conversion Edna, coming in the front door of my house in Merchantville, New Jersey, scarf pinned in parachute formation atop her crown to protect her carefully curled set against morning dampness. What a relief that I had long ago outgrown the desire for fashionably sized curls in my own hair along with the need to look like everyone else! No religious experience had been necessary to convince me that a life without hair curlers was much simpler and far more pleasant.

Warm under the blanket and quilt, and smugly satisfied with myself for being where I was and at the same time, so perceptive, I dozed a few minutes longer in the quiet. When I woke again, the room was much lighter. And the girl was still there beside me, slumbering away with her face now turned fully in my direction.

She was much younger than Edna but older than Wendi. No more than eighteen or nineteen, I guessed, studying her features more closely. Thick black lashes lay peacefully upon cheeks the color of smooth chestnuts. She had arrived the night before on her own, I'd been told by the woman of this house. She was from someplace in Georgia. And now here she was, in Selma, Alabama, in the same bed with a complete stranger she had not yet met nor even, judging by the depth of her slumber, laid eyes upon.

My daughter Wendi, on the other hand, was only fifteen. She had wanted to come along with me; indeed had begged me several times to let her come. "Suppose something happens to you, Mom?" she had implored, as if she alone could prevent that. And I had stated flatly that nothing bad was going to happen to me. That her father needed her here at home to help him with the younger kids over the weekend, and that was that.

The sleeper on the other side of the bed dreamed on, oblivious to my visual inspection. One hand was flattened under her cheek to ease the pressure of the mammoth pink curlers. She lay differently from the position in which she had been when I crawled under the covers beside her the night before. Then, her well-fortified head had been only half-turned toward me. Would she be frightened, I asked myself now, to open her eyes and find a caucasian woman nearly twice her age, a stranger, staring her in the face from only inches away? Surely not a thing that had happened to her before. Just as this whole bizarre situation was an entirely new experience for me.

What had I done? Why was I here?

Lifting my head soundlessly so as not to disturb my bedmate, I tore my eyes away from her face and cast them about the unfamiliar room. I noted the faded wallpaper, the simple mahogany veneer bureau and chest of drawers in 1920s style, the face of a Negro man hanging on the far wall. My borrowed knapsack lay in a crumpled heap against the old bureau, nearly buried by my discarded clothes from a few hours before. My purse with the long shoulder strap topped the pile. I should have put that thing somewhere not so visible, I scolded myself. Or at the very least, taken my wallet out and put it beneath my pillow before I went to sleep! And the sleeping bag, also borrowed—good grief, where was it?

And then I remembered. I had loaned the sleeping bag to the rabbi!

We had sat together for hours, Rabbi Friedlander and I, seatmates on the chartered bus ride from New York City to Montgomery. Today should be Saturday, should it not? It had been Thursday, late in the evening, when I left home. But he and I hadn't actually made each other's acquaintance until the next morning's breakfast stop, and that was Friday. Yesterday? Twenty-six hours on the bus, and I had almost lost track of time and which day was which.

After one entire night and the following day—yesterday—and well into last night on the charter bus, Albert Friedlander and I and three other white men had been driven the fifty-four miles from Montgomery to Selma through the blackness and the rain. Maurice, the rabbi who had met us and taken us there in a borrowed car, had been careful never to exceed the speed limit, or do anything else to attract attention, he explained. We had arrived in Selma past midnight, and had been taken immediately to a church in the so-called "Negro Compound," the several-block area where virtually all of Selma's black residents lived.

The rabbi named Maurice had told us as he drove that our most urgent order of business before all others was to register with the March organizers. Exhausted and famished though we were, he had nonetheless dropped three of us—Albert and me and a white man working for a "trade sheet," as he called it—at the side entrance of Brown's African Methodist-Episcopal Chapel, a church simply referred to as Brown's Chapel. We had been welcomed at the door and steered into the dimly lit church office by two young Negro men who seemed to have been waiting up for just this purpose—to greet any and all newcomers. From the cluttered desk behind which they now took a seat, each of us was handed a mimeographed half-sheet of paper which we were asked to fill out. I could see that the form with the faded words on it had been hastily compiled and run off.

Peering at it in the dim light, I was just able to make out the questions. They were similar to the ones I had answered on the bus when I first boarded it a thousand miles away in South Jersey. Name? Address? Home phone number? Next-of-kin, in the event of serious illness or injury? Whom should be notified if bail money had to be posted to get me out of jail? Crazy, I told myself through my exhaustion; such a preposterous idea, my going to jail! But I had gone along with the game, as I had from the beginning. I had pushed aside an ashtray overflowing with cigarette butts to make room on one corner of the desk, and had bent over, legs aching, to print my answers with the pen I had brought along in my shoulder bag.

"Mrs. Gwen Gain. 304 Volan Street, Merchantville, New Jersey." For next-of-kin I had of course written down my husband's name, William Gain, and had supplied his office phone number in Philadelphia and our home number in Merchantville. In answer to the bail question, I printed the name of the Unitarian Church in Cherry Hill, with the minister's name of Edwin Lane beside it. Though my church hadn't sent me here officially, they might be willing to bail me, a long-time choir member, out of jail if circumstances required it. Supplying all this information to someone, even to these two dark young strangers, gave me an immediate sense of security. Somehow it provided a link to that safe life in South Jersey I had left behind.

Speaking casually, the older of the two Negro men had given us three newcomers instructions as he took back our completed forms. If we should be arrested, we should ask to make a call to Dr. King's group, the Southern Christian Leadership Conference Office here in Selma. (Philip Savage, Executive Secretary of the Tri-County NAACP in Philadelphia had already told me that, over the telephone back home. Whom else to call if I were arrested? Keep my number with you, he had said, and use it if you have to.) In the meantime, offer no one any temptation to arrest us. Stay away from the white residential sections of town, as well as the business district, our SCLC advisor now said.

It was especially dangerous to go into the business district, he further warned us. At this, I nodded my head up and down. I knew that was where the Rev. Jim Reeb, the white Unitarian minister from Massachusetts, had been murdered a week ago. But if for some reason we had to go there, the Negro man admonished us now, be sure to let someone at the SCLC office here in the Negro Compound know about it so we could be traced if something went wrong.

We should keep well within the boundaries of the Negro Compound, an area easy to recognize just now because of the police barricades blocking off each street leading into the white areas. Wasn't he aware that the main blockade had been taken down, just tonight? We had learned that from our driver, the trade-sheet man said now.

My brain last night felt ever more frazzled and confused. *No more chit-chat! Please hurry and finish, you guys. I'm so tired! I jus want to find someplace to lie down!*

"And oh, yes, most important!" Now the younger Negro man took over. "Report without fail to First Baptist Church tomorrow morning at ten. Ask anyone how to get there. We require all new arrivals to take orientation in the philosophy and techniques of non-violence. There will also be a mass meeting tomorrow evening beginning at seven here in Brown's Chapel. At that time we'll give everyone the instructions you'll need for the March on Sunday. Keep an eye on the Negro churches' bulletin boards for any changes in plans." He reached into the desk drawer. "Here are your meal tickets for dinner at First Baptist Church tomorrow—I mean today—at five. Don't lose them, it's your only way in." He handed each of the three of us a small card, a ticket converted from some long-past social function at a school I had not yet heard mentioned in press reports: Selma University.

And then the same young man consulted a list on the desk in front of him and made a quick phone call. They had a bed for me with the Sims family in the Negro housing project close by, he told me as he hung up. He would take me there at once. As for the two men in my party, the rabbi and the trade-sheet man, they'd have to sleep on the floor of the church basement, he said, with some of the other out-of-town men who had come to Selma in response to Martin Luther King's plea for help over national television. There were no longer any beds available for the men in private homes, he said. He was sorry.

Albert Friedlander, my new friend from the bus, had merely smiled his cherubic smile, eyes bleary behind the super-thick lenses of his good eyeglasses. "That's fine!" he said cheerfully. "Thank you!" And turning in my direction, he said, "Good, Gwen!" about the sleeping arrangements for me.

Looking back into Rabbi Friedlander's tired eyes, I remembered the spare pair of eyeglasses tucked away in his breast pocket, the ones he had brought along from his home in New York City, he'd told me, in case anything "well . . . happens to my good pair." Except for the small shaving kit dangling by a strap around his wrist, he had brought with him no luggage at all.

"I'm afraid we're fresh out of cots downstairs," the young Negro man apologized, referring to the church basement. "More folks showed up than we counted on. I can give you each a blanket, though . . . ." And his Southern black patois trailed off in obvious embarrassment.

That was when I had told the rabbi to take my sleeping bag, for heaven's sake, that I obviously wasn't going to need it. And gratefully he had untied it from beneath my knapsack. Making hasty arrangements to meet again on the morrow so I could retrieve the borrowed sleeping bag, we had parted. He and the other white man had gone with the older Negro to find empty spots to spread out their blankets on the basement floor.

As for me, I obediently followed the lanky second young Negro man out of the dark and empty church. He loped shyly along in the damp and cold March air, setting our direction, my knapsack perched like a featherweight upon one of his shoulders. By this time my legs from thigh to ankle were protesting with aches with every step I took.

At least the rain had stopped, I noticed with relief as we crossed a muddy street and went down half a block to our destination. Maybe a good omen for the March from Selma to Montgomery, scheduled to begin on Sunday morning. Tomorrow!

*   *   *

2.

> "Born equal? When so many—
> "Look 'round you—are inferior?
> "In God's name, who believes—?
> None but the superior!"
> —Mark Van Doren, American poet and historian
> (From my collection of "Words To Live By")

So I had been brought to this apartment in the George Washington Carver Homes, a low-income housing project, shortly after midnight. Thin and tawny "Miz Sims" had gotten up from sleep and stood waiting at the back door in misshapen robe and age-vented slippers to give me welcome. Her yellow-tan face had remained serene as she thanked my Negro escort and bade him good night, just as calmly as if being presented a white woman overnight guest from the North at twelve-thirty in the morning were an everyday occurrence.

She had told me her name was Adelaide, and then she had taken my knapsack from my unprotesting hands and put me in a chair at her kitchen table. She had gotten out hard cheese and bread and a glass of cold milk. She had sat down at the table with me while I ate and drank. Smoking a cigarette, she listened attentively while I told her where I'd come from.

"New Jersey," I said. "South Jersey, actually. Just across the Delaware River from Philadelphia."

And how many children had I left behind? "Four, and a husband as well." And I told her how my equilibrium was temporarily out of whack because of the long bus ride, and other details of my life similarly unimportant considering the lateness of the hour.

"How long you been trav'lin, Miz Gains?" she had finally asked. No sense bothering to explain to her just then, I told myself, that there was no "s" at the end of my last name. No "e," nor "es" either. Not the time to say, the way I often had to do, *It's just plain Gain, like in the soap powder. The opposite of loss.* No, not if we were going to be on a first-name basis with each other, as I fully intended should happen. One thing at a time, I told myself.

She was waiting for me to answer her question. "I don't know how long," I said. "Let's see, I'm not sure. Twenty-seven hours, I guess. Without stopping for more than a few minutes at a rest stop every now and then." I explained to her that a charter bus had come down the New Jersey Turnpike from New York City. That it had picked me up at ten o'clock Thursday night, at one of the exits in South Jersey close to where I lived. "Ten o'clock Eastern Standard Time, that is. We're an hour ahead of you in New Jersey. So I'm not really sure how long . . ." I let my voice trail off. "Do you have children, Adelaide?" I asked.

"Yes, ma'am. Six younguns." No mistaking the pride in her voice.

"Six! You've got me beaten by two. Any little ones?"

"Oh, yes, ma'am. There's Willis, he's ten now. An' George be eight. The baby Oscar—he be two last month. My other three is teenagers. Charlie, he's the bigges' one. Charlie's gonna go to Atlanta soon to be a fieldworker for SCLC." She told me this last in a conspiratorial tone, words pouring forth in a rapid staccato made even more difficult to comprehend by her Alabama drawl.

"Don't you have any girls, Adelaide? I counted four boys' names," I said.

And Adelaide said, "Yes, ma'am. Cissy and Claire. Cissy's fourteen and Claire, she's jus' thirteen." And I said, "I've got two daughters too. They're fifteen and five. Wendi and Julie. My boys are twelve and eight. Their names are Kenny and Scotty. But listen, Adelaide—I wish you wouldn't call me ma'am. You don't have to, you know."

"No, ma'am . . . . Miz Gains," and she grinned self-consciously as she corrected herself. For the first time I noticed that one of her eyes failed to focus correctly, turning inward when it shouldn't. It was out of synchronization with the other one. The strange, cross-eyed look it gave her was not unpleasant. Just unexpected.

"No—please! Call me Gwen. Unless you'd like me to call you Mrs. Sims?"

"Oh, no, ma'am! Everybody in Selma call me Adelaide," she said.

"Okay, then!" I said. "It's settled, all right? You'll call me Gwen, and I'll call you Adelaide. And please, Adelaide, no more 'ma'am'?"

"No, ma'—Gwen," but I could tell it made her uneasy to say it. Maybe I should not have pursued that just yet. Good lord, I'd been in this nice woman's house for fifteen minutes and already I was setting the rules.

Trying to alter the caste customs of more than three hundred years, and making this kind soul uncomfortable in the process. Albert Friedlander was right; I was indeed an iconoclast! I should shut my trap and eat, so we could both go to bed.

But my hostess seemed in no hurry to end the conversation. Pressing upon me my second round of milk and cheese, she told me her husband did day labor for a factory just outside of the city. She herself worked as a janitress for the Selma school system, cleaning the rooms of one school on a regular basis and sometimes helping out in the cafeteria. The colored people of Selma had been fearful lately, she told me, of losing their jobs. They'd been told by the superintendent of schools that any school employee seen participating in the voter registration drive sponsored by Martin Luther King's Southern Christian Leadership Conference here in Dallas County would be fired immediately.

But the children, the colored children of Selma, they just wouldn't listen to their elders, Adelaide bemoaned. Her Charlie, in particular. He had been outspoken about his right to help in the Movement, as they called the SCLC's civil rights campaign to win the vote for Southern Negroes. As a result, he'd been beaten and arrested, trying to march to Montgomery Sunday before last, "and he be only a child of seventeen . . ." Adelaide's words trailed off.

By this time feeling comfortably full, I had taken my turn to listen, and I had done so with horrified admiration, gazing across the table into the intelligent face etched with worry lines and calm no longer. Adelaide's expression bore a mixture of pride and apprehension as she spoke of the stubborn courage of Selma' s colored children, her own son in particular. At times, words and whole phrases were unintelligible to me, as my ears were not yet attuned to her speech, which was slurred at times, and overlaid with the accents of the Deep South.

But there was no mistaking the message in that face. Something big was being played out here in Selma, and Adelaide was, if only vicariously through a mother's concern, playing a part in it. Something dangerous, true; but also something potentially full of nobility. Listening and watching and asking a question now and then, I had fought back memories of our colored maid Unity, of the beloved brown-skinned face that had been such a part of my childhood in South Jersey. I tried not to focus on the pain I had brought to her features when I, with ten-year-old naivete, had once demanded of her, "*Unity, why don't you nee-groes just get together and tell the movie manager you're not going to sit in the balcony any longer? Maybe the kids could do it, if the rest of you are afraid to . . . . Nobody would hurt children, I don't think . . . ."*

It had seemed such a good idea to suggest to her, back then. And Unity had told me bluntly that she never went to the movies, her religion didn't permit it. And I had tried to imagine a life without Shirley Temple and Tailspin Tommy and *Gone With The Wind.*

But that was long ago, and I was here in Adelaide Sims' kitchen in March of 1965, and it was past one a.m. by her kitchen clock—two, by my body's time—and I remembered I was dead-tired. Adelaide apparently realized it at the same instant. She stubbed out her final cigarette, and first rinsing my glass and plate in the sink that doubled as a laundry tub, she led the way through the darkened living room. In a drawled whisper, she had pointed out the way upstairs, and told me to go in the bedroom door straight back at the end of the hall. She whispered an apology that I'd have to share the bed with a girl who'd arrived for the march only a short while before, that same evening. I hadn't stopped to ask if the girl had any idea she'd have a bedmate.

I murmured back, "Good night, Adelaide. See you tomorrow."

"Night, Miz Gains. You sleep well, hear?"

"Thanks for everything." Again in a whisper.

"Don' say no more. I must say, I'm so very happy you came to me."

With those murmured words of gratitude in my ears, I had crept up the wooden steps in the shadowy light from the bare bulb in the ceiling. I had clutched knapsack and shoulder bag tight to my breast as I moved, analyzing the while that this entire project, this march-for-voting-rights business, seemed a bit like playing a game of Underground Railroad, only in the twentieth century when people were supposed to be civilized, for Pete's sake. The problem was that in this kind of game—in spite of what the rabbi had said to reassure me on the bus—a person really could get hurt. Tired though I was, I had to force myself to face that fact and to remember that I was far from home, among strangers. From now on, I should make myself exercise some degree of caution and stop trusting instantly every person I met.

Resolving thus, I had flicked on the overhead light in the bedroom at the end of the hall, sized up my surroundings and bedmate in brief seconds, and flicked the switch to off again. I had undressed and located my flannel pajamas in the depths of my knapsack by feel in the dark. I had climbed in beside the silent brown figure in the weird pink helmet, and hoped for the best. My resolve to be more cautious had been overcome by my fatigue, and I had slept with the abandon and innocence of childhood, until dawn came.

*   *   *

3.

"If you had gone to college when you were eighteen, instead of getting married, you'd have done all this then. This is something that kids do."
—Aunt Hazel McCalley, my friend and mentor (Post-Selma comment from one of my favorite folks back home)

By morning light from behind tattered window shades that Saturday morning, I could see that it must be Adelaide's own room I and the pink-curlered sleeper were sharing. I guessed that Adelaide herself was probably downstairs on the living room couch. There had been no sign of her husband the night before. But he could be in another bedroom, or in the kids' room, perhaps. Who knew

No use for me to try to sleep longer, in spite of the fact that I'd gotten to bed so late. For two years now, since becoming a Continuing Education student at the University of Pennsylvania, I'd been accustomed to getting up at four in the morning to study. And my internal clock would not be fooled for long, even in this foreign environment. I could barely see the hands of my watch, since my reading eyes were going bad, but I decided it must be close to seven. My stomach was growling gently, demanding food again, and I was worried the girl beside me would hear, and be alarmed.

Sliding out of bed carefully so as not to squeak the springs more than absolutely necessary, I gathered up most of my belongings and tiptoed down the silent hallway and into the bathroom next door to get dressed. I washed with a washcloth I had brought with me, and combed and teased and pinned up my long hair into its customary French twist. I put on the clean double-knit blue dress I had also brought along, folded carefully in the bottom of the knapsack in a paper bag from the A&P. As I did so, I remembered the debate I'd had with myself before my departure from home.

Should I take another dress besides the one I'd be wearing on the bus? Or would a pair of slacks and a shirt be more appropriate? I had finally decided on the blue dress, my reasoning being that I was going South, where people were more conservative. So perhaps I should try to convey the appearance of being a lady. (What matter whether I was or not, as long as I *looked* like one? I had asked myself coyly.) Who would take offense at an innocent-looking white lady walking down the street, even in the company of a few hundred other, like-minded "outside agitators", and wearing a dress? I wanted to present as slight a threat as possible, at least as an individual, to the already angered white citizens of Alabama; the ones who might otherwise take it into their heads to beat me, as they had the Selma Negro women and children two weeks earlier on national television. It was the same reasoning that had impelled me to wear my good black coat with the fake fur collar, instead of the older, colorful red one. Not because the black was warmer, though ordinarily, that would have been my first consideration, since I hated to be the least bit cold. No, let's face it: I had chosen the black coat this time in order to be inconspicuous, to blend, to make myself less of a target for some white racist's gun.

I smiled into the bathroom mirror with a mouthful of toothpaste, recalling that mental debate I had had back home. Silly, I saw it now, to think they'd attack a woman of "their own kind," no matter how she was dressed. Furthermore, maybe our presence (there would surely be other white women there) would exert a calming influence. Perhaps we'd remind them of their own mothers and their renowned Southern code of conduct would stay their hands, and keep them from attacking anyone among us, male or female.

That was why I had come. Wasn't it? To remind them?

No one was going to get hurt anyhow, we all felt pretty sure of that now. We had gotten the message on the bus on the way down. One of the SNICK youths from New York City had picked up the news report on his portable radio, and it had quickly been passed from the back to the front of the bus, row by row, quietly but with elation. Even though most of the passengers had come not to march out of Selma, but to stay in Montgomery, the capital of Alabama, to help with the ongoing voter registration drive.

"President Johnson has called out the Army troops from Fort Bragg," the message went. "They'll be there to protect the marchers on Sunday!"

"Wonderful news! So you see, Gwen, no one's going to get hurt," the rabbi had told me from his aisle seat beside me. He had brought nothing along with him but an extra pair of eyeglasses and a shaving kit with a leather wrist strap, just so he'd be certain to have both hands free (to break any falls, I assumed he meant). Thursday evening he had gone home from his office where he was Jewish chaplain at Columbia University in New York City, kissed his wife Evelyn and little daughter Ariel goodbye, and left to catch the charter bus leaving the city at five p. m. I could not help but admire his ability to rise higher above the need for material comforts than I had done. And at the same time, I was happy that I'd brought the sleeping bag along to lend him when we'd arrived in Selma last night.

As for me, I'd tried to keep my own accouterments to a minimum. I surveyed them now where they sat in a neat pile on the toilet lid. My well wrinkled clothes from yesterday's long journey, the paper bag still containing a second change of underwear and stockings. A comb and some bobby-pins and a tube of lipstick. A toothbrush and paste, and the flannel pajamas I'd just climbed out of. An old washcloth and towel from our camping gear back home. And last but not least, the item I treasured most, a very small loose-leaf notebook with a blue vinyl cover.

These few things would have to do me for the entire four days I expected to be away from my home in Merchantville. As I packed everything back into the knapsack, I told myself with smug assurance that it was a good thing that as a child I had learned to be adaptable. Just one of the many rewards of growing up third in a large family of nine sisters.

I kept the small notebook out and slipped it into my shoulder bag for safer keeping. That notebook was my "Bible," the only Good Book I had ever needed, or wanted. It was an agnostic's thesaurus of beautiful sayings, gleaned from everywhere and copied onto sheets of lined paper in my awkward left-handed cursive writing, one to a page. There were inspiring insights recorded there, from Thomas Jefferson and St. Francis of Assisi, from Jesus of Nazareth and Ro'bert Frost and Martin Luther King, Jr. and you-name-it, even one from an often perspicacious lesbian schoolteacher I had befriended a few years back.

For a long time I'd been collecting my favorite literary gems into that notebook, my bits and pieces from the wisdom of the ages. Those entries gave me an awed sense of oneness with great minds, no matter when or where or how their owners had lived. I called them *My Words To Live By*. I even dared include an occasional gem of my own making. Not out of arrogance, but in recognition of my innate link with thinking and feeling humanity. Because I, too, had a brain. One that produced such pseudo-sage literary observations as: "I am a composite of so many qualities: Intelligence. Ignorance. Simplicity. Complexity. They fight in me and make of me a Neutral, a Nothing. June 1962."

Yes, that little notebook was indeed my treasure. I had begun it ten years earlier at the time of my father's death, when my older sisters and I had discovered a similar little book in his top bureau drawer. After the funeral I had bought my own little book at the dimestore, and copied some of his favorites onto my own blank pages, to give me a start. I'd brought my notebook along with me on this trip not, as one might suppose, for reinforcement of my passionate idealism, or even for inspiration, since I carried on the tip of my conscience too many exhortations to right society's wrongs as it was. I brought that small but inspiring treasure with me only because at the last minute I'd decided I might need something to make notes in, and there were still plenty of blank pages in the back.

I realized now that I hadn't been very smart to do that. Suppose it got lost? Or worse, someone took it forcibly from me? I'd have to start all over again, and much of its carefully selected contents would be lost to me forever. Best to keep it here in my shoulder bag which I always held close to my body, instead of in the bulky knapsack.

At last, on that new day in Selma, I considered myself ready to greet the world—this one insignificant part of it. I stood for a moment in the middle of Adelaide Sims' bathroom, listening to the peaceful silence of the sleeping house. Feeling a little frumpy in my sturdy tie shoes and nylon stockings and wrinkled blue dress, I was nevertheless grateful that this had not been, for me, the wrong time of the month.

I had long wondered how female ballet dancers managed in that condition, especially if they also suffered from abdominal cramps—how vulnerable and weak they must feel, and how unflinchingly they had to hide their condition, doing their job so well that their audiences could never tell. Women who wanted to be civil rights demonstrators fell roughly into the same class, I supposed. They too had to be, like ballet dancers, "on their toes" at all times, and tell themselves to heck with monthly female complications, life must go on. But I was still relieved that I had that one less problem to deal with. Chuckling beneath my breath at the pun I had just made to myself about being on my toes, I examined my face again in the mirror above the sink.

An ordinary person with a pinky-beige WASP face stared back at me with the familiarity born of long acquaintance. She was a person considered by others for all her days to be a white female, Anglo-Saxon, Protestant. The body that stood beneath the face in the mirror was a little pudgy, I guessed, but I told myself that you couldn't have everything. One-hundred-

and-thirty-five pounds were distributed fairly pleasantly, I thought, over my five-foot-five frame.

I was definitely no Debbie Reynolds; but then I had never aspired to be. My mousy-brown hair was worn that year in my own version of a French twist, one that required only a minute or two to twist around and bobby-pin in place at the back of my head and swirl in a circle at the top. I had no indication yet of the double chin I felt sure would be coming some day far in the future. And people still gasped—in genuine disbelief, surely!—when I told them how old I was. Yes, there in the mirror, I did look somewhat younger than my thirty-five years, I had to appreciate that. But it wasn't because of anything I did, or had done. My mouth, too, met with my approval as long as it stayed closed; but when I smiled, the top row of my not-quite-even teeth revealed a slight flatness across the front. As if someone had bashed me once for talking too much.

In the mirror my eyes looked strained, reminding me again that these twenty-twenty wonders of my youth could no longer discern the whorls in my fingertips and that I would probably have to go soon for reading glasses. Maybe just as soon as I got back home. Presbyopia, at thirty-five! I hadn't counted on that. Well, at least it wasn't amblyopia, the crossed eyes that poor Adelaide Sims,my hostess here in Selma, appeared to have. At least I didn't have that! She'd probably never had a chance at good eye care, poor thing. She hadn't been one of the privileged, as I had been. For one moment, I hated knowing that.

I held up my fingers in the faint light of the bathroom to search the tips again for whorls, and noted instead that most of my unpolished fingernails were too short to be glamorous. I deliberately kept them short so as to be able to type fast without too many errors. But the skin around them, I now saw, were ragged with flecks of dead cuticle. The calves of my legs, I knew without having to look, were just as unsmooth beneath the nylon stockings. I'd had varicose veins swelling both calves since the birth of Scotty, my third child. Occasionally, when I had to sit for any long period of time, my legs throbbed with a distracting intensity, as they had begun to do on the bus yesterday on the way south to Selma, Alabama, one thousand miles away from Merchantville, New Jersey.

My reflection was still there in the bathroom mirror, looking impatient to be off. Ceasing the inspection of my hands, I looked up again and for the first time since leaving home, I inquired of my image looking back at me in the glass what a thirty-five-year-old woman with poor circulation and bad veins in her legs and pollen allergies and a tendency toward indigestion was doing here in this place? Especially one who hadn't been prudent enough to bring along either Alka-Seltzer or anti-histamines?

Why was I not home where I belonged, tending to my children and my husband and my house and going to my job and my classes at the University of Pennsylvania? Taking letters in shorthand from my wonderful boss, Connie Richardson? Choosing my college major? That decision had to be made by the end of March, I had been told by my college advisor, and I was as far from a decision as I had been when I started out half-time at Penn two years ago. I should be busy this very minute outlining the research paper on interracial marriage I had to write for my American Government class and turn in by the end of the semester in May. I should be translating the next two chapters of *I Promessi Sposi* (The Engaged Couple) for my Italian professor, who always beamed at me because I could read passages of it so well when he called on me. Mental athletics were what I had always handled best. Not this physical endurance challenge.

Listen, the stern eyes in the familiar face said back, you're not all that hopeless a human being. You can still walk a few miles, and stand on your head for two minutes, and parallel-park a car in one S-swoop backwards. And you do belong here, you know that. You're familiar enough with the wrongs of American society when it comes to the treatment of Negroes. My Darling Nellie Gray came along when you were two or three. Then there were the haunted eyes of those Negroes after the race riot in Detroit when you were thirteen. The lynching picture you saw in a magazine when you were ten. The sad faces of that handsome Negro couple who wanted to rent the apartment you viewed with them last year as a volunteer. The Negro children at the movies in Woodbury, where you grew up; the kids who could only sit upstairs in the balcony. Unity, whose nephew in the Navy could not do anything better than wait on a white admiral. And another nephew who flew P-51 fighter planes with red tails in World War II and guarded the big bombers on their runs. Lots and lots of other scenes cropping up from the whole of your past. And not just Negroes. You've been getting conditioned much of your own life to what it's like to be discriminated against, just because you're a female.

Mr. Rafferty*, please, I want to play my flute in the marching band!

Besides, this is Saturday morning, remember? And if you were home at this very minute, you'd be dressed in jeans and T-shirt and down in the kitchen, just starting your second load of wash with three more piles of dirty clothes to go. You'd be getting out the vacuum cleaner, and feeding the cat, and helping Julie with her breakfast. You'd be making out a grocery list for this afternoon, and setting up papers on the dining room table, preparatory to writing out checks to pay the bills that would come due by the first of next month. Bill would be out on the sun porch just off the living room, drafting up a set of plans for a client. And your other three children would be going happily about their Saturday pursuits, glad for two whole days off from school.

So what kind of contribution would all that ordinary mothering stuff be doing toward improving the lives of suffering humanity? *"Never send to know for whom the bell tolls. It tolls for thee."* The English poet John Donne had written that. So get going, girl! Those other obligations can come later, after this unpleasant business here in Selma has been taken care of.

*   *   *

<h1 style="text-align:center">4.</h1>

"The God who gave us life, gave us liberty at the same time,"

—Thomas Jefferson
(From Gwen Gain's "Words To Live By")

The brown-skinned girl in the pink plastic helmet was awake and eying me when I sneaked back into the bedroom to leave my packed knapsack in a corner and get my coat. Her sleepy eyes followed me as I moved across the room. I noted she had turned onto her back and propped her head forward against the pillow so the fat curlers would take less of the weight.

"Hi!" I said. I slipped my arms into my coat and buttoned the buttons.

"Hi," she said, barely loud enough for me to hear.

"I'm Mrs. Gain," I said. "Gwen, that is." *That's right. Don't pull any age rank on this person either. But you in the bed there—please don't say, yes, ma'am!*

"I'm from New Jersey," I added, when she said nothing back. "I got in pretty late last night. I hope I didn't disturb you."

"No, ma'am." She smiled shyly back at me, lighting up the pretty face inside the wreath of curlers. "ma'am". A response taught to all Southern children, be they black or white.

"What's *your* name?" I asked. I slid my shoulder bag, over my head and one arm.

"Dorothy," she replied. *Never any last names. As if they still aren't entitled to one.*

"Where you from, Dorothy?" was my next question. *She's still sleepy. I'll bet she wishes I'd drop dead—or at least, go away and let her sleep.*

"Tuskegee. I go to the Institute," she said. I had learned in my Race Relations class at Penn that the college she referred to had been founded by the famous black educator Booker T. Washington. The girl had pronounced the name Tuskegee with a hard "g", and thereby cleared up for me one of my life's minor mysteries. I had seldom heard the word pronounced before.

"I came on a charter bus," I volunteered. "How'd *you* get here?"

She required two syllables to produce her response in her soft Southern drawl.

"Hee-itched," she said.

This baby! Hitching rides—! If she were my daughter . . . ! And then I got a mental picture of myself, standing here in the bedroom of a Negro family's apartment in Selma, Alabama and guessed what my own mother, a widow who lived in Florida with my two youngest sisters, would have to say about what *I* had done.

My hand on the doorknob to go out, I smiled at young Dorothy and told her she might want to consider the wisdom of going back to sleep, it was still quite early. I said that I was a morning person and just could not help being one, no matter what time I went to bed at night, and that I was well aware it was annoying to other people. I told her that I'd see her later. Tonight.

Without another word, not even so much as a timid "yes, ma'am," Dorothy rolled gratefully over to her position of the night before, only the tips of her pink curlers showing above the hem of her blanket. I had had to choke back the impulse to tell her how lovely her hair would look for the march tomorrow. A remark like that might sound too much like Wendi's mother. Dorothy might take it for sarcasm, the way my daughter Wendi almost certainly would have. Or "You're just saying that because you're my mother," Wendi would have said, implying that my opinion didn't count for anything.

Stealthily I tiptoed through the hall to the steps I had ascended only a few hours earlier. Through a wide-open door to a bedroom as I passed by, I caught a glimpse of another double bed, widthwise across which were sprawled, in various postures of sleep and with blankets askew, a covey of Negro children. My eyes registered four heads. Some of Adelaide's six,

I guessed. The three young boys and one of the teen-aged daughters, I suspected.

Questions came rushing to my mind. Did they usually sleep like that, all in the same bed? Where did Adelaide's other two children sleep? Were there other guests behind the closed door of the third bedroom? How far had this large family put itself out to welcome strangers invited in on such short notice? Thus pondering, I continued down the stairs as quietly as possible. I crept past a blanket-shrouded figure on the living room couch. Adelaide? Her husband? Or the older boy just out of high school?

The kitchen was unoccupied and showed no signs of use since Adelaide and I had parted five or six hours ago. My hostess had given me instructions as to where to go for breakfast. Still walking noiselessly, I went out of the apartment, pulling the back door shut as quietly as possible behind me.

The basement of the Tabernacle Church, one of the places in charge of providing breakfast that weekend for all Northern visitors, was teeming with activity that must at any other time have been unusual, even for a Saturday morning. It was true the Negro residents of Selma had had little advance notice in which to prepare for the white inundation they hoped was coming in answer to Martin Luther King's televised plea for help a few days ago. But they had quickly and nobly recognized that the first order of business for assuring the success of an army of any kind was food. They had found a way to assuage somehow, on a regular and continuing basis for no one knew how long, the hunger pangs of this peaceful army's collective stomach.

Negro men and women, members of the Tabernacle Church as well as of other churches in the surrounding Negro Compound, were in the final stages of preparing and setting up for a morning meal they intended would not soon be forgotten (at least not until lunchtime). The tantalizing smell of eggs and bacon and sausage and biscuits filled the air. The big room was already teeming with visitors, both black and white. Most were standing around and talking with each other. The orderly pandemonium was both comforting and soul-stirring to a refugee from a long and confining bus ride. On our swift journey of a thousand miles, hot food, as well as time to eat it, had been in short supply.

I expected to have to wait patiently in a long line for something to eat. Barely had I walked through the double doors of the basement hall, however, than I was steered by an elderly gentleman to a serving counter, where I found myself confronted by platters and pans of savory delectibles. Standing behind it, ready to assist me, were women in aprons, as well as a few men. Most of the serving staff were Negro, a few of them white, each server with a skin of a different hue. Their faces were invariably split with smiles. They spoke to me in accents of Southern black or Northern white, all their words vibrant with cordiality as I passed along the serving line.

"Kin ah he'p ya, ma'am?" "Do you need butter for that biscuit?" "Dese sauges be raht good, ma'am. Kin ah give ya some?" "The coffee's over here, it's good and hot!"

The Negroes behind the tables needed no explanations as to why all we white visitors were there, in their town and in their church. By their welcoming smiles and kindly voices they conveyed that they were grateful we had come. Squirming inwardly as I loaded up my plate, I wanted to apologize to all of the Negroes, for not having taken a stand beside them sooner. I yearned to be able to tell them what I had been doing back home to try to help. But of course I could not, not then. The line had to keep moving.

I ate the first grits of my life that morning at the Tabernacle Church in the Negro Compound of Selma. I relished the steaming pile of rather tasteless white lumps along with the familiar taste of warm scrambled eggs and buttered toast and two plump sausages. A paper cupful of hot black coffee and a freshly baked doughnut finished off the meal.

Being among the earliest arrivals, I thought I could take my time sitting at one of the long folding tables set up all over the low-ceilinged room. But as the cafeteria line near the service counter grew longer and the chairs filled to near capacity, I hurriedly finished my last bites and turned over my knife and fork and plate to the eager hands waiting to take them to be washed for use by another guest, newly arrived.

"Is there anything I can do to help?" I asked the person who took my dirty eating utensils.

The question had popped out before I knew it, the habit of seventeen years of being a grown-up female responsible for looking after the needs of a husband and children. Not that I particularly enjoyed the doing of what was considered "women's work" It was the assisting of another woman to get through hers that would give me pleasure and a sense of accomplishment. I could look into the small kitchen behind the service counter and see that it was already jammed with bustling women and that several of them back there were white.

"Wait raht there, honey." The buxom brown-skinned woman in the huge apron went into the kitchen. She was back in seconds.

"Not jes now. But can ya come back in an houah, honey?" she said. "We'll be needin' someone then to he'p put the grits on the plates."

"All right," I looked at my watch. That would be nine-thirty. I would come back then.

"Better not sign up for anything that late," a male voice said behind me. "The orientation meeting starts at ten over at Brown's Chapel. They have two a day, but you're supposed to make the first one after you get here."

The man who had spoken up at my elbow just then was one of the white strangers who had been in the car from Montgomery the night before, when I had been half asleep. Yet I was awake enough to hear him telling the driver that he was a trade sheet reporter from New York City. His body had been permanently scarred by cigarette burns inflicted by police during the time he once spent in the Birmingham jail. They didn't cotton to nigger-lovers, was the excuse they gave him. Now he too was turning in his plate and silverware.

"But—but the grits !" I stammered back "I said I'd help!"

' "This is more important, believe me," he said. And he went off to find a corner of a table where he hoped he could sit undisturbed to write his daily report for his publication. He had been here for several days, he had told me; enough time to know the ropes. I should have asked him why he was in the borrowed car last night, taking the trip with me from Montgomery to Selma. He had needed to go to Montgomery to file his reports, perhaps?

I turned back to the dirty-dish handler, who had been listening.

She said, "Thas all raht, honey. Don't ya worry none, ya hear?" and she turned away, too busy to talk further.

I was disappointed. It would have been nice to meet some of the people working in the kitchen. Nice to find out if any of the white women there had left four young children at home a thousand miles away, as I had done.

Other than the conscientious reporter, I had spotted no one I knew among the ever-increasing numbers of white faces coming into the basement; not one person, black or white, I could greet in even faint recognition. I had unreasoningly assumed that Albert Friedlander, my rabbi friend, would be up early and eager to get about, the same as I. I choked back my disappointment at his continued absence.

And then I scolded myself. What had I expected when I first set out on this wild adventure, anyhow? A constant companion to lend me moral support? Someone to whom I could verbalize my doubts and my guilts on a regular basis? I should use my eyes and ears more, and my mouth less, and stop pathetically searching every face I encountered, looking for a friend.

Outside once more in the chilly March air, I watched two Negro kids taking canned goods from the open kitchen window of the church and tossing them up, one by one, to two other boys standing in the back of a truck parked alongside. One of the necessary preparations for tomorrow's march? I guessed. Everyone here seemed to have a task to do but me. Everyone seemed so organized. Everyone but me.

I walked several blocks alone under the cloudy sky and budding tree limbs, forcing myself to observe, for a change, instead of analyzing. I nodded only a friendly hello to the occasional strangers, both black and white, mostly men, who passed by me. All of them were obviously converging with empty stomachs upon the Tabernacle Church, the designated place for visitors from out of town to get breakfast that morning. As they hurried along, they seemed scarcely to notice me. None of them came in groups. They walked along singly, or in pairs. Middle-aged, mostly. Clean-shaven types, some wearying white clerical collars. Most of them appeared groggy with sleep and not anxious to communicate with anyone until they'd had that first cup of coffee.

The white women I had wondered about since leaving home? They too were there, hastening along in their tweed skirts and head scarves. They looked to be straight out of the pages of their church directories up North, their names listed under "Social Action Committee" (a member of which I was not). Younger, college-age characters of both races and sexes were also hurrying toward breakfast, their faded jeans and khaki shirts their only bulwark against the cold. There were a few white girls with straggly hair to their shoulders; white boys with stubbles on their faces from not having shaved for several days.

A few of the Negroes hurrying by me looked to be a different sort, not like visitors. Middle-aged and older, they were mostly neatly and conservatively dressed, with intense expressions on their faces for the most part. Church members, I surmised, maybe assigned to the serving line? But had they gotten out of bed too late and now felt themselves to be in disgrace for not being at their "battle stations?" How could I know? I resolved to talk to as many people as I reasonably could, from now on. I'd have conversations with people from both races, in order to get more insight into what circumstances brought them here, to this place, at this time. And maybe I could also find out what was going on.

Funny thing. As long as I stuck to the center of the Negro Compound, I felt secure and unafraid, even relatively inconspicuous in spite of my caucasian face and pinky-beige skin color. I wandered up one unpaved street and down another, examining the houses on either side as I passed by. The one-story wood structures were huddled close together in an odd assortment of shapes and colors. Very small they were, all of them badly in need of paint. Most of them had ramshackle porches built onto the front. Most of the porches looked bowed down and over-powered by the ancient trees that hung low over their roof tops. Budding green shoots on long branches were beginning to shut out the sun, now that spring was almost here.

The houses in the Negro Compound were for the most part antiquated and neglected, settled close on either side of the dirt streets. It seemed to me the houses were still imprisoned, like the Negroes who lived in them, by the slavery shackles of the past. Only the George Washington Carver Homes, a relatively new public housing project of six or seven two-story red-brick buildings, appeared sturdy enough to survive the next quarter century. Those, and the several old brick churches scattered here and there. And none of the streets I wandered that morning were paved. Not a single one.

But the houses, humble as they were, were homes, and I guessed they'd be around for decades to come anyhow. Negro families lived in them, and would continue to live in them, come what may. I spotted colorful curtains at some of the windows; lots of old chairs on the sagging porches for sitting in at day's end. Children lived here too; children who had not yet grown and whose dreams had not yet died. Stifling the sudden twinges of loneliness caused by the mental picture of all these unseen families I was passing by, and none of them mine!—I reminded myself that I ought to be a little grateful for this unexpected time of freedom.

For I was indeed free. So completely and unchallengingly free, here in the confines of Selma's Negro Compound, that it made me as uneasy to recognize the fact of it as Adelaide Sims had been the night before, when she'd tried to stop calling me ma'am and use my first name instead. Free of my own middle-income customs: the dishwasher to load and unload, the checks to write out for the never-ending pile of bills, the mysterious forms waiting back home to fill out in order to pay any federal income tax due by the first of April.

I was free of the never-ending weekends spent running too many clothes for six through an automatic washer and dryer, with the Sunday evening folding and sorting still ahead. Free of the vacuum cleaner that had to be run through seven rooms and up a flight of steps, all of the rooms at least twice the size of any of Adelaide's. And yes; my college requirements superimposed upon all of that. Today I was free of books that had to be read and assignment papers researched; free of dictation to be taken and letters to be typed for my boss at Penn. Free, too, I had to remember, of the confining and defining police barricades, the ones that until this morning, had separated us SCLC march recruits from the streets where the white folks of Selma lived. I had not had to see those barricades, and now had no idea in which direction they had been erected.

All at once I noticed that not a human being, Negro or white, was in sight. There was no sign of life anywhere around at this moment. It was strange that no dogs barked; no cars moved along the mud-streaked street in either direction. My instinct for survival aroused, I looked furtively around for hints of danger. Had I wandered too far? No; no evidences of white prosperity were anywhere. The streets were all rutted dirt, in every direction. I was safe. But here, several blocks from the Negro churches where all the activity was centered, the area was a ghost town, and I, it seemed, was the ghost. I had been transported from my accustomed aura of responsibility and set down, voiceless and invisible and without duty, in this foreign place.

Still amazed at the truth of my new and surprising freedom, I sat down gingerly on a crumbling brick wall at the edge of an empty, weed-strewn lot. And for the first time since leaving home a day and two nights ago, I permitted myself to give more than mere passing thought to the four children I had left behind, children with dreams of their own.

*   *   *

5.

"*My* first duty is to my children."
—Mrs. Sally Wilson*, Member,
Unitarian Church of Cherry Hill, New Jersey
Post-Selma comment from one of the folks back home)

Past nine o'clock Central Time, by my wristwatch. So it was already past ten, back home in Merchantville. And since it was Saturday morning, I figured my kids would have gotten up about an hour ago, allowed by their father to sleep later than usual since there would be no school nor Sunday School today.

In my mind's eye, I envisioned my husband trying to persuade the four of them to eat breakfast faster and get themselves dressed, to round up their dirty laundry for washing, and to help with the other Saturday chores around the house. My imagination panned to a close-up of my indecisive husband standing in helpless frustration in the middle of the kitchen floor, trying to guess how to divide the week's wash he had piled on the tile floor into the most efficient loads to go into the washing machine. He would be openly annoyed, expecting too much cooperation from his children and as a result, getting little, or none at all.

Julie would, as usual, not be able to find her shoes.

A familiar pang of guilt stabbed through me, pushing away the feelings of loneliness. I knew all too well what it was like, having to face on a Saturday morning the prospect of an entire weekend spent catching up on the jobs that had been neglected all week. Because the mother of the house was too busy with college and part-time employment to pay anyone to help her, even if there had been money to spare. As the delinquent mother in question, I had accepted the never-ending load of responsibilities as the price I had to pay for becoming at last a person. This time, though, I had dumped it all on my poor husband Bill, who was a person already, and had no such perceived debts to settle.

But Julie would be "helping" him, I shouldn't forget that!

She would be underfoot the entire time, begging him to let her sort the clothes and load the dishwasher and fry the French toast and perform all the other bits of domesticity an enthusiastic five-year-old girl considers herself an expert in. Twelve year old Kenny and eight year old Scotty might be teasing her to the brink of tears, meanwhile cluttering the house with dropped possessions almost as fast as their father could straighten it up.

Wendi, on the other hand, would most likely be engaged in meeting her once-a-week challenge of getting out the door to a friend's house without straightening her room. Either that, or tying up the telephone so Bill, a newly licensed architect doing small jobs at home on the weekends, could receive no incoming calls. Yesiree, I could picture my teen-aged daughter at this very moment, sprawled on the floor in the front room by the piano, wearing on her head the ubiquitous pink curlers, and giggling at some hilarious secret nobody but she and the person on the other end of the telephone were allowed to know.

"But why can't I go with you?" she had demanded for the third and final
time when I told her goodbye last Thursday evening, up in her bedroom.
There had been no giggling then. For once, she had been dead serious. I
had picked up a curler and rolled it at the back of her neck, the spot she had
the most difficulty reaching, but even that hadn't lessened her resentment
at not going. In the end, she had promised to help me by helping her father
and not arguing with him; but by now, the promise had almost certainly
been forgotten. Maybe even *I* had been forgotten. Would that be bad, I
asked myself, under the circumstances?

Little Julie had been the only one of the four children who had come
all the way down the stairs to the front hall when I left. Wendi had stayed
up in her room, sulking and upset, and had slammed the door behind me.
Kenny and Scotty had positioned themselves before the television set in
the second-floor sunroom, and had seemed absorbed in a Western movie
rerun. They were two whirlwinds stilled in one of the temporary lulls that
overcame them now and then.

Each of my sons had given me a casual flip of the hand, trying to look
nonchalant that their mother was actually going off on a civil rights march
a thousand miles away in Alabama. Watching them for a moment from
the doorway, I had wondered how much they comprehended. Numbers of
miles and names of states meant little to children their age. So did causes.
That which at the time I had taken for feigned nonchalance, had it in
actuality been indifference? (Someday, when they grew up, I promised
myself, I'd ask them.) And then Kenny had unexpectedly caught me on
the landing, and with a few carefully selected words he had let me know he
understood quite well.

"I know why you're going, mom," he said. "Somebody has to do it.
Look what white people did to the Indians." Which made me remember
that I, twelve years old when Pearl Harbor was attacked, had been made
very aware from then on that there was evil in the world.

"Thanks, Ken," I said. He did understand. Maybe it was time he
graduated to that more adult nickname for Kenneth.

Julie, as I had feared she would, clung to my presence until the last
possible moment. Brown pony tail flouncing behind, she had torn down
the stairs at my heels, kissed me ten times as I got into my coat. Then she
hung out the storm door as Bill and I went down the walk to get into
the VW sedan for the ride to the New Jersey Turnpike to meet the bus.
Her small treble voice had wafted after me on the air, heartbreaking in its
innocence and intensity:

"Bye, mommy, Bye!"

I had almost turned back, and stayed home. How could this little one possibly understand what I had told her? How could I have expected her to grasp that her mother felt compelled to leave for what would seem to a child of her age an eternity, simply because far away from here some people of the darkness of Edna, and the lightness of Julie, and various shades in between, were being cheated of their right to vote? Had been assaulted because they had tried to challenge that denial?

She knew what the act of voting was. Bill and I had always taken her and the others to the polls with us to witness the overt mechanics of the democratic process. It was the underlying significance of that simple act I shouldn't expect my little daughter, at five, to comprehend. How Negro votes could ultimately change the face of America for the better. Nor indeed, how could she possibly grasp what the Jim Crow segregation laws of the American South had to do with us here, living in the North. Nor what a farce our own voting rights became, if they could be taken away from anyone so easily.

No! I had to go! It was partly for my own children I was doing this. The world they would inherit in the future, a so much wider and vaster world it would be than their father's and mine had been, that world that was coming was crying out for change. How could I expect my children to believe in those fine American phrases in our national anthem, "the land of the free and the home of the brave." When half of that noble sentiment wasn't true?

"I'll be home soon, Julie," I called out to her. "Go on in now, sweetheart, and close the door! It's cold outside, and you're letting out the heat!"

But the little voice had continued calling until we pulled away from the curb in front of the house. And now here in these grey and brown surroundings in Selma, with no other person to relate to, I heard the voice again and again, echoing persistently through the recesses of my memory: *"Bye, mommy, bye!"*

Why did I now have to feel guilty about this, too? I was one thousand infinite miles from home. What good did it serve anyone now for me to feel guilty? Hands thrust deep into my coat pockets to protect them from the chill, I ordered myself to forget about Julie and the older children back home. To dispel the mental picture of picaresque Scotty going through the Sears catalogue, picking out a thousand dollars worth of presents he wished he could get for his ninth birthday next Sunday. With no mother around to confer with about that annually important decision he had been told to narrow down to ten dollars.

I had to refuse to see in my mind's eye academic Ken, trying to type with two index fingers his history report, done with such love on the subject of the Lenni-Lenape Indians, a tribe that had lived in South Jersey before the white man came. I had to reject the mental vision of sensitive Wendi, getting her best clothes ready to wear to a party this very evening with a boy who had already stood her up once, and might again. And finally, to block from my ears all remembrance of worshipful Julie's last plaintive farewell.

I commanded myself, there on that cold brick wall in Selma, not to conjure up in this present situation so much as a hint of that one young face, much less the childish and much cherished voice that went with it. I would not do that again, not until my mission had been accomplished. hen I could think about all four of my offspring, and wallow incessantly in my guilt regarding them, if I still needed to.

Realistically though—and here came the question again—what indeed was I doing here? I had always considered myself conscientious about duty, even to the—enth degree; a person basically of more reason than rhyme. But perhaps it was neither my sense of responsibility nor my physical capabilities I should be examining as a result of this latest venture, but rather, my emotional bearings.

Altruistic impulses translated into words which in turn managed to stir up glowing emotions in others were fine, as long as I kept them inside a little blue notebook to be taken out once in a while and admired for their shining glimpses into mankind's better nature. Those splendid sentiments such as "They are slaves who fear to speak, For the fallen and the weak," and "It is better to light just one little candle than to curse the darkness." Though certainly not mere platitudes, they were never seriously meant to prompt a woman to action. Were they? Like verses of Holy Writ, they were only to be used to console one when life seemed too cruel or too niggardly. It helped to know there were others out there with noble thoughts like mine. But like Jesus' naive preachment to "turn the other cheek," those grandiose outpourings of the idealistic and the altruistic were not for the real world. Everyone knew they were just part of a game!

Everyone, it seemed, but me. All my life I had been falling for them. I still believed, in spite of all reason to the contrary, that they were directed at me, and that the real world could be a better place if I paid them heed.

But that "real world"—where was it? How could it possibly be here, in spite of these indications of life all around me? Shivering with a sudden spasm that sprang from somewhere deep inside me, I pulled the fake fur collar of my coat tighter against my neck and hopped up from the brick wall. Time to head for the Baptist Church and the scheduled orientation session. Time to learn to be truly non-violent; to find out from experts how to turn the other cheek in the most effective manner.

This was not the first time since leaving home that I had been gripped by a sense of utter unreality. The first time had been last night close to midnight, when after that body-wearying, mind-numbing, marathon bus ride from New Jersey, I had climbed into a stranger's car to be brought at last to Selma. Brought in stealth to this town with the mellifluous and effeminate name in the heart of an innocuous-appearing Southland. "Dream-like" is the only term to describe my mental state during that last stage of the long bus trip. I had felt as if I had taken one final move in a string of moves in a Southern Monopoly game. Or like Alice, had fallen down the rabbit hole into Alabama, with matters getting "curiouser and curiouser." True, the protagonist of this game was not an Alice. But it was that sweet name Selma that had lent the entire affair its most unreal and curious-sounding quality.

*   *   *

END OF PART ONE

PART TWO

GOOD SENSE

6.

"I shall be telling this with a sigh,
"Somewhere ages and ages hence:
"Two roads diverged in a wood, and I—
"I took the one less traveled by,
"And that has made all the difference."
                    —Robert Frost, American Poet
            (From Gwen Gain's "Words To Live By")

Selma, Alabama. I had heard of it only once before in my lifetime, and that one time, quite recently. Just last semester I had read in my American History book at the University of Pennsylvania that during the Civil War a great munitions factory had been situated in Selma. Cannon had been turned out there for the Confederacy until the city's capture in April of 1865, the very month the four-year War ended.

For one hundred years thereafter, Selma had lain, somnolent and obscure, on the banks of the Alabama River, fifty-four miles almost due west of Montgomery, the state capital. And then suddenly it had shot again into prominence, as the site of the Georgia-based Southern Christian Leadership Conference's latest efforts to break down Jim Crow discrimination in the South. Martin Luther King, Jr., and his cohorts had chosen Selma, the county seat of Dallas County, as a likely place to push a voter registration drive. And white Alabama, determined to uphold the status quo, had pushed back.

But Dr. King had set his sights high. He was aiming for nothing less than capitulation by the entire South, on a state-by-state basis if necessary, to the Constitutional guarantee of citizen suffrage. It was a guarantee that had been circumvented by whites since the end of Reconstruction in 1875 on up to the present, by keeping Negroes in Southern states in a constant state of fear. Or where that had failed, by using the device of a so-called "literacy test" to eliminate potential black voters from the polls. If you were black, no matter how smart or well educated you were, you automatically flunked the registration test and therefore could not vote in an e lection.

To bring about a change of the magnitude the Southern Christian Leadership Conference (SCLC) envisioned, Dr. King and his colleagues in the non-violence movement were well aware they had to raise the consciousness of sympathetic Northern whites. They would have to persuade those outside the Southern system to bring to bear the necessary political and economic and moral pressure that was needed to produce change. The problem was how best to accomplish that.

Then fate, in the guise of Dallas County Sheriff Jim Clark, played into their hands when they least expected it. "Over my dead body!" Sheriff Clark had declared when told that Selma's Negroes were determined to register to vote and then go to the polls. And the contest was on.

Over a period of weeks in New Jersey, I had been pulled to the six-thirty television news each evening as to a magnet. I, along with millions of other watchers, had several times been hypnotized with anger and disgust by the sight on our screens of dignified Negro citizens, some of them with more formal education than most of us viewers had, being turned away from the Dallas County courthouse in Selma where they had gone to try to register. Having little time nor inclination for watching television of any sort (my reaction to many boring years of it, evening after evening), I had nevertheless been ensnared by unfolding live events in the South. In horror I watched the scenes of brutality against Negroes that were being played out regularly on the national news.

I had watched as Reverend C. T. Vivian, a black minister from King's Southern Christian Leadership Conference, was violently and openly shoved down the county courthouse steps in Selma by Sheriff Clark. His "crime" was attempting to lead a group of Negroes into the registrar's office. According to Walter Cronkite of CBS news, Rev. Vivian, like Martin Luther King, was not only a minister of the Gospel but also had earned a PhD from a Northern university.

News had come next of the death of a young Negro, one Jimmie Lee
Jackson, after a beating at the hands of white thugs. He had been in his
hometown of Marion, twenty miles away from Selma, demonstrating with
other Negroes for voting rights in conjunction with the SCLC. He was
only a boy in his teens, not old enough yet to vote. The news reports said
that he was killed while trying to protect his mother from a similar violent
attack.

Next came that infamous deed on Sunday, March 7th, 1965. A group of
several hundred Negro residents of Selma, made up largely of women, old
men and teen-agers, had set out to walk the fifty-four miles to Montgomery,
the Alabama state capital, that afternoon. Led by Hosea Williams of the
SCLC, their avowed purpose was to publicize the presenting of a petition
before the Alabama state legislature, one that protested the discriminatory
withholding of voting rights from Dallas County blacks. All three of the
television networks were there with their cameras, waiting to document
whatever might happen.

The attack had come just after the marchers crossed the Edmond Pettus
Bridge that led out of Selma and onto U.S. Highway 8O, the route called
the "Jefferson Davis Highway" after the President of the Confederacy
during the Civil War. The peaceful, unarmed group had been halted by a
battalion of helmeted and gas-masked state troopers, stretched clear across
the highway. The Negro marchers had quietly hesitated, uncertain what
to do.

And then, at Sheriff Clark's command, they had been trampled to the
ground by his posse of volunteer deputies, who were mounted on horseback
and swinging bullwhips. The Negroes had been tear-gassed by the troopers
and beaten over the head with billy-clubs. Many of the Negroes had been
arrested; scores of others were injured. The ones still on their feet had been
chased back across the bridge to Selma and into the Negro Compound.

I had witnessed on my television news daily this cruel, sickening
confrontation. I had seen it live, in black-and-white, and then many times
afterward in subsequent evenings as it was replayed, over and over. The
marchers' screams of terror and pain had been received with surprise and
shock by many of us Northern whites, we who prided ourselves on our liberal
racial attitudes. Most Northerners had until then not fully comprehended
the extent of Southern intransigence in matters of race.

For my part, I had looked on and listened in horrified silence, knowing
a little about this state of affairs all along. When I was a child growing up
in South Jersey, Unity, our Negro maid, had told me in bits and pieces

about the quiet discrimination going on there in my home state, in matters of housing and employment, education and entertainment. (With crosses being burned on Negro lawns from time to time, courtesy of the outlawed Ku Klux Klan.)

And after I'd grown up and still lived in the same general area, sweet Edna, my newly converted Black Muslim housekeeper, had reinforced Unity's tales. And then there was feisty Barbara, who came out from Camden on a bus weekly, two years in a row, to help me with child care and ironing. Barbara, who had six children already and lived in poverty, had told me plenty about the way welfare recipients were treated. And there were tales from others of my Negro friends, well educated and prosperous, whom I had met on the Camden County Human Relations Conference or while I was volunteering in fair housing efforts. From them I had learned details of the discrimination they faced when trying to move to the suburbs outside Camden, the big city across the Delaware from Philadelphia.

But seeing this outright violent bigotry in action in Alabama was something else again. On my way home next day from the University of Pennsylvania, where I worked part-time as a secretary in order to earn my tuition and other expenses involved in going to college in my thirties, I had deliberately taken a different route so as to drive around City Hall in Philadelphia. And they were there, all right, as I had heard reports over my car radio they would be: the Philly marchers.

Two dozen or so brown-faced men were wearing heavy winter overcoats over their suits and ties, so I could barely make out their features. They were pacing slowly in front of the massive Victorian-style building with the statue of Quaker William Penn, founder of Philadelphia, on the very top. (By City ordinance, developers could not build any building in Philadelphia taller than the top of William Penn's hat.) The demonstrators walked in an elongated oval of a hundred feet or more, strung out on the sidewalk in an orderly line as mandated by law. It appeared to me they were all businessmen. Most carried picket signs, some of which proclaimed their membership in the Philadelphia Chapter of the NAACP (the National Association For the Advancement of Colored People). Other of their signs declared in large black headlines messages like "Freedom Now!" and "Justice Dead In Alabama" and "Give Selma Negroes The Vote.".

On an impulse, I parked my blue VW beetle along a curb nearby and walked over to join them, choking back my life-long aversion to cold. My decision to join in the action had not resulted from a sudden insight or spark of emotion at sight of the grim marchers. It sprang, rather, from a surge of empathy that had reached a new peak.

All my life, as long as I could remember, I had been especially attuned to the plight of America's Negroes. According to every rationale I could muster, they were entitled as much as any of us to the privileges and responsibilities of American citizenship. The Fourteenth Amendment to the U. S. Constitution, passed by Congress and ratified by the states in 1868, had made that perfectly clear. But Negroes in the Southern states had always been seen as malevolent or undeserving intruders in a country not of their ancestors' choosing.

This NAACP Chapter had already won my particular admiration. Headed by an outspoken black lawyer named Cecil Moore, the chapter had recently been instrumental in breaking down racial barriers at Girard College. This was a Philadelphia private boarding school of old and proud vintage, whose buildings at the present time and for a long time were nearly surrounded by black neighborhoods. After long months of protest demonstrations and legal maneuverings, the Chapter had in the end won a favorable United States Supreme Court decision. Basically, the ruling said that the school, opened under the terms of the will of its benefactor Stephen Girard to white male orphans only, must now admit Negro boys as well as white. Girard had been a much-respected signer of the Declaration on Independence back in 1776. But today was today, and under the circumstances of the school's location, the bequest no longer made good sense. No one could expect the terms of a bequest to be honored for hundreds of years into the future.

Having seen and heard Mr. Moore railing at length on television, not once, but many times, I recognized him instantly, where he was today walking with several others at the head of the line. Bellicose in speech, abrasive to the point of constant rudeness in dealings with his adversaries, thoroughly despised by most whites I knew and by many prominent blacks as well, Mr. Moore's tenacity of purpose in the face of great odds had nevertheless won a substantial legal and moral victory for the members of his race. Not to mention a boost up the economic ladder for a few of those fatherless Negro boys. The definition of "orphan" at the time of the bequest had specified a boy who had lost his father only. He could still have a living, breathing mother. (In the debate about whether a Negro boy could enroll at Girard College, no one ever mentioned for consideration a fatherless girl.)

With a shy smile, I made a point of shaking Cecil Moore's hand before falling into line near the rear.

"Glad to have you with us," Mr. Moore had said mildly, not sounding at all like the "monster" he deliberately portrayed on TV.

And I had said, "Thank you," gratefully, not knowing what else to say. Nor had the other marchers indicated either resentment or disapproval at sight of my white face and my female attire. They had made me quietly welcome, and for an hour I had circled with them, and had sung along with them, to the tune of "Amen," their own version:

"Free-ee-ee-dom! Free-ee-ee-dom! Free-ee-dom, free-dom, free-dom!"

We chanted the same phrase over and over as we circled in front of City Hall. A few policemen of both races looked on but no one else seemed very interested. And then, toes and fingers numb with cold, I went home and warmed up.

But the pain and indignation over the most recent Selma developments as they were shown on television had not left me. I thought I knew the helplessness, the humiliation, the bewilderment of rejection reinforced by violence that was utterly unfair to the receiver. At the age of nine and in small measure, I had gained some personal insight into that kind of irrational rejection. I guessed that I knew how it felt, knew how it could become the basis for reciprocated bias, as well as keep the emotions enslaved long after the body had been liberated. And knowing all that, my walk in front of Philadelphia City Hall that day had served not as a catharsis, but as a catalyst.

*   *   *

7.

"Let no man make you sink so low as to make you hate him."
—Booker T. Washington,
Negro American Writer and Educator
(From Gwen Gain's "Words To Live By")

Nothing in my life previous to the age of nine had prepared me for the sting of unwarranted hostility directed at my person, followed by the realization that I, and all others like me, were somehow considered by our society to be inferior.

Growing up, I was the middle daughter of seven girls and knew little of boys. The social and cultural ambience of my young life had been broad, I realize today, for a family living through the Depression years. My sisters and I had received a wide variety of innocent experiences, which included Sunday School and Church every Sunday, books and poetry read aloud by our mother, classical music over our father's radio, croquet matches with our sisters in the back yard. Games of kick-the-can in grassy backyards with the other kids on the block. Sled rides and homemade fudge and popcorn in winter. And in the summer, an aging cabin cruiser on the Chesapeake Bay, so many weekends as to be almost intolerable for me, the daughter who yearned to see more of the world. We girls had lots of relatives and family friends, most of them females. But no exposure of any extent to the male mind, except to that of our father, a college graduate and chemical engineer.

Dad, we children knew, was more than mortal man. He was to us, and deservedly so, only one rung below the Lord God Almighty. He was a genius, our mother constantly reminded us. If he was ever unhappy with the lopsided monotony of an all-girl family, he never let on. The family disciplinarian, he would have been treated as king-of-the-castle in any event. We, in our youthful innocence, never dreamed that being female implied being something less than male.

Our parents would go on to have two more girls after the first seven before his untimely death in 1955 at the age of 51, and when our youngest sister was but a year-and-a-half old. Our mother had always picked out the name for their son long before the culmination of each pregnancy. Their agreement at the time of their marriage had been that she would name all the boys they produced together, and he, the girls; and she had stuck through thick-and-thin ahead of time with her choice, "John Carl." Our father had simply smiled like a Cheshire cat. For our mother to deliver a son, we children always concluded that inscrutable smile meant, would be to ruin the Great Joke the two of them had made together, one in which they had allowed us to participate. And he would never select his name for a new baby girl ahead of time, he always told us. Not until he had first seen what she looked like. "I have to wait and see what her personality is," he told us in all seriousness if we ever tried to press him. That was a rule he had. A girl, even a newborn girl, was entitled to that sort of consideration.

Growing up in such a family, I hadn't learned my "place," in the world, even by nine. There was no way I could have guessed it from my home life as well as my disciplined life at school.

But I had been forced to recognize the terrible truth that year I was nine, while crossing a vacant lot near my home. I had been returning from my flute lesson close to suppertime of a bright spring afternoon in 1939. It was the same year the world across two oceans was really going crazy, preparing for war—but what was all that to me? A group of boys were playing on one end of the empty lot their own informal pick-up game of game of baseball, with few rules. (That was the way it used to be before frenzied adults came along to further organize the already-in-group of kids into neat little pools of superskilled, impenetrable malehood. Those were halcyon days, sure enough, for white male children. Those times before Little League and Pearl Harbor changed the world.)

But I knew nothing of that. I stood still in the path that ran catty-cornered across the lot and watched the boys play baseball. My flute case lay cradled in the bend of my right arm. My left hand was free to be held behind my back so I could imagine I was up at bat. That hand was itching to hold the bat, something I had never had the opportunity to do before. My genius father was an egghead, not an athlete, nor was he interested in professional sports teams.

This day I stood and observed the technique of the boy who stood at bat, telling myself I could do it too, if only I had the chance to participate in a real game. It looked so easy. But the boys had ignored me, their unrecognized features and flailing limbs had come from another neighborhood than my own. Except for one, the kid standing farthest from the batter and closest to me. He lived only a block away from me. We had been in school together since kindergarten, but seldom had anything to say to each other. He was a poor student, always getting into trouble with the teacher for chewing gum in class or not handing in his homework in time. And I didn't yet like boys.

He fielded a fly ball, tossing it with a graceful flip of his wrist back to the pitcher. I had followed the ball with my eyes, had watched the batter hit, trying to make first base before the catch, my own legs churning vicariously in imagination. (In those days, I liked to run, but only in short bursts of speed.) The batter knew he was "out." He started back toward home plate at a trot.

"Hey, girl!" It was Dan, the boy from my class at school. I turned toward the sound, wondering at the contempt in his voice as he called out those two words "hey, girl!", wondering why he had even used them. He knew my name, as I did his. His arm was flashing down to his side, as if he had tossed the ball again, and he was grinning at me. But the pitcher had already received the ball . . .

Wham! Something thudded into my head from Dan's direction, hitting me just below the hairline. Something hard and sharp. It spun off and dropped to the ground at my feet. I looked down and saw what it was, a jagged piece of cinder stone. Blood came quickly. I felt the wound stinging and the blood oozing out. The other players looked at me for the first time, and seeing what had happened, and realizing what Dan had probably done, they laughed.

They laughed! Dan laughed even louder than his friends did!

Turning without a word or a sound, I continued along the dirt path toward home, everything but my legs frozen in horror at the sting in my scalp. My legs worked fine. But the sight of the blood that came trickling down the side of my cheek and dripping off my chin onto my black flute case scared me. I refused to wipe it away, however, or to cry until I was in my own backyard, and into my house. And then the tears flowed forth.

Questions, one upon the other, with no satisfactory answers, came pounding into my brain for a long time after the blood had been wiped away by my oldest sister Jackie. My heart still hurt. How had Dan guessed? Had it shown on my face? That I longed to be more than a mere spectator at their game? And if it had shown, why did he care? Why had he called me "girl" in that demeaning manner, instead of using my name, which he knew well? Why had he thrown a sharp cinder stone at me? And smiled when it hit its mark? None of it made sense.

And those other boys, who didn't know me—they had laughed right along with Dan!

It was too much for me to comprehend back in 1939, and there was no one I thought I could ask to explain it to me. Later, years later, I would wonder if the violent action I had provoked by my staring presence had truly been resentment at my gender, or had it been simply a revenge of sorts on a far better student. And the laughter of the other boys? Perhaps embarrassment at the stupid deed of a fool?

I only knew then, at nine, that for some reason girls couldn't play, should never even think about playing. And I knew that I would despise the game of baseball forever.

*   *   *

8.

"Congratulations, Gwen, on being valedictorian of your high. school class. Never forget that superior intellect carries with it the obligation of social responsibility."
—June 1946 letter to me from Rev. Paul B. Irwin, former pastor of Central Baptist Church of Woodbury, New Jersey. (From Gwen Gain's "Words To Live By")

By February of 1965, when Selma, Alabama was making an infamous new name for itself in the annals of American history, I had finally acquired second-semester-sophomore status as a Continuing Education for Women student at the University of Pennsylvania in Philadelphia. I had begun classes when the program was brand-new in the fall of 1963.

My boss, Constance Richardson*, was a former marriage counselor who had come out of semi-retirement that year to organize and implement the University's program to encourage older women to return to school. She had hired me at the very beginning of the program that February of 1963 as her part-time secretary, to begin the following autumn. For my part, I would be coming to her fresh from a full-time job as secretary to the Editorial Director of *Holiday* magazine. Scarcely able to believe my good fortune, I became one of the original sixty-two "guinea-pigs" in the Continuing Ed Program when it got off the ground in September.

My part-time work as Connie's secretary earned me barely enough to pay Negro Edna Wilson for the care of Julie, my little one still not in school a full day, and for doing some of the housework while she was there. The job at Penn came with free tuition for up to three courses each semester. Since I also worked twenty hours a week, I was unable to take more than three courses at a time anyway. But by going to classes the summer of 1964, and having received credit for a semester completed at Penn when I was seventeen, I had managed to accumulate the required number of course units to be considered a sophomore.

Then in September of 1964, my little Julie had started to kindergarten in the mornings, and my housekeeper Edna, who had worked for me nearly full-time for the past two years, had been amenable to coming to my house from her home in Camden for the afternoons only. Her husband Eddie had recently found Allah and Elijah Muhammed, leader of the

Black Muslims in America. As a result of Eddie's new religious creed and improved self-image, he wanted his wife to stay at home like a proper Black Muslim woman. Our new arrangement had seemed to Edna a reasonable compromise between their purse and her husband's conscience.

Thus it was that my days by March of 1965 when I was thirty-five, were a blur of housework and University classes, and shorthand-and-typing at my job, and my children's and my husband's needs and my own studies. Not to mention the tiring commute across the Delaware River to Philadelphia five times a week. Every morning even on weekends I arose at four a.m. to do my school work while my mind was still fresh. At four a.m., I had long ago realized, no one would be likely to call me on the telephone or need help with homework, or would play a radio or the television when I was trying to concentrate. It meant I had to be in bed myself by ten at the very latest, an hour after the younger children were tucked in bed.

I never questioned why my husband Bill never offered to help me with my arduous and unrelenting schedule. It was the way American society was structured, back then. No question about it, a man's wife was obligated to take care of house and children. If she wanted to do more, she had to find a way to work it all out herself, and do it all without complaint.

But difficult though the pattern of my life was, it was the way I wanted it. I was living, I told myself, really living again. And if I could hold on long enough, if I could keep from physical or mental collapse, I'd eventually earn a bachelor's degree from an Ivy-League institution. In what, I wasn't yet sure, since I had not yet selected a major. I only knew I wanted to learn, and learn, and learn. I yearned to take every liberal arts course in the college catalogue; dip into every possible subject. And if it had been possible, to read all the fascinating non-fiction paperbacks I saw in the campus bookstore when I bought my many textbooks.

During the 1950's, the entire decade of my twenties, I had stayed at home, kept house, borne four children—and read exactly one book! That one exception to the long night of my bookless existence had been, I well remember, *The Caine Mutiny.* The novel stood out in my memory ever after, and now, in the 1960's, it remained an oasis in the intellectual desert that was my brain during those child-bearing years before *Holiday* magazine in 1961, and before my return to Penn in 1963.

I remember the volume was hundreds of pages long, and weighed close to a pound in the hardback edition I was reading. In spite of that, I found I could not put down *The Caine Mutiny* for hours on end. The circumstances of how I happened to come by this gem are gone from memory. I do recall that I had started reading it early one morning after Bill went off to work, intending only to steal a glance at a chapter or two before getting the children dressed and starting the washing machine and running the vacuum cleaner.

Lugging the heavy book around with me, I had cared for the young children presently romping around at my feet (Wendy and Kenny, who were home from elementary school getting over colds) and for baby Scotty in his crib. And I had somehow managed to keep reading. My eyes almost riveted to the pages, my entire emotional being had been transported to the all-male crew of that hapless Navy destroyer in the Pacific Ocean during the Second World War. I had soaked up words and scenes and chapters like a giant sponge.

Ensconced in a stuffed chair in the living room of our match-box development house, my legs draped over one arm of the chair in cozy abandon, I read on and on, blocking out children's sobs and games and squabbles and the ticking of the clock; feeding them lunch with book still in hand; turning off dirty little faces and the plaintive meowing of the cat. Changing Scotty's diapers and giving him his bottle only when he—and I—got desperate enough. I had managed to keep my precious charges alive, yes, but doing nothing else that did not demand to be done for them to survive. I had even succeeded in blocking out the guilt feelings that struggled to take possession of me as they had so often in the past, whenever I had selfishly tried to separate my own existence from those other three so dependent and so beloved little beings.

(I picture her now as I write this: that housewife-woman in the chair, hypnotized by *The Caine Mutiny*. What had happened to her all those years since high school? She had been so bright, everyone had said. The little girl who had gotten her library card at seven and by seventeen had gone through every interesting piece of fiction from the Woodbury public library she could lay her hands upon. She had such a good mind, everybody had said back then. She would go places.)

For two days and one evening I had read, putting the ponderous volume down only long enough to go to bed to sleep. I was deaf to questions and pleadings and the perplexed demand from my husband: "What have you been doing all day, honey? This house is a mess." And just before time to get dinner on the second day, I had finished.

In a daze, I had turned over the back cover for the last time and surveyed the wreckage and human misery that lay all around me. A huge dose of guilt had swept over me then, in waves of self-hatred, and I had gathered my little ones to me in apology and had told myself, never again. Newspapers were okay, they were made for quick reading. But no more books. I got too absorbed in books, and wives who were also mothers couldn't do that, not when their kids were little. And it wasn't worth it anyhow, considering those yearnings for more when a book was all over, and the feelings of incompetence that followed the state of ecstasy a good book could induce.

Guilt, I was beginning to suspect, was a much more effective deterrent to participation in living than any amount of physical force, even vicarious living through someone else's imagination. I hadn't tried reading again for a long time; at least not an entire book. Not until *Holiday* magazine's editorial department had moved from Philadelphia to New York, in June of 1963, leaving me behind, unemployed and thus free to go to college once more. That is, if I could work out the complications.

Actually, it had been *Holiday* magazine, with its "meaningful" and "provocative" travel articles, that had turned on my thinking mind again. But this time, I had discovered the joys of non-fiction. "Real life" was even more fascinating to me than well-written novels, I discovered, once I had accepted the inevitable slanting of the truth in any writing, depending upon who the interpreter was.

And now that I was back into "real life" again, on a first-hand basis, I told myself I had little need nor use for make-believe tales of any kind. Furthermore, I would attempt to rid myself of as many personal hypocrisies as I possibly could, when it could be done without injuring others. As for the world out there beyond the doors of my house—for all its frustrations and inadequacies this was surely where "things were at." Some of my many hypocrisies could also be changed, and should be changed. But to do that effectively, I'd have to know more. And that piece of paper, a diploma from a top-of-the-line University like Penn, an Ivy League school, should give me that chance.

I had begun to be something of an agent for social change, albeit a quiet one, even before college. A narrow escape from death at the time Julie, my youngest, was born in 1959, nearly coinciding with the milestone of my thirtieth birthday, had opened my eyes to the intellectual limbo of my daily existence. It had made me see that I was playing a game by rules I no longer accepted. And ultimately, and in spite of the guilt, it had propelled me out of the house and into a job, and put me into association with adults again on a regular basis. I had no way of knowing then, in 1960, that I was part of a silent revolution about to find voice in a book called *The Feminine*

Mystique. "The problem that has no name," author Betty Friedan would label the state of discontent with my own existence, along with that of millions of other American women. Though I did not know that yet.

Over the next three years in the early 1960's, I had worked at two different full-time secretarial jobs. Together, Bill and I had also found time—it was amazing what time you could find if you really wanted to—to join several others in our New Jersey County of Camden in the founding of a Human Relations Council. This was an organization of volunteers dedicated chiefly to ending practices of racial discrimination in housing. A small interracial group lacking both power and influence, the Council nevertheless hoped to use reason and persuasion on real estate offices in our end of the state to end the perpetuation of segregated housing patterns in our area., particularly in the township of Cherry Hill, a sprawling and hitherto-neglected geographic entity. Over the past decade, Cherry Hill had undergone an astronomical increase in the development of middle-and upper-middle-income dwellings. It had become the "bedroom community" Mecca of South Jersey for people who worked in Philadelphia, as my husband did. But only white families were able to buy a home there.

Not meeting with any visible success in our contacts with the County's unbending white real estate bloc, our little organization, meeting only monthly in the evenings, taking turns in the homes of different members, had joined in struggling along with other like-minded citizens across our state. Particularly in North Jersey, fair housing councils had been using white couples and black couples to test houses for sale and apartments for rent in order to prove rampant discrimination against black buyers. Problem was, the black testers we used were seldom legitimate seekers of housing and thus not eligible, under current New Jersey law, to bring charges of racism.

So the North Jersey Human Relations Councils had turned their attention to demanding the passage by our legislature of comprehensive, strong open-housing legislation for our state. This included the establishment and funding of a new state agency, a Division on Civil Rights, to be based in Trenton, the capital of New Jersey, to handle housing discrimination complaints—as well as the right of black couples to bring complaints, regardless of whether or not they actually wanted the property in question. But so far, the Councils' demands had fallen on deaf ears.

During the past few years, my husband and I had several times gone into a real estate agency's office escorting black homeseekers who truly were interested in buying the houses we inquired about, and who also had the money for a down payment as well as an income sufficient to keep up the mortgage payments.

In every case we had gotten nowhere. Bill and I had signed affidavits on behalf of the Negro couple afterward, outlining all the lies and deception we suspected had taken place. We had witnessed with our own eyes and ears what happened to black would-be buyers, as opposed to the respectful treatment Bill and I always received from real estate brokers when we went into their offices alone. By 1964, we had helped to file several complaints of outright discrimination with the finally established New Jersey Division on Civil Rights. But nothing ever got resolved. In the end, there were no consequences leveled on the lawbreakers, who were given only a warning. There were no teeth in the New Jersey law. And the investigations took so long that the houses in question were sold elsewhere, always to whites.

I had looked into the sad, bewildered faces of the Negroes we were trying in vain to help, and they haunted me. Since starting at the University of Pennsylvania, however, I had had little time to be active in the Council's endeavors. And the awareness of my neglect, however well justified, bothered me. The right of American citizens of any race, color or creed to buy or rent the housing of their choice, based only upon the color and quantity of the money in their wallets, was a concept to which I had long been committed. Only the knowledge that growing numbers of more outspoken white citizens than I were showing concern about the problem assuaged my conscience in that direction.

And now, in March of 1965, this had come along when I least expected it—this string of events in Alabama that little by little unveiled the Great American Hypocrisy for all the world to see. The denial of the right to vote based on race made a mockery of all the democratic principles I had long held dear, and for which thousands of American Negroes had fought during World War Two. And there was nothing I, or any of us could do, it seemed, but stand by and watch.

So I viewed the nightly television news reports from Alabama in fascinated revulsion. The violence-filled drama continued to be played out, day after day, photographed by the main television networks and put promptly onto a national stage. The Southern Christian Leadership Conference, I suspected, had counted on that. Dr. Martin Luther King, Jr. had flown to Selma from his SCLC headquarters in Atlanta immediately after the beating of the women and children on that day now-referred-to as "Bloody Sunday", March 7th, 1965. It was there he announced that he would personally lead a protest march from Selma to Montgomery, the capital of Alabama, to publicize the glaring voting inequities of Dallas County. He had attempted to lead it himself several times during the days immediately following March 7th, and each time had been turned back by the Sheriff of Dallas County's legal maneuvers.

It was while resisting efforts by the white power structure to prevent another march, first by street barricade, then by court injunction, that Dr. King had gone on national network television to make a plea. He had issued an invitation to America's religious leaders of all faiths and races to join him in Selma. By last weekend, several hundred clergymen from across the country had answered the call.

The next victim in the Selma drama had not been long in falling. The Reverend James Reeb, a young white Unitarian minister from Massachusetts, had gone to Alabama in that first wave of ministers, priests and rabbis. Struck in the back of the head without warning by a 4-x-4 board wielded by a Selma white man on a downtown sidewalk of the city, Reeb died shortly afterward, leaving behind a wife and two children. Pledge-paying Unitarians ourselves for the past few years, Bill and I had gone to our church in Cherry Hill that next Sunday and listened to our own Unitarian minister eulogize his fellow clergyman.

In a sermon of simple eloquence, Reverend Edwin Lane stated: "Jim Reeb was my personal friend. He understood that his liberty and your liberty and mine are on the line in Alabama." He had praised Rev. Reeb's commitment to justice translated into the supreme sacrifice, the giving of his life. Rev. Lane had ended his remarks with the final lines of a poem: *So that if he fall, it will be with a song in his heart.* I had long been a sucker for simple eloquence and poetic lines taken out of context. I added that stirring sentiment to my little blue notebook of "Words To Live By" when I got home from church that Sunday of March 14th.

That afternoon, my husband Bill and I took our four children with us to Moorestown, a middle-class community close to Merchantville that dated itself back to pre-Revolutionary days. There we joined free-thinking Quakers and liberal Baptists and other Unitarians in a silent white march through the venerable and non-threatening streets, wearing black armbands in mourning for Rev. James Reeb and the young boy from the town near Selma, Jimmie Lee Jackson.

My daughter Wendi (now spelling her name with an "I" on the end and not a "Y", following President Johnson's daughter Luci's lead) came home from high school the next day, Monday, bringing with her the news that the martyred Rev. Reeb, the white minister killed in Selma, had been first cousin to her choir director. I knew the director slightly, this man who could extract from the throats of Merchantville High's lackadaisical white students a rendition of "The Battle Hymn Of The Republic" that brought tears to my parental eyes. The Selma affair, strictly non-fiction, was touching ever closer to our home. But even then, I had not seriously considered that one dead Unitarian should be replaced by a live one. Least of all by me.

*   *   *

9.

"I wish my countrymen to consider, that whatever the human law may be, neither an individual nor a nation can ever commit the least act of injustice against the obscurest individual without having to pay the penalty for it. A Government which deliberately enacts injustice, and persists in it, will at length even become the laughingstock of the world."

**—Henry David Thoreau, American Writer
(From Gwen Gain's "Words To Live By")**

It had actually required only another two days for the idea to burgeon within me. Thus it had jelled by the Wednesday before the now-scheduled date of Sunday, March 21st, decreed by Federal District Judge Johnson as the day for the march to take place legally and without opposition. Like a silent message from some unknown deity (or more likely, from the ghosts of the framers of the United States Constitution), it whispered that there was no good reason why I, Gwen Gain, American citizen, could not go to Alabama and join Dr. King's non-violent army. He had expanded his invitation only the day before to include anyone in sympathy with the civil rights movement's methods and goals now being referred to as "non-violence." He had meant to include not just clergymen, he said, but anyone who shared his vision of justice.

The revelation that he had meant me had come to full bloom in my American Government class at Penn, about ten o'clock on that Wednesday morning. And once formulated in my mind, it pushed me, inexorably and without let-up, over the brink of indecision and into action.

I had signed up that semester for an "honors" section in American Government 2, which meant a smaller class as well as a more challenging atmosphere, according to Dr.Robert McLeod,* the professor who was teaching it. It also meant my taking a hard look at the Bill of Rights, which referred to the first ten amendments to the U.S. Constitution, and doing a research paper on some aspect of same, utilizing materials from the nearby University Law Library. Our teacher was an attorney, who was in his mid-thirties just as I was. A specialist in Constitutional Law, he was also a strong believer in the "natural rights" theory of democracy, we, his students, quickly surmised.

Throughout the entire dismal month of February and into blustery March he had us devoting almost all our class time to a discussion of First Amendment rights. Millions of words and multitudinous volumes had been written, our neophyte class of Constitutional Law studiers discovered, about those forty-five words that begin the Bill of Rights: *"Congress shall make no law respecting an establishment of religion, or prohibiting the free exercise thereof; or abridging the freedom of speech, or of the press; or the right of the people peaceably to assemble, and to petition the Government for a redress of grievances."*

It was a particular arrangement of words I was already somewhat familiar with, having once, as a thirteen-year-old freshman in high school, had to make a three-minute extemporaneous talk on that same amendment before a packed auditorium of my peers. The occasion had been the American Legion Oratorical Contest; and I had that same morning made my ten-minute prepared speech on the glories of the Constitution itself. The First Amendment had been the choice I had made right afterward by drawing a slip of paper from ten folded-up numbers placed in a bowl by Woodbury High's principal. Back then I had understood neither the amendment's ramifications nor its import. There had never, in my entire short life of thirteen years, been any reason to understand them. So I did the extemporaneous explanation badly, wandering around in my words, not altogether sure what I was saying.

By the time I was thirty-five and in that honors section at Penn, matters had not been altered to any extent. I had found the necessity, over the intervening years, to claim for myself a measure of the religious freedom guaranteed me, and which I had long exercised within the privacy of my own thoughts. But though members of my extended family had been shocked and disappointed by my to-their-thinking heretical conclusions, no one had seriously tried to deprive me of my right to hold them.

I had changed in another, sadder way, however, since high school. After nineteen years of playing the role of housewife, I found myself unable to stand up in front of a group of people and express an honest opinion on any topic whatsoever. At least not without stammering with embarrassment, or flushing crimson and forgetting most of what I wanted to say.

When seated, however, I could generally pull it off. Debating an issue with close friends, for example, was no problem. Nor was discussing ideas in a classroom of fellow students I had come to know and felt at ease with. I had acted in numerous amateur plays, both in high school and afterward, in "little theater" groups, in which I was taking someone else's words; pretending to besomeone else. But let me get up on my feet and try to communicate an idea of my own to a roomful of people whose eyes were fastened on me, and all my composure vanished. Especially if they were males, or if it meant competing with others for the floor. Yes, in that sense I had changed for the worse.

But still, in all those years of my nice, safe life, while I was playing my role and losing my argumentative skills and later being a behind-the-scenes worker for what I considered social justice, I had never had cause to fully understand that First Amendment to the United States Constitution. Certainly I had never forced anyone to invoke its privileges because of any action of mine; nor had I claimed them for myself. There had been no need. So protected had I been that for years I could not have stated with surety what a "First Amendment issue" was. All I knew was that the right to housing of one's choice if accompanied by the ability to afford it was not one of them. Not if your skin was brown.

But now, after sitting in that American Government class three times a week, for how many weeks? Discussing cases from a textbook having to do with free speech and freedom of assembly issues? My mind kept drawing parallels, calling my attention again and again from those textbook cases, already resolved by decisions of the U.S. Supreme Court, to the events taking place at that very moment in the South. The newspapers and the television news were full of them.

The light of realization was slowly dawning in my brain. This, then, was what "civil rights" were all about! This was why those simply-stated restraints in the Bill of Rights had been thought vital by people like Thomas Jefferson: *"Congress shall make no law . . ."* The first ten amendments of our Constitution were there to protect the individual citizen, the minority, from the capriciousness and the oft times cruelty of the majority! No longer just fine words, but concepts I now understood!

If you already had power, or belonged to the group that was already in charge; or if no one ever questioned your right to do and say certain things, you had no need of First Amendment protection. But the outsiders did: the rebels and the questioners, and beyond them, the weak, the powerless, the despised. These were the beings for whom those words in the Bill of Rights had been penned. And so far, I had not had occasion to be numbered among them. Even regarding my religious freedom so vital to my self-concept, I had always had the privilege of taking them for granted.

Professor McLeod led the class skillfully from one obvious conclusion to the next. Individual states in our country had often tried to abrogate, or do away with, the protection afforded certain of their citizens. And particularly vulnerable had been those guarantees of the First Amendment. Often a state had gotten away with its deliberate misuse because no one had effectively protested the circumvention of those rights. Governments of Southern states, in those counties considered to make up the Black Belt, had been especially clever at using ordinances and statutes that were clearly unconstitutional under the hard light of the First Amendment. Thus, they managed to keep Negro majorities segregated and in their second-class status through "legal" means. The "Jim Crow" laws, they were called, and they segregated the two races in nearly every area of life.

By selective enforcement of the requirement for a "parade permit" and similar devices, the white South had thus far effectively prevented its black populations from petitioning their state governments for "a redress of grievances." Just as the white registrars' trumped-up or insulting "literacy tests" at the white-run county courthouses had kept Southern Negroes effectively away from the polls. The white South knew that an easily identifiable group such as Negroes, unable to vote and with no legal means of protesting that deprivation, would never be able to change its status, no matter how much education or financial wealth it attained.

That is, until the Reverend Martin Luther King, Jr., with his non-violence direct action movement, came along and said "Enough!"

All told, the civil rights movement had been struggling for freedom of various types for a long time now. 1954 had seen *Brown vs. the Topeka Board of Education,* the famous Supreme Court decision that declared that "separate but equal colleges and schools were inherently unequal." I was the mother of two small ones by then. In 1956 and 1957, while I was bearing my third child and being swamped by dirty diapers and baby bottles, the Movement, with a young Negro minister at its helm, was organizing a black boycott of the city buses in Montgomery, Alabama. That was when the names of Martin Luther King, Jr. and Rosa Parks came to light up the world for the first time. Mrs. Parks was the young Negro seamstress who set off the boycott when she refused to move to the back of a city bus and give up her seat to a white man. Dr. King was the man who responded to her arrest. Which resulted in the successful year-long Montgomery bus boycott by the city's Negroes.

Next it was the white lunch counters of the South who were forced to end discrimination on the basis of race. This was accomplished by Negro youths using non-violence direct-action tactics. At about the same time those brave young men were taking their first beatings for daring to sit on stools at the lunch counters in the Woolworth's dime stores in Birmingham, Alabama, I was recuperating from the birth of my fourth child Julie. I had nearly died from "childbed fever" in September of 1959. Swift hospitalization, along with antibiotics, had saved me.

Early in 1960, I had found a baby-sitter and gone out to work as secretary to the owners of a tire retreading plant very close to my home. We needed the money; I needed the mental stimulation. In 1961, I was struggling to learn my second job as a secretary at RCA in Moorestown, New Jersey, where I typed letters about ICBMs (intercontinental ballistic missiles) and worried about how I would get home to my children in the event of a nuclear attack. Meanwhile the Civil Rights Movement's black youths, along with their equally young white companions, were taking "freedom rides" on Greyhound buses to challenge racial segregation of interstate bus lines. They had been attacked by white bullies waiting at bus stations and badly beaten. But ultimately they had won a Supreme Court decision in that area as well.

It was on my third job in 1962 and half of 1963, while I, still a secretary, was placidly helping my boss to purchase those "meaningful and provocative" articles for the slick pages of *Holiday magazine,* that Dr. King and his organization had mounted their racial integration campaign in Birmingham, Alabama. After much turmoil and thousands of arrests and several deaths, including the murder of four little black girls in the bombing of a church one Sunday, the SCLC had finally been able to rid Birmingham, "the toughest city in the South," of its Jim Crow laws and segregation practices. The Movement and its demonstrations had been directly responsible for the passage by the United States Congress of the Civil Rights Act of 1964, triumphantly signed into law by President Lyndon Johnson. The Act had made racial segregation in places of public accommodation and in employment illegal all over America. But still more, much more, was needed.

That same summer of 1964, called "Freedom Summer," by its organizers, three young men, two white and one Negro, had been working on a voter registration drive in Philadelphia, Mississippi. They had been picked up by the police, taken to jail, and later released that same evening—only to be kidnapped and murdered by members of the Ku Klux Klan, their three bodies buried at the foot of an earthen dam outside of town. I had started my second semester at the University of Pennsylvania by the time that happened, and had begun to feel a stirring deep inside me of more than just sympathy. I was getting angry.

And now, in the spring of 1965, Dr. King and his followers had given notice that Alabama's blacks would no longer accept being denied their right to the franchise. And white Southerners were fighting back in blind panic by refusing to let the Negroes march en masse from Selma to Montgomery to petition the Alabama legislature for *a redress of grievances.*

Just how had the South gotten away with these blatant injustices for so long? my American Government class had demanded of Professor McLeod. One hundred years had passed since the end of the Civil War and the end of slavery in the United States. In 1868 had come the passage by Congress of the fourteenth amendment giving all male citizens, black as well as white, in every state in the Union, the right to vote. In all that time, why hadn't enough people seen and understood? we students wanted to know. That the entire fabric of our precious and much-touted democracy was being sabotaged? Why had no one stepped up to remedy this in all that time?

Our professor had simply shrugged. He seldom advanced a personal opinion, usually leading us into a certain conclusion by the Socratic method of asking us questions, by making us think. Now he made a statement, but it was a roundabout reply. This is when he told us, quoting a remark by Mark Twain, "An American is someone who has freedom of speech and the right of assembly, and the *good sense* not to use them. To which we also might add: And the sense not to demand them for anyone else."

"Good sense! Good lord!" My indignant voice rising higher with each word startled even me. The several other members of my American government class turned at my outburst to stare at me. And mortified that I had revealed my disgust so openly, I felt my face turning red.

"Well, you can afford good sense, can't you, if you're white," I stammered. "If you're white, and if besides that, life has given you all the

goodies to start with! Did you ever think of that, Mark Twain?" He had
been utilizing sarcasm, I was slow to recognize, and my words trailed off
in embarrassment. When life hadn't done that, if you were born black in
America, what you needed most was courage instead, I thought but did not
say, in order to claim your birthright of freedom. It was plain to see that,
in this day and age. And maybe, if you had some white friends who would
stand beside you . . . .

At first shot, I had placed a literal interpretation on Twain's sardonic
homily, and embarrassed myself in the process. He had of course not meant
it to be at all a praise of American citizens. Now that I thought about
it, I recalled that Mark Twain the writer was famous for his humorous
expressions of contempt for the average American's political indifference.
As for Professor McLeod, I was already well aware of his liberal bent, try
as he might to conceal it behind Socratic reasoning. He reminded me of
my Problems of American Democracy professor whose name I could not
recall, during my Senior year of high school back in 1946.

Okay, so I lacked the guts to say very much in public, now that I finally
had recognized the truth for what it was and had found something to say.
Maybe I lacked the power and the money to have influence on legislators
and businessmen. But I was an American, wasn't I? A female, to be sure;
un'americana, as we said in my Italian class. *Io sono amerioana,* I am an
American woman. Not as physically strong as a guy, *un'americano,* perhaps.
But I had two legs and a body, and I could walk, couldn't I? I had empathy
and I had courage. *Who says I can't play?*

Sitting there in class with my still-hot face and really grasping the
importance of those First Amendment issues for the first time, I found
the cruelty and hypocrisy of Alabama's discriminatory voting practices and
parade-permit devices too much to bear in silence. "Give us the ballot,"
Martin Luther King had said many times, referring to the Negroes of the
American South, "and we will change the history of this country."

In the depth of my soul, I yearned desperately to help give him . . . .
them! . . . . that chance. It was my country too. *And to hell, for once, with
having good sense!*

*   *   *

END OF PART TWO

PART THREE

FINDING MY WAY

10.

"In general, people who want to change the world are just frustrated individuals who don't know how to live with themselves."

—One of Gwen Gain's sisters
Post-Selma Comments etc., etc.,,,,)

Back at my desk in the College For Women offices that Wednesday afternoon, I weighed the question of how I could possibly manage it. I would have to be in Selma by Sunday, if I wanted to march out of town with Martin Luther King.

In those days, I had very little money. It was stretching our financial resources to the limit just keeping me in college part-time, not to mention the other expenses incurred by a house, two cars, and four children. I had no contacts, not at the University nor at home, who would be able or willing to help me financially, or even have information as to whether and by whom any "march stipends" were being given out. (Who would chip in for me anyhow, to help me do such a crazy thing?)

And then I remembered Cecil Moore, the NAACP attorney whose hand I had shaken during the protest demonstration in front of Philadelphia City Hall. This was the man who had successfully breached, with his frequent demonstrations and constant legal challenges, the thick stone walls of "lily-white" Girard College. Surely he had already devised a means for sending large numbers of non-violence protesters South to Alabama, now that King had sent out a plea for them.

My boss Connie Richardson was in her private office next to my desk with the door closed. She was interviewing yet another middle-aged woman for the Continuing Ed Program; one who was probably by now unburdening her tortured soul to Connie with confessions such as "I'm up to *here* with volunteer work! I want to be *paid* for what I do, just like men are. And to get a decent position, I need a formal education!"

These women kept coming, without surcease, in ever greater numbers each semester, ever since I began working there two years before. Ever since Betty Friedan's book *The Feminine Mystique* had been published in 1962, Connie had told me. *The problem that has no name,* Ms. Friedan had called it in her book. It had been my problem too, though I had never admitted it out loud.

I picked up my desk telephone and with hands trembling and surprised by my own boldness, I called the Philadelphia Chapter of the NAACP. I had gotten their number from Information.

"Would you know," I inquired politely, staring at a pot of lily-of-the-valley I had been nurturing on my desk for some time, "if there will be a special plane going to Selma from Philadelphia in time for the voting march on Sunday?" *Is that really my voice, asking such a ridiculous question?*

The equally polite female voice on the other end of the line seemed to find my query a reasonable one, in spite of my own reservations. The charter plane leaving for Montgomery on Saturday was already filled, she told me regretfully. And it would cost me well over a hundred dollars to book a regular flight on a commercial airline, she supposed. If I could even get a seat on one at this late date.

I'd have to get money from somewhere, especially if I went on a commercial vehicle. "Could I please speak to Mr. Moore?" I asked.

Cecil Moore, she informed me, was in court. But I could talk to Philip Savage, the NAACP Tri-County Executive Secretary, simply by phoning his office next door. And she gave me his number.

Mr. Savage was blunt. There was no money at all available for that sort of thing, at least not for sending white housewives on commercial airlines whenever they took it into their privileged heads to risk their necks down South. And besides, he wanted to know, if I hadn't paid my NAACP dues since a year ago July, as I'd just admitted, how could I claim to be a member at this point?

I was by this time thoroughly ashamed of having asked him for help. And equally ashamed of not having kept my membership up to date. And of course, as he said, there were definitely more vital needs for their money than subsidizing the likes of me.

"We pay for things like lawyers, bail money, fines," Mr. Savage explained, and his tone was more kindly now. "Let me tell you this: If you do get there and you get arrested and put in jail, contact Dr. King's Southern Christian Leadership Conference, and I'm sure they'll do their best to get you out."

I thanked him for his advice and got off the phone quickly. Who was he trying to kid? Demonstrating was one thing. But the idea of my actually going to jail was as ridiculous as imagining a snowfall in Philly on the Fourth of July. It was too utterly preposterous a situation to consider. Jail was for law-breakers. Criminals. But sometimes, indeed, quite often, it had happened to civil rights workers. *But it wouldn't ever, not to me. I'm too lawabiding.*

Unwilling to give up yet, I next tried phoning the University of Pennsylvania's Christian Association office. I knew that Reverend Perez, the young white minister who worked there, had come back from Selma a couple of days before—early, he said, because his wife was expecting a baby any day now. "I was afraid if I didn't come back and she had a girl, she'd name it Selma, just to punish me," he had quipped at the campus meeting I had attended yesterday on a first-time basis to hear him speak.

I'd talk to the Reverend, find out if he knew of any subsidies, or any sponsors. Because by this time, I really, really wanted to go.

But when I called, I got the usual female office worker on the phone, and the customary response. Reverend Perez was "out." Could she take a message? Without much hope—indeed, feeling more than a little foolish—I told her I was trying to fly to Selma by the weekend but had no money for the airfare. Did she know . . . ?. Was it possible . . . . ? Would the Christian Association . . . . ?

She was the second person that day who had not thought my questions the least bit odd.

"Are you a student here?" she asked me.

"Yes. I am." Could she tell I was older? "Well—only part-time right now." That I was older probably wouldn't matter anyhow, I told myself. I felt certain the Movement needed all the warm and committed white bodies it could get.

"I understand a charter bus is leaving for Montgomery, Alabama, on Thursday evening—tomorrow—from New York City," the refined voice said. "There might be room left on it for you. And it would certainly be much cheaper than flying, I should think." And she gave me a number to call in New York. That's the number of a group called the NCSM, she said, not having the faintest idea what the letters stood for.

I thanked her for her help and hung up.

Thursday evening. Tomorrow night! A long shot. And even if they'd hold a seat for me, I'd still have to get myself the ninety miles north to New York City. But swept along by the polite atmosphere of business-as-usual I had so far been met with, I called the long-distance number, and it was indeed the office of NCSM, the Northern Christian Students Movement, a group I had never heard of until that day. But the name sounded reassuring, even to a religious skeptic like me. After all, the "C" could have stood for "Communist," which would not have been good, not good at all. Dangerous, in fact. The SCLC, Dr. King's organization, was already being accused of being the tool of communists.

There was no one in the NCSM office at present who knew the details of the bus arrangements. Could someone please call me back around five o'clock?

I left my name and home phone number with the switchboard operator. And that same day, just before supper and Bill's arrival home from work, just when I had decided I wouldn't be going to Alabama after all; no one was going to call me and I was probably quite lucky; a Miss Stassen phoned me from the NCSM in New York City.

"Am I speaking to Mrs. Gain? Mrs. Gwen Gain?" she asked. Hooray! She had it right! No attempt to add an "s" sound to the end of my last name, for a change! The accent and tonal quality of her speech seemed to indicate that she was Caucasian and had grown up in the North.

"Yes, this is she. I'm trying to get to Selma by the weekend," I replied, and I described to her the difficulties I had been encountering.

"Yes, of course. No problem," she said in answer to my inquiry about the charter bus. "We'll reserve a seat for you. We're leaving New York tomorrow night at seven. We should get to Montgomery, the state capitol, on Friday evening about nine. We'll leave from there Sunday evening to come home. Be back by late Monday."

As I listened to her matter-of-fact voice, I gulped, my mind a whirl of as yet undigested facts. Leaving New York City—by seven tomorrow evening! Another—figure it up quick!—twenty-six hours on a bus after that! And then we'd still not be in Selma. It lay yet another fifty-four miles further to the west, as we all knew from the news reports of the five days it would take the marchers to get to the Alabama state capital Montgomery on foot. And I wouldn't be able to stay past the first day of the march itself. But Sunday would be the crucial day, wouldn't it, after all was said and done? Sunday would be the walk out of town.

"What will it cost me, Miss Stassen? The bus ride, I mean?" I might have been inquiring about a cruise ticket to the Caribbean, my tone so matched hers in calm.

"Forty dollars round trip," she said. "We're sorry about that, but there just aren't any funds to give out . . . ."

"That's quite all right," I told her. A forty-dollar passage there and back was peanuts compared to what a round-trip plane flight would have cost me. And then she threw in the clincher. She told me there was no need for me to go all the way up to New York City to catch the bus. There was no reason they couldn't stop somewhere on the way south and pick me up!

"Where would be a good place to meet you?" Miss Stassen asked me with the same matter-of-fact manner she had used all along. As if matters with me were all set. "We'll be coming down the New Jersey Turnpike," she said. "Are you close to that?"

I drew in my breath and held it a moment. She needed to know now, right now, in order to hold a seat for me on that charter bus. Forty dollars *was* a bargain, wasn't it? I could make that amount up easily, a little at a time, couldn't I, by stinting on my grocery shopping later on? I'd be home again by Monday night, if we started back on Sunday. Only four days in total, and I'd have to miss only two days of my classes, on Friday and Monday. The job should be no problem—I had vacation time coming, and Connie Richardson was a very understanding boss.

"The Turnpike would be fine," I said. "At Exit 4. It's not too far from here. I'll be waiting at—at the southbound toll booths, the last one to your right. Is that okay?"

"Great!" she said, not skipping a beat. "We'll see you tomorrow night, Mrs. Gain. At Exit 4. Around nine o'clock. Please don't be late!"

Oh, I wouldn't be, I assured her calmly, and I thanked her just as calmly, and hung up the receiver, my heart pounding at the enormity of the step I had just taken.

But there were too many matters that suddenly needed my attention for me to dwell upon the wisdom of my decision for long. Once I had so decisively made up my mind, the thing was settled. I couldn't back out now. My first challenge was to convince my husband Bill of that.

As it turned out, Bill was easy. It took only a few minutes together in the kitchen that evening to convince him that his wife belonged in Alabama this coming Sunday to support Martin Luther King. I would be representing the family, as it were. Bill and I had joined the Unitarian Church at the same time, seven years earlier—the church of Ralph Waldo Emerson and Henry David Thoreau. Of Thomas Jefferson and Louisa May Alcott, and of Michael Servetus, the first Unitarian, who had been burned at the stake during the Spanish Inquisition because of his religious heresy. His crime was insisting there was but one God, and not a trinity of the Father, the Son, and the Holy Ghost. And for that, he had to die!

Both Bill and I were humanists, reacting against the no-longer-believable religious tenets of our Protestant childhoods. My husband well knew of my deep sympathy for underdogs of any kind, and for Negro Americans in particular. Not one to grieve over injustices as strongly as I did, he'd nevertheless helped start up the Camden County Human Relations Conference and nearly always accompanied me to the once-a-month evening meetings at the homes of different members.

My husband's home life as a child had not been one of learning tolerance for minority groups. Quite the contrary ! Nor had he had regular contact with Negroes as I had had. But to my great relief, he had risen above all that and continued to show ample signs of open-mindedness. As a teenager he'd been a camp counselor who taught Negro Boy Scouts to swim, during the one week the segregated black troops living in South Jersey got to use Camp Roosevelt each summer. (The Negro boys, Bill once told me, got the undesirable first week of the season when the water was still chilly and the detritus at the bottom of the lake needed to be stirred up and settled.)

Bill had gone to Woodbury High School with several dozen Negro students, just as I had done two years behind him. They always sat in their own little clique at assembly, in the two back rows of the auditorium. My husband even had a good black friend, a fellow architect who drafted in the same office with him. Several times we'd gone to racially mixed parties in Charlie Parnell's* posh bachelor apartment, furnished much more elegantly than anything we'd ever had. Not at all envious or even very surprised, Bill was happy for Charlie that he was doing so well.

Nor did my husband register much surprise when I told him of my plan to go to Selma. He usually went along with my projects, anyhow, and found them exciting even when he was unable to embrace them as wholeheartedly as I did. There was seldom any need to argue or cajole; nor was there this time. If I told him it was safe for me to go, then it must be safe. His attitude, as I expected, was that he'd be happy to take my word for that.

Helping me load the portable dishwasher in the kitchen that evening, with the children dispersed to other parts of the house, he even voiced his own inclination to go with me.

"Forty dollars is a lot of money," he said, "or we could both go."

I handed him a bunch of silverware. "You'd lose your job if you did, you know you would."

He was head man in the office of a Philadelphia architect. He was what he considered a "glorified draftsman" when it came to salary, even though Bill himself was a registered architect, with a degree from Drexel Institute of Technology. He'd never dare take time off on a whim, however, especially one as controversial as this one.

"You're right. They'd fire me there if they found out," he agreed.

"Besides, we can't both go away from our kids for four days," I said. "And listen, Bill, nothing's going to happen to me down there, of course. But just suppose—well, just think if something did . . . . ? I mean, life is a gamble. So *both* of us couldn't go. Do you know what I mean?"

He said again, "You're right. We can't." And then musing, he added in a low voice, "I wonder what my dad will say?"

I grimaced at the sudden thought and said, "Oh, boy! Do you have to tell him?"

Bill grinned, and shook his head. "Not if I don't have to."

I told myself that I had to divert him from thoughts of parental wrath to come. His parents still lived in Woodbury, only ten miles away from Merchantville. Of course they'd find out. But by that time, I'd be long gone. Poor Bill would have to face their ire alone. That didn't seem quite fair . . . .

"I'll need some things to take with me," I said quickly, to change the subject. I added the powdered soap to the dishwasher. I watched as my husband hooked the hose to the faucet and turned on the hot water. "I should probably take a sleeping bag, don't you think, if I'm going there without a definite place to stay?"

Bill pointed out to me that the zippers were shot on both of ours. "Let's try to think of someone you can borrow one from," he said, once more back in the spirit of things. "You wouldn't want to take a new one there, Gwen, even if we could afford to buy it."

"That's a good idea, honey. Thanks!" I said. "Let's think."

Bill was a good man. A kind man. We had been friends for a long time, ever since high school days in Woodbury when he had run around with a crowd that included my two older sisters, Jackie and Jocie. He and I had met again the summer of 1946, when the Second World War was over and his two-year hitch in the Navy was finished. I had just graduated from high school and had a whole summer to kill before starting at the University of Pennsylvania in the fall on a four-year, half-tuition scholarship. After one semester commuting to college across the Delaware River from New Jersey, I had been physically and mentally exhausted. I had dropped out in February of 1947 and taken a secretarial course at Peirce School of Business in Philadelphia instead, finishing up in six months well ahead of schedule.

Bill and I had dated heavily for over a year. And when I turned eighteen and he was twenty-one and a college student attending Glassboro College under the GI Bill, we had married. Since then Bill had earned two college degrees, one in math at Gettysburg College, and one in architecture at Drexel Institute of Technology, taking classes at night. And during that time I had given him four children and a lot of moral support.

I wondered now, as we finished cleaning up the kitchen together, if he ever guessed how depressed I had often been over wanting to leave him these last few years, before I started back at college instead? He had never shown the slightest indication of recognizing my discontent, at least not since we had gone for that one session with a marriage counselor a few years ago. We had both found the visit a demeaning and demoralizing experience, one we could not bear repeating. We had dropped the close examination of our relationship after that, returning to our habit formed over many years of being nice to each other. We never argued. And soon after, in the fall of 1963, I had begun my studies at Penn in the Continuing Education for Women program.

I felt sure Bill hoped I had forgotten my unhappiness. But when I had time to think about it at all these days, I was secretly amazed at his lack of awareness. Our marriage had descended still further into boredom, and super-niceness, and an utter dearth of communication on a personal level. This was an undeniable fact about which my husband of nearly eighteen years seemed to be completely oblivious. Our time spent together had become one long siege in front of a television set. Only my college studies had been able to liberate me from that, and from a constant desire to flee from the hypocrisy of my own life. Being at Penn made it easier now, the waiting. The waiting until the children grew up . . . .

That Thursday evening in our kitchen, my boss Connie Richardson's face took shape in my mind all at once.

"It's incredible how many of these Continuing Ed women are coming back to school instead of getting a divorce!" she had said to me one day while dictating a letter for me to type. "At least half of them, Gwen, from the stories I hear in my office." Now I cringed inwardly, remembering the day she had told me that. Wondering if she had yet guessed the truth about me. That I was one of those women. That I too suffered from "the problem that has no name."

Pretending now to be absorbed in sweeping the kitchen floor, I observed my husband as he poured himself a glass of milk from the refrigerator to go with his nightly Twinkie. Yes, he was a sweet man, a kind man, still a good-looking man. But should sweetness, and kindness, and a fit body and face, be enough to contribute to a relationship with a spouse that you had intended to be with for fifty years or so? And should a good sexual rapport be enough? Shouldn't there be a mutual pooling of enthusiasms, each partner bringing to the other some stimulation as to the wonders of life? It shouldn't be all one-sided. The Big Ideas didn't matter, as long as basic premises were agreed upon. I cared not a whit that Bill was not a deep thinker who liked to argue vehemently with others about the meaning of existence. I knew men like that; and after a while it got tiresome listening to them.

It was the little times that mattered most to me; that really made up a marriage. The hours and days spent together that could be—ought to be—rich in companionship and the sharing of interesting pursuits. Bill seemed to have reneged on those "little times" years ago. The switch to the television set was too close at hand; too simple a way to fill the hours in the evenings until time to go to bed. More than that: I wanted moral support, not just for the adventures, but for the hard places as well. I never seemed to get that when I most needed it, and as a result had stopped telling my husband years ago when problems and disappointments really bothered me.

I knew what had happened. For so long I had hated to even frame the idea in my consciousness. But sometimes it materialized, in spite of me. We had married too young, he and I—before either of us had completely broken the emotional ties with parents and home. Bill had been the cherished only son, the second-born of two, with a sister much older. I was the third of nine sisters, growing up in a family where older siblings helped care for all younger ones. Gradually, over time, the behavior patterns we had each brought to our marriage relationship had solidified. Until now I had come to feel like my husband's mother.

I had had no time to dwell on that awful realization for months. And now, before my resentment toward Bill could grow, turning inevitably, as it always did, to guilt and self-hatred, I went upstairs to our bedroom to gather the articles I thought I would need for my trip to Alabama.

Afterward, Bill drove me to Cherry Hill, to the home of Fred Clever, one of the men in the Human Relations Conference, and we borrowed his Boy Scout son's sleeping bag, and at the father's insistence, a knapsack as well. "You'll need this, Gwen, to carry a few things like food and clothing, just in case," Fred said. "Especially if they put you in jail."

                    *   *   *

11.

"We must love our white brothers no matter what they do to us. We must make them *know* that we love them. *Jesus* still cries *out* in words that echo across the centuries: 'Love your enemies; *bless* them that curse you; *pray* for them that despitefully use you.' *This* is what we must *live* by. We must meet *hate* with love."

—Martin Luther King, Jr.,
Minister and Civil Rights Agitator
(From G G.'s "Words To Live By")

Upon our return from Cherry Hill that Wednesday evening, while Bill worked at his drafting table on our sun porch, I packed away my few necessities in the borrowed knapsack, making a test trial on my back to see how heavy it would be. I took out a book from my Italian Literature course, the book from which I was supposed to be translating several pages by Monday. Then I took out an extra pair of shoes in order to further lighten the load. The children were all there with me, upstairs in the bedroom, and casually I explained to them where I would be going next day. Only Wendi seemed to comprehend that there might be danger lurking there.

"I thought they were killing people down in Selma," she said, frowning at me. I guessed that the fate of her choir director's cousin was etched vividly in her memory.

"I'll be perfectly safe," I said. "I'll be with a busload of other people, don't you see?"

"Yeah," said my older son. "Mom's always doing stuff like this, and she's never gotten hurt." Stuff? What did he mean by that? Though Kenny was traditionally our worry-wart, he seemed not overly concerned at the moment for my welfare.

I laughed and said "Yeah." And cool-man Scotty said, "I think it's neat! You'll be back for my birthday, won't you, Mom?"

"Don't worry about that, honey. I'll be back Monday night. In plenty of time to get ready for your birthday," I assured him. "You have your present picked out by then." Scotty always began dreaming about his March birthday present as soon as Christmas was over.

Julie climbed onto my bed beside the knapsack and sleeping bag, bewildered that I was going anywhere at all. I sat down beside her, and took her on my lap. I tried to explain to her, to all of them, actually, what my intended journey was all about. I told them I wanted to help make our country an even better place than it already was. So they could say the pledge of allegiance to the flag every morning in school without resenting the words "with liberty and justice for all," the way I had always done. I told them that the phrase was not yet true, because in a large part of our country, in the states that made up the South, Negroes like Edna were not allowed to vote. And if you couldn't vote, you couldn't make things better.

When I was done, my youngest patted my face affectionately.

"Okay, Mommy. I want Edna to be able to vote. I like Edna, Mommy."

Kenny said, "She already can vote, silly! Because she lives in New Jersey. She just doesn't believe in voting, 'cause she's a Black Muslim now."

I was surprised he knew Edna's new views on voting. "Mom—my Lenni-Lenape Indians report—it's due next Monday; remember?" Kenny said.

"I'm sorry, Ken. You'll have to print it in in ink this time. Or type it up yourself."

Kenny, at twelve, loved doing research reports. His face always glowed with joy when he was working on one. He liked them to be beautifully done as well as factually correct. Which was why I had always typed for him the final copy.

"Okay, Mom, I'll do it that way," and he went off whistling to pick up his plastic tanks and soldiers from the hall floor, without coercion. Scotty followed soon after. The two girls hung around for a while longer, both of them still apprehensive. Wendi had been asked out to a party for Saturday evening. The boy who had invited her had asked to take her to a movie the previous weekend, but had never shown up for the date.

"Suppose he does it again, Mom . . . ?" *And you wouldn't be here to help me bear it,* the tone of her voice implied.

"He won't, Wendi. I'm sure he won't. He seemed to have a reasonable excuse for last Saturday." But I wasn't sure. And neither was she. "And if he does, I know you can handle it," I told her. "I know it would hurt—but you wouldn't bother with him again if that happened, would you? I hope not."

"No. I guess not," Wendi said. She had been loving the boy from afar for a couple of weeks now. How many hurts would it take? And so we went on, saying words to each other we didn't really mean. Not saying what we really felt inside, about anything.

And when all four of my children came to kiss me goodnight and went off to bed, one after the next over the course of that Wednesday evening, I wanted to tell them how much I loved them, and how proud of them I was, and how grateful for letting me go without argument. But I didn't. I feared I might frighten them if I sounded too serious. (In those days, parents didn't say "I love you" to members of their own family on a daily basis. They assumed their children, at least, always knew it.)

Alone in my bedroom, I had mulled over at length the problem of whom I should tell about my going. My housekeeper Edna, certainly. I'd have to call her that night, since I wouldn't be seeing her on the morrow. Thursday was one of her "early" days to come to us, and she'd be leaving for home as soon as Wendi got home from school to be with her little sister Julie. My boss Connie Richardson? Since I'd see her tomorrow at work, I could wait until the last minute to tell her in case she tried to dissuade me. There was Jim Clemson,* my engineer friend. I was scheduled to have lunch with him next day, and I'd tell him then. He was always terribly amused by my "shenanigans," as he called them. This one would really make him laugh! Other than informing those three, I'd make no farewell calls to anyone, I decided. No; no goodbyes.

With the exception of my sister Jocie, who lived only thirty miles further south in South Jersey, my eight sisters were scattered far away along the Eastern Sea Board, with the two youngest of them still living with my widowed mother in Florida. We were lucky if we saw each other once a year now; and in the meantime, we married ones sent what we called "potty chair letters" to each other in Round Robin style, kept going by our mother by means of timely reminders. ("Little Linda sat in her potty chair for fifteen minutes again today and finally did something," a sister in Georgia might write. Or "Tommy and his daddy went to Indian Guides together last night; they're carving totem poles for a special project." Or This, from a sister in Virginia, with one of mine, tacked on: "Wendi's fifth grade teacher says her grades would be better if she'd stop looking out the window and day-dreaming." Light stuff like that, sent around over the years, keeping us all in touch.)

It was an unwritten rule among us sisters that we never discussed the truly heavy stuff in writing or over the phone. We each had different interests and opinions anyhow. And much as we cared about one another, I was aware they all considered me to be "far out strange," in matters of politics and religion. I'd tell them all where I had been, once I was safely back from Selma. And there was no point in worrying my mother either. She had problems of her own raising two little girls alone without her husband, our father, and she had been dealing with Parkinson's disease since her twenties.

My friends these days were scattered too. My best friend Marion at college, and my best friend Doris in Merchantville—it seemed that lately I only saw them or spoke to them on the run. I'd had equally little time for church associates. And my neighbors and I merely waved to each other as I raced in and out of my front door. Edna my housekeeper, my boss Connie and my engineer friend Jim, I realized, taking stock, were the only regular contacts I had had all this school year outside of home and the classroom. I felt no obligation to give advance notice of my absence to anyone else.

*   *   *

Black and beautiful in spirit long before anyone had coined the slogan of "Black is beautiful," Edna Wilson had been my full-time housekeeper and baby-sitter for the nearly two years I'd worked at *Holiday* magazine, and again, during my freshman year at the University. I saw her less frequently than I wanted to, now that she was coming afternoons only, in order to be with Julie after morning kindergarten and until Wendi got home from school each day. But we remained fast friends.

It must have been sometime during the previous spring or summer that I began to notice a subtle change in Edna, and by and by she had explained it to me. She and her husband Eddie had become Black Muslims, followers of Elijah Muhammed, the leader of the Nation of Islam in America. Edna's entire outlook toward her own life had improved as a result, she said. We had discussed it often after that; in the days when she was still coming full-time and had gotten to my house early enough to share coffee with me before I left for work. She had taught me the Arabic words that all Muslims use to greet one another.

She had given me literature to read and had explained to me that the Black Muslims did not go around trying to eliminate "white devils" from the face of the earth, in spite of newspaper stories to the contrary. But they did believe in fiercely defending themselves if attacked, whether by white people, or by anyone else. Her new religion had done for her and Eddie, she said, what years of Christian doctrine had never been able to do: made them feel proud, given them dignity; taught them to love themselves and each other. And listening to Edna, I had never found the slightest reason to fear for the safety of my children when they were left in her care.

"*Ah-salahium-salaam*, Edna," I greeted her in Arabic that evening when she answered her phone. *Peace be with you.*

"*Malakium-salaam,*" she said back, without skipping a beat. *Peace to you, too.*

"Guess what!" I said, letting myself sound excited. "I'm going to Alabama on a bus tomorrow evening, to march with Martin Luther King in Selma, Alabama."

"Oh?"

I knew she wouldn't, couldn't approve. Black Muslims heartily resented King's use of techniques of non-violent passive resistance borrowed from India's Mahatma Gandhi, the Hindu lawyer who had successfully used similar tactics to end British rule in his country after World War II. Muslims felt that the end did not justify the means. The use of non-violence seemed to them to further emasculate black males, who needed instead to have their aggressive instincts sharpened for their own and their families' survival. Furthermore, the ends in this case they considered equally reprehensible. Muslims refused to vote at all in a white-controlled society, where their votes would be meaningless. Dr. King, they claimed, was raising false hopes.

But I was counting on Edna's grasping my intent, however misguided, and helping me if she could. I told her my plans.

"So I won't be home by four as usual on Friday afternoon, Edna. Is there any chance you could stay later that day, until Bill gets home from

work? Could you fix their supper, maybe, so my kids won't be too upset?"
Bill could do that, of course. Wendi too could do it. But I'd be better able
to go off with a clear conscience, if I knew a woman of Edna's calm abilities
was in charge. I could be sure there'd be some kind of order, at least for
Friday evening. *Day after tomorrow!*

"I'll be happy to do it, Gwen, Edna said. "I'll stay on Monday too." I
had told her I would be late getting home that evening.

"I was hoping you'd say that!" I replied. "But listen—I'll have to pay
you what I owe you for this week when I get back, since I won't be at the
office to get my pay-check on Friday . . . ."

"Don't you worry about it. We can manage," the sweet voice said in
my ear. She had become my friend over the past two years and not just my
employee.

"Are you sure . . . . ?" I had never been late with her pay before. I could
only guess how badly she and Eddie counted on it every two weeks.

"Sure, I'm sure." And then she added, teasing me, "Gwen, I only want
to tell you one thing before you go. When the bullets start flying, hit the
deck!"

She was getting even with me for telling her not too long ago the same
thing. We giggled together, remembering the Black Muslim convention she
and Eddie had attended in Chicago only a couple of weeks ago. Malcolm
X, the militant rebel who'd broken with Elijah Muhammed some time
before, had been assassinated in New York City in February. He had been
shot down in cold blood while he was standing behind a podium up on a
stage preaching peace with the white man. And all the news reports had
implied that the Black Muslims had been responsible for his murder.

Since then, Edna had told me, there had been retaliatory threats
against Elijah Muhammed's life from followers of Malcolm X. Members
were concerned there might be an attempt to kill their national leader at
that upcoming convention in Chicago. So the day before Edna left with
her husband for the convention, I had expressed my concern for her safety,
telling her that if she insisted on going, she should "Remember, Edna,
when the bullets start flying, hit the deck!" We shared impulses in common,
she and I. We felt tough and we felt brave, as we laughed in the teeth of
potential danger.

Now I said, "Don't worry, I'll remember! But there aren't going to be
any bullets, Edna. Besides, remember what you told me when you left for
Chicago? Who would want to shoot a woman, you said."

*   *   *

At the University of Pennsylvania next day, when I reported to work, I found that Connie Richardson was ill at home. Instead of calling her there, I decided to leave a brief explanatory note on her desk for her to find when she returned, telling myself I ought not concern her with this at her home when she wasn't feeling well. Whereas deep down my real reason was that she would read the note only after I had left and couldn't be stopped by her cool reservations. She'd understand when she'd had time to think it over, no need to worry about that.

Connie was all for women taking their rightful place as first-class citizens in American society. Though we had recently discussed the Selma situation superficially—indeed, I had given her no indication of the inner turmoil I was suffering because of it—surely she would approve of my taking such a stand. Surely she would realize that I had done it for everyone who couldn't go, but wanted to.

The note I wrote said, "Connie. Gone to Selma to walk with M. L. King. Back Tuesday a.m. Wish me luck. Love, Gwen."

But the curt message on the note looked presumptive, lying there on my boss's desk blotter at lunch-time, when I was preparing to leave the office for the day. It looked a little bit arrogant, too, not to mention a lot foolish. Because suppose I changed my mind and decided not to go after all? Anything could happen between now and tomorrow evening. One of my children might get sick, or I might get sick. And then, when I came back to the office on Friday, after having *not* gone to Selma, I'd have to explain that ridiculous note. I couldn't really be sure I was going, could I, until I was actually on that charter bus?

I tore up the note and put the pieces in my coat pocket. I'd ask Bill to phone my boss tomorrow morning, tell her my trip had been completely unexpected. Surely he wouldn't mind doing that for me. He should feel no embarrassment in vocalizing it after the fact: "Gwen has gone to Selma." He would probably be proud. Wouldn't he?

Constance Richardson was a rock; she was like one of the staunch rocks upon which our republic was founded back in the old Colonial days, and I admired her tremendously. Rocks did not go out on protest marches, no matter how commendable the cause. Rocks of democracy worked quietly behind the scenes with no reward except the knowledge that they were pillars of a society based upon enlightened self-interest. Moderate at all times in their activism, rocks seldom got angry at circumstance they considered beyond their control. They always tried to understand the other guy's point-of-view, even if they did not at all condone his or her behavior. They knew innately that lasting social change took time to come about. They were also convinced that their special brand of reliability kept democracy from foundering.

If they were impossible to move to extremes of righteous action, rocks were equally impervious to being swayed by demagogues. I had until lately prided myself upon being in this category, in spite of my long-range commitment to the as yet unpopular cause of Negro rights. Now I feared that if I did not go to Selma, but Connie found out I had attempted to, our friendship would be diminished by one small iota. And all for nothing.

Once, Connie Richardson had given me what was the supreme compliment to a person resolved to be a hypocrite no longer. "You're one of the most truthful people I know," she had said to me only a month or so ago. I had cringed inwardly because of my lie of omission about my marriage. And now, remembering her words, I still couldn't bring myself to leave the note.

I cleared off my own desk, almost as if parting from it for the last time. I dusted the bookends and the telephone and around the typewriter. I watered the plant in the pot. That darned lily-of-the-valley, I thought with a nagging sense of being betrayed. *That darned thing's going to bloom while I'm gone.* I picked up the notebook in which I took notes in shorthand at my classes. I'd have one class this afternoon before I'd be free to go home. And get ready.

The outer office of the College For Women was nearly empty when I went through it to get to the outside. Gina Allesandrini*, a young clerical worker handling student files, was sitting at her desk marking time by the telephone until someone came back from lunch to relieve her. She called goodbye to me, as she always did when I left for the day. I called goodbye back at her, as I always did. But this time I lingered with the open door to the outside in one hand, debating in my mind whether or not to tell her . . . . what I was planning to do.

"Gina ?"

I could go over to her, tell her calmly where I intended to go that evening. I felt certain she would be sympathetic because we had discussed the situation in Alabama several times over the past week. But—how sympathetic was it possible for a young girl to be with an Italian last name like Allesandrini? Gina was the product of an ethnic group I was particularly fond of. The affectionate regard in which I held it was the main reason I had decided to make Italian my required language at Penn. But I was also well aware that this particular ethnic group was still struggling to pull itself up the social ladder of American society. They were still hoping to assimilate themselves into our culture while making as few "waves" as possible.

Traditionally city dwellers since their arrival en masse in the early nineteen hundreds, Italian-Americans were the most affected by the spreading blight of urban black ghettoes. They seemed to feel the most threatened, the ones caught in the middle. Being shocked about the beating of fellow human beings was one thing. The murder of a white man-of-the-cloth could easily instill feelings of disgust and revulsion. But understanding why a white mother would go off a thousand miles to a hostile environment on a half-cocked mission of mercy to Southern "niggers"? Well, that was something else again.

"Hmmm?" Gina looked up quickly, disturbed by something in the way I had said her name. She sat with comb poised in her long dark hair, waiting for me to continue.

I said, "Would you—could I ask you to please water my potted plant next week? In case I don't get in?"

"Sure thing, Gwen," she answered back.

And I let the door close slowly upon her puzzled face.

*   *   *

12.

"I could see you just had to get it out of your system."
—James S. Clemson*, friend and chemical engineer
(Post-Selma comments from the folks back home)

By March of 1965, Jim Clemson* and I had been meeting for lunch on an average of once every couple of weeks for going on two years. We'd gotten acquainted while acting the lead roles in a play about Egypt for a little theater group in Cherry Hill. Jim had played the sun-god worshiper Pharoah Akenaton, while I had been his proud and doting wife, Queen Nefertiti. (Happily, I had never suffered from my customary indecision and embarrassment while pretending to be someone else in a theatrical production. I always knew my lines and was able to project them with confidence so all could hear.)

Jim and I had quickly become fast friends behind the scenery in spite of his mother. She was a roly-poly little woman who looked to be half her only son's height, with thinning hair dyed blonde to match the color of her son's hair. Daisy Clemson* had successfully devoted the past few decades of her life to seeing that her only child James never got married and left her. In line with this noble goal, she had never missed a play rehearsal. Sitting in the front row of the theater practically on top of the stage, Daisy had supervised our every move on stage with scrupulous concentration. Even I, safely married and the mother of four, acting a part on a stage—I obviously constituted a threat, to Daisy. I saw daggers in her eyes when she looked my way.

Backstage in the wings, waiting for our cues, Jim and I would giggle about it. We even managed in those few stolen moments to compare notes, making the interesting discovery that while he lived in another county from mine, his engineering office was located beside the South Jersey highway I took on my drive home to Merchantville. And long after the play was over, there was something deliciously risque about the two of us meeting for lunch every other Thursday behind Jim's mother's back—even when it was so innocuous an affair as a hurried hour in a diner near Jim's office. So innocuous had it been that in the beginning I hadn't even bothered to mention it to Bill. And later, I hadn't wanted to. It was my little secret; a pleasant break in my life's hectic pace.

Aside from our both being left-handed and loving to study foreign languages that we'd never ever get a chance to speak, Jim and I had discovered one important bond: we needed each other. A bachelor of thirty-nine when I met him, Jim had long recognized that his existence was severely limited by his life-term commitment to a jealous, demanding mother. He realized that because of this he had given up a chance at all the good things life was providing other people: romantic love, children, a family of his own.

The poor fellow never went anywhere, except to work, without his mother. Incredibly, all his evenings and weekends were spent, without exception, in her company, and because she was too lame now, to go anywhere, Jim never took a vacation from his job except to paint the house he and his mother lived in. He had once dated women years ago, he told me, but there had always been too much hell to pay; too many screams of rage and threats of suicide from Daisy. Jim the henpecked son was too dominated to fight back.

Jim Clemson the engineer chafed continually under the terms of his imprisonment at home, and he told me so. But he no longer attempted to escape. However peripherally, I was one small bright light in his otherwise generally dull existence; the one contact he cherished to help him remember he was an interesting human being in his own right.

It flattered me to realize how much Jim looked forward to those diner lunches with me every couple of weeks, for which he always picked up the check. And we chatted occasionally on other days over the telephone. He seemed to enjoy hearing my stories about the children, my tales of going to school at a great and thriving Ivy-League university, my attempts at civil rights involvement. I shared with him the excitement of my courses at Penn, the nuances of my secretarial job with the Director of Continuing Education for Women. All on his own, he took up the study of Italian—a language I had seemed to select almost arbitrarily.

Equally peripherally, Jim was the emotional bulwark missing from my own life. I knew, when things looked dismal and there was no one else to tell them to, that I could reach him over the phone at his workplace, Monday through Friday. I knew that he would even come for an unscheduled lunch on an emergency basis so we could talk things over. It was Jim who had listened to my anguish when President Kennedy was shot in November of 1963, during my first semester at Penn. Both of us were Republicans then; he, a far more avid one than I. He had "never cared for the man," was his comment about Kennedy. But I had called him at his office in tears that Friday afternoon after the news came from Dallas, and he had come rushing to the diner to meet me.

We sat across from each other in our customary booth, I wailing that "he was our president, our elected leader, regardless of what party we belong to. How dare someone do this to our American democracy?"

His own voice breaking, Jim had soothed my sobs of grief and rage with "I know, Gwen, I know how it hurts," all the while patting my hand across the table and passing me his clean white handkerchief to wipe the tears from my cheeks. And then I went home to reassure my husband and children that while it was indeed a scary time for America, everything was going to be all right.

It was Jim Clemson too who had consoled me when I'd received the results of my first mid-semester test that fall after seventeen years away from high school. The time I got a D—in Race Relations.

"Race Relations! Can you imagine, Jim—Race Relations?" I had blubbered. "I started out with that because I thought it would be easy. Because I already knew a lot about the subject . . . ."

He had said, "I know, Gwen, I know," and again had handed me his clean white handkerchief. "Look: you have to learn ahead of time what each professor wants, what kind of tests he gives. Then you'll have no trouble. Get to know a couple of the students in each class, Gwen. They'll tell you what's out there on the grapevine."

He had been right, of course. I had followed his advice, and from that time on I had made only A's and B's in my courses. More importantly, I had gotten to know a few of the college-aged kids in my classes. I had become friends with several of them and found I was wrong to have supposed they wouldn't want to be bothered with me, a woman much older than they were. They seemed to like and respect me, and supposed that because I was older, I had more wisdom than they had. I let them think that, anyway.

For a little while I had even fancied, because of the emotional vacuum that existed in my own life, that I was falling in love with Jim. I was willing to overlook the fact that he was tall, and blond, and looked like a politician, all of which I considered definite negatives. But time had quickly divested me of any delusions that Jim Clemson had just been waiting for the right woman to come along to give him courage. He had truly dedicated himself to his mother's service for as long as she lived. And the idea of his choosing to leave her for a woman with four young children, even if I hadn't had a husband . . . . well, that was too ludicrous a notion for me to entertain for very long. As for a possible affair? Well, I had no time. Jim had no freedom. So I got over him. I settled for having a comforting friend instead.

Time had further shown me that compatible as Jim and I were in left-handedness, and academic and linguistic interests, we were poles apart in other areas. Particularly on the issue of race. Essentially a brave man, there were but two human beings in this world whom he feared, he told me sardonically. His mother, first of all. And next came Negroes.

I was a few minutes late for our luncheon date at one o'clock on Thursday of the day I was scheduled to take the bus trip to Alabama. I had trouble finding a parking spot behind the busy diner for my VW beetle. I was chilled in my light jacket and out-of-sorts when I got inside. Jim was already there, sitting in our customary booth. He had ordered coffee for both of us and the two cups sat steaming, still too hot to drink. Piling my jacket and purse on the seat beside me, I slid in across from him, giving him a fake smile in greeting.

"What's up?" He could always tell when something was, just by looking at my face.

"You'll get a real kick out of this, old buddy, you're really going to laugh," I said, and with no further preliminaries I added, "I'm going to Selma. Tonight, on a charter bus."

He had not laughed, not at all. Instead his lips drew tight over his mouth. "You can't be serious!" And then, when I continued to sit there silently smiling at him, he added, "Yes! You *are* serious, aren't you?"

"Perfectly." I kept right on smiling, unable to stop.

"But . . . . in God's name, Gwen . . . . why?" There was no answering smile from Jim, not even in his eyes.

"I think I can help down there," I said. "Oh, I don't mean *help* help. Just *be* there. They're going to need a lot of us down there, you know. They need bodies. Particularly white ones."

"So you're going to offer yours? For what purpose?" Jim spat out. "Don't you realize that King and his bunch are making dupes of all those white people going down there?"

I knew he didn't mean white Southerners. He meant the young Caucasians going down from the North to work with Negroes to change things. He meant the ministers and priests and rabbis who had answered Dr. King's first call a week ago. Jim's voice had lowered to a tone that was almost threatening. His face was reddening. He looked like a seething volcano about to explode.

"I—I thought you'd think it was funny!" I stammered, sober at last.

"Funny! The whole thing is so unnecessary! Don't you know that there's a bill in Congress right now which would give Negroes down there their voting rights? Johnson sent it to the Hill three days ago, didn't you know? There's no earthly need for a march now, just to prove a point, goddamn it!" Jim seethed.

And I retorted, "I know all about that. But don't you see, we have to make sure—that the bill passes in both the Senate and the House of Representatives. That has to happen, you know, before the president can sign it into law. We have to *make sure* . . . . !"

The waitress came for our orders just then, and Jim calmed down long enough to ask for our usual tomato soup and cheeseburgers. While we waited, I told Jim of my arrangements. I told him that I had them all made except for drawing out the necessary funds from the bank, and I'd do that on my way home this afternoon. I'd stop at my bank and still get home in time to be there when Julie got there from school at two-thirty. Edna was going to stay late tomorrow and Monday, I told him.

"Look, Jim," I wound up, and I was still trying to keep things light, "I know you don't at all share my concern for the plight of American Negroes. You've always made that perfectly plain, and . . . ."

"I don't know anyone else who does, not to the extent that you do, Gwen," he interrupted me. "I think you've lost the good sense you were born with!"

There it was again, that business of lacking good sense.

I told him I knew I couldn't expect him to understand why I was doing this. "But—please, believe me, I'm doing this for you, too! For all of us!'

"Don't do me any favors." His voice dripped sarcasm.

I said I was doing it for every one of us Americans. I said that we, as a nation, had an obligation to straighten this mess out. To give Southern Negroes their rights, let them be recognized as first-class citizens like the rest of us, so we could all move on to other things. Such as what was happening to our young men being drafted and sent to Vietnam, a disproportionate number of whom were Negroes.

We owed it to ourselves, if to no one else, to right matters, I went on. He and I had discussed the Selma situation many times during past weeks over our diner lunches. We had never fought over it; we were both too polite to argue vehemently. Up to the present, when our words had begun to take on more than an edge of annoyance, we had both known it was time to change the subject.

"Gwen," he said, and he was pleading now. "Don't go. It's not our business down there. Let the South take care of it."

"Jim," I said, "I know you think it's none of our business. I know you think these things take time. But Jim . . . . not everybody has your patience . . . I mean, I don't know *anyone* who is as patient as you are . . . ." Waiting for an old woman to die, I meant, and he knew it. Waiting for that old woman to die before he could live. How could I convince him, in a few brief minutes, of the truth of what I had been learning in school? What words could I find so as to share with him the insights I had gained into the predicament of black Americans? So many times and over so many years in my life, going as far back as I could remember? *Oh, my poor Nellie Grey, they have taken you away, and I'll never see my darling anymore. I am sitting by the River and a-weepin' all the day, for you're gone from the old Kentucky shore* . . . .

But then, I had been telling Jim Clemson these things for quite a long time. And it was the one tragedy for which he had never once said to me,

"I know, Gwen, I know," and pulled out a clean white handkerchief for me to use to wipe away my tears.

We glared at each other over our cheeseburgers. We were full of quiet horror at the chasm that had suddenly yawned between us. Our eyes said, let's not fight. Not now, when tonight I would be gone. But we were at an impasse. Neither of us knew how to settle it, and get beyond.

Jim broke first. Cooking his head to one side in that winning way he had, he said gently, "I know why you feel you have to do these crazy things. It's because you're a Libra. A left-handed one, at that. Nothing worse than a left-handed Libra. You people are always trying to make life fair. You can't accept that it just can never be."

"Oh, for God's sake, Jim . . ." He was only teasing me, trying to find for me a way out. Why couldn't I take his offer with a laugh and leave the matter alone? Drop it before it destroyed our friendship for all time?

"Let's see, Jim. I've known you for all of twenty-two and a half months now," I said with my most pleading tone of voice.

And Jim said, still trying to cajole me, "There goes the statistician again."

"All right; so I'm a statistician. But in all that time, haven't you heard one word I've been saying? Haven't you gained an ounce of sympathy? Some of our cities are in shambles enclosed by invisible walls of prejudice; black ghettos full of poverty and misery and violence. And now they're starting to have riots . . ." I knew I should stop lecturing him, but I couldn't.

"You're even afraid to drive into Philly after dark, you're told me that! And yet more and more black families continue pouring into our Northern cities every day, the fathers mostly unskilled Negroes who are coming up from the South hoping to find a decent job, and maybe a little dignity along with it. Don't you see that if they had the vote down South, maybe they could change things enough that they wouldn't want to leave. From a practical point of view, did you ever think about that? . . . . And I've been telling you about educated Negroes. Some of them are even better educated than you and I, believe it or not. Some of them have good-paying jobs and are rolling in dough—and still they have to live in places, right here in New Jersey, that you wouldn't be caught dead in!"

Warming more and more to my subject, I was getting my social problems mixed up, and thus mixing for Jim a potpourri of Negro complaints.

"You know all this, my friend," I said in as quiet a tone as I could muster under the circumstances. I leaned across the table so as to be sure he heard my every word. "I've been telling you all this for the past twenty-two-and-a-half months. And you can still sit there and tell me it's none of our business. Why, if you can't sympathize with their plight, can't you at least grasp that it's the North that's being duped? By Southern politicians, who are very cleverly sending their so-called Negro problem up here to us!"

"Who said I can't sympathize? I just don't want them living next to me." His voice in reply was colder than I had ever heard it.

"Because of your mother! She'd have a stroke!" I blurted out.

"Because of me," Jim said. "And keep your voice down. People are looking at us."

I stared across at this stranger in the business suit and tie, wondering if I had ever really known him. The blue eyes were cold and unwavering. How could a person so intelligent, so educated, so considerate and self-confident, so utterly decent, I had discovered over time, how could he be so blindly prejudiced? Before Jim, I had thought I had it all figured out. Before Jim, I had thought that prejudice was the crutch of little people, white men who were basically mean and cruel, people who had little reward in their lives to make them feel worthy, and thus they had to feel better than someone. Better than a person born with brown skin.

Take my father-in-law's prejudices. He hated so many groups with such passion. And not just Negroes. He hated Jews. Catholics. Republicans. You name it. Any group he didn't belong to himself, he hated. Yet the individual members of those groups that he happened to know personally? They were exempt from his hatred. Yes, even a Negro, here and there. Like his yard man. "You'd never find a better fella than Sammy," I had heard him say more than once. "But all the rest of them . . ."

I had come to understand, after these eighteen years of marriage to Bill, some truths about his father. Having only a tenth-grade education, he was a Philadelphia Navy Yard machinist who had never made much money or had much ego-satisfaction. I had come to see that my father-in-law had to feel better than somebody just to get through.

But this man, this Jim, my friend? This peaceful, gentle man who had been given all the material advantages American society had to offer? Did he not also realize first-hand what psychological slavery was, and that he too was a victim of it?

"What would you do," I asked him, quietly earnest, linking my fingers above my plate of half-eaten food and leaning toward him again so no one else in the diner could hear what I was about to ask. "What would you ever do, Jim Clemson, if you had to shake hands with a black man? Suppose a

Negro engineer from Harvard, say, with a master's degree and dressed like you, came to work in your office? At the desk right next to you? And you were standing there that first day, being introduced to him as he came in the door with your boss? What on earth would you do if he held out his hand? Would you shake it?"

Jim laughed aloud for the first time, a ripple of genuine mirth. "I'd do it, of course. Sure. I'd shake his hand."

"There, you see! One point for me! I guess you're not totally hopeless. Now if we can just go on from there, that's a beginning!"

"Of course, I'd have to wipe my hand off afterwards," Jim said, a grim expression on his face. "I'd shake his hand. But then I'd have to put my hand behind my back and wipe it off."

I could only stare at him, too shocked to speak.

Well, I had asked for it, hadn't I? I'd been condescendingly, insufferably self-righteous. He could not have meant those sickening words. Not really. He had just been terribly deprived, all his life, with no chance to associate with minorities. But wait! He had grown up in Missouri, the very same state that my own parents came from. And it was they who had raised me without prejudice toward any group of people. And Jim had been an ensign in the United States Navy during World War II. Surely he had met black sailors on board ships whom he had liked, and even come to know? No; President Truman had not integrated the Armed Forces of the United States until World War II was safely over.

But why did Jim insist upon baiting me so ruthlessly? And why could I never make him understand anything, no matter how hard I tried? *He would have to wipe off his hand,* he had said . . . . ? I stood up, on the verge of tears, and slipped my arms into my jacket. And then I sat down again just as abruptly.

"The trouble with you," I said, "is you like to play games. You like to pretend you're the Southern gentlemen, there in your big house with your mother and your fifty windows. Which makes a total, statistically, of twenty-five windows apiece." Now I was truly on a roll, delivering to him my farewell speech. "Jim, do you know there are people in this country who, when you average it out, don't own even one window? That there are children, little black children, who go to bed knowing rats may run across them while they sleep? May even bite off a finger or toe, so I've heard? And there's never, ever any hope of their getting out of those terrible conditions! Because no matter how much money their parents ever make . . . ."

Jim was amused by me now, just as in the old days. A half-smile creasing his unblemished Caucasian face, he sat quietly, sipping his second cup of coffee.

Hey, wait up!" he called out as I got up abruptly and turned to leave. "How much money you taking with you?"

Why should I tell him? I didn't have to tell him. "Seventy-five dollars. Forty of it is for my round-trip bus fare." My eyes on the buttons of my jacket, I refused to look at him. How could I ever have thought I liked him, much less loved him?

"I don't need very much," I said. "I'm taking a sleeping bag. And some food."

"A sleeping bag!" He pulled a single bill from his pocket. "Here, you crazy nut. Here's another twenty, it' s all I have with me after I pay for our lunch. You might need it."

I didn't want to take it. But I didn't want to leave him like this, either. It would be ridiculously melodramatic of me to go stalking out of this diner without so much as a goodbye. I'd take his money, in case of emergency. Mail it back to him when I returned. And never ever have lunch with him again.

"Thank you." I reached out and took the money from his fingers. I hesitated a moment longer. "See you on television," I said with a forced grin.

"I hope not," Jim said. His voice though sober was kind. "Be careful. Don't do dumb things." He did care about our friendship, he truly did!

"I won't," I said, looking back into his now softened blue eyes. "I won't do dumb things."

"And Gwen—I've got to say one thing for you. You may not have much good sense. But you've got guts!"

I wouldn't mail the money back. I'd bring it back. I wouldn't give up on him. Not yet. After all, wasn't he, when you got right down to it, just like nearly every other white man I knew?

But one thing was certain. I had to go to Selma now, come hell or high water. My friend Jim Clemson had seen to that. He thought I had guts.

* * *

END OF PART THREE

PART FOUR

JOURNEY OF A THOUSAND MILES

13.

"....I believe that man will not merely endure: he will prevail. He is immortal, not because he alone among creatures has an inexhaustible voice, but because he has a soul, a spirit capable of compassion and sacrifice and endurance."

—William Faulkner, American Writer,
accepting the Nobel Prize for Literature, 1950
(From G G.'s "Words To Live By")

My husband Bill and I were at Exit 4 on the New Jersey Turnpike by eight forty-five that Thursday evening of March 18th. We sat in the front seat of the VW beatle for awhile, and then we got out and stood on one of the concrete curbs that separated the four toll booths, after first explaining to the toll collector that I was there to meet a bus. We conversed with each other in short, pleasant sentences as we always did, speaking of mundane family matters. I gave him some last minute reminders as to the care and feeding of our children.

"The world won't come to an end if they don't brush their teeth twice a day, Bill," I counseled him. "And they really don't need to take a bath every night, unless they want to. So don't worry about all that, okay?"

"I know that. I won't," he said.

"I just hope you won't get upset at them. Remember, we're trying to raise them to be adaptable human beings. I'd be more concerned with whether the two boys were teasing Julie." As I spoke, I kept hearing her piquant little voice calling after me as I left the house to get into the car. *"Bye, Mommy, bye!"*

"They drive me nuts when they do that," said Bill, gritting his teeth in mock anguish. "She screams at them in frustration, and then they both swear to me that the other one did it." My husband was a good-looking man. Sturdily built, with a flat stomach and firm muscles in his arms. No sign yet of a receding hairline. The brown crew cut and the innocent eyes under the heavy brows made him a youthful-looking man for thirty-eight. All four of our children resembled him, people said; much more than they did me.

He was only a few inches taller than I, but I liked that. I liked not having to bend my head back on my neck, like some kind of doll-child, to look up into a tall man's face. Surely there must be other wives who felt that way too. And other women who would find Bill attractive, in more ways than that one. And in case I decided to leave him permanently someday, he wouldn't have to live alone for very long, I suspected.

"Maybe the bus has forgotten you. It's getting late. Looks like its almost ten already," Bill said, consulting his watch in the dim light of the toll booth.

I said, "No, I'm positive they'll be here. Bill—I just remembered something! Kenny has a dentist appointment Monday after school! Will you be sure to remind him about it before you leave for work that morning? He forgot the last one, and if it keeps on, we're going to start getting charged for missed appointments."

"Maybe I should write Kenny a note?" my husband said.

"Good idea," I said, wishing for my sake that he would sound more positive. Never before had I asked him to look after the daily needs of our household and our children for as long as four days at a time. That had always been my job. "And whatever you do, honey, don't forget to call Connie Richardson, huh? Tomorrow morning, before nine? Tell her this trip came up suddenly. Very suddenly. And that's why I didn't call her myself."

I cringed inwardly at my cowardice while Bill took pencil and paper from his pocket and ran over his check list once more. Why, in the face of such diligence, could I not feel secure that something important wouldn't be forgotten? Bill tried so hard, once I had gotten through to him that a thing, an idea, a project was really important to us. We never argued.

But that had always been our problem: my making him understand, really understand, that certain aspects of life were very important to me.

Like encouraging our children to read instead of watching television. Like deciding where we should live based on our preference and not the circumstances of our birth. Like planning to spend some of our modest income on travel someday instead of on material possessions. Matters of that nature mattered a great deal; at least, to me they did. I so yearned to see more of the big, wide world before I died. Bill cared not a fig about that. He had served two years in the Navy and had seen a few Pacific islands.

He had thought to fix me some food to take on the bus, his own idea when I had repeated to him one of Miss Stassen's remarks to me: "No time to stop for steak dinners on the way down. And we'll be keeping our food and rest stops to a minimum," she had said.

Bill had been so sweet while rummaging around in the kitchen, assembling for me what he had labeled a "picnic lunch," for want of a more fitting phrase. One peanut-butter-and-jelly sandwich, two spot-peeled raw carrots, two bruised apples and a can of vanilla Metrecal powder.

"You might need this for energy on the march," he explained about this last, "There's no telling how long you might have to go without food, and all you'll need for this stuff is some water and a glass to mix it in." And I had nodded solemnly and hadn't pointed out to him that those two things—water and a glass—might be the hardest items of all to find. The lunch had gone into a paper sack and had been added to the top of the assortment in my knapsack, and I had been grateful to Bill for his concern.

Now I said, "Scotty's birthday is a week from Saturday, He's deciding on his present already, as usual. Did you know he wants a flying machine? Not a plane, mind you, but something he can strap on his arms and legs and really fly with."

There came once again Julie's high-pitched voice in my head: *Bye, Mommy, bye!*

"He's a real character, that kid," Bill said with an indulgent chuckle. "He probably thinks we can buy one for $9.98 at Two Guys."

Before leaving the house that evening I had taken my younger son's chin in my hand and had told him to look at me and listen carefully. "Now, Scotty," I had said to the pixie face with the cup-handle ears, "Don't you go getting into mischief while I'm gone. It's impossible for me to think of all the things you're not supposed to do and tell you ahead of time. Just use your imagination when you want to do a particular thing and try to decide if I'd like it or not. If it would be safe to do or not."

"I will, Mom," he said, and he had smiled back at me that sunny smile. I had never been able

to develop a blanket rule to cover all the schemes for adventure this child could manage to concoct in his active little brain. Even now he might be planning something dangerous. Never cruel or mean, he was genuinely interested in every challenge, every titillating bit of excitement the world around him had to offer. For an eight-year-old going on nine, that could often be a dangerous business.

"And you're to come straight home from school tomorrow and not go picking through people's trash cans along the way, okay? Edna will be here after school, and she's making you that meatloaf and macaroni you love for supper."

Now, at the turnpike entrance, I told Bill, "See if you can convince him there's nothing on the market to help kids fly without wings. At least, not yet. And Bill—keep a special eye on Wendi, okay? She's worried about my going on this trip. She asked me several times tonight if she could come with me, did you know that?"

"Bye, Mommy, 'bye!"

'Wendi had stood at my mirror that evening, her comb and curlers and bobby pins scattered across my dresser top, and precipitated one of our usually congenial disagreements.

"I should really be going with you, Mom," she had insisted, "because of the principle of the thing."

"You can't go, of course," I had told her. "But thanks, honey, for offering. I appreciate that."

"But why can't I go? I'm fifteen!" she had declared.

"That's exactly why," I told her calmly. "If you were eighteen, I might let you decide for yourself, though you won't be legally an adult until you're twenty-one. But fifteen? No. And you're not doing all that well in school this year, you know that. And you've got band practice on Monday for the spring concert. And what about that party you're invited to on Saturday night, to go to with what's-his-face? And how could you ever get along without your hair curlers for four whole days?"

She had ignored my attempt at humor with the mention of the curlers. "Fifteen is practically eighteen. You've said so yourself, Mom." Her voice trailed off. And then, "I would give up the dumb party if you'd take me along. And no one would care if I missed band practice. I wouldn't care."

I had given her my silver flute when she was in Junior High. She took private lessons for awhile and went into high school last September. She had been able to join not only the orchestra, but the Merchantville High School marching band. I had been so thrilled for her. I had played flute while in Woodbury High School, but only in the orchestra. Girls were not allowed nor welcomed into the all-boy band when I want to high school back in the 1940's. I had so longed to be able to wear a blue-and-gold uniform and cap and march around the football field in patterns, playing my flute, stepping high and proud. And now my daughter had been given that opportunity, and she wasn't thrilled, not one little bit. She wanted to be a pom-pom girl instead.

"And if you took me along, there'd be two of us," Wendi was saying. "We'd stick together, and no one would want to hurt us."

So it was my safety she had been worried about, all along; just as I had suspected. Nothing else would have kept her away from the chance to go out with one of the school's glamour boys. "No. It's out of the question," I said. "And no one is going to hurt me, honey." I quoted to her what Edna had said to me three weeks ago before she left for her Black Muslim Conference, "Don't worry about me, Gwen. Nobody would want to shoot a woman."

But my daughter had had to make one last stab at it. "If you leave me here with Dad, Mom, we'll just fight," she said matter-of-factly.

"You'd just better not, young lady! You'd just better help him, that's what you'd just better do!"

"Now, now, Mom! You don't believe in violence, remember?"

"I don't. You're right. But I could easily make an exception in your case!" I had said with a dramatic snarl.

And my daughter had grimaced, and groaned, and gone back to rolling her blondish hair—getting herself primed to try asking again later, I feared. Five-year-old Julie had put the cat down long enough to race around the upstairs for five minutes, searching for a plastic rain bonnet she had decided I should take with me.

"Julie," I had told her when I was at last ready to go downstairs and get into the car, "Don't come down to the door this time, sweetheart. You'll only give the dog a chance to run out. How about I open the window for you up here so you can wave goodbye?"

But there had been such disappointment in her face that I had relented and let her come down to the entrance hall and watch me go out the door. I had hugged the two boys in the upstairs den and instructed them to get into their pajamas and go to bed when Wendi told them it was time. Eyes glued on the television, they had nodded, their heads wobbling wordlessly up and down. So far my departure hadn't been at all like a Greer Garson-Walter Pigeon war movie, with the whole family lined up on the front stoop keeping stiff upper lips, while stirring violin music played in the background.

"Gee whiz!" I had pretended to fume at the boys' backs, "this is a great group! Just you fellas wait until *you* get to go on a trip—am *I* ever going to ignore *you!*"

But I was secretly relieved that my sons hadn't wanted to discuss the matter. The only thing that had really hurt was Wendi's attitude. She was angry at me now behind her closed and locked bedroom door.

"Come on," Bill had said. "If we don't get going, you'll be late meeting that bus." He had carried the sleeping bag and bulging knapsack down the steps. Julie had gone back for my chap stick in the bureau drawer when Kenny stopped me on the landing.

"Listen, Mom," he had said with sober dignity, "don't mind that dumb Wendi. She'll be okay after you've gone. She's just afraid you'll get killed or something,"

And I said, "What about you, Kenny? Are you worried about that?"

And he said, "Yep, I guess." His cheeks and chin had quivered a second, unmasking his own previously well hidden fears. "But I think you should go anyway." And then he added, "*Somebody* has to."

We had looked at each other solemnly, my older son and I. Maybe it was because he was small for his age that I had assumed he hadn't known what it was all about, this problem in Selma. Maybe there was more to his thirteenth year of life than playing with toy soldiers and making good grades. (There certainly had been, to mine, when I was Kenny's age.) This was the kid, I had all at once remembered as I stood there on the landing, staring into his anxious eyes, this was the kid who cried over dead birds . . . .

*   *   *

Nine-thirty at the tollbooths. The charter bus was very late by now. A fine rain was falling, and Bill and I had run out of things to say. I told him I'd better call home to see if something had gone wrong, and leaving him by the tollbooths to watch for the bus, I ran across the lanes to an outdoor phone booth and dialed my home number.

"Oh, hi, Mom!" said an icily-calm Wendi at last, in answer to many rings, "A lady called a long time ago from New York, just after you left. She said the bus would be over an hour late because they were just leaving."

"Oh? Was that all?" I said.

"And she said she was supposed to tell you to wait at a Howard Johnson restaurant on the Turnpike instead. Because the bus driver said he couldn't go off the Turnpike like that to pick you up. And then I told her you'd already left and I didn't think you'd call, and she said never mind, if you did call, to tell you to stick to the original plan and she'd talk the driver into it. She sounded nice," Wendi wound up.

"Oh, lord!" I groaned. And then I said, because the young soprano voice was unmistakably cool in its delivery, "Look, Wendi, someday you'll understand why I feel I have to do this."

"No I won't." She was respectfully adamant. "I never will." Ordinarily, when she was adamant, she neglected to be quite as respectful. Which is how I knew this was serious anger on her part.

"Listen, Wendi. Remember when you felt you were the one who had to talk to that boy in school who kept beating up Kenny? I couldn't do anything about it, you said, because I was an adult. But you said that *you* could. And you did. It's the same thing, don't you see? Sometimes a woman can do things and go places in safety that a man can't. And sometimes she should."

"But you're a mother." Her tone was accusatory, no doubt about it.

"All the more reason. And I'll be perfectly safe. No one wants to hurt mothers who go on marches," I said calmly. How to make Wendi accept the principle that only an animal could be expected to feel no higher duty than to its own offspring? That it was *because* I was a mother . . . and because I knew so many things that were wrong and needed to be corrected . . . ? Because I wanted her and all American children to be able to pledge allegiance to our flag in school each day and know that the last few words of the pledge were true . . .

"*. . . with liberty and justice for all.*"

But this was not the time, nor the place; and my fifteen-year-old was a long time away, I hoped, from becoming a mother. So how could I expect her to understand?

I sighed in resignation. "Be good," I said. "Help Dad. I'll be back Monday night, I promise you."

When I went back to his side and reported on Wendi's news, leaving out her and my subsequent conversation over the phone, Bill said, "All of a sudden I'm worried about you doing this, Gwen. Going off all alone like this, I mean." He scratched at his crew-cut, the way he did when he was bothered about something.

I said in reply, "I'll be fine, you'll see. After twenty-four hours on a bus, I won't be what you'd call 'alone' when I get there. By that time, I'll even be friends with the bus driver! And statistically speaking, Bill, I'll probably be safer this weekend in Alabama than all the rest of you will be, driving around in all this crazy traffic up here. And that reminds me. If you take the kids anywhere in the VW bus, be sure that sliding back door is closed tight, won't you?"

"Okay," he said. I half-expected to see him write that down on his Remember list.

* * *

14.

"A journey of a thousand miles begins with one step."
—Old Chinese proverb
(From G. G.'s Words To Live By")

About ten o'clock that Thursday evening there it came at last, a steel-shaped, silver behemoth owned and operated by the Greyhound Company, looming out of the misty darkness with its two huge yellow cat-eyes seeking me out. Almost at once, even before I glimpsed the big "CHARTER" sign above the enormous expanse of window glass in front, I recognized that the big bus had come off the Turnpike just for me. Though most of the inside lights remained off, we could make out the figure of a woman standing at the driver's elbow, pointing in our direction.

With a squeal and a gasp, the vehicle came to a stop in front of the tollbooth beyond which we stood waiting. The driver swung open the bus door. He called out a few words of explanation to the toll collector, who passed the vehicle through with a wave of his arm. It came to a second stop only halfway through, but directly in front of Bill and me. The woman standing beside the driver stooped over from the top step to regard me with a questioning smile.

"I think you're looking for me," I said, peering up at her.

"Are you Gwen Gain?" I immediately recognized the voice over the phone, my contact in New York City. And she had used my name correctly again! No "s" on the end; no "es" and probably no just plain "e". Then it hadn't been just an aberration, that first time over the telephone!

"Yes. I'm she."

The young woman thrust forward a hand intending to help me up the two steep steps. "I'm Keene Stassen," she said. "Here we are, we made it at last. Sorry to be so late—did you think we were never coming?"

I said, "We *were* beginning to wonder. Wait a minute, please. I'll be right there."

I turned back to my silent husband, feeling the old guilt sweep over me again. But this time it was with a new twist: guilt because I loved him less than enough to be sorry he wasn't coming along. After all, he agreed with my convictions, and had often come with me on my civil rights adventures.

Our lips brushed lightly as we kissed goodbye.

"Be careful, honey," my husband said.

"I will." I said. "Take good care of our kids, honey."

"I will," he said. "Call me when you get back. I'll come pick you up."

"I will," I said. "I'll try to get off at that Howard Johnson just after Exit 3 on the Turnpike Monday night. So I can wait for you inside the restaurant. In case it's raining."

Cold sprinkles falling from the sky above brushed our cheeks. I lifted one foot and stepped decisively up into the bus. Bill handed my borrowed equipment up to me. The knapsack, when I hefted it, now seemed to weigh much too much. I called down to him, "See you soon! And don't worry!" I said it softly enough so I wouldn't wake the sleepers I glimpsed sprawled in the bus seats to my left and right and further on back.

"We'll be watching the TV news on Sunday! Be sure to wave!" he called back in the same exaggerated whisper. He backed away, grinning and waving as if I were off to Hollywood to be on a quiz show. With a fierce grinding of gears, the bus pulled all the way through the toll booth, turned left across all four lanes, and turned again, and headed back through the entrance onto the Turnpike. Only then had the steel door slammed shut with grim finality, letting me know I was at last on my way to Alabama, one thousand miles away, and it was too late to change my mind.

I was glad there had been no time for final, sentimental goodbyes. I was glad that the bus business had happened quickly, when Bill and I had almost stopped expecting it. No one had wept, or clung. I was thankful for that.

Shoulder bag clutched to my side, I turned toward the recesses of the darkened bus and became aware of a many-shaded congregation of sleepy faces blinking back at me in the gloom, from what seemed dozens of rows of seats. The driver had forgotten me already, but the young woman named Keene, tall and friendly and big-boned but not at all fat, flashed another bright smile and told me it looked as though the only empty seat left was at the very back of the bus. She picked up my sleeping bag and lurched ahead of me down the long aisle. I followed with the knapsack, glancing at the many faces, both black and white, turned up toward me from either side.

Keene helped me store my gear on one of the luggage racks overhead. Then she looked on approvingly as without a murmur of disappointment, I settled myself into the center seat, the middle one of five places that stretched across the back end, directly over the motor. The bus was too old, I saw, to have a restroom built into the usual spot at the left rear corner beside the back door. I hoped that would not present a problem for me.

Stooping down in the aisle at my feet so her eyes would be nearly level with mine, the young woman introduced herself once again. I could see she was white and looked to be in her mid-twenties. She had shoulder-length brown hair, worn in a casual flip.

"Mrs. Gain—I'm Keene Stassen, but everyone call me Keene. We're happy you could join us."

I assured her that I was happy too. "And please—call me Gwen," I said.

"Fine. This is Tom Courtney," Keene said, indicating the black man sitting to my right. "He's the SNICK primary leader for the bus. His co-leader Bill Morris is up front. Tom will fill you in on our plans, okay? But first I need to get some info from you."

Still stooping there before me, her elbows braced on the seat against the jiggling of the bus, she took down my address on the clipboard she held in her hand. She already had my phone number from our long-distance conversation of the day before. Keene. Strange first name for a female, I was thinking. Smothering back a question, I watched her write as she scribbled down the information I gave to her.

Keene Stassen? Stassen was a familiar name, especially to those paying the least bit of attention to the political scene. Harold Stassen was the ex-governor of Minnesota who during the nineteen-fifties had tried twice to capture the Republican nomination for President of the United States. He had been beaten out twice in the primaries by General Dwight Eisenhower. Everyone the least knowledgeable about black civil rights knew that the

Republican Party cared more about law and order than about individual
civil rights or the plight of the poor, I reminded myself. Everyone of us
working for more civil rights for black citizens thought that the party of
Lincoln had sold America's Negroes out to big business interests a long
time ago.

Yet I myself was a registered Republican, and had been, ever since
attaining the age of twenty-one and becoming old enough to vote in the
1952 presidential primary. Being Republican had seemed the natural
thing for me to do, as daughter of two midwesterners transplanted to the
east, from Missouri to New Jersey. And my father had served as assistant
manager of a Dupont chemical plant during World War II and had naturally
remained a Republican. But I had mentioned my party affiliation less and
less often of late, until I had finally gotten to a point where I was almost
ashamed to mention it at all. Certainly I'd never admit it to the people on
this bus . . . !

But one question popped out after all. Feebly, by way of apology for
even thinking such a thing possible, I inquired of Keene, "Stassen? Are you
any relation to Harold?" Not likely, I told myself, especially since she had
come on the bus from New York City and not from the Midwest. But I
had to ask.

"Sure! I'm his daughter! See you later, Gwen," and touching my arm
companionably, she went off up the aisle to her seat by the alternate bus
driver in the front. Leaving me to wonder if any of the young people dozing
in the seats to left and right in front of me had any idea their presence here
had been arranged for by the daughter of a twice-Presidential nominee,
and a Republican to boot. Most of those faces had looked too young to
have even recognized the name without a history course.

Well, so what? Why should they have been impressed? Wasn't Keene
Stassen just an ordinary person, like the rest of us?

But it would become obvious to me as the hours passed that she wasn't.
I got to know her better during that long bus ride and found her to be
anything but ordinary. For one thing, at twenty-five years old, she was
teaching elementary school in a New York City ghetto area. A teacher!
Of course! No wonder she was so aware of the correct pronunciation of
names. And she still managed to be actively involved in the activities of the
NCSM (the Northern Christian Student Movement). And financially, she
appeared to be making it on her own. Once she told me with a wry laugh
in answer to my pointed question, "Sure, I'm a crusader, Gwen. But I'm
certainly not affluent!"

My main memory of Keene Stassen, however, has nothing to do with the apparently boundless physical energy she demonstrated, nor her quiet leadership skills, nor her commitment to justice for American racial minorities. I remember her best for her cool ability to take everything, absolutely everything, in her stride. I see myself stepping over the unpretentious lump of her body as she lay sleeping in the bus aisle during the hours after midnight, while the steel spaceship in which we were encased hurtled endlessly south through the blackness and the rain.

Keene lay there in blissful repose on the hard floor, with only my spread-out sleeping bag for padding. She was covered by her raincoat against the chill on the floor and seemed oblivious to discomfort now as well as to any danger that might lie ahead for her. Or even to the immediate possibility of being stepped upon by a clumsy fellow passenger taking a walk up the aisle as I had done to keep the blood circulating in my legs. For the time being, Keene's job, that of trip organizer and passenger recorder, was held in abeyance. Truly a "pragmatic idealist" as President John Kennedy had claimed to be before his assassination two years ago, she was making the most of her chance to lie down and sleep.

The rest of us did our best to sleep sitting up in our seats because the hard and vulnerable, and probably dirty, floor seemed a less desirable alternative. Even if I had wanted to chance a bed in the aisle, the fact that I was wearing a dress and my good coat would have held me back. Later, at the first rest stop, I noticed that all the sleepy girl students lined up for the one toilet in the Ladies Room were wearing jeans or slacks. I'd been a fool, I told myself, not to have done the same.

And I found myself to be in a particularly unenviable position. The last, long seat across the back of a bus, alas, has no mechanism for leaning the seat back, nor any inside arm rests, and I had to sit almost bolt upright, elbows tight at my sides lest I bother one of these strangers beside me. If I fell asleep, the movement of my head jerking to one side woke me instantly. The young travelers on either side of me seemed to be taking it all in stride, including the fact that we were sitting directly over the throbbing engine. Two, in fact, were curled up in the back corners like cats on a warm stove, and were snoring gently.

As Keene had promised, and before we had slumped down for the night, Tom Courtney, the black SNICK primary leader who sat just to the right of me, had given me further details of the journey ahead. I already knew that "SNICK" was a phonic for SNCC, the Student Non-Violence Coordinating Committee. I knew that this was an organization formed in the early nineteen-sixties as a student counterpoint to the Southern Christian Leadership Conference headed by Martin Luther King, Jr. I was also aware that its membership had been heavily involved during the days of the Freedom Rides on the interstate bus lines and the lunch-counter sit-ins all over the South. For the past few years, the daily newspapers had been full of reports about SNCC campaigns.

I would have to be assigned to one of the bus's secondary leaders for my own protection, Tom explained to me as I strained my ears to hear him above the purr of the bus motor. The problem was, they were somewhat short-handed in that department. He spoke in a barely audible, rather formal undertone, but with perfect English and no black accent as he told me this.

"Maybe I could act as a secondary leader," I volunteered.

"I beg your pardon?" He sounded surprised by my suggestion.

"Well, I mean—I'm thirty-five, older than most of the others here, from what I can see of them," and I motioned toward the rows of seats in front of us.

"Age isn't important here. It's experience that counts. What experience have you had?" He might have been interviewing me for a respectable job in an exclusive business office.

"Experience? Well, I've been a mother for some time now . . . ."

To his credit, he didn't laugh. Patiently he elaborated. "How many demonstrations have you participated in, Gwen?"

"Demonstrations? Oh, one—no, two. Just little things you wouldn't want to count." I grasped now that he was referring to non-violence passive resistance affairs in which people often got beaten and thrown into jail. And I'd never been in any of those, thank heavens. And when Tom told me dispassionately that he was afraid I didn't actually qualify for a secondary leadership role, I was gratified to be relieved of that responsibility.

He gave me a piece of paper to fill out my name and address at our next stop and return to him. It was important I do so, he emphasized, since there might be trouble when we got to Montgomery.

And that was when I found out. That this busload of passengers, carrying mostly students from various high schools and colleges around New York City, was bound, not for Selma, but for the Alabama capital of Montgomery to help in canvassing the black neighborhoods of the city. Their goal was to see if it would be feasible to start an Alabama Freedom Democratic Party, a black political party similar to the one that had recently been organized in Mississippi. They had been summoned down from New York City by John Lewis and James Forman, Co-Chairmen of the Student Non-Violence Coordinating Committee, explained Tom. SNICK had been actively working in Montgomery for several months already.

"Then—*none* of you are going on to Selma for the march on Sunday?" I asked just as calmly. I thought I did well, there in the blackness of the bus, at concealing my surprise and disappointment. What had Keene told me over the phone yesterday when I reserved a seat on the bus? Hadn't I listened? Or had I just taken their ultimate destination for granted?

"No. Just one guy, I believe, sitting up near the front there. The rabbi—maybe you noticed him when you got on. You're headed for Selma, then?" Tom said.

"Yes. I thought you were too. All of you," I said.

"No, not at all. See, Gwen—this trip has been in the works for some time now." Long before, he hastened to explain, the recent developments in Selma had precipitated Dr. King's nationally televised invitation on the news broadcasts. Nobody, really, could possibly have foreseen the startling events of the past two weeks, nor predicted that the march from Selma to Montgomery would finally get the go-ahead for this very same Sunday. That was just a coincidence. Besides, Lewis and Forman and the other SNICK leaders were not in agreement with Dr. King's tactics in regard to the Selma situation. They did not approve of his constant hesitation and apparent willingness to let illegal injunctions deter him.

Tom's terse explanation came to me as a second unwelcome surprise. I had not been aware of philosophical and strategic differences of opinion between the two major components of the non-violence movement. It seemed so other worldly to be sitting there in the unlit interior of this bus and listening to this young person as he talked low and slow beside me. Because his skin and his clothing were so dark, I could not make out his features, nor his frame. All he seemed to be was a monotonous voice in my ear, telling me things I did not want to hear.

And therefore, Tom Courtney went on, this busload of students would continue with the original plan. They would be assigned to go door-to-door in the black neighborhoods of Montgomery, asking questions to find out how many residents would be eligible to vote if they could once get registered. It would be a dangerous assignment, since the Montgomery police were constantly on the look-out for "Northern agitators," be they black or white, male or female.

"Besides," Tom wound up grimly in my ear, "we wouldn't be all that effective in Selma at this juncture. Most of us here on this bus are black. You now, you're white . . . ."

He did not need to go on, as I had caught his drift. At this juncture, Dr. King and his organization needed plenty of white faces to accompany them on that walk out of Selma on Sunday, in order to make their point. The fact that many American Caucasians were on their side.

The black youth who had been snoozing on the other side of me stirred uneasily in his seat. "Shit, white folks is no damn good!" he muttered beneath his breath, just loud enough for me to hear. Then he opened his eyes and blinked at me once or twice in the dim overhead light as if he had just realized next to whom he was sprawled. "I don't mean you. You're a white nigger," he said. And with a soft moan he squirmed around to face the other direction and went back to sleep.

White nigger. It was a term I would hear many times before all this was over. But that first time, applied to me there in this busload of strangers in the eerie dark—I could not be certain as to whether the remark had been meant as a compliment. Or as an apology for what the fellow had said before.

It seemed to fall into the same nebulous category as my friend Jim Clemson's send-off sentence to me: "Gwen—I've gotta tell you—you've got guts."

*   *   *

15.

"I read in the Congressional Record that there was a good deal of fornicating going on down there. I seriously doubt that was true."
—Henry Ridgway, Quaker and white member of the Gloucester County, N.J., Human Relations Council (Post-Selma Comments from some of the folks back home)

All through that long night on the bus, I found it impossible to sleep. Every hour or so, while the flat plains of Delaware and Maryland flew invisibly by, I took a stroll up and down the aisle to keep the circulation going in my legs. I stepped carefully over the slumbering Keene. And

I kicked myself mentally, over and over again, for my stupid choice of traveling outfit. Why had I assumed that I had to wear a skirt?

The carrying of four babies inside my body during the decade of my twenties had brought on the nuisance of varicose veins in both my legs. For years I had known the importance of keeping the flow of blood to my calves as unrestricted as possible. Yet here I was, facing this long journey and physical endurance test in—*what an idiot you are, Gwen!*—nylon stockings and a somewhat restrictive garter belt. What could I have been thinking of, to do such a stupid thing? At least I had worn sensible shoes, my brown leather oxfords with the shoelaces to match. I told myself it was a wonder I hadn't worn my black dress-up pumps with the two-inch heels! At least my feet could be comfortable and let me walk on solid heels and soles when the time came for marching.

During the three a. m. rest-and-gasoline stop somewhere in Virginia, while waiting for my turn in one of the toilet stalls, I leaned against the restroom wall and filled out on my shoulder bag the SNICK form Tom Courtney had given me. Along with the expected identification info like name and address was the question, "Willing to go to jail?" I thought it over for a moment and then printed carefully on that line, "Would rather not."

Carl, the relief driver, had been napping in the front row of the bus, but now it was his turn to take over for number one driver, Jeffrey. We women were barely out of the restroom before Carl was there in the restaurant door in his rumpled uniform, telling Keene the bus was ready to move on. By the time the first haze of daylight had touched the eastern sky, my eyes were burning from lack of sleep, my normally sturdy back ached, and my legs seemed to throb in rhythm with the motor beneath me. Even when George, the young man who had called me a white nigger, woke up for an hour at dawn and played Hangman with me on the back of my filled-in SNICK form, I hadn't been able to completely forget my physical misery. At our next stop I returned the form to Tom. I was grateful to him for folding it up without reading in front of me my equivocating response about my willingness to go to jail. Nor did he seem to notice our irreverent Hangman diagrams on the back of the form.

In spite of my physical discomfort brought on by constrictive clothing and lack of sleep, I made it a point to introduce myself to the rabbi during the breakfast stop around six-thirty in North Carolina. I had noticed him sitting unobtrusively on a stool at the restaurant counter amidst the subdued clamor of hungry male passengers. They were all placing their orders, while we women and girls from the bus, about twenty all told, went to form our customary line in the little room in the back marked "Ladies." (The guys always got in and out of their separate facility and were deep into meals before we females could even get started.)

I came out of the restroom at last and found the rabbi still sitting there at the counter, waiting patiently for the attention of one of the two scurrying waitresses. He was easily recognizable as the man Tom Courtney had mentioned, since he wore the customary black skull cap, a *yarmulke*, on his head. Judging by the looks of his profile that his age was somewhere near my own, I took strange comfort in his presence. Not because he was a member of the clergy. I had long ago outgrown my awe of officially sectarian personages. But there was something reassuring about the comfortable manner in which he wore his somewhat rumpled black suit and his *yarmulke*. He also wore an air of sedate serenity that conveyed both warmth and self-reliance. I went to stand behind him, waiting for a stool of my own. Clearing my throat, I struck up a conversation.

"I understand you're going on to Selma for the march on Sunday. I'm on my way there too," I told him in an undertone so the waitresses behind the counter could not hear. *Can I really be here in the state of North Carolina saying such a ridiculous thing to the back of this strange man's head? Impossible!*

"Good!" He turned on his stool to look up at me approvingly, dark eyes magnified behind thick lenses. "Yes, I'm on my way there," he said. "Most of these others aren't, I've found."

"I discovered that too," I said. "Hi, I'm Gwen Gain. No 's' on the end, please. No 'e' or 'es' either. It's just plain Gain. You know. The opposite of loss." I told myself to stop rambling.

He nodded. "Yes. I heard Keene say your name when you got on the bus last night, and I noticed she didn't put an 's' on the end," he said. He held out a hand to shake mine. "I'm Rabbi Albert Friedlander." Rounded facial features only faintly Semitic blended into a wide smile that lit his entire face and set me completely at ease. I felt, in that first moment of meeting as I grasped his hand in mine, that I could tell this man anything, *anything* that I felt or thought, and he would not be shocked.

"In just a minute," he said, "I'll turn this stool over to you. I think the waitress there is about to take pity on me. Listen, can't I order you something too?"

I moved up closer and touched his shoulder lightly in gratitude. "That's okay. I haven't the faintest idea what I want."

"There's little else than coffee and buns at this early hour, I'm afraid. Better grab something while you can," he said. And that was how our friendship began.

The small wayside restaurant, a typical "greasy spoon" along the side of the four-lane highway, was ill-equipped to handle a bi-racial busload of starving-but-in-a-hurry adventurers at that early hour. I settled for coffee and a cheese Danish, ordered for me by the helpful rabbi. He managed also to get two small paper cups of orange juice, one of which he handed over to me. And then he got up and insisted I take his stool while we ate.

"Not because you're a woman," he explained with a twinkle in his eyes. "Just because it's your turn. You look worn out." He had apparently sized me up in a few brief minutes of conversation. I noticed that he wore a dark grey cardigan beneath his suit coat. He, as I, had given thought to the possibility of cold weather.

"Thank you! I've not been able to sleep a wink," I said. "I should be exercising my legs right now instead of eating."

Back on the bus once more, the edge barely off my hunger, I bade the rabbi Albert Friedlander lgoodbye and resumed my place at the rear. None of my four seatmates were as yet alert enough to want to talk, but all nodded in friendly greeting as they lurched toward me down the aisle. Throwing themselves down in their usual, much roomier seats, they easily went back to sleep.

And then, miracle of miracles, as we started to move, an empty seat! Three rows forward, equipped with an adjustable back and footrest! After observing over several vibrating miles that no one else intended to claim it—that it apparently belonged to one of the bodies lying in the aisle where Keene had been before—I moved forward and lowered myself into it with a silent shout of relief.

At last, if only for a little while! And finally able to lean back in my seat, I hooked my sturdy heels over the foot brace and got my first sleep in more than twenty-four hours.

Intermittently throughout the morning I napped, seeing little of the North Carolina foothills that now lay outside the windows. I roused myself only briefly at first, to exchange a few words with my seatmate by the window. He was a freckle-faced, super-energetic white boy who looked t be of Irish extraction who told me he was on his way to Alabama simply because there had been nowhere else for him to go that weekend. His father, an alcoholic who belonged to Alcoholic Anonymous but seldom went to the meetings, had thrown Peter out of their apartment in New York City the week before. Simply because he had taken home for dinner two black friends, two guys he knew from the local college he was attending.

Feeling responsible for Peter's plight after his unceremonious eviction from his own home, the two Negroes had told him about this trip to Montgomery, and had scraped up for him the forty dollars for the fare, plus a little more. His two buddies, I learned, were in the two seats across the aisle from us.

Peter obviously needed to talk, and I forced myself to stay awake a few minutes longer. "My mother was kind of upset when I phoned her last night to say goodbye," he said.

"I'll bet she was !" I exclaimed.

There was no need to look at Peter as we talked. We both reclined in our seats with our heads supported by the back rests and our eyes closed.

"I told her I was only going to help my friends make a survey, but she guessed what it was about," Peter said. "She made me promise not to get involved in any of those racial demonstrations. She told me, 'now don't you go getting yourself mixed up with that crazy colored minister!'"

I had to laugh out loud, right along with him.

He would call his mother Monday night when we got back, Peter told me. That would be after his father had had time to cool off. He told me, "Look, I'm wearing the brand-new, bright blue wind-breaker Mom gave me for my eighteenth birthday last week. After my father threw me out."

"My children were the ones who got a little upset with me," I volunteered. "At least my oldest one did."

Peter sounded surprised. "How come?" he wanted to know.

"She wanted to go on the march with me this Sunday, to keep me from getting hurt," I said. "Isn't that a riot? She's only fifteen, and *she* wanted to protect *me!*"

Peter's doe-eyes widened as we turned our heads to look at each other for a second or two. "You going all the way to Selma?" he asked.

"Um-hmm. That's why I came. To join the march on Sunday. I didn't know anything about this SNICK project in Montgomery," and tired of talking, I drifted off to sleep once more. When I awakened again, it was to hear my seatmate asking in my ear, "Aren't you scared?"

"No. I'm not scared." I hadn't had time to be, I told him. And now I was too tired to care.

"You're going to walk all the way to Montgomery?"

"Can't." I said dreamily. "Wish I could. Gotta get home by Monday night. Be back at my job at the University of Pennsylvania by Tuesday morning."

Peter turned his upper body in his seat in order to regard me straight on with open admiration. His look said, lady, you're something, for a woman of your advanced age! And a mother with a job, on top of it!

"That's tough," he said, using the new expression for "swell." "That you're going to Selma, I mean. Hey! Maybe I'll find some way to get there too! Right now I've got to stay with this gang."

I said, "I'll watch for you, Peter. Just in case. Maybe we can be in the march together." And he said "Cool!" as if he truly meant it, and I dozed off again, the morning sun through the tinted window glass beyond his head shining bright on my eyelids.

The rustle and jostle of Peter rummaging through his windbreaker pockets woke me an hour or so later. "Hungry," he said, seeing me open my eyes. "Sorry if I woke you. Those buns back there—not nearly enough grub for a growing boy like me!"

Taking pity on him, I got up and rescued Bill's picnic lunch, forgotten until now, from the knapsack on the rack above our heads. I offered the mashed sandwich to Peter, but he shuddered. "Ugh, no thanks! Peanut-butter-and-jelly!" he said with a look of loathing. "I hate peanut-butter-and-jelly!"

"It was all we had in the house," I told him apologetically. "How about a carrot?" But these, too, he viewed with distaste. He settled finally for one of the bruised apples while I, wide awake now, chewed noisily on a carrot and told him if he was going to be a civil rights demonstrator, he should seriously consider going into missionary training.

"Missionary training! Is that what you said?" Peter replied. He was obviously puzzled.

"Yep. Missionary training," I said, more than a little amused by his reaction to those two words. "One of my brothers-in-law used to be a fussy eater like you. But then Bob decided if he wanted to be a missionary to the Philippines when he got out of college, he'd better learn to eat everything or he might starve. So he went into what he called his own private missionary training, and from then on, we never knew whether or not he liked something we fed him." The apple almost gone now, Peter eyed my lunch bag with renewed interest. "Of course, when the time came for him to go to the Philippines, he couldn't," I wound up. And waited for the inevitable question.

"Why not?" my eager young friend wanted to know. He *had* been listening!

"Well, it turned out that he and my sister were pre-milleniums and the missionary society was post-millenium. Or was it the other way around? I don't remember what those terms mean. Something about Jesus, when he would be coming back to earth. Besides, my brother-in-law also found out he was dangerously allergic to bee stings, and the Philippines are rife with stinging insects. But by that time, he really did enjoy eating almost everything my sister put before him."

"You're putting me on," said Peter, laughing quietly in my direction. But he decided he'd have the other raw carrot after all, and when I got around to unfolding the wax-paper that encased the dreaded sandwich, he held out one unturned palm in front of me.

"Half?" he asked with a compromising grin.

*   *   *

16.

**"The men made this mess, Gwen. Let *them* straighten it out.
We women shouldn't get involved. It's not feminine."
—Charlotte Scott Finlay,*
Continuing Education Student, U. Of Pa.
(Post-Selma Comments, etc., etc . . .)**

At noon I bolted down a tuna fish salad in another wayside restaurant, since by this time it was necessary to fortify the carrot and apple and half a peanut-butter-and-jelly sandwich. I ate sitting crammed onto one bench of a booth with Keene Stassen and Rabbi Friedlander on one bench and facing three young black students from the bus.

One of the latter was Donna, a bright, round-faced girl of barely sixteen who told me she was a junior at Science High School in New York City. Keene interrupted her to explain to me that this was a special public school to which only those who did exceptionally well academically were admitted.

Wilma, Donna's seatmate on the bus, was more slightly built. While we waited for our food, we learned from her that she was a twenty-four-year old from Harlem who had a secretarial job in a Manhattan office. She had planned ahead and taken vacation days to come on this trip. Donna and Wilma had only just met each other for the first time on the bus last evening. But they appeared to be already fast friends, united in a common cause for the betterment of all of us. Larisha, the third young woman squeezed between them in the booth until she was almost invisible, had little to say as she nibbled nervously at her French fries.

Very few of the forty-six passengers, Keene pointed out to Albert Friedlander and me, had known anyone else before this trip. Peter and his two black comrades were an exception, as were the white couple, a husband and wife in their fifties, I judged, who sat halfway back in the bus. They both nodded pleasantly each time I lurched past down the aisle, but otherwise kept to themselves.

Gradually a picture emerged, as Keene talked, of many individuals, some white, some black, almost everyone strangers to one another. They had converged upon our chartered bus last night in answer to notices posted on many school and church bulletin boards in New York City, their reservations made well in advance. They were not the cohesive collection of NCSM or SNCC members I had originally, at least last night, assumed them to be. Tom Courtney and Bill Morris, his white co-leader who alternated with Tom in a seat behind the driver, were apparently the only official contact with SNICK, the Student Non-Violence Coordinating Committee. Just as Keene Stassen was, with the Northern Christian Student Movement.

Gradually more and more of the other riders were taking on the characteristics of distinct personages in their own right as I got to know more about them. The young white male with the longish blonde hair in the aisle seat directly in front of me? A social worker from Harlem whose brother was a minister in Montgomery. He fully expected to be fired from his job when he got back to New York. The dignified Negro man with the white hair ringing his head like a halo, who waited with me at a cash register to pay our lunch checks? He turned out to be a professor from the religion department of Drew University in North Jersey. The fifty-ish white couple was also from North Jersey, I learned from the husband. Their children were grown and working in the Peace Corps in Africa. A black girl in jeans and dangling earrings and sandals who loaned me her copy of the New York Times later on that day? She was a reporter for her college newspaper.

"You're assigned to my group now, Gwen," Keene had said to me during our noon wait in the line outside the toilet stalls in the Ladies' Room. "Be sure to check with me before you cut out from the rest of us," and I assured her that of course I would. As matters now stood, I had not the faintest idea how I was going to get from Montgomery to Selma. But somehow it seemed the time was not yet ripe to bring up that little detail with anyone else. I feared I'd be seen as a worrier as well as a drag on the rest of them.

No one came after lunch to claim my seat beside Peter, or even to look at it longingly. Delighted, I accepted the knowledge that it was probably now mine. Barely aware until then that the colors outside our windows had been changing, I began to notice the grey-brown loam and muted winter landscape of my home state of New Jersey had become the red clay and feathery green foliage of the almost-spring-like South.

I spent a great deal of time in sober reflection during those afternoon hours with Peter snoozing beside me as we sped through South Carolina. The vibration of the bus and the warm sun through the window glass had not been conducive to reading a borrowed newspaper for more than a few minutes at a time without bringing on a headache. And one could look at scenery along a superhighway or seek oblivion in restless sleep for only so many hours at a time. I had little choice but to be caught up in my own thoughts.

And memories. In the proverbial manner of the drowner's last seconds before going under for the third time, the major figures and faces of my entire past wanted to parade through my imagination. Many of them had been gone from my daily life for years now. I forced myself to concentrate instead on my college career and its related problems. There were so many decisions to be made when I got back, and made within a fairly short time.

What did I really want to major in? To become? And why couldn't I settle on a topic for my honors-class research paper in American Government? I had to get going on that, and soon! But nothing particularly interested me. That is, *everything* did. The older I got, the stronger was my urge to put knowledge of all sorts into my brain. In choosing to concentrate on only one aspect of my country's unique government, how could I bring myself to leave anything out?

Thus tortured but able to arrive at no conclusions, I was pleased when Keene declared a half-hour dinner stop just over the border into Georgia. And even more pleased when Rabbi Friedlander suggested that he and I try to get seats together afterward so as to continue the conversation we had begun in the lunch booth. When next we boarded the bus, then, a few seconds of good-natured finagling on his part led to some seat-swapping that seemed to satisfy everyone concerned, especially Peter, who could now fold his tall young body over two seats instead of one and finally get some sleep. And quickly I found myself sitting in a window seat in the second row right, just behind Keene Stassen and Carl the relief driver. I was both astounded and impressed at how fast it had happened.

Albert and I talked on and off, but mostly on, throughout the remainder of daylight and into the evening, the two of us becoming ever more loquacious as the miles continued to pile up behind us. First we exchanged even more detailed information about ourselves. Those are the additional facets of one's personal portrait that one thinks are suitable to reveal to acquaintances with whom one has already established a certain rapport. I had already told the rabbi about my four wonderful children, and about my husband who was a licensed architect. Now I felt perfectly free to explain that no, Bill didn't have his own business, he worked for another architect and the pay was lousy. We weren't the millionaires most people assumed we were when they heard that glamorous word "architect." At the place where he worked, my husband was little more than a glorified draftsman, I said.

Albert had told me already that he was presently a Jewish chaplain at Columbia University. He spoke now of his small daughter Ariel, not quite two, and of his concert pianist wife Evelyn, who was a British subject and had grown up in London. He had married late, he said. He was now in his upper thirties, but Evelyn was not yet twenty-five. If she had her way, they'd move to England tomorrow to be near her family. And to make her happy, he was considering it. He was fast becoming a citizen of the world.

I told Albert that I was a late bloomer too, if not in matters of the heart then in the mind. That I had become a college student at the ripe old age of thirty-three and was still going strong and loving it. We commented on the coincidence of our both being at Ivy League schools. Though of course, we had to quickly insist to each other with grins on our faces, "the prestige of being at Penn or Columbia really means nothing!"

Albert revealed that he and Evelyn had only the year before left a synagogue in Chicago to come east. And he said that he found the post at Columbia University more in keeping with his major interests than ministering to the spiritual needs of a well-heeled and rather spoiled midwestern congregation. Opening up further, he told me still more about himself.

"I was born in Germany, a German citizen," he said. "I spent the first twelve years of my life in Berlin."

"No kidding! Then you. must be fluent in German . . . !" I exclaimed. "I'm envious!"

He nodded. "As a matter of fact, Gwen, I translate German theological literature into English," and he named as his specialties a couple of author-philosophers I'd never heard of, and I wasn't afraid to tell him so. He went on to say that he had lived his teenage years in Mississippi, of all places. When Hitler had begun his active persecution of German Jews, Albert's entire family had had to hide in the attics of Gentile friends until their escape could be arranged.

They had fled Germany, Albert went on, by way of Switzerland and England, arriving in the United States just before its entrance into the Second World War with the bombing of Pearl Harbor in December of 1941. They had ended up somehow in Mississippi, where his father had been offered a job. It was in the deep South that Albert Friedlander had become a naturalized American citizen. It was there, too, that he, a Jewish lad already well sensitized to the evils of blind prejudice, had developed a lasting concern for the plight of American Negroes. He had gone to both college and seminary in the North, and had thus escaped the blatant social malignancy of the South's Jim Crow system after only six years of living there. But the exposure, he assured me, had been quite long enough.

His quaintly precise manner of delivering his words intrigued me. It was as if he found traces of consonants to pronounce that native-born Americans did not realize were there. Nothing definite I could put a finger on. I remarked that he had scarcely a trace of a foreign accent. His accent seemed neither German nor Southern. I told him I'd read somewhere that a person has to learn a second language by the age of fourteen, in order to speak it without an accent.

"Small wonder I don't have a British accent, living with Evelyn," Albert said with a chuckle. He talked again about his wife's hunger to return to England to live. If she finally succeeded in talking him into it, he didn't think he would mind overly much. Much as he loved his adopted country, the United States of America, he'd seen England when he was a child seeking refuge, and had found it a less tense existence than any he had ever known. That had been, of course, before England had been drawn into the War against Hitler, and had had to fight a ferocious six-year battle for its very survival.

"What about you, Gwen Gain without an 'e' or an 's'? I'd be willing to bet you've had a very interesting life," the rabbi said.

"Pleasant, yes. A happy childhood, but not all that exciting. I've spent all my life in little old South Jersey, except for one year when my husband Bill and I lived in a trailer at Gettysburg College in Pennsylvania." And telling him more about myself, I finally managed to insert the unique fact that I had eight sisters, no brothers. We were nine girls altogether, I told him. And I was able to assure my incredulous listener that "no, indeed, my father was anything but hen-pecked! He was king of the castle!"

"It was my one claim to fame, that accident of my birth, and a sure-fire conversation piece in many instances. As was my custom, I made the most of it.

"Nine girls!" Albert exclaimed. "So you have eight sisters?"

"Yessiree, I do! Did you ever know anyone who bought identical 'Happy Birthday, Sister!' cards a dozen at a time? Well, you're looking at her!" And I went on to tell him that we Simon girls had all been given names with a "lyn" sound on the end. I ran down the list of nine without drawing a fresh breath in the middle. "Jacqueline, Jocelyn, Gwendolyn, Marilyn, Caroline, Lynn, Kathlyn, Pauline and Ellyn."

"Wow! I don't believe the whole thing!" He meant the names, this time.

"Believe it! My father, who got to name all the girls, thought it would be a good joke. My mother, on the other hand, always hoped for a 'John Carl.' She was to name all their sons, you see."

My family's list of names all sounded so trite, suddenly, in light of what I had just learned about Albert's childhood. The Jewish boy had been a victim of Nazi persecution because of the very fact of his Jewishness. At twelve, he had been forced to hide in attics; then had to leave his homeland forever. Now he was a grown man, with a very good, very personal reason for caring about justice for everyone. Anyone could see that. But what was mine? I felt a stab of envy. Why couldn't I, too, have had some genuine justification for being here?

Around six or seven, a city of light loomed up ahead of us in the gathering dusk. "Atlanta," someone murmured to his neighbor across the aisle, and the rabbi and I paused in our conversation to look out the bus windows. A few minutes more and we were hurtling through the very center of the Southern metropolis, whizzing between modern high-rise buildings at sixty miles an hour, and at the same time caught in a web of traffic in just as big a hurry as we were.

"Peachtree Street," said a sign marking an exit off the superhighway. I remembered Scarlett O'Hara and Aunt Pitty-Pat, those fictional characters from one hundred years earlier. In the movie, they had been portrayed as almost hysterical with terror in front of the little house on Peachtree Street, because the Damned Yankees were coming! I had managed to see *Gone*

With The Wind at least half a dozen times since I was ten, and had read the book twice too. And I had that particular scene in the movie memorized right down to the white-washed picket fence.

This time, I reflected with glee, the dreaded Yankees comprised a busload of racially mixed, mostly still-wet-behind-the-ears young students bearing not the weapons of the conqueror but bringing hopes for peaceful change. Besides the students who came on the SNICK project, we were the schoolteacher daughter of an also-ran Presidential candidate; a middle-aged housewife with a pollen allergy and varicose veins; a far-sighted rabbi who had spent his early years in Nazi Germany. And don't forget the two grey-headed Caucasian bus drivers who methodically swapped off their turns behind the wheel every few hours and had no interest in social causes whatsoever. They wanted only to make a legitimate buck taking some forty-six kooky types safely to Montgomery, Alabama and getting them safely back home to New York City again.

Atlanta, Georgia, and the thoughts of the dreadful Civil War that the sight of it engendered, turned my seat companion and me to the subject of the political situation currently in the South. We spoke of the coming march and what it might possibly accomplish, now that the federal court decision had finally cleared the way for its legal start. President Lyndon Johnson had sent a Voting Rights bill to Congress only days before; and afterward he had addressed a joint session of the House and Senate concerning it. "Their cause must be our cause too," the man from Texas had said with calm conviction. "Because it's not just Negroes, but really it's all of us who must overcome the crippling legacy of bigotry and injustice. And we *shall* overcome!"

Albert and I discussed that astonishing finale, which we had both witnessed on the television news. But neither of us knew whether the bill had a chance of being passed by Congress and sent back to the President for his signature, or whether it was strong enough, or whether it could be effectively enforced. Would the march itself, successful or not, attacked or not, spur Congress to take action?

"What do you honestly think will be the outcome of all this, Albert?" I asked at one point in our discussion. "This march, I mean."

He said, "I can't imagine. What I do know is that we're sure to get blisters on our feet if no one tries to stop us."

And I chuckled and said, "Seriously. I mean—will a new law do any good? Bring about real change? Or just alienate Southern white people further?"

"I wish I could tell you. That Voting Rights bill is crucial I think. Its passage depends upon the aroused conscience of this entire nation. And I'm not sure its conscience will be aroused enough, when the chips are down. But you and I, Gwen, and all these others," and he waved his hand to indicate the passengers of the entire bus, "we still have to try. I think the march must go on."

I wanted to hug him, so elated was I by his final words on the subject. But of course I didn't. Rabbis weren't for hugging.

Albert had decided to come on this mission only yesterday afternoon, when he had belatedly learned that some of his colleagues from Columbia University and other New York City institutions of higher learning were planning to fly to Montgomery on Friday, which was now today. He had been unable to book a seat on any plane, and in the end, this bus had been his only option, as it had been mine. He had had just time enough after work to walk to his apartment near the Columbia campus for a quick supper and that extra pair of glasses. He had left his gold watch, a gift he particularly cherished, in the bureau drawer where the glasses had been kept. He had stuffed socks, shorts and nylon shirt into the shaving kit, along with his toothbrush and razor. His wife Evelyn had not been particularly surprised by his spur-of-the-moment decision to go on this mission, Albert said. She had not tried to stop him.

It was dark in the bus once more. The overhead lights above each seat were on here and there, beams directed downward, allowing people who wanted to read, light enough to see. The sun had gone half-circle, from east to west, since we had left home, and night was upon us and still the bus hurtled onward.

The rabbi sat looking in my direction. I knew he was searching my face through the semi-darkness. He was barely visible to me as he talked, nodding his head from time to time as I responded to a remark from him. The lenses of his glasses were twice as thick as any I'd ever seen before, even my father's. Earlier, by daylight, I had noted that. The rabbi had told me earlier that he was blind as a bat without them. And yet, knowing that, he had been willing to risk losing his glasses, and his ability to see clearly along with them. He was willing to risk having them torn or knocked from his face, maybe even destroyed, and the spare pair along with them.

You and I. Gwen, we still have, to try. Mom, somebody has to go. Bye, Mommy, Bye!

I absorbed Albert's narrative for a moment, and then I said, "How come she wasn't surprised? Evelyn, I mean."

He said, "I guess she knows me pretty well by now. She would have come too, but . . ." He paused.

I said softly, "Of course. You have a young child."

"It was more than that," Albert said just as softly. But he didn't say what. And I didn't ask. I was too busy asking myself why, if Albert's wife knew him so well, my relatives didn't know me?

*   *   *

17.

"I like your Christ, but not your Christianity."
"Mahatma Gandhi, Lawyer and Civil Rights Crusader,
Leader of the non-violence campaign for independence,
To free India from the British Empire.
(From G G.'s W.T.L.B.)

I suppose it was inevitable that from politics the rabbi and I would go almost non-stop to the subject of religion. Inevitable, that is, given the fact that we were still over three hours away from Montgomery, and given the fact that we had both been interested in theological issues for a long time. He, as a rabbinical student; then as spiritual leader of his own synagogue, and finally, as a translator of German philosophers and a college counselor to questioning young Jewish students. I, as the perennial doubter, the restless skeptic, the humanist Unitarian. I had spent an equally long number of years debating to myself where I stood theologically, or if I stood anywhere at all. Or needed to.

The bus had fallen into quiet lethargy again. Lights were off and most of the steel giant's riders were sleeping. Some sat staring out the windows or talking softly to seatmates. Keene was up in front chatting with Carl, the second bus driver, who had been relieved by Jeffrey at the dinner break. Those of us who were wide awake felt the suspense in the air, the eager excitement of knowing we were approaching our destination. Comparatively speaking after so long a ride, it wouldn't be long.

At my request, Albert began to explain to me his standing in the Hebrew faith. He was a Reform Jew; in practice and belief somewhere between Orthodox and Liberal. The Reforms, for instance, were not required to eat only Kosher foods, he said. On the other hand, they stayed conscientiously away from pork. For Liberal Jews, the sky was generally the limit when it came to menus and a few other things.

I told him I was a Unitarian by belief. Not a "birthright" Unitarian, but a converted one. Most of the Unitarians I knew, I told him, were fallen-away Catholics or Baptists, or come to think of it—Jews!

"And you?" Albert asked. "What did you fall away from?"

"The Baptists. The Northern ones. As long ago as I can remember I was one. As a child I was in Sunday School and church every Sunday, unless we were away from home. The whole bit."

"So—what happened?" my new friend asked.

"I'm not really sure," I had to confess. I told him that my husband Bill was a math major when we lived in a trailer in Gettysburg, Pennsylvania for a year, back in 1948. Because German was then the language of science and mathematics, Bill had had to take two years of it at Gettysburg College. And I had studied it right along with him in order to help him, because languages were not his forte, whereas I had always been good at them. He and I had read Albert Schweitzer's *Leben Und Denken* (Of My Life and Thought) in the original German, in order for Bill to fulfill his requirements for graduation. In that book we had read much about the philosophy of Unitarianism, and been impressed. But still it had not moved us to do anything about it.

It was so easy to sit there in the darkened bus and speak to this congenial rabbi of sensitive issues long since resolved in my mind. Sensing that he was truly interested, I felt free for once to speak slowly, and choose my words carefully. I, personally, had been disillusioned with my own church long before my introduction to Schweitzer, I told him. As a Baptist, I had secretly questioned from an early age many of my church's doctrines and miracle stories. But the final, permanent break had to await the ultimate disillusioning moment.

About ten years ago before our third child was born, I explained, Bill and I had taken our two children, Wendi and Kenny, on a car trip to St. Petersburg, Florida to visit their grandmother. We had stopped at a gas station in South Carolina to use the toilet facilities. And there, lined up along the side of the building, had been the "Jim Crow" signs to indicate the rest rooms: "Men," "Women," "Colored". To me, it was like implying that Negroes were dogs, or worse. Not fully human. Right then and there I had put two and two together and come up, for a welcome change, with four. And I had said to myself, this is Baptist country, isn't it? And therefore were Baptists accepting—even perpetrating—this cruel nonsense? And mentally I had resigned my church affiliation on the spot. I no longer wanted to play that particular game anyway, and this gave me the impetus to stop being a hypocrite in at least this one important area of my life.

We crossed the state line into Alabama while I was expounding upon all this heavy stuff to Albert. But so engrossed were we in conversation with each other that we scarcely noted it. Nor did we notice that the drizzle we had been driving through for hours had turned into a hard rain, and the bus's giant windshield wipers had been turned on high. Word came back from the driver Jeffrey by way of Keene that we were in a different time zone now, Central Standard Time. Without missing a beat in the conversation, I reached up, switched on my reading light, took my watch off my wrist and set it back one hour. The rabbi, I now remembered, had brought no watch with him to worry about.

"By their fruits you shall know them?" Albert was asking, referring to the South Carolina Baptists and their rest room signs. (He was quoting—at least I thought he was—from the Christian New Testament. When everybody knew that Judaism was accepting of the Old Testament only.)

I acknowledged that I had indeed thought something like that. "Unitarians accept the teachings *of* Jesus, but we reject many of the teachings *about* him. His divinity, the virgin birth, his bodily rise into heaven, and so forth," I said. I told him there was one aspect of Unitarianism I had particularly liked when I first learned about the denomination. Its subscribers claimed to believe in "praying with their hands." By which they meant *doing* good works instead of merely talking about them.

"Whatever constitutes good works," I said. "Unitarians claim to believe, purely and simply, in brotherhood, and reverence for life, and being caretakers of the earth. They don't need all the magic and the gobbledy-gook of traditional Christianity. For that reason," I explained, "a lot of denominations don't consider Unitarians to be 'Christians.' As for me, I have no concern for that, one way or the other. Thomas Jefferson was a Unitarian, you know," I ended up my lecture. "He was really naive, though! He wrote that he trusted every intelligent young man of his generation would die a Unitarian. I don't know what he thought about the women!"

"I'm familiar with that quote," Albert said. I could sense him nodding his head.

"You are? You know a lot!" He had probably known all of it, all along, but he had let me go on and on.

"It's my business to know things like that," he said. You people are kind of 'fellow travelers' with us, you know," he said, comparing Unitarianism to Judaism, "And as you pointed out earlier, you've been raiding our territory upon occasion." His voice in the darkness was teasing me. "Let me think a minute. You Unitarians believe in unity, you claim, as opposed to trinity. In one God, instead of the Father, the Son, et al. And a lot of you aren't even sure about that. So if you do ever pray with words instead of works, it's to—let me think how it goes—it's to 'one God, at the most,' isn't that so?"

I snorted with amused appreciation. "Actually, Albert, it's more like 'to Whom it may concern'." And it was his turn then to laugh.

When next I flicked on my reading light to check my watch, it was ten-thirty, Central Standard Time. Which meant eleven-thirty, back in New Jersey. Long past my bedtime again. The two of us seat companions rode along in silence for awhile, more aware now of the falling rain and swishing windshield wipers. We were scarcely able to comprehend that the first lap of this interminable journey would soon be over.

Sitting there beside my new rabbi friend, I began to worry that I had given him the wrong impression. Had I inadvertently led him to believe that I was something I was not, or not something that I actually was? I started up the conversation again, confiding to him that I'd been going through another period of disillusionment lately, and was even considering leaving my new church and becoming a fallen-away Unitarian.

"And believe me, Albert, that's about as far away as a person can fall and still be on the faith charts!"

Having been handed a tidbit like that, the clergyman in Albert wanted to pursue it further. "What's been the problem?" he asked me, and he still sounded interested; he really did!

"I dunno. My Unitarian guys say all the right things. At least, as far as I'm concerned. Brotherhood. Peace and justice. The sacredness of life. The recognition that life itself is miracle enough. But it seems to me most of them are just as inclined as all the others to sit back in their comfortable pews and congratulate themselves on being the true believers."

"We Jews are that way too, I'm afraid," Albert said.

"If you say so, I wouldn't know. And then too, I find I'm not much of a believer in anything anymore. Sometimes I think the whole thing, our existence on this planet, is some Warped Genius' idea of a joke." Could I really be voicing these things aloud? Playing a little game of shock-the-rabbi? Or did I simply desire that he understand the basis for my being here on this bus was perhaps not the same as his? That no Messiah and no Jehovah had sent me. I had come completely on my own say-so. Democracy; being an American citizen with pride and without hypocrisy of any sort, was the only religion I aspired to. I plunged on, too far into the matter now to turn back. "Do you know that famous quote by Thomas Hardy about the Vast Imbecility?"

"No. Thomas Hardy, you say?"

This well-educated and knowledgeable person was secure enough to admit to me that he did not know everything. I genuinely liked him.

"You know. The nineteenth-century English writer," and when I saw him nod his head in recognition of the name, I said, "I'll give you this special little gem as a present from me, Al. You could probably work it into one of your sermons, or whatever it is you rabbis give in synagogues."

"Tell me."

So I did. I quoted by memory from my little blue notebook. "It goes like this. 'Has some Vast Imbecility, mighty to build and blend, yet impotent to tend, framed us in jest, and left us here to hazardry?' That's it, and what a concept, huh? A 'Vast Imbecility'!"

He wasn't shocked. Hadn't I guessed long before this that I could say to him anything? But I had to test his tolerance still further. I told him I intended, when I had the time, to develop my own theory of the nature of the universe. I had as much right as anyone else to do that, I said.

Groping around in my brain for something funny to say, I came up with the ultimate shocker. God, I informed Albert the rabbi, could be a—a—a cockroach, for all we knew! I'd call it my Cockroach Theory of Non-Evolution, I said. And when Albert gave a soft hoot of laughter, I said no, seriously, hadn't he ever noticed how ubiquitous cockroaches were? They were all over the place, everywhere. Even in New Jersey.

Albert went along willingly with my nonsensical spiel. "Especially in the South, Gwen. I once lived in Mississippi, remember?"

"Yes, of course. Then surely you've noticed how impossible it is to wipe the abominable creatures out, no matter what you do to them. You step on one cockroach, and another crops up someplace else, as determined as ever to run things. Or at least run over them. Don't laugh. I read somewhere that the cockroach has been around in its present form longer than any other living organism. With no evolutionary changes of any kind! Wow, doesn't that arouse your suspicions right there? And as I said, you find them everywhere. No neglectors of rich or poor; black or white. Especially down

South, where at the present moment God is probably most needed! Did you ever think of that?"

I had him really laughing now, with quiet chuckles from deep in his throat so our sleeping neighbors on either side of the aisle wouldn't be disturbed. But I knew I should stop. Cease this tongue-in-cheek bantering before I really did offend him. Or worse, convinced him I was some kind of unstable wretch. Which I knew very well I was not. When I stopped to draw in a breath, Albert said, "Gwen, your dialectics make perfect sense! In Mississippi, the cockroaches grow as big as tarantulas."

Like Keene Stassen, he seemed unflappable. And the longer I carried on in this vein, the more he seemed to enjoy it, and the friendlier we became. I felt invincible; in control of my life again as I hadn't been since I was nine years old and found I could not play baseball with boys, or at thirteen discovered I could not play my flute in the high school marching band.

For one thing, there had been, during the last few hours, no time for guilt, or painful memories. And quite by luck, I had found me a congenial companion, someone else intending to go on to Selma. Go on in the middle of the night, for god's sake! For one fanciful moment, I imagined I was Huck Finn, floating on that raft down the Mississippi River with his Negro slave pal Jim. Only in this case, "Jim" was a Jewish rabbi.

Albert said, with a final chuckle before he got serious again. "You're quite an iconoclast, Gwen."

If he could be humble, so could I. "Whatever that is," I said. I really didn't know.

"One who tears down false images. Other people's, of course," he said.

And I said, "That's true. I guess I do like poking holes in other people's cherished religious inanities when they don't seem to make sense. My last line of defense is to come up with my own!"

"I'm working on a book you might be interested in." Albert's voice came to me clearly from out of the darkness. "It's a compilation of essays centering around the widespread disillusionment of today's college students with traditional religious values. So you see, my friend, as a student questioning faith you are right in step with the times."

"For a change, thank god! With a small letter 'g', that is. Tell me more about your book, please." And I listened as intently to him as he had to me.

His book, he explained, would thoroughly investigate the role of campus chaplains confronted with the radical changes in student religious thought and attitudes that had surfaced during the first years of the 1960's. The book, a collection of essays by various rabbis, would question the chaplain's function, and his purpose on campus. It would posit the viewpoint that a campus religious counselor, whether Catholic, Protestant or Jewish, should refuse to be a policeman for parents. He should act instead as spokesman for the students' secular, not sectarian, needs and concerns. Such a course, the book's introduction would argue, would ultimately fulfill the chaplain's religious function.

No, he hadn't selected a title for it yet. But he had a definite commitment from a publisher. I told him my boss at *Holiday* magazine, where I worked several years ago, would have found his proposal for the book both "provocative" and "meaningful". As editorial director for the magazine, Harry Sions had had lots of contacts with authors, and those were his two favorite adjectives when he dictated letters of approval for me to send to them.

Provocative and meaningful, he always said their literary creations were.

*   *   *

18.

"There are times when history and fate meet at a single time in a single place to shape a turning point in man's unending search for freedom. So it was at Lexington and Concord. So it was a century ago at Appomattox. So it was last week in Selma, Alabama."

**—President Lyndon Johnson, March 15, 1965
(In an address to Congress requesting
Voting Rights Legislation)**

"Guess what, Mom! Linda's mother found out you went to Selma, and now Linda's not allowed to come over to my house any more. Oh, well."

**—Wendi Gain, daughter
(Post-Selma Comments, etc. etc.)**

It was while Albert and I had our heads close together, quietly engrossed in these serious mental exercises, that an important message came murmuring forth from the bowels of the bus, jumping rapidly from row to row like an electric current until it reached the front rows. Someone back there had brought along a portable radio. And the local Alabama station was reporting that President Lyndon Johnson had just federalized the Alabama National Guard troops and was sending them to Selma to protect the marchers on Sunday!

That was when Albert had made a reassuring comment to me that it looked like no one going to get hurt, after all. I said back to him, grinning into the darkness, "What wonderful news! I love that man!" referring to our Chief Executive, the president. We were going to be protected, we were going to be all right! And Keene Stassen, from the aisle seat in front of us, had sighed in utter disgust at the fate that was preventing her from continuing on to Selma with us. She had made a commitment to SNICK's Freedom Democratic Party project, she explained, turning onto her knees and leaning over the back of her seat to talk to us. She couldn't renege on her responsibility to that, she said, nor to the students in her charge.

"How will you two guys get into Selma anyhow? It's at least another fifty miles or so past Montgomery, I think," Keene said.

"Fifty-four, to be exact," I said. I had read that figure days ago in the Philadelphia Inquirer that was delivered to our house each morning. "Could there possibly be a public bus service running a trip there tonight, I wonder . . . ?"

I had no idea what I was talking about. And what would a bus trip cost, anyhow? Did I even have enough money to pay for one?

Albert spoke up then. "I have friends who flew down from New York this morning," he said. "They promised to try to find some way to meet this bus in Montgomery. If someone shows up there to meet me, Gwen, you can go into Selma with us."

It was almost too good to be true! First, the National Guard to look after us on the march! And then a ride with Albert and his friends into Selma tonight! And so, without my having to lift a finger, the main problem of my immediate future had been resolved. At least I hoped it had . . . . !

Bill Morris, the white primary co-leader for SNICK, stood up at the front of the bus in the aisle just back of the driver and faced the now wide-awake and attentive passengers. We were rumbling through the outskirts of a city now, so large that it could only be Montgomery. With all the stopping and starting of the bus at traffic lights, he had to grasp at a seat back to keep from losing his balance.

"At our last meal stop," he announced in a nicely audible voice so all could hear, "we phoned ahead and learned that our Montgomery contact was arrested downtown today during a demonstration. We don't know what we'll find when we get there tonight. We had expected that we would all be put up in a dormitory somewhere, but now—well . . ." and he shrugged. "The important thing right now is for you to stay in your seats after the bus stops, and wait for instructions. Remember! Don't leave the bus 'til you're told to! But then be ready to move quickly!"

He sat down amid a stunned silence. No beds? It was already nearly eleven o'clock. Everyone except me had been on the bus for twenty-nine hours since leaving New York City. It was raining outside. The two big wipers were frantically pounding back and forth *swoosh, swoosh, swoosh,* over the bus's enormous glass windshields. No one had brought blankets or sleeping bags or ponchos for just such a contingency as this. I thought of the dignified, graying couple from my own state who were sitting halfway back, and of the Negro professor with the circle of white hair atop his nearly bald head sitting close by. I thought of my young friend Peter, in his new blue windbreaker. I thought of me. I had no guarantee that even if I got to Selma this night, I would fare much better than my fellow travelers would, even with a sleeping bag in my possession.

Tom Courtney now took Bill Morris's place at the front of the aisle and made a few animated remarks about staying with our secondary leaders once we got off; about never going anywhere, even to the bathroom, without telling our assigned team leader beforehand. It was very important, he reiterated, that we stick together. On the morrow there might be police, there might be tear gas. We should behave with dignity at all times and not panic. I felt left out of things, all of a sudden; almost like a deserter, with my plan to leave the group and go on to now-safer Selma.

When Tom had finished, I left my seat beside the rabbi and stumbled to the back of the bus to make sure my gear would be ready to go when the time came. Peter helped me re-roll the sleeping bag Keene had used into a tighter bundle. Then he took his shiny blue jacket down from the luggage rack and zipped himself into it.

"Pretty sharp, huh?" he murmured to me. He patted its softness against his chest. "Warm, too. Just right for this type of activity."

In spite of his grin, I knew he was serious. In his unsoiled attire and neat, short, blond haircut, he cut the perfect picture, it seemed to me, of the coddled blue-collar child whose heart was nevertheless in the right place. He showed me the clean blue duffle bag he had brought along, which included another pair of shoes, two complete changes of clothing, and a transistor radio that wouldn't work on the bus. He had gone back home and smuggled the bag and its contents out of the apartment night before last, after his father had gone to bed. Against orders, his mother had unlocked the door and let him in.

Peter carried my knapsack and sleeping bag to the front of the bus and stored them on the luggage rack just above my seat. I got into my own coat and put my shoulder bag strap over my head and one arm. So I was ready now, I told Albert Friedlander, ready for anything.

Jeffrey, our head driver, had no problem finding his way to the Benmor Hotel located in a Negro section of Alabama's capital city. First putting on his uniform cap, he pulled alongside the curb before the hotel and brought the bus at long last to a complete and wheezing stop. The street was almost deserted in both directions. By the neon light over the canopy announcing the hotel's name, we could see a white man in a black raincoat and *yarmulke* waiting below at curbside, jiggling up and down on his soles in the drizzle, his arms wrapped around his chest to keep warm. Had he been waiting there since ten? Or perhaps even nine, if you took the time differential into account? And now it was after eleven o'clock at night, Central Time.

The anxious look on the man's face disappeared at sight of Rabbi Friendlander smiling down at him through the glass window of the bus. He lifted one arm in a wave of recognition.

"Wait here, Gwen." Getting nods of permission from our two primary leaders, Albert grabbed up his shaving kit and was out the door and on the curb with his friend, clasping hands. The two of them spent a hasty minute or two in consultation. Then Albert looked up at my window and motioned frantically for me to come along. It was not like him to be frantic, I knew that by this time. I jumped up and yanked my gear down from the luggage rack above my head. It was time for me to move on.

The other passengers meanwhile had not budged from their seats. They were obediently awaiting instructions. All except for Keene, who had followed Albert out and was conferring with a young black man who had materialized out of nowhere. Now she climbed back aboard and helped me down the steps with my knapsack and sleeping bag. She grasped my hand in tight farewell. And then she became my secondary leader again.

"Goodbye, Gwen. Don't forget—the bus leaves for home at eight o'clock sharp on Sunday evening. That's written into our contract with the bus company. We'll be waiting right here at the Benmor. Better memorize the name so you don't forget it," she said, looking deep into my eyes as if to impress me with the importance of what she had just told me.

For a few brief seconds I was an anxious Cinderella. "I'll remember. I'll be here in time, I promise." I'd have to be, wouldn't I? Albert had already told me he hadn't decided yet how he'd be going back home, or even when. It would all depend upon how the march went on Sunday. But there was no alternative open to me, I had told him. This bus was my only way back to home and family and job and school.

"Take care of yourself, Gwen," Keene said. "And good luck on the march."

I was well aware that she longed to be in it too. "Thanks, Keene. You too, with your survey," I said.

I stood in the rain and stared back up through the bus door, not caring that the fake fur collar on my Sunday coat was getting soaked. It had all happened so fast, my leaving the group. I had had no chance to bid the others a formal goodbye and good luck: Donna and Wilma and the other Negro girl, the excited three I had met in the lunch diner. Sweet Peter, who had merely needed a place to go after his father threw him out for bringing two Negro college students home for dinner. Tom Courtney, the brave black man, and Bill Morris, the brave white man. And Jeffrey, the good-humored white driver, and Carl, his relief driver. No matter. I'd see them all again on Sunday evening. Be back by eight, my fairy godmother had warned me. Else I'd turn into a pumpkin? No; else the bus would leave on the return journey without me, which would be much, much worse.

"Come on, Gwen!" It was Albert, breaking into my fairy-tale reverie but not unkindly. "My colleague is here in a car he borrowed, and he has to get it back." Dangling my gear in his two hands, along with his shaving kit, he was impatient to be off. Pleased at the ease with which we'd made our connection, he was probably concerned about the late hour, and about keeping his faithful rabbi friend up, and about the fact that we still had no guaranteed place to sleep. At least that's what I figured it was at first. So I threw one last quick wave toward the bus and trotted after him.

Three other white men were waiting in the back seat of the car with the Ohio license plate parked further down the curb away from the Benmor Hotel. The dome light of the car did not go on when the door opened, so I was unable to see if the others were rabbis too. As I slid into the front seat, one of the men in the back was explaining through the window to Albert that it wasn't safe these past days for anyone from up North to drive anywhere alone.

Nor was it safe for us to hang around the Negro bus depot for long. They had already been waiting down the street for over an hour, hoping the City police, or someone worse, would not spot them or their borrowed car from up North. They had counted on the bus being late, the man said, but not this late! And we should hurry and get out of there right now. This very minute.

The rabbi who had met us tossed my things into the trunk of the car, and hurried around to the driver's seat. Albert quickly climbed into the passenger side of the car beside me. He had brought nothing with him but the shaving kit, not even an overcoat, and thus he had no luggage to concern himself with.

As the car started forward, we caught sight of our companions from the charter bus. They were out now, empty-handed for the most part, walking along the sidewalk in some semblance of discipline, a straggly band of innocuous "outside agitators" with the invincible, seemingly tireless Keene leading the way in the rain. Albert, who had been in on the discussion beforehand, told us they were being taken to a Negro church close-by where they would be able to spend the night on the hard basement floor. It was a last-minute, make-shift arrangement, yes. But according to the young black man from SNICK who had met the bus, it was the best thing that could be done under the circumstances. Most of the volunteers on the bus were just kids; kids could sleep anywhere.

I sank gratefully into the padded seat back of the late-model sedan, too weary for once to feel guilty for having such comfort beneath me and behind my head when my bus mates must be so miserable out there, walking in the rain, soaked and facing a basement floor to lie down upon. The bus lurched off around a corner and out of sight, all the suitcases and backpacks and other large luggage presumably still in its belly. The black SNICK stranger had been standing up front by the driver, pointing in order to guide him to what I assumed was a suitably safe parking place.

So this was how I came to Selma, Alabama, that dark and drizzly night in March of 1965. Along unlit and now notorious U.S. Highway 8O, sitting in the front seat of a borrowed car, wedged snug and secure between the sturdy shoulders of two Jewish gentlemen of the cloth. My head bobbed sleepily, but I forced myself to stay awake and listen to the conversation of the men.

". . . . work for a trade sheet in New York City. Came down here to get a story . . . . two years ago, worked down South." One of the men in the back seat was leaning forward, talking to Albert over the seat back beside me, telling him a story.

". . . . Northern advertising firm at that time . . . . making special film in collaboration with a Negro college near Birmingham . . . . secretary nice Southern lady, seemed sympathetic to the project. One night, returning to motel in Birmingham from the college . . . . picked up by police and charged with vagrancy, since I didn't have the required $50 cash on my person . . . . only allowed one phone call . . . . called my secretary, asked her to contact my firm in New York immediately for bail money . . . . Cops took away all my clothes and put me naked into a jail cell with a group of Southern "rednecks" and told them of my activities at the Negro college. They left me in there for four days before they let me go."

"What happened to you in there?" another of the back-seat men seat asked. Wide awake now, I stiffened my back, waiting for the reply. Heart pounding, I steeled myself for the shock that I felt sure was coming next.

My body is covered with scars from where they put out their cigarettes on my bare skin. And my navel is now non-existent. As for that faithful secretary—she never bothered to phone my company at all. And when I went to my office in Birmingham after my release from jail, she had completely disappeared. I never saw that nice Southern lady again, but I'm pretty sure she was the one who turned me in in the first place."

Unreal. Who could believe a tale like that is true? Surely he made some of it up.

But only last summer—those three young men picked up by the local sheriff and murdered by the Ku Klux Klan down in Philadelphia, Mississippi. Just because they were trying to help Negroes register to vote. Bodies buried in dirt beneath a dam. Who could believe a tale like that was true? Yet it was! It was! And even worse: the bombing of that black church in Birmingham, Alabama a couple of years ago, in which on a bright Sunday morn those four innocent little Negro girls had been killed . . . four children around the same ages as my own . . . .

The rabbi behind the wheel had been giving us a running commentary as he drove.

"You may have noticed the overhead light is turned off. That's so we don't stand out like sitting ducks when we open the car doors," he said. And later: "Here is where the march will end up next Thursday, right here in front of the state capitol building. If they make it that far." And still later: "This is where interstate 80 narrows to two lanes for quite a long stretch. It's also the most desolate part of the route, full of swamps. The

Montgomery powers-that-be are trying to make it part of the court order that only a certain number of people can go all the way from Selma to the last-day part of the march."

Slumping back into the soft padding once more, I again let my muscles relax as I stopped fighting the urge to fall asleep. Wedged in as I was, I told myself, at least my head couldn't loll around too much and embarrass me. But suppose I snored? Or whistled through my nose? Or talked in my sleep?

And finally, after what seemed ten minutes but had to have been nearly an hour, "Wake up, Gwen," Albert said, nudging me gently with his shoulder. "You'll want to see this."

"We're coming into Selma," our driver Maurice said. "We may have to go in the back way after we get across the bridge."

He had slowed the car down as we approached the outskirts of the small Alabama city that had captured the nation's headlines over the past two weeks. "If the roadblocks are still up, the Selma police could delay us for hours before they let us into the Negro Compound. They've been ordered to remove them, but now they're threatening to prevent any more outsiders from joining the march," Maurice said. "Which is quite a switch, threatening to keep people out whereas before, they were trying to keep people in."

I opened my eyes to look, but so far there was not much very visible all around us in the dark. I had seen television photographs of one of the roadblocks, the one set up just before Brown's Chapel, the Negro church that had become famous almost overnight as a meeting place for the march strategists and their followers. This roadblock was the barricade over which Selma police and civil rights activists had confronted one another nose-to-nose for many days.

Our tires, turning slowly now, crunched across the Edmond Pettus Bridge into the city and through the empty wet streets. There were no signs, none at all, of the police barricades, our rabbi driver noted with relief. He would take Albert and me, and the trade-sheet man in the back seat, straight to Brown's Chapel, he told us, to the church office through the side door where we could register with SCLC (the Southern Christian Leadership Conference). And at the same time, we could make arrangements with people posted there who could, he hoped, provide us a place to sleep.

He and the other two men, the two nearly silent rabbis in the back seat, had already been billeted in one of the Negro apartments in the subsidized housing buildings practically across the street from Brown's Chapel. He had brought them along tonight to provide safely in numbers, Maurice said. Only a few hours had passed since his own arrival yesterday into Selma, and already Albert Friedlander's rabbi friend Maurice from New York City had become a tour guide. For now, behind the wheel of someone else's borrowed car, he was the unchallenged expert on this small piece of Alabama and on the march itself, delivering his spiel to us with a decidedly Long Island accent.

Almost hypnotized as I was by the on-coming headlights of an occasional car, the spatters of rain on glass, and the swish of the windshield wipers, I scarcely saw the "places of interest" he was pointing out. "You two got in just in time," Maurice kept saying. "The police will be turning people away, when the sun comes up."

Through a mental fog, I kept telling myself this was not a bizarre dream I was having; that I must actually be experiencing it. I kept telling myself that my great adventure in the pursuit of justice was only just beginning, and already things were not going according to plan. When I left home, I had expected to be going into Selma with a busload of other people, and now look! I should make myself wake up all the way and stay alert.

And someday, I told myself—no, absolutely just as soon as I got back home!—I would write everything down so I would never forget it.

*   *   *

END OF PART FOUR

PART FIVE

SELMA SOJOURN

19.

"I say unto you, if a man smite you on one cheek, turn to him the other also."
                    —Jesus of Nazareth, teacher and healer.
                    (From G G.'s W.T.L.B.)

I found it a curious thing that Saturday morning in Selma, Alabama, that I, Gwen Simon Gain, third of the nine daughters of Kenneth and Helen Simon, had to be taught to be non-violent. True; at the age of twelve back in 1942, I had longed to be a fighter pilot in the United States Army Air Corps so I could get me a few Japs or Nazis for the glory and revenge of my country. At fourteen, I was still making models of fighter planes cut from balsa wood and hoping to do duty as a volunteer airplane spotter if the Second World War should last until I grew up. But the two atomic bombs had been dropped on Japan in 1945 when I was fifteen. The terrible Second World War had been ended by the Allies for once and for all that year, and I was much relieved that the killing was over, and I no longer wanted to be a hero, or a killer, of any sort.

And somewhere along the way I had either matured or grown soft, depending upon who was looking at the issue. From the age of sixteen on, I was convinced that my survival, as both a woman and a human being, depended upon the triumph of the world's brains over its brawn. What was there to know further, then, about believing in non-violence? Either you did, or you didn't, and I wholeheartedly did.

I dutifully reported that Saturday morning in Selma, however, to the First Baptist Church in the Negro Compound, where Albert and I had been instructed the night before to go for our orientation. My stomach was comfortably full, my legs and mind sufficiently exercised by my early walk through the quiet streets. Well before the designated hour of ten o'clock I was in a pew close to the pulpit, sitting behind a row of six Catholic nuns in formal back-and-white habits.

I saw no sign of my new friend the rabbi, and attendance seemed poor, since only the first few rows of pews were filled. Newcomers filtered in through the back doors, one or two at a time over the next few minutes. I could hear the faint rustle of their bodies as they slipped into places behind me. Every few seconds someone coughed nervously, needing a cough drop of some sort to quiet down.

At last a balding young man with a boisterous manner and a light-tan skin the color of hazelnut stood up to face us, his arms akimbo, on the wood floor below the pulpit. He introduced himself as the Reverend James Bevall.

"That's B-e-v-a-l-l," he pointed out, and announced that he was in charge of orientation that morning. We would please pay close attention to what we would hear from him because our lives, and the lives of others around us, would perhaps depend upon it. They ran these small sessions several times a day, he said, for people coming to Selma from everywhere to take part in the march on the morrow. Because it was vital that everyone involved in the Movement understand the philosophy behind the Southern Christian Leadership Conference's strategy for change.

And it was equally as important that we learn how to handle ourselves in an organized and orderly fashion, and to know what to do when confronted by a threatening situation. Though we bore no arms, each one of us should think of ourselves as an important link in an army of peace, and act accordingly. "Because," he said, "in our unity lies our strength."

"Mom, if there are two of us there together, nobody would try to hurt us." My daughter Wendi's voice, sneaking into my consciousness, begging to come with me.

Appearing to be quite young for all his self-confidence, the Reverend Bevall looked for all the world like a refugee from a movie depiction of a Georgia chain gang. He wore faded blue denim trousers and a ragged, short-sleeved shirt that displayed his well developed biceps. But when he opened his mouth, Southern syllables flowed forth with perfect grammar and syntax, as rapidly as his drawl would permit him to get them out. I took my pen and my little blue loose-leaf notebook from my shoulder bag, found a blank page toward the back, and prepared to take notes in Gregg shorthand of everything he said and did.

"There are four parts to orientation," Rev. Bevall explained, striding passionately back and forth on the stage before us as he pounded out with one fist into the open palm of the other fist each important point. He said as he paced, "The first deals with your responsibility to SCLC. The second, with security precautions to take for your own survival. Thirdly, we'll give you a demonstration of non-violence direct action techniques. And finally, an explanation of the unique philosophy of non-violence. Each part is equally important, and we urge you to stay for the entire session."

Faced with this dynamic charmer, I thought, who would even think of leaving before he told us he had finished?

"First, the responsibility of you visitors, the large majority of you white, to the Southern Christian Leadership Conference, the make-up of which is largely black. You owe us your allegiance while you are here Don't make more problems for us than we have already."

Another name for Selma at that moment, he went on, was "Rumorsville," and he admonished us against believing unverified reports of upcoming events. By that he meant there were not, repeat *not*, to be any demonstrations held anywhere whatsoever without SCLC approval. "The way you can tell if something has been officially approved is simple: There will *always* be a mass meeting before any project or demonstration. And those mass meetings are *always* held right here in Brown's Chapel, where you are to assemble this evening at seven o'clock."

He swung around at the end of his paced loop once more. "You have left your structured environments behind you. You'd better go home right now, you white folks, if this upsets you—being away from your structured environment. While you've here, you must depend upon us for the major decisions. The SCLC staff is constantly in touch with what is going on, but they have to play everything by ear, and you will have to accept that," he lectured us soberly. "The Movement is always going on. This Alabama project has been going on for two years now, even when you weren't here. Here, you are the Indians and the SCLC staff are the chiefs. Regardless of *who* you are, back home!"

No problem for me, Rev, I'm a nobody.

Another swing, heading back in the opposite direction: "Instead of trying to run things while you're here in Selma, spend your time getting to know the local people in the Negro community. Especially the kids. *Especially* you should get to know the kids!"

I envisioned the small, dark-hued bodies sprawled all over the big bed at Adelaide's house that morning as I crept by the open door. They were the only "kids" I had seen as yet, and they were all asleep. Where were all the others?

A subdued shuffling to my right and Albert Friedlander slipped into a seat on the pew beside me. In his sober black suit, the ever-present *yarmulke* perched upon his wave of black hair, his clothing presented a solemn and dignified contrast to the ebullient reverend up front. But I could tell at a glance that Albert was anything but dour. He must have slept well, and eaten well, too. He seemed delighted to see me again. I gave him a fleeting smile of welcome and went on with my note-taking.

"Now, as to security precautions," Reverend Bevall went on, still pacing, "In spite of the holiday spirit that exists here, it is not the same story in the white community. In fact, it is extremely tense in the white community of Selma. Hostilities are at a fever pitch. There are certain precautions you must take for your own safety."

We sat in outwardly calm silence. No one was leaning forward in the pews. All were sitting back, listening with both ears cocked as we tried to play it cool. Albert watched in mute fascination as my left hand continued forming the curly shorthand squiggles across the page of my little blue notebook, moving back and forth like the reverend in front of us.

"Saturday in Selma is going-to-town day," Rev. Bevall continued. "And eighty percent of both whites and Negroes downtown could be drunk. Don't be fooled into entering an explosive situation. Don't go into the white community at all unless you go on a project sanctioned by SCLC. When you made your decision to come to Selma, you made your decision also to give up your freedom for awhile. You can't buy cigarettes downtown or go to the post office to mail a letter. They know very well who you are. They can spot us before we spot them.

"One white boy from up North was beaten up yesterday when he went downtown to take pictures! Keep your private ambitions and anxieties to yourselves and don't get yourselves in trouble. I believe there is a heaven, and I believe I'm going to go there. But I want to go because my Maker calls me, not because one of you, doing something foolish, sends me there!" His voice grew louder as he warmed ever more to his topic.

I knew he meant every word he said. And he had our undivided attention now. This was heavy stuff, this talk of life and death and people actually getting beaten up. This was the kind of material that made newspaper headlines back home, but always seemed so remote from everyday living.

"Today the main blockade is down," he informed us, referring to the infamous blockade thrown up by police between the white and Negro communities of Selma the week before to keep a new march from taking place. "Be careful of any cars driving through these streets. They may throw bottles or even shoot at you. Keep your eyes open. Cars may try to run you down. A car is like a gun, just another way to get rid of a 'nigger,' or a 'nigger-lover;' and that's what you white folks are while you're here."

I thought of my walk that morning and shuddered inwardly. I had seen an occasional car moving along the quiet unpaved streets, but it had never occurred to me to correlate an Alabama license plate with the race of a driver to see if danger lurked.

By now, Bevall's arms were gesticulating wildly as he looped about the small raised area at the front of the church between apse and audience. Sincerity shone forth from his brown face. Obviously intelligent, very articulate, often eloquent, he was our friend, trying to keep us well-meaning, potentially careless do-gooders from grief.

Where, oh, where, I wondered as I sat there, were the shuffling, ignorant "darkies" of my childhood in Woodbury, New Jersey, the ones with the slurred and almost incomprehensible speech? The ones who hung out in front of that run-down bar in Woodbury's own Negro section of town, their breaths reeking of whiskey, while they shot craps on the sidewalk and waited until time to pick up their hard-working wives from the kitchens of white households. The ones who had led me to conclude all Negro males were like that, even though I had always understood innately the reason why. Because they couldn't get jobs of their own.

"I tell you sincerely that white faces don't mean a thing to the local white population here in Selma. To them, you are a 'white nigger'. These people are feeling backed into a corner now. Their whole lives have been built around the idea of segregation. You gave up the security of your white faces when you came to Selma. To them, you are the enemy."

Next Rev. Bevall ran down a check list of things we should do, and should not do. Carry identification and money on your persons at all times, he told us. In case of being stopped by the police, you need to be able to show both, or they can get you for vagrancy. In case of arrest, call the SCLC office in Selma, at 872-4469.

We should write that number down, our instructor said, and memorize it well. If it happened, SCLC would post bond for us and provide the legal counsel we would need to be released. We should leave knives and nail files in our luggage, not in our purses or pockets. These could be called a "concealed deadly weapon," and be an excuse for arrest. Those of us who were here in our own cars should remove the dome light from the interior if we drove anywhere tonight. We ought to be very careful what we said to the press. Especially in trying to interpret the success or failure of a demonstration. Every demonstration was a carefully planned part of a total scheme to win our cause. We should be honest with the press if we were interviewed, but not exaggerate.

"I repeat: in case you leave the Negro community for any reason, let SCLC know you are going. Check in at the office, at that phone number I gave you. If you are arrested, give your own home address, and not, whatever you do, the address of your local hostess! You folks can always go home when all this is over, but the Negroes of Selma will go on living here. If you like, you can use Brown's Chapel as your address. Avoid conversation with white citizens of Selma. Don't try to explain anything. Let President Johnson take care of it.

"Choose a spokesman for your group in case you are confronted or arrested. Be calm, courteous, and look the person right in the eye. Be gentle, but firm. This is *very important.* The philosophy of non-violence is not to destroy the other person but to bring out the best feelings in him. *Don't* provoke him into a violent action. In a racially mixed group, the police may try to take just the Negroes. In that case, lock arms and insist upon being arrested with your Negro brothers and sisters."

When Rev. Bevall paused for effect, I took the opportunity to whisper to Albert, "How did everything go last night?"

"Just fine!" he whispered back, not hesitating to beam that big, friendly smile in my direction. "That sleeping bag was a life-saver!"

Good thing I had thought to bring it with me! Or had that been my husband Bill who suggested it? No matter. Whoever had thought of it, that inanimate object had won a friend for me in this place of strangers.

*   *   *

20.

"In an age of thermonuclear weapons, the choice is no longer between nonviolence and violence, but between nonviolence and nonexistence."
—Martin Luther King, Jr.
(From GG's WTLB)

A casually dressed white kid of twenty or so had joined Rev. Bevall at the front of the church. The two of them proceeded to demonstrate for us the most effective techniques of nonviolence, with the white kid pretending to be the attacker and Rev. Bevall, the jostled and ultimately set-upon demonstrator. The latter kept up a running commentary as he was knocked to his knees several times by various fake blows, cudgeled over the head with a rolled-up newspaper, and spat upon in pantomine.

"You nuns," Rev. Bevall said, indicating the six women who sat in front of me, wearing their black and white headdresses, "they may jerk on your white collars. Don't stop the line if that happens. Step to the side. Monitors will come to protect you. If someone is hit, fall down," and taking another fake blow from his tormentor, he followed his own instructions. We in the audience stared spellbound at the empty spot where Rev. Bevall had just stood.

"The one in front falls across you, then the one behind." His muffled voice issued from somewhere on the floor in the vicinity of the front row of pews. The young white helper had fallen on top of his head. And then Rev. Bevall was springing up again, like a jack-in-the-box, to explain the rationale of his latest tactic: "Better for each to take one lick than for one to take all! If a white woman will fall to her knees and beg to take some of the beating, the attackers will probably stop. *Don't,* whatever you do, and no matter what happens, throw up your hands! It might be construed as an aggressive move, not a defensive gesture."

A woman in one of the side pews raised her hand and asked about the possibility of tear gas.

"Glad you reminded me to mention that," our trainer said. "Tear gas is very light in weight. If they use it, get down on your stomach with hands linked behind your head, make an air pocket between your elbows and chin, and take short breaths. Use a handkerchief over your eyes, if you have one. Lie there, until the gas has a chance to rise, and say a few holy words from yourself to the Man Upstairs. Horses? Never run from them. You haven't a chance of winning a race with a horse. Stay on your feet. If you're knocked down, keep your eyes open after you fall so you can roll either way to avoid the hoofs. And please!" He held up his hands in mock resignation. "Don't ask me what you do if they use tear gas and horses at the same time! I just can't answer that!"

We all roared with laughter at this admitted but improbable impasse, forgetting that just this dilemma had faced the Negro marchers here two weeks ago. Laughter relieved the tension all of us newcomers were feeling, and then seeing that the demonstration part was over, we applauded with much enthusiasm for both Rev. Bevall and his white partner.

An exceptionally thin Negro went up front as the demonstration couple ran off. He introduced himself as Dr. Vivian. He was the brave minister we had all seen on television, I remembered, being shoved bodily down a flight of stairs by Sheriff Clark, right in front of the Dallas County Court House building where he had gone to try to register to vote. Dr. Vivian proceeded to talk to us about the philosophy of non-violence, tracing its roots from Jesus and Mahatma Gandhi to the success of Martin Luther King, Jr. and his associates in organizing the Montgomery Bus Boycott nine years ago in 1956.

"We have all come here to demonstrate," Rev. Vivian said. "Demonstration is a means of communication. After negotiations have failed or broken down, then one demonstrates. It is a means to an end.

"As we walk down that street and across that bridge tomorrow, we are saying to the white power structure and the white residents of Selma, 'We love you, and we are willing to suffer to see that the kind of community we want comes about. This society is evil.' We are saying, ' Look! We have nothing in our hands. We have only a desire to speak love to our fellow man.' This tells something to the community. The truth was not told until people became willing to lose something; to say, 'Now we demand justice of you!'"

If anything, he was an even more eloquent speaker than Rev. Bevall had been; and certainly he was more solemn, talking to us in a voice that was almost funereal. He wore a small mustache on his upper lip and appeared to be in his forties, very tall and gangling in a suit and tie. Standing quietly to one side of the center pews, down on our level, he spoke to us of the guilt feelings of white society toward the Negro, feelings that led to fear that the Negro would take over if he got the chance. And if he takes over, whites reasoned, he will then treat us the way we have treated him.

"But we do not demand retribution," the tall minister said. "The Negro does not want to own society, but only to share in it. Our attitude cannot be self-righteous. This is not a struggle between black and white, but between justice and injustice, right and wrong. We have no right to be self-righteous. Love, truth, justice is what we seek in a new society."

The Rev. Dr. Vivian continued his remarks in the same vein, and I honestly tried to concentrate on every word he was saying. But emotionally exhausted by what had gone before, my mind wandered. A single phrase uttered by young Rev. Bevall early in his introduction kept pushing its way into my consciousness, ludicrously persistent. "In unity lies strength."

That word unity. Of course! That name Unity! In Unity, the dignified Negro maid of my childhood, there had always lain strength. She had been one of those needing to be picked up at a kitchen door—ours!—now and then by her husband, usually when her old car had broken down and needed to be fixed. But picked up, in her case, not by a drunken bum with no job, but by a gentle, white-haired black man with wrinkled skin, at least thirty years Unity's senior, who preached in a Negro church on Sundays, Unity had told me during one of our frequent talks.

Drat, I had done it again. Let my thoughts be dragged back—no, they had flown back—to other times and places. Not to the recent past, because I was being successful in my resolve not to let live ghosts populate my memory. Instead, my mind insisted upon retrieving, against all my best efforts to concentrate on the here and now, events from the distant past that were long dormant, often buried, in the far recesses of my brain. These trickles of memory were being played back by the dozens since I arrived in Selma, set off when I least expected them by the multitude of sights and sounds and impressions so different from my customary surroundings.

Normally, back home, the business of fulfilling my many responsibilities occupied nearly all my waking moments. That, and the abundance of new and fascinating concepts I was being introduced to in my classes at the University of Pennsylvania. Personal memories of another, longer-ago time had no place in my frantic schedule. But the floodgates of my past had apparently begun to swing open during those long hours of meditation on the bus ride to Selma. Before I'd moved up to a seat beside Rabbi Friedlander and occupied my mind with other, more absorbing ideas.

Perhaps all this remembering was a defense mechanism, I told myself. A protection against the uneasy reality of the present moment. Or perhaps, as my father had been fond of suggesting to me in those days of my adolescent awakening to philosophical and ethical concepts, mind is the only reality. "How do you know that you are actually alive?" he would pose to me. He would be stretched out on his studio couch in the privacy of his den whither I had gone at my mother's instruction to read to him from Dostoevsky's *Crime And Punishment.* Or Tolstoy's *War And Peace.* Or a book by Dickens. Or one by Dumas.

Maybe all this, the present, is just a dream, Dad more than once proposed to me with a grin. And I would get these chills flashing up and down my spine—*and I could feel one coming on me now!*—and after a few minutes more of discussion I would plead with him to stop, the idea he had just posed to me was so incomprehensibly eerie. My father's presence was now, alas, the past; just a ghostly memory as he himself was. He had been dead for ten years last February at the age of 51, felled, we in his family guessed, by an elusive derivative of petroleum poisoning after thirty years of working for the DuPont Company. This here, today, this moment, was the only true reality, and I had better pay attention, Dad would have said. My survival tomorrow might depend upon it.

Dr. Vivian was still speaking, quoting Bayard Rustin, the Negro Quaker who has been actively seeking rights for his race in America since the thirties and forties. The reverend was enlarging upon Rustin's theme of the "indestructibility of the non-violent participant." And then, suddenly, he was finished, and I was on my feet with the others, giving him a standing ovation. To my surprise as I looked around, still clapping, the church behind me was half-full.

Back at his old stand before the pulpit once again, Rev. Bevall began making a fervent plea for help before dismissing his audience. Telling us drolly that he didn't need more people to march and get on CBS-TV; he was in need of people now who would do some work and get on NBC. "Here is your opportunity to be Indians, for a change, instead of chiefs. Go to the SCLC office and sign yourself up on one of the two lists they're keeping there: 'Set Up' and 'Break Down'. That's for those of you who have cars and can help with the march campsites being set up along the road to Montgomery.

"None of the things that are happening now were supposed to happen," he said. "As a result, our staff has been going crazy. We've had no chance to look beyond the five-day march that's coming up. But we ask that all of you think about what kind of resources you can mobilize back home for the people of Alabama. They've been boycotting the business district of

Selma for some months now, and they need so many things. Food, money, clothes, books—whatever you can send. Get in touch with the SCLC office here in Selma, at 21 Franklin Street, and let them know what you have, or can get together back home. Remember; we must stay united after all the marching is over! In unity lies strength."

Once again Unity, the Negro woman and friend of my adolescent years, is here. I hadn't thought about her in a good many years until the Selma events, not for almost a decade. I'd had to miss her funeral back in 1955, but I had eventually stopped feeling guilty about that. I was expecting a baby at the time, and was very pregnant, so what could I do? Strange, though, that I had never dwelt much on her passing, especially when she had been such a strong and enduring personality in my life from the time I was twelve years old.

She had materialized at my parents' house every weekday morning and a half-day Saturday for fifteen years, driving fifteen miles each way in her old jalopy. She came to help my harried mother with the housework when the majority of us nine sisters were young. Small and wiry, still muscular in her mid-fifties and with a keen native intelligence, Unity had seemed to me capable of any task. But it was her aura of dignity that impressed me the most. Her chocolate-brown face, topped by a film of fuzzy greying hair, maintained an expression of composed determination through what seemed to our family to be a never-ending string of her own family's adversities. Deaths. Accidents. Divorces. Separations. Illegitimate babies. Deserted grandchildren for her and her husband to take care of . . .

Only once had Unity lost her dignity in front of my family. It had happened one hot summer morning in 1944 when a casual friend of my mother's gave my baby sister Lynnie a colored baby doll. Unity had taken one look at that doll and another at the white woman's smirking face. And visibly shaken, she had walked out of the house, apron and all, and driven herself home, refusing to come back to work ever again.

When the problem was relayed to my mother, she was only too happy to get rid of the offending article, the brown-skinned baby doll. Mother, who didn't drive, had talked her insensitive friend into driving her the fifteen miles to Unity's house in the country, since they had no telephone. And she made me go with them.

Unity met my very pregnant mother at the back door of her farmhouse. We hadn't known, my mother explained feebly to Unity's set jaw. In no way would we have deliberately offended her. But we kids all guessed that Unity knew what the rest of us had known from the beginning. Reluctant to register our own objections to the "gift" and thus create an issue, we had hoped Unity wouldn't realize it. That she wouldn't know that the woman who brought the doll to Lynnie was a person with very racist attitudes who had done it as a condescending joke.

Unity may have once longed for Negro dolls for her own children in the years when there was no such thing available anywhere. No, it was not the doll itself but the motivation behind the gift. We all breathed deep sighs of relief when Unity forgave our mother her cowardice, and came back to us, and the subject was never again mentioned, in our house or anywhere else.

Unity's unshakable and wholehearted faith in traditional Christianity never rubbed off on me, however. I had rejected it, secretly, but just as unshakably and wholeheartedly, in my eighth year, one fine day at Sunday School. But her commitment to the ideal of universal brotherhood had reinforced my own growing awareness of the interdependency and essential sameness of the human race.

We had had many contemplative conversations, Unity and I, during my growing-up years, discussing a wide range of issues that never failed to end up on the topic of race. If I deliberately withheld my religious heresy from her, as I did also from everyone else, I made no attempt to hide my indignation at the unfair and demeaning treatment Negroes consistently received in matters of jobs, and schools, and places to live. Right there in my own hometown of Woodbury, New Jersey!

Sometimes, when it became my job to scrub the kitchen floor on my hands and knees every Saturday morning without complaint, Unity would give me a closer glimpse into her personal life. Tell me how she had been forced to marry at the age of twelve (I could not even imagine the horror of being married at twelve!) to a man over forty. A minister of the Gospel, she always said with pride, though he'd had very little formal schooling. She would confide in me stories about her seven grown children and their mish-mash of marital problems; and about her youngest child Mariah, aged ten, who made good grades in school and would be the first person in Unity's family ever to graduate from high school. What was more, Rydie was going to become a nurse someday! If it was the last thing Unity ever did, she would see to that, she told me.

And then Rydie would sometimes come to the kitchen door with her father to pick up her mother in his farm truck, and she and I would smile shyly at each other before she lowered her jet-black eyes in embarrassment. Rydie was only a year younger than I. How on earth, I would ask myself when the three of them had left, would that shy girl ever get enough self-confidence to become a nurse? Why, she looked as if a mere shadow would scare her! But Unity had spoken, and I knew that somehow in some way it would be so. Because Unity, Rydie's mother, was a veritable pillar of strength and determination.

* * *

21.

"Go freely with the powerful uneducated persons, and with the young, and with the mothers of families. Re-examine all you have been told in school, or in church, or in any book. Dismiss whatever insults your own soul."
—Walt Whitman, American Poet
(From G.G.'s WTLB)

Our required training and orientation session over and done with in the Negro Compound of Selma, it was still only midday, and a whole afternoon lay ahead of us. The mass meeting in Brown's Chapel was still several hours away. Albert and I left First Baptist Church together and found our way to the Southern Christian Leadership Conference office, based in an old storefront. The big need was for automobiles, we were told when we tried to volunteer our services. Had we driven to Selma, and did we have a car for various transportation needs?. And since we hadn't brought one with us, and all the other tasks were already assigned, we thanked the woman who had been typing at the desk and went out.

"It seems odd," Albert said as we strode along side by side, going nowhere and with nowhere to go, "to be so utterly free." I knew he meant, for that moment.

"You said it!" I agreed. "I usually have a whole raft of weekend commitments at my house that have to be taken care of!"

"Our other lives seem such a long way off, don't they?" Albert said. "Even the Vernal Equinox is going to take place up North sometime this evening. Without us."

"Spring, you mean?" I asked.

"Yes. It won't wait for us to get home," Albert said.

I laughed. Since we were much further south, there was more spring here, than there. "It better not wait! I hate winter!" I said. And then, not wanting to interfere with any plans he might have made with his new friends here, I asked, "What will you do now?"

"I need to look up the other rabbis sometime later today, but for now, there's nothing. I feel useless, Gwen," he said.

That was my cue to say, "Albert, there's someone I'd really love for you to meet!" and with no further need for persuasion, I took him "home" with me to the George Washington Carver Homes and introduced him to my hostess, Adelaide Sims. We ended up eating baloney sandwiches and drinking coffee at Adelaide's kitchen table and spending half the afternoon in her company and that of the three Sims children who were teenagers.

Adelaide's husband worked all day Saturdays, we learned, and would not be home until dinnertime. The two-year-old baby Oscar napped on an upstairs bed most of the time we were there. The two little boys, Willis and George, hung around us with wide and curious eyes for a few minutes and then, bored with inspecting the white folks in their midst, went out to play bare-footed in the scruffy yard between two of the several brick buildings that made up the George Washington Carver apartments.

Adelaide had been cleaning house when we arrived, but she ceased her labors and announced she would fix us some lunch. She sat down with us at the kitchen table, refusing my offer of assistance to help fix the food. I couldn't help noticing how tired she looked, nor help wondering how relieved she would be when all this "strife and stress" and worry about her children, was over. I knew from our conversation last night that for the past tern days she had been putting up guests from the North in the double bed—my bed!—where she and her husband usually slept.

Her housework bandana still tied around her hair, Adelaide eyed the door nervously as it closed behind her two little boys' backs. She had cautioned them to stay close by, and now she lit up another cigarette and explained.

"Two weeks ago, the day the colored people was beaten and tear-gassed, the deputies on the horses followed them all the way back here. They was 'spectin' 'em to head right straight for Brown's Chapel—that's just down the block from here, y'all know. But the colored people was tired and couldn't run no more. So they come in the yards here at the Homes, tryin' to get away. And those men come after 'em on their horses, hollerin', tramplin' down the bushes, ruinin' the grass. Hollerin' at everybody to get in their houses and stay there. We had some nice bushes out here, until they come around! My place here was filled up with Selma Negroes, yellin' and screamin' and terrible upset." She stopped to wipe the sweat from her forehead and take a deep breath. We guessed she was not yet finished with her story, so said nothing.

"My Claire—she's my thirteen—was outside playin' in the yard when they come ridin' up, and I went runnin' out to get her, and this big man, he rides right up on the porch there outside my door and won't let me by. He hollers at me, 'Get back inside, nigger!' So I holler, 'you crazy? My baby's out there! I'm not goin' in without I get my baby!' And I pushed me 'round that big horse and there was Claire, cryin'. She was right scared, Miz Gains. I must say, I found her real quick, lucky for me!"

I could better understand her speech patterns by now, and as she told her story in rapid-fire bursts of emotion, I could almost feel her fear and panic. Adelaide was not a heavy woman. She was taller than I, but much thinner, almost frail in appearance. I had a mental picture of her defying the white sheriff's deputy on horseback, and could only guess at the courage it must have taken for her to do that. But wouldn't I have done the same thing, in a like situation? For Kenny? For Wendi? For any one of my children? Especially for my two little ones, Scotty and Julie. For my little sisters when I was growing up? I hoped so. But then I wouldn't have been considered an "uppitty" black woman, daring to provoke my white masters by defying their orders.

"Things are pretty bad down here, we know," said the rabbi, sighing at the fact of the cruelty and injustice we had just heard about.

"Yessir, times is hard." Adelaide nodded her head thoughtfully in his direction. Some of her short, straightened hair was visible beneath the bandana at her forehead, and I could see that strands of gray had begun to creep in. "I won't deny it's hard," she said. "The Selma colored people needs jobs, they needs clothes. My two little boys there—" and she motioned with her head toward the small voices of Willis and George at play just outside the kitchen door, "they needs shoes real bad."

"Shoes are indeed a problem," I agreed with a groan, thinking of the four young pairs of feet needing to be constantly re-shod back in my own home in New Jersey. The need for larger shoes, it seemed, was the one item that always seemed to ruin my own family budget. And Adelaide had eight members of her family to procure them for, on a lot less money than I had available to me on Bill's modest wages.

"But it's the other that's most hard," Adelaide said.

"The other?" Albert said.

"The white people here in Selma. They way they talk to us," and then she told us a surprising thing. "I'm from the North, you see. I notice things, more than them others. I means to say, I gets bothered more . . . ."

"The *North*, Adelaide?" I broke in, unable to hide my astonishment.

"Yes, ma'am. Pittsburgh. Been down here 'most twenty years now." And she went on to describe, in her quick, short bursts of speech, the visit she had made to a Selma laundry a few days ago to pick up some sheets left there by a friend. She had answered with a simple "yes" to a rude question put to her by the white woman behind the counter.

"I'm a white lady! Don't you dare 'yes' me! You say 'yes, ma'am' to me, do ya hear, or ya don't get these sheets! You can see I'm a white lady!" the woman had screeched at Adelaide in a rage.

"What did you answer back?" Albert asked.

"Nothin'. I jes turned me 'round and got me out of there. Told my girlfriend she'd have to pick up her own sheets! First time I was ever brave enough to do somethin' like that since I come here."

"Good for you, Adelaide!" Albert and I said in unison. I couldn't get over her actually being from up North. That might explain the rapid speech delivery beneath the Southern drawl. But not the deferential manner she still used in addressing my companion and me.

The downstairs of the modestly furnished apartment was cramped, but clean and neat. A party of sorts had already been in progress in the tiny living room when we arrived. Several young people, including Adelaide's two teen-aged daughters, had gathered to listen to pop music on the radio. As we ate the sandwiches Adelaide fixed for us, we could see them through the wide-open door. They were sitting around talking in subdued voices, long brown limbs draped over chair arms or across the steps leading upstairs.

Just then eldest son Charlie, an extroverted lad of seventeen, came into the kitchen through the outside door. At his mother's urging, after the initial greetings and shaking of hands, he displayed to us the wide and thick four-inch scab running down the back of his head, a result of the ugly wound received at the hand of one of those mounted sheriff's deputies two Sundays before. He had been tear gassed and billy-clubbed that day, along with lots of others among the several hundred marchers, many of whom were women and children. He sat down at the kitchen table, ate the modest lunch his mother had prepared for him, and described to us in more vivid detail the scene we had already viewed on television several times back home.

Between bites, Charlie told us the marchers would probably have turned around as ordered by the sheriff and gone back peacefully, but they had been given no time to do that. He recreated for us in colorful phrases the pervasive misery of the tear gas, the fear the marchers had of the horses' hoofs and of the bullwhips some of their riders carried. The sounds of women's voices screaming in surprise and terror, the clubbing and scattering of children without mercy. Some of the children were only in elementary school. And Charlie, narrating all this to us, was, at seventeen, little more than a child himself. He had been arrested, and held in the Selma jail overnight, the back of his head bleeding all the while. He should have had stitches, I thought, viewing his scalp.

As he related his story, I remembered that once I had been hit in the head with a cinder rock instead of a billy-club, just because I stopped in an empty field to watch some neighborhood boys playing softball. I remembered how traumatic an experience that had been. And I had not been taken off to jail. Nor sprayed with tear gas. Nor humiliated publicly, nor been wounded to such an extent. The entire drama of the attack had been played out in a matter of barely minutes. The whole irritating mess, Sheriff Clark must have reported with satisfaction to his superiors at the County Court House, had been taken care of in short order.

But as events were continuing to prove, the sheriff had been extremely short-sighted. The cruel episode had played into the hands of the Selma Negroes who, with the help and support of the Southern Christian Leadership Conference, had been struggling in vain for many frustrating months to make inroads in their attempts to vote. Their goal was to lay before the conscience of the entire nation the issue of denial of Negro voting rights in their county and state. And now it had happened! The issue they had been hoping and planning and waiting for had been highlighted! And by the man who wore the "Never!" button, Sheriff Clark himself!

At first the Movement had hoped to do it the "simple" way, as they had in 1956 when a black woman, Rosa Parks, had gotten fed up on a Montgomery bus and had refused to make her weary feet give up her seat to a white person. Dr. King, his friend Reverend Ralph Abernathy, and others had organized the Montgomery Improvement Association back then as a result of Ms. Parks' arrest. After more than a year-long public bus boycott by the Negroes of Montgomery, they had finally won the contest. The white power structure in Montgomery, faced with economic disaster, had at last been forced to capitulate, and the South's Jim Crow legal system, long supported by the United States Supreme Court's "separate but equal" doctrine formulated in 1896 with the *Pleassy vs. Ferguson* case, had begun to crumble.

The deciding factor, however, had not been the specter of economic ruin, but a new Supreme Court decision making segregation of Montgomery's city buses illegal. Other Southern cities, including Atlanta, Georgia and Birmingham, Alabama, pressured by newly-begun Negro boycotts and the implied threat of more Supreme Court decisions, had desegregated their own municipal buses.

Another notable result had been the birth of the Southern Christian Leadership Conference in 1957. A consortium of activist leaders, mostly Negro, from all over the South, had unanimously elected the Rev. Dr. Martin Luther King, Jr, its President.

Segregation of lunch counters and water fountains and interstate buses throughout the South had been the next target. The student Non-Violent Coordinating Committee, or "SNICK," as it came to be called, had a hand in that campaign, after the organization's formation by the SCLC in 1960. The goal had been accomplished by a series of sit-ins and Freedom Rides over a three-year period by black and white students together; affairs that had become bloody confrontations with white policemen and enraged Southern white citizens. Forced to confront the unjust and morally reprehensible situation at last, the Congress of the United States had finally passed the Civil Rights Law of 1964, outlawing the segregation of public facilities, as well as job discrimination, all over the United States.

The issue of voting rights had proved to be much more difficult; with the Movement's adversaries even more intransigent. In flying to Selma after that abortive try on March seventh two weeks ago, Dr. King had obviously hoped for wide-spread publicity to aid the cause. He was, after all, A Nobel Peace Prize winner in 1964, and thus internationally famous. But what happened next had exceeded all of the SCLC's expectations and challenged all their resources. Dr. King's attempts to lead a second march to Montgomery had been turned back not once, but several times—first by hastily flung-up street barricades, then by court injunctions. But each frustrated attempt had brought still greater news coverage.

Counting on his hunch that "out there" on the other end of the television air waves, countless Americans who valued democratic principles were watching in shocked disbelief, Dr. King had finally issued his television invitation—first, to religious leaders across the country, and later, to any sympathetic white citizens, begging them to come and walk with him. To come to Selma and march to Montgomery with their "black brothers and sisters." The injunction forbidding a march had been lifted by a federal court judge. And at long last, the proposed march to Montgomery had received the court's permission to begin on Sunday, March twenty-first, two weeks to the day after Sheriff Clark's fatal miscalculation.

Adelaide's son Charlie knew a great deal about all the events leading up to that day, starting with the beginnings of the civil rights movement in Montgomery. Now a senior in high school, he had been working with the voter registration drive for some time, he said. The day after the March 7th beatings, he had been released from jail along with open threats that the police would be watching him. Charlie was beginning to worry now, he told us, about the effect of his activities upon the safety of his family.

"Mr. Wilson Baker, he not so bad," chimed in Adelaide. "He be the Selma police chief. But that Sheriff Clark is a mean one! Him, and that Al Lingo!"

"Head of the State Highway Patrol," Charlie explained. "But it was Sheriff Clark sicked the posse on us!" I was getting accustomed to *his* drawl as well. Getting to like the sound of it.

"Tell 'em, Charlie," his mother prodded him. "About—you know."

The boy lowered his voice conspiratorially. "I'm waitin' to hear about if I'm goin' to Atlanta this summer! SCLC wants to train me to be a field worker with them. Get paid, and all. I sure would like that," he added almost wistfully.

Albert nodded his approval and said, "Good! We'll be hoping you make it, Charlie." (I had noticed that everything was always "good!" to Albert the optimist.)

"Adelaide," I said, while she poured me more coffee, "will you be walking with us in the march tomorrow morning?"

She looked startled, as if she had not even considered such a thing. Then she shook her head. "No, ma'am, Miz Gains. I'd lose my cleaning job at the School, sure as shootin,' if they found out."

"Is it true? Would that really happen?" I still found these things hard to believe.

"It's true." Charlie scraped back his chair and got up from the table. Once again we could see the ugly scab on the side of his head where he had been struck with a billy club. "It's true, sure enough!"

Adelaide said, "Some of the Selma colored people already be losin' their jobs." But then her face brightened. "But don't you worry, I must say, I be there in Montgom'ry next Thursday, marchin' in your place, Miz Gains. Too many of us to make all our pictures then, so's they can fire us from our jobs." She already knew that I couldn't stay past the first day of the march, that I had to go home on the chartered bus leaving Montgomery tomorrow evening. "I be there if my shoes hold out, I guess," she added, almost as an afterthought.

"Please, Adelaide. Call me Gwen? What do you mean, if your shoes hold out?"

"I got me no decent walkin' shoes, Gwen," Adelaide said, downcast once more.

"It's the boycott," Charlie interjected. "The black people aren't buying in the Selma stores anymore."

"Oh, of course! I forgot about that!" I said. Rev. Bevall had told us about that, only this morning at the training session. And I guessed that the money for new shoes would be a problem, as well. Mr. Sims a day laborer, Adelaide Sims a kitchen helper and cleaner, with six children to raise! I made a mental promise that when I got home, I'd see what I could do about collecting some good used clothing and sending it down. There were probably women in the Unitarian Church of Cherry Hill, where Bill and I were members, who'd want to take it on as a project. And maybe there would be some money somewhere, too, for a pair of new shoes for Adelaide. And maybe the shopping boycott wouldn't have to last much longer.

"But don't you give it no mind," Adelaide was saying, looking from me to Albert. She began lighting up another cigarette. Smoking, a habit I had always easily avoided, was apparently one of her few luxuries. "I'd walk barefoot to Montgomery, just so's my kids can be free!"

Albert and I exchanged triumphant glances with each other across the chipped-enamel table top. The looks said that we were deliriously glad we had come to Selma. Adelaide asked Albert if he wanted to stay at her house instead of trying to walk all the way to Montgomery on the march. Or, she said, he could go Thursday or Friday to Montgomery and the final ceremonies. Charlie had heard just this morning, she said, that the federal court had decreed only three hundred people would be allowed to go on after the first day, and most of these had already been chosen. Even her son Charlie had not been among them.

This was news! Albert declined her invitation with thanks and regret. "I'd love to stay with you, Mrs. Sims," he said. "But our bus leaves for home tomorrow night, and I have to be on it." He chuckled. "I don't want to lose my job either," he added.

Good, good, and good again! He's apparently made up his mind. He's going back the same way he came. With me!

*   *   *

22.

"You don't know, Gwen, what it's really like down there. You didn't realize you were just being used, poor thing!"
—Marion Sommers,* my good friend in the
Continuing Education For Women Program at Penn
(Post-Selma Comments, etc. etc.)

"Folks, get to know the kids," the Reverend Bevall had advised us at orientation. "Especially the kids." Now Albert and I were about to find out why that was considered so important.

Cissy, Adelaide's mod-looking daughter of fourteen, came into the kitchen to get crackers and Kool-Aid for herself, her sister Claire, and their three friends. Feeling more comfortable with the presence of our white faces in the next room, the young people in the living room had turned up the volume of the pop music on the radio. Not loud enough to be annoying; but we could tell that an obviously black male singer was wailing in falsetto voice about the anguish of unrequited love, this to the throbbing strains of a rock band accompaniment.

Or was the singer so "obviously black"? How could anyone know for certain, these days? How could we even know for sure that the singer was male? I asked myself, smiling inwardly. Through the doorway I caught glimpses of bobbing bodies in the living room, several Negro kids in varying shades of brown skin, in the throes of a wild dance. Not an African village stomp, oh, no; this dance was the American twist! Except for their bushy Afros, or hair cut short and straightened, they could have been white kids, cavorting with Wendi in the living room of my own house back home.

And yet—only two weeks ago, remember?—some of these same kids had walked across that bridge over the Alabama River. Had dared to face Sheriff Clark's "volunteer deputies," on horseback, and Al Lingo's troopers with their tear gas and billy-clubs, in order to say by their presence, "Look at us. We are people, like you. We think, we feel, we hope, we believe."

Included in the First Amendment to the Constitution . . . . *The right of the people to peaceably assemble, to petition their government for a redress of grievances* . . . . All the people. Not just the colorless white folks. The brown people too. The joke was on our slave-holding Founding Fathers, I thought with a smile.

Talking to Charlie in the kitchen, all the while observing Cissy and Claire and the others dancing in the living room, I marveled again at this strange turn of affairs. These children in Selma had found the necessity to stand up for something; but there lay the chief difference, it seemed to me, between them and privileged white children of the same age! Until now, I had been largely unaware of the similarities of Negro children to my own, both culturally and in appearance. But the vibrant strains of the music issuing forth from the record player in the living room only served to demonstrate that sameness. I did not know the tune, but I felt certain that Wendi did.

I studied Charlie where he stood at the kitchen sink, getting himself a glass of water and swallowing it down in three long thirsty gulps. Bright and articulate in his narratives and opinions, he had never failed to look me in the eye when he spoke to me. I was reminded of something my Negro housekeeper Edna had once told me. In the South, she said to me, black mothers taught their sons never to look a white woman directly in the eye. Negroes had been lynched for such effrontery. Charlie Sims, apparently, had not learned that lesson.

There was a boy from Chicago, name of Emmet, fourteen years old, last name of Till. Kidnapped, tortured and murdered by the KKK in the 1950's, his body thrown into the river . . . his crime that he had whistled at a white woman . . . .

Still in the first blush of manhood, the bulk of Charlie's dark young face had not yet caught up in size with his nose. When he had no need to be serious, when he wasn't talking about the Movement and could relax, he gave the impression of being, by nature, a friendly puppy-dog. Personality-wise, he was a larger, older version of my happy-go-lucky eight-year-old son Scotty. And he had the same short haircut, the same loose, non-committal stance, the same impatient way of gulping liquids as my twelve-year-old Kenny. When Charlie talked to Albert and me, he used some of the same slang expressions Kenny was now into. "Get it together," and "Right on!" and "tough!" instead of "terrific!" The visible differences between the two boys—those of shape and shade and height—seemed somehow trivial.

Except for the cocoa-brown of her skin and the jet-black of her straightened hair, Charlie's sister Cissy reminded me even more of my own daughter Wendi in looks and mannerisms. Even her facial features were somewhat similar. She had delicate lips and a small nose that tipped up on the end. Beyond that, the same flipped-up-on—the-ends hairstyle, the same casual jeans and T-shirt, the same friendly grin nearly hiding an underlying insecurity. The same abominable taste in music, too. The same giggle even, sometimes forced, and sometimes artificially prolonged. Only the accent and pitch of her speech was different from Wendi's and my own. Cissy had a low, pleasant Southern drawl, but her grammar, at least when she spoke to me, was, like my daughter's, very nearly perfect.

On a mission all his own, Charlie bade us farewell and left by the front door. Excusing herself, his mother went upstairs to check on the baby. The rabbi and I drifted into the living room, whereupon the children graciously made room for us on the well-worn couch and turned down the sound of the music. As a consequence of our asking them the usual polite adult question as to what grades they were in, we found ourselves deep into a conversation about Selma schools. These black kids, we soon discovered, had definite opinions about the value and the implications of a segregated education.

"We're getting short-changed," a handsome Negro lad named Donald whom I hadn't noticed before told me emphatically. "Our books in high school are second-hand from the white schools and they're 'way out of date by the time they get to us."

Their teachers, he went on, had received inferior schooling to start with, which limited what they could in turn do for their pupils. It was a vicious circle from which it was impossible to escape. At least here in Alabama. A black person would have to migrate either to the North or the West of the country, and then accept the certainty of having to live in a slum, and with no guarantee of a better education after all. It was obvious that young Donald had given the matter considerable thought before this.

Cissy Sims, it soon developed, was a spelling champion in the segregated grade school where her mother worked as a janitress and kitchen helper. It was Cissy who told us now of Selma University, the name printed on our meal tickets for dinner that evening. The place was a joke, she said. She wanted to be a teacher someday; but Selma University, a college for *Negroes,* (she pronounced this word with a sneer that twenty years earlier would have cut my Unity to the quick) was the only place she could go for training, "And when you come out," she said, "all you're good enough for is teachin' in a segregated school!"

.... *Separate but equal is inherently unequal . . . Brown v. Board, 1954. But this was 1965 . . .*

Adelaide had earlier told Albert and me about something that had happened to her daughter Cissy. She had been jailed overnight after an earlier demonstration outside the Dallas County Courthouse. Forced to sleep overnight on a damp cement floor at the Selma recreation center, with no blanket or cover of any kind, the girl had become seriously ill with tonsilitis for days afterward and was still not completely over it.

"They call it a university, what a laugh!" Donald was saying with contempt, his mind still on the inadequacies of Selma University. "With only six teachers! And only two of them are PhDs. And the professors don't care about any of this. The Movement and all. They're just scared for their jobs. They keep tellin' us, 'Things 'll get better if you just wait and be patient.' But they never do. Get better."

Hearing this, thirteen-year-old Claire Sims spoke up for the first time. "It's the white folks who make them so scared, Donald." She turned her long-lashed gaze on me from where she sat cross-legged on the faded living room rug. "Why are they so evil? The whites, I mean?"

It was plain by the child's look and tone that she was exempting us, Albert Friedlander and me, from the pejorative label of "evil whites." I had already learned that the use of the adjective "evil" by Negroes meant nasty, or mean, not necessarily sinful. But it was "*They,*" whom she had asked about, looking me right in the eye. "Why are *they* so evil?" I couldn't help remembering some of the white people I had known over the years, expressing their negative opinions to me about the so-called Negro problem. Which was really a white problem, at bottom, if you examined it honestly enough. But I could never convince them.

So many times I had heard one of them say to me something on the order of, "I have to admit, my girl Dottie (or my Pearl, or my Mildred) who comes to clean for me once a week, why she's the most wonderful human being you could hope to find anywhere, even if she is colored. She'd never take a thing from me, she's so trustworthy and clean. But the others . . . they could carry nasty germs, you never know!" And yet another white acquaintance might say, "Our Calvin (or Jacob or Horace), who mows our lawn? (Cleans our storm gutters? Takes care of our garden?)

He's as fine and honest as the day is long. But the rest of them, I wouldn't give you a plugged nickle for. They're utterly worthless! Admit it, Gwen, most of them just don't want to work." Showing the speaker's ignorance of history, and the centuries-long toil of slaves in America.

Long ago I had made myself stop arguing with those myopic white friends because it never did any good. So I wasn't going to dispute this little black girl's opinion of the white race now, or tell her I had given up trying. I wasn't going to tell her of all the wonderful white people I knew; people without prejudice. She probably wouldn't believe me, in the midst of this Selma thing.

"I don't know, Claire," I said gently. "And I'm sorry. It doesn't make any sense, I know." As I continued sitting there, looking around at the roomful of Selma black children and listening to their angry words, I was noticing something else.

What had happened, I wondered, to the grating, high-pitched speaking tones of nearly all the Negro voices, male and female, young and old, of my growing-up years? As if the men were trying to sound like women, in order to make themselves seem less threatening? Like flutes, instead of bass violins? I had long assumed there was something wrong with their vocal chords. I knew better now.

And where today the Rydies, the little pickaninny girls made ridiculous in the movies with their pigeon-toes and their mass of pigtails in all directions and their scared, clasped-together fingers? Where, the knobby, close-scalped boys with the downcast or rolling eyes and the "yes, ma'ams" and "no ma'ams", in barely audible, squeaky voices?

Somehow, between the then and the now, the children of America's largest racial minority had gone from being colored to Negro (with a capital N) to black (with" black" being a brand-new synonym for a sense of pride in one's color). And in the process many of them had learned to speak like the rest of us and dress like the rest of us, and certainly to think much like the rest of us, as well. Take these kids of Adelaide's. They didn't accept, didn't seem to even entertain the notion, that they were *inferior!* Some benevolent circumstance of their lives seemed to have spared them the internalizing of such a concept. When had that happened?

No matter. It just had. "Get to know the kids," Rev. Bevall had emphasized to us only this morning. So this was what he meant! Black kids had changed. Where had I been, all these years? Asleep in my cave, like Rip Van Winkle?

I thought back to the hot-pink hair rollers on the head of my bedmate Dorothy when I woke up this morning. How they had struck me as a fitting symbol of that merging of cultures I, for one, had not realized had occurred. How was it possible that I, a delinquent-in-my-dues member of the NAACP as well as a volunteer champion of fair housing, had overlooked the signs of that merging for so long?

Nor could I have guessed, that eye-opening day in 1965, that just around the corner, sociologically speaking, lay a still newer time: the time of the bush Afro, on both male and female black heads, as the most highly visible symbol of new racial pride. Or that, just as certainly, long, straight, usually unkempt hair on white youths of both genders would become the mark of their own avowed independence from the cultural inheritance of their own past. How could I have foreseen that a phenomenon so superficial as a common hair style would no longer unite the two groups, our brooding children of both races?

Instead, a much deeper sharing of values would very soon come to bind them together. Those values would divide them from my own generation at the very moment in history that the two groups, so long and so assiduously kept apart by their elders, had begun their meeting of the minds. Young white anger against the injustice of the War currently being waged in Vietnam would be matched by young black outrage at the overt and miserable and de facto racial discrimination rampant in America's cities. Not too far beyond this Selma year of 1965 there lay ready to surface that far grimmer age, the machinery already set in motion and gathering speed. But few of us, as I say, could have guessed how fast it was coming upon us.

This quiet day in Selma, none of us dared conjecture either as to what extent and how soon our hopes for Negro voting power and the death of Jim Crow, the South's racial segregation laws, would ultimately be realized and our country changed. Nor could we swear for certain that our "new day," with all its perils and hostilities, was truly ushering in a ray of sunshine for the entire South. After all, as my father had also liked to remind me upon occasion, "The road to hell is paved with good intentions." And another of his favorites, "There's many a slip twixt the cup and the lip."

We three adults sitting in this room—Adelaide had come to join us—we three might not live long enough to witness any tangible improvements, even if our immediate cause prevailed. My Dad had had his own sage admonition: "Don't make too many plans for tomorrow; you may be dead by then."

Don't make too many plans for tomorrow, Gwennie. You may be dead by then.

It did seem, however, that Fate, or Whoever, had inexorably merged the three of us together there in that apartment in the Negro Compound of Selma. The Jewish chaplain. The two mothers, one white and one black. One of us two women the Bible-believing Baptist, the other, the agnostic humanist Unitarian. Fate had brought the three of us together there for one golden moment of peace before danger.

And it further appeared as if, in some wonderful way that my skeptic's heart could not yet fathom the extent of, these children had been the reason. These Negro children, almost grown now, were poised to go on the world's stage as fully participating, decision-making members of the total American society. It was clear to me, as it should have been made clear to everyone else, that they would no longer be denied.

Why do you Nee-groes always sit up in the balcony at the movies, Unity? Why don't you just tell the manager you want to sit downstairs? Tell him you can't see well enough from up there? Or hear well enough either?

We Nig-groes like the balcony, Gwennie. And I don't go to the movies anyhow, remember? It's against my religion.

But—but—that's not the point, Unity. It's the principle of the thing! Doesn't it cost your people the same as us white people to get in?

It's the way it's always been, Gwennie. Can't change it.

But if you'd all do it together, Unity. Maybe the kids could do it . . . .

Those funny, pathetic, obsequious Nee-gro kids of my yesteryear back in New Jersey—they could never have done it. But a new day was surely upon us. Something had happened to the whole of American society when no one over thirty was looking. Just as surely as ante-bellum Southern culture had been swept away in the nineteenth century by the Civil War, so the segregation-preferring and patronizing mores of my childhood years had been rendered anachronistic by far-reaching technological advances and better education and rapidly-disseminating social ideas of a racially-more-liberal cast of characters.

And by cars! The great equalizers!

That "safe" and insulated pre-World War II depression-haunted world had been swept away forever by this new wind. Not swiftly, by the Second World War's death and destruction, which had ended twenty years ago, and in which so many colored men had fought and died in segregated units. But slowly, slowly, behind our backs since then, the great cultural revolution had begun to take place.

Today, don't forget, Unity's shy, scared little Negro girl Ridie was a self-confident, well-educated, and much loved doctor, a pediatrician working in Philadelphia across the Delaware River from where I lived with my husband and four children. After she graduated from high school in South Jersey, my mother had made long-distance calls to nursing schools until she finally found one that would accept a black student. My parents had paid Ridie's bus fare to Harlem Hospital in New York City. After finishing the nursing program there, she had gone on to medical school in Philly. I had attended her graduation from there sometime during the 1950's—after Unity, my beloved Negro friend, had died following a stroke. But her miracle, and my mother's, had begun long before.

I sensed Albert looking at me. Turning my head, I met his eyes with a half-smile, wondering if he had caught the message too. Then I told myself that of course he had. As a Jewish chaplain at Columbia, a major and much honored university in New York City, he must have seen the harbingers of change long before this. I had been too busy to look and listen as I tried to keep pace with my own hectic existence.

Most white Americans of my acquaintance had not yet awakened to the fact of the new day's dawning, much less learned to accept its illuminations. This rabbi and I, on the other hand, had come here, two solitary citizens among many, to acknowledge our own growing awareness of that something special blowing in the wind. We had come to state by our presence our personal convictions that the old ways were no longer valid, if they ever had been. By our presence, we were saying that denial of the right of the franchise to any American, based purely on skin color, had no place in this new nation we had all created together.

Next time perhaps, when this issue has been resolved, Dr. King would tackle the desegregation of schools. The Supreme Court had declared eleven years ago in 1954 what the children in this room, born about that same time, had caught on to for themselves: *"Separate-but-equal is inherently unequal."* As a nation, we were to integrate our schools "with all deliberate speed." But these children—these children here in Selma—why, they were half grown! Their parents must be able to vote in order to change things in a big way for them.

Another awesome idea occurred to me as I sat on Adelaide Sims' sofa, musing even as I conversed with these Selma children. Another unheard-of little community, Gettysburg, Pennsylvania, where I had long ago lived a year of my life while Bill pursued a college degree, had become, eighty-five years after the famous battle there, the symbol of the high-water mark of the American Civil War. The bloody battle that had been fought there over three days was now considered the turning point of the deadly four-year convulsions that had ended legal slavery in this country forever. No one realized it, at the time. It was only afterward, looking back in retrospect, that it became obvious the battle at Gettysburg in 1863 had been the turning point of the Civil War. The "high-water mark," it had subsequently been labeled.

But de facto slavery had gone on, right up to the present day. What if this little place, this Selma, Alabama, would one day represent to future generations of Americans who would study about it, another high-water mark? The beginning of true equality in the United States of America? The idea was so exciting it almost took my breath away.

Thus went my silent social analysis as I sat in the warmth and security of Adelaide Sims' home, making new friends of her children. Surrounded by good will and the happy, hopeful faces of these Negro adolescents, I had listened intently as they spoke of their frustrations with the present and their dreams for a better future.

After awhile, Adelaide got up and went upstairs to fetch from his nap her two-year-old, a thin, squirmy child with handsome features and wide, curious black eyes. She sat on the sofa between Albert and me and fed Oscar a baby-bottle of milk while we admired the child's tiny bare feet and curly black hair. Albert told fatherly stories about his little Ariel, close to the same age, whom he had left behind in New York City with his wife Evelyn. Two babies, who might someday help to change the world.

"He looks so smart, Albert. Wouldn't it be wonderful," I said as I watched precocious little Oscar squirming in his mother's arms, wanting to get down, "if this little boy could grow up without having to believe he is inferior. Also, without being denied any of the opportunities my own four kids will have." I had lived during the Second World War, and was well aware of the treatment of Jews in Nazi Germany and Europe when I was growing up. "Just like your little girl will have, Albert," I added.

For two time-suspending hours spent in the George Washington Carver Homes, I had made myself forget that there were numerous others out there beyond these fragile, cracked and faded walls of Adelaide Sim's apartment, who did not in any way, shape or manner agree with me when it came to people with brown skin.

*   *   *

23.

"Be ashamed to die until you have won some victory for humanity."

—Horace Mann
(From G G.s WTLB)

In mid-afternoon the rabbi and I left Adelaide Sim's apartment to wander about the so-called Negro Compound, sampling the various denominational religious caucuses that had sprung up over the past two weeks. The various churches were mostly close-by. By means of little notes posted on several of the church bulletin boards, the caucuses had advertised word of their existence and whereabouts.

Now that the two of us had accepted the fact of our not being needed by the Southern Christian Leadership Conference except to join in their march on Sunday—we were, after all, very-latecomers to the proceedings—it was a relief to be able to be Indians, Albert remarked to me, instead of chiefs. (I didn't point out to him I had never been a chief, except in my own household.)

First we visited the Episcopalian priests, who were celebrating communion for the members of their denomination throughout the day in one of the George Washington Carver Homes like the Sims lived in. Then we went to talk to the rabbis, who had gotten together in the house of a Negro family on the next street and were making themselves available to give counsel to the many Jews they knew would come to Selma. After all, Jews knew as well as anyone what discrimination based on skin color or background was like.

And lastly, we both reported to still another house, to the Unitarian Sign-In, where I put my name on a list with the dozens of other Unitarians who had come there to help from all over the country. In return, I was given a telephone number for yet another apartment in the George Washington Carver Homes. That was where, I was assured, I could reach a Unitarian minister day or night if I needed one while I was here.

The Catholics and the Presbyterians and the United-Church-of-Christ adherents were busy with their own flocks someplace else. I found it both amusing and awe-inspiring to discover that these clergymen of all faiths never stopped working, and apparently were unable to stop working, even thousands of miles from home base. I couldn't help wondering how Albert had managed it.

A Presbyterian preacher we spoke to assured us that at seven o'clock that evening, these white cliques of individual denominations would begin to come together as one physical unit, joining forces with those who professed no faith at all, or had no use for organized religion. They would gather, all of them, at Brown's Methodist-Episcopal Chapel on Sylvan Street for the mass meeting that always preceded a demonstration. Their black counterparts from all over the South would be there too, along with lots of Negro citizens of Selma. By eight o'clock there would be "standing room only," so be sure to arrive at seven, we were advised by everyone.

Also attending would be the Congregationalists, and the Baptists, along with the many non-practicing doubters, both blacks and whites, who had yet to be convinced by Martin Luther King that the non-violent way was the best way. The old and the young of both races would gather there. But especially, this time, there would be many more of the white middle-aged, such as Albert and I were. We both were sold on the concept of non-violence for protesting injustice.

The mass meeting was scheduled to begin at eight o'clock that evening, but long before that, Albert and I had heard many things through the constantly circulating grapevine. Most important were the ground rules as stipulated that day by federal court judge Prank Johnson. They had to be followed to the letter if the march were to take place the next day.

The defeated state and county authorities had grudgingly laid the rules out to the Southern Christian Leadership Conference (SCLC) leaders. Chief among the rules was the proviso that after the first day, no more than three-hundred marchers could continue down the highway toward Montgomery. Since four more days would be required for the fifty-four miles to be covered on foot, the judge's reasoning went, an important east-west highway like U.S. 8O could not be tied up by possibly thousands of people, along with their many food and sanitation and medical needs, for that length of time. Particularly over the long, empty stretch of road where 8O narrowed to only two lanes.

The three hundred to go on toward Montgomery after the first day would of course be carefully selected from among the most faithful and hardest-working of Movement members, including of course Dr. King himself. Many would be Dallas County Negro residents. There would be a sufficient number of whites among the three hundred to make an impression, but for the most part they would be chosen from among those who had already been deeply involved in the voter registration drive in Alabama. If Albert Friedlander had been disappointed by the news that he wouldn't have been allowed to continue past the first day anyhow, he hadn't registered it with me. But that ruling, I guessed, must have influenced his decision to go back on the SNICK charter bus with me.

Any number of participants would be permitted to join the march once it had arrived at Montgomery, on Friday morning after the last day's walk. Through the city it would go, straight to the steps of the Alabama capitol building. (Atop it, the flag of the conquered Confederacy was daily being flown side by side with the stars-and-stripes "as a symbol of pride in Southern culture," the white folks said. Never mind the half of the state's population who were black and had hated that culture. Everyone knew it was actually a defiant warning not to trifle further with Alabama's "peculiar institution" of Jim Crow segregation.)

On Friday to come, the expanded march would enter Montgomery and walk the same streets where, up until a little over a decade ago, Negroes had had to sit in the back of the buses. Back in those days in the 1950's before Rosa Parks' feet had gotten too tired for her to get up and give her seat to a white man. In the square before the capitol that last day, there would be final ceremonies led first and foremost by Dr. King. A petition for "a redress of grievances", namely, the right to vote being denied to Dallas County Negroes, would be handed to the governor or to a representative of the Alabama state legislature.

Just as we had learned in the bus coming down, President Johnson had even "federalized" the Alabama National Guard to watch over the marchers. So Governor George Wallace would know who was boss, the rumors went. "We *shall* overcome," the president had said while addressing the nation on the matter a few days ago.

So the governments of the City of Selma, of Dallas County and of the State of Alabama had been forced by court order, based on the First Amendment, to capitulate. The Selma grapevine provided us visitors, away from our customary radios and newspapers and black-and-white television sets, with the latest reports. Sadly, it could not answer the questions each of us held secretly in the privacy of his or her own bosom. The questions that none of us, out of consideration for our fellows and the need to put on our own brave front, could bring ourselves to voice aloud.

What of the white citizenry of Selma and surrounding areas? Had the worst of them capitulated? Aroused to a frenzy of fear and hatred by recent events, according to Rev. Bevall's account of only that morning at his demonstration of non-violence techniques, would some of them decide to take matters into their own hands? Would a mob of the most paranoid KKK members be waiting on the other side of the now infamous Edmond Pettus Bridge, for instance? Waiting with guns or clubs or other weapons, even explosives? Waiting for the "uppity niggers" and the "outside agitators" to dare to pass over their bridge again?

Would there be snipers hiding in buildings or behind trees along the route? Would law enforcement officials refuse to intervene if we should be attacked, as they had often done in the case of the Freedom Riders traveling into the state on the interstate buses? The possibility further existed that even the Selma police or the Alabama state troopers, eager for an excuse to get revenge, would also attack us, justifying their actions on the grounds that they had to keep order. Would someone else, even a lot of us, be injured or killed? "Would someone, God forbid," try to assassinate Dr. King? It had happened to Mahatma Gandhi, martyred in India in 1948, soon after his non-violence campaign to win his country's independence from Great Britain had been won.

How many white supporters of Negro voting rights would have the courage—or the foolhardiness?—to show up? How many Negroes? ("There is safety in numbers," my mother always said, reminding us nine sisters, her daughters, to stick together whenever we were outside the safe walls of our house.) There was as yet no way of telling how many people of either race would dare to face the possibility of Southern white rage.

No mere mortal could look into the future and know the answers to any of these questions. But President Johnson had called out the National Guard to give us safe passage. And he *was* the boss, wasn't he? Literally the whole world, this time, would be watching on instant-eye TV to see if he truly was.

Only one ingredient was so far lacking in sufficient quantity. It seemed obvious to those of us who had come to Selma singly or in pairs, not knowing any of the others, that a sense of spiritual unity would also be needed. In unity, spiritual as well as physical, lay strength. And who knew better than Negroes nurtured in the emotion-rousing religious traditions of the old South how to achieve that?

*   *   *

24.

"... The rabbi ... who refuses to be the policeman for the [student's] parents, but becomes the genuine spokesman of student needs, ultimately fulfills his religious function."
                                    —Rabbi Albert H. Friedlander,
                                         Friend and companion on
                                              my adventure in Selma

I remember little about the dinner menu that Saturday evening, served in the Sunday School room of First Baptist Church of Selma. The meal preceded the Southern Christian Leadership Conference mass meeting that was scheduled to begin in Brown's Chapel at eight p.m., with the gathering beginning at seven. The meeting itself managed to erase from my memory forever most of what came just before.

I do remember that someone at the dinner table passed along the word to me that the number of would-be participants pouring into the town had swollen to such proportions that a third church had to be pressed into service to handle the overflow crowd of hungry diners. Reports like this never failed to hearten us visitors. The more who came, the unspoken rationale went, the safer each one of us would be, come the next day. And even more important, the greater the chance of the march's success.

No one asked about the reports of Selma police keeping many would-be marchers out.

Our meal tickets, held close to our persons since we received them on our arrival in Selma last night, were never collected. Albert left the dining hall early, after telling me that he and several of the other rabbis from New York City were planning to conduct a short Passover service that evening at Brown's Chapel. That is, if they could convince the more conservative Jews among them it would be no act of disrespect to their faith. I asked him why they might think that. Because Passover was approaching but was not yet here, Albert explained to me. Besides, the rabbis lacked the proper essentials for conducting a service. And the proposed place of worship was inside a Christian church.

"As to that last, I figure it's the same God, so why should it matter?" said Albert, finishing up the food on his paper plate. "See you over there at seven, Gwen," and skipping dessert, he got up from the narrow banquet-length table bench and went out. Remembering my resolve to talk to as many different people as possible, I made a point to introduce myself to the young woman who sat two places down from me, on the other side of the spot Albert had left empty. And I was almost immediately sorry.

Tiny-boned and dark-olive-skinned, Maria Romana* was a bitter woman. She looked like a high school girl in her bandana scarf and the leather jacket she kept on all during the meal, and she was stuck around the clock with the many disfiguring pimples on her face. She quickly informed me she had left her eight children back home in Boston and had come officially to Selma to do stories for a Negro newspaper back home. It was soon obvious that she had come for much more than that.

Maria was nursing a long-pent-up grudge against anyone who fell into the category of Caucasian, and now it was my turn to pay for being one. She was polite in her choice of words, even confidential at times. But there was an ill-concealed hostility in her tone that could not be completely credited to the fact that she had been walking around Selma for two days with a fever that had occasionally, she said, gone up to 103 degrees. She knew this last because her hostess at the George Washington Carver Homes where she was staying had insisted upon taking her temperature every time she showed up there.

"I'm on the verge of pneumonia," she assured me with a touch of pride in her words as well as the implication that she would never give up until she dropped over dead. But the biggest frustration she faced at that moment was the knowledge of the mistake in judgment she had made the day before. Sick with nausea and chills, she had nevertheless gone with a group to Montgomery, intending to get herself arrested in a demonstration. She wanted to write a first-person account of jail experience drawn from real life, she said. But she had arrived there just too late for the big one.

Meanwhile, during her absence from Selma, a group of Negro demonstrators in the Negro Compound had set off for the mayor's house in twos and threes; and as a result, more than three hundred of them had been arrested and detained in the Selma recreation center overnight. Eyes glowering at me like burning coals over her dish of fruit cocktail—all she had been able to eat, she swore, for the entire day—Maria described the experience as she had gotten it second-hand from one of the participants.

"The first ones who went were never intendin' to have a demonstration. But some of them just wanted to see what the mayor's house looked like from the outside. They figured there wasn't nothin' illegal about goin' there in small groups. But they were picked up and charged with creatin' a disturbance, and when the others waitin' back here, the ministers and some of the others, found out about it, they also set out for the mayor's house, knowin' they'd be arrested too! The police wanted to put the Negroes in the jail and detain the whites in the recreation center, but they all just locked elbows and refused to budge unless they went together. So they all ended up in the recreation center. They sang freedom songs all night long. Those ministers, I hear, were the best sports of all! And by this mornin', the police were just beggin' them all to leave!"

Surely Maria realized that those ministers whom she apparently admired so much, and who were trying to be chiefs instead of Indians without consulting SCLC, were largely white. "And I had to miss it all," Maria ended with a moan. "It was my one chance to go to jail."

Jail! The very one-syllable word made my privileged liberal blood run cold. She was hoping to go there? But then, I wasn't Maria. All the empathy at my command could never make me a Maria. And there was something about the woman that defied any further attempts on my part to feel her pain.

"My father was Spanish," she said, though I had expressed no curiosity about her ancestry. "And my mother is only half-Negro."

"Why that means—" I began in all innocence, certainly not from any desire to commiserate, nor to generously bestow upon this cynical young mother any of my "superior white blood", but merely to state a fact. I had been reading in my American Government class at Penn about the definitions different states had come up with to determine who was "colored" and who was not. "That means, Maria, that you're only one-quarter Negro. Actually, you're—"

But Maria had laid the trap for me, and I was not allowed to finish my naive analysis. "Don't tell me that! Don't tell me that! Don't you dare tell me that!" she hissed at me between clenched teeth. "I'm Negro! I'm one-hundred percent American Negro! That's the way I'm seen to be, and that's the way I want it!" With that, she turned her face away from me and began to pick at her paper dish half-full of fruit cocktail.

Well, really, how could I blame her? I inquired of myself. For the past weeks and months and even years it had been creeping over me with increasing intensity like an incoming tide: the awareness that had fate bestowed upon me a darker skin and Negroid features, I could never have been able to stay in my inferior "place" either. At least not the person that I was today. Rather than endure patiently the indignities suffered daily by America's racial minorities—rather than accept prejudice and poverty with Christian love, as my much-admired Unity had done—I too would surely have run to embrace the even more painful way: defiance. Buried there in my own nature, I suspected, were the genes of the revolutionary.

No, I couldn't blame Maria for her verbal attack on me. But that didn't mean I had to like her.

Lela Hamilton was as big and husky and brown as Maria was small and wiry and light-skinned. She sat on Maria's other side, and it soon became obvious that the two of them were at the dinner together. The three of us walked the several blocks to Brown's Chapel after our meal and I had a chance to get to know Lela better. There was a placidity about her manner and outward appearance that fooled me at first. As with young Peter from my bus, she seemed at first to have ended up in Selma on that precise date because it was something to do.

And then I learned from her that her husband, a native of Montgomery, had been drafted and sent to Vietnam only the month before, and Lela, not an Alabaman by birth, had been preparing to go to Chicago to stay with her family. But after watching the television coverage of the people being run down with horses and beaten with billy clubs, she had come instinctively to Selma instead. So that if her soldier husband survived the fight for people's freedom on the other side of the globe, she told me, he could perhaps find a little more of it when he returned to his own backyard. Lela had previously been too young and too disinterested to want to vote, but now she wanted to help make it possible for the two of them to go to the polls together when her Clyde came back to Alabama.

"Tell me, please: how do you two feel about all this? This Vietnam business," I asked Lela, astonished at her unquestioning acceptance of her husband's army duty. "How does your Clyde feel, being sent to fight for a country that treats him the way it does?"

She gave me a straight answer, her full lips curving into an ironic smile that put dimples in her cheeks. "It's his country. This is his home, and mine. It's still the best place, America. Of course he wants to fight for it. We just keep hoping things in Alabama will get better."

I braced myself, waiting for the inevitable tirade from Maria, or at the very least, a snort of supreme disgust. But nothing like that was forthcoming. It was as if Maria, too, accepted what Lela had said. Or maybe she really was too sick to care.

*   *   *

END OF PART FIVE

PART SIX

OH-H, FREEDOM!

25.

"The arc of the moral universe is long, but it bends toward freedom."
                                    —Dr. Martin Luther King, Jr.
                                    (From G.G.'s Words To Live By)

"Didn't you see a lot of hanky-panky going on?"
"Between the coloreds and the whites, I mean?"
                                    —Arthur M. Penhurst,* DDS in
                                    Woodbury, New Jersey
                                    (Typical Post-Selma Question)

The mass meeting the SCLC threw for us and with us that Saturday night in Selma was notable not only for the spirit of comradeship it forged. That spirit was enough to carry us over for a lifetime, we felt. But the carefully crafted performance was noted also for the colorful cast of characters who contributed to an ever-more-motivating sequence of events.

Nothing in Selma ever started on time, we had been told. Suspecting as much, Albert Friedlander and I were nevertheless in our places at Brown's Chapel by seven, in a center pew about six rows from the front. His part in the Passover service, Albert told me, would come later—by which, I assumed he meant, after the mass meeting.

The deep-red-painted, old brick building that was Brown's African Methodist-Episcopal Chapel had been made famous by the television coverage it had received over the past two weeks. Its distinctive outer facade with the twin white bell towers and white quoins and arches was the central point around which much of the civil rights furor in Selma had swirled. Within the building we could see, now that we were seated and had time to look around, the church boasted a balcony that stretched around two sides and across the rear and could hold several hundred people. Several hundred more would manage to cram themselves into the three sections of pews on the main floor before the evening was over, and their numbers would overflow onto the floor.

The raised stage up front was set off by one distinctive piece of decoration. A tall Roman cross, made of wood and outlined even further by a double row of bare electric light bulbs, reached from the stage almost to the ceiling. Nothing here of stained glass windows or silken altar cloths! An ancient upright piano standing on the far right side of the platform was the only other piece of furniture besides the undraped wooden podium.

Inspired by the sight, I took out my small blue notebook and with my pen whipped off a few lines in longhand.

"Selma, Alabama, March 20, 1965," I wrote. "The most incredible experience of my life! Had anyone told me four days ago that today I would be sitting here in Brown's Chapel, waiting for tomorrow's march to begin, I should have declared that person stark, raving mad. Yet here I am—and it still seems to me like an impossible dream, a bizarre joke. And at the same time, an experience that has marked me forever. I almost dread going home to face those 'outsiders' who can never know the joy of being here. But return I must; and I have to speak out now, every chance I get . . . ."

The bare-bulb cross was turned on just then, one glaring surge of light to which my eyes were soon adjusted. Expectantly, I put the notebook away in my purse. And just then two enthusiastic young men in their early twenties—one black and one white—ran up in front of the stage with guitars and started the audience singing a freedom song. Albert and I put our heads close together and guessed they were deliberately either "warming up the crowd," or stalling for time.

But no matter. For a half-hour or more we in the audience all sang our hearts out, our combined voices booming off the soffits of the church ceiling and echoing back at us in splendid waves of sound; the two guitars twanging; the hundreds of hands clapping in unison—gently at first, with stiff wrists and elbows held close at our sides. We white folks of many years standing were not used to this overt display of inner emotion. A few choruses were required for us to really get into the rhythm and mood of the music. But then we had it, arms swinging forward with each explosive meeting of palm against palm, elbows swinging back to put as much force as possible into the next sharp clap.

> "This little light of mine, I'm gonna let it shine!
> "This little light of mine, I'm gonna let it shine!
> "This little light of mine, I'm gonna let it shine!
> "Let it shine, let it shine, let it shine!"

Still louder, clapping harder, on the next verse. And now it was okay, we were far from home and we could let some of our acculturated inhibitions go. All over that packed church, on the main floor and in the balcony, people were caught up in the same rhythmical frenzy.

> ". . . . All over Selma, I'm gonna let it shine!
> "Let it shine, let it shine, let it shine!"

Albert and I exchanged joyful grins in the middle of a verse, our elbows banging companionably together at the end of each clap. Collectively, we in Brown's Chapel then let our little lights shine all over Alabama, and all over Sheriff Clark. Over Police Chief Wilson Baker, and over Highway Patrol Chief Al Lingo. All over Washington, D.C., too, and all over America; and then people called out some of the different states they had come to Selma from, and we let our lights shine over all those places as well.

Other songs of the Civil Rights Movement in the South were shared with us too, that evening. Some were songs I'd never heard before, but which were a cinch to catch on to, with their simple words and melodies.

> "Woke up this mornin' with my mind—stayed on freedom!
> "Woke up this mornin' with my mind—stayed on freedom!
> "Woke up this mornin' with my mind—stayed on freedom!
> "Allelu, allelu, allelu-u-u-uia!"

And yet another:

> "Oh-h, freedom! Oh-h, freedom!
> "Oh-h, freedom over me!
> "And before I'd be a slave,

"I'd be buried in my grave,
"And go home to my lord
"And be free!"

These repetitive outpourings set to simple tunes were nothing like the beautiful anthem of the NAACP, *"Lift Every Voice And Sing."* That was a song I had sung to its stately cadences several times back home, ever since I had joined the Camden Branch in the early sixties and attended some of its membership meetings. The combination of stirring words and stately music had never failed to bring tears to my eyes. But today this was different. This was an outpouring of determination, laced with love, and delivered with the joyful gusto that comes from knowing an up-to-now unfair battle of wills was about to be joined.

"Ain't gonna let nobody turn me 'round,
"Turn me 'round, turn me 'round!
"Ain't gonna let nobody turn me 'round!
"Keep on a-walkin'! Keep on a-talkin'!
"Goin' to the Promised Land!"

And then, "Ain't gonna let no sheriff turn me 'round! . . ." Followed by, "Ain't gonna let state troopers turn me 'round! . . ." And "No tear gas" and "no horses" were gonna accomplish that either, our song's next two verses declared.

And still another. Comparing ourselves to trees that stand by the water, we declared emphatically in song such facts as "Marching out of Selma, we shall not be moved!" And, "Goin' to Montgom'ry, we shall not be moved!" And always, back to that overriding topic again: Freedom! Freedom! Freedom!

We mentioned all our obstacles in song, over and over, varying only a few of the words, whenever necessary, to fit the occasion. We sang all the familiar songs; all of them, that is, but the unofficial "creed" of the Civil Rights Movement that began back in 1955 with the Montgomery bus boycott: *"We Shall Overcome."* We all knew without having to be told that we were saving that soaring tune for last.

A frail-looking, elderly Negro gentleman in black suit and white clerical collar walked regally onto the stage and raising his arms for silence, brought the frantic singing and clapping to a close at the end of a chorus. He had come there from his church in Florida, he announced when all was quiet, and he would be in charge of the formal service. We would begin with a hymn from the hymn book, he said. A Negro woman from the Brown's African Methodist-Episcopal Chapel congregation took her place at the piano. And most of us nearly sung-out whites simply listened, enthralled, as the minister from Florida led the remainder of the audience in the words of the hymn, unfamiliar to me. Those of us from the Northern tradition of dignified self-control in religious rituals had never heard an anthem rendered in quite that fashion before.

Slowly, majestically, the blacks' voices rose and fell in measured cadences, while the dynamically firm voice of the old preacher wandered off by itself into soulful improvisations at the end of each line. After several verses, while many of us were still mesmerized with admiration, he brought the hymn to an end and launched into a prayer. A long prayer, exhorting "Oh, Lawd" to look after us on the morrow, and backed up by loud and spontaneous "amens" from a handful of older black worshipers in the audience.

Next on the list of surprises came the Passover Seder. My rabbi left my side to go up on the stage to join three other rabbis who had gathered there. They arranged themselves in a semi-circle around the pulpit, with the glaring bulbs of that Christian cross for a backdrop. Each spoke in turn, each adding something to what the previous rabbi had said.

My rabbi, Albert Friedlander, went first. In a low-key delivery that matched his calm personality, Albert talked to the now packed-to-overflowing church building about the need for us to be there in Selma. He described the ruthless persecution of Jews during his own boyhood in Germany, and how it had affected him and his family when they had to hide from the Nazis in an attic in Berlin. He told us that freedom was a precious gift to be constantly cherished and guarded, for ourselves and for others.

A second rabbi explained the origins of the Passover Season. God, he said, had spoken to the Jews through Moses, instructing them in the way they should protect their first-born sons against the plague he would soon visit upon the Egyptians, who were keeping the Jews in bondage. Jewish households were thus "passed over," and eventually, so his story went, their God had delivered them out of Egypt to freedom, precious freedom. Thus, the origins of Passover.

Rabbi Weismann,* one of the two remaining rabbis, spoke next. He was the same man who had met Albert and me at the bus depot in Montgomery last night and had been our tour guide when we drove into Selma at midnight. He described the Hebrew ceremony of asking God's blessings upon us for the days ahead. He displayed on the podium the makeshift supplies he had garnered from his Selma hostess's kitchen cabinets. Two birthday-cake candles had been twisted together to take the place of the customary tall tapers in the Jewish ceremony. A can of common household herbs was there in place of the specially prescribed ones he would have had available for his use back in New York City. A paper cup filled with water represented the ceremonial wine. The picture of self-confidence, he stood up there behind the podium and taught us the simple Hebrew chant that always ended the Passover service.

"Sha-vua-tov!" we found ourselves testing awkwardly on our untrained tongues. In Hebrew, the rabbi explained, the words meant "Good week!" The nuns tried chanting it with him, and the non-singers tried singing it out, and the black kids from Selma, their mouths held open like little birds, tried it too, never taking their eyes off the rabbi's face.

"We need not one good day for the marchers tomorrow, but five! Almost a week, to get to Montgomery by Thursday evening, walking fifty-four miles. So we can sing 'Shavua Tov!'" With uplifted hands he started us off with the chant. And Jew and Gentile, agnostic and atheist, we had responded in unison with equal fervor, our voices soaring magnificently through the melody over and over, while the fourth rabbi lit the twisted candle being held in Albert's fingers, and held the herbs in a tablespoon over the flames, and sipped symbolically from the cup of "wine." The Hebrew plea for God's blessing concluded with a final "Shalom!"—"peace"—from the four rabbis to us, their make-do "temple congregation," from all over the United States. It was followed by a resounding "Shalom!" from all of us in reply.

A minute later, an ecstatic Albert joined me in the pew and leaned over to murmur in my ear, "I *told* Maurice we could do it very nicely with substitutions! I think it was quite appropriate for the occasion, don't you?" and I nodded my head in enthusiastic agreement. I'd tell him later how superb a part he had played in it.

Rabbi Maurice's telltale Long Island accent was replaced almost immediately by the indignant Southern black drawl of the "Selma Historian," an articulate middle-aged Negro man. No doubt for the first time in his life he had a captive audience with a large component of white people, and was thus unable to resist the chance to chastise us a little. I thought of Maria Romana, my dinner conversationalist, sitting somewhere else in the church. I pictured the look of satisfaction that must be on her feverish face as she listened.

"Don't you folks come here to Selma," admonished the Historian from the podium, "and rub elbows with the lowly and then go back to your homes and forget they ever existed! And don't ever, ever forget about the children of Selma! History will engrave their names in golden lights on the white clouds of heaven! These children shucked off the shackles of tradition because they wanted to be free!"

Tomorrow, he reminded us, we were going to walk together out of Selma, across the Edmond Pettus Bridge over the Alabama River. The slaves had called it "Shame River," he went on. Legend had it that this name had come about because of an Indian squaw, back at the beginning of our country's history, who had drowned her baby in the river rather than let it be sold away from her by the white man. The River had caught the tears of countless Negro mothers since that time and had done that for over two hundred years, he told us. And it had often received the bodies of their helpless, murdered children, during the time of slavery and up to this very day. Nobody knew, in fact, how many Negro bodies had ended up in that River.

But now, the Historian went on, it was the children of Selma who had dared to stand up not only to the white power structure, but to their own parents as well. Enough! they had said. The old traditions of bowing down and accepting injustice would have to go. It was they, the children, who had refused to give up many months ago when their elders had gotten discouraged and frightened and wanted to quit. It was the children, who had insisted on making that first attempt to walk to Montgomery. The Negro mothers of Selma were proud now, of their children's courage and perseverance. Justice was ultimately going to prevail. No one knew how, just yet, but it would. And when it did, there would no longer be a need for tears. And Shame River would at last be cleansed.

I am twelve and I am scrubbing the kitchen floor. Why don't all of you tell the manager you don't want to sit in the balcony anymore, Unity. Maybe the kids could do it . . . .

The Historian was winding up his talk, his anger at us for being white and privileged sufficiently vented. His voice softened then, and his final words to us as he bade us "goodbye and good luck" brought a lump to my throat that wouldn't swallow for a long time afterward. "As for us, the Negroes of Selma—we will remember you, as the Indians say, 'as long as the river flows'."

I couldn't help thinking that Maria Romana must be furious, sitting somewhere in the audience, listening to what she would surely consider a cop-out such as this!

Tears and a river. The first true memory of my life.

While the Selma Historian was leaving the stage to take a seat in a pew, I let memory carry me back to that time when I was young; so young it seems I could not yet have had conscious knowledge of being alive, much less have grasped the concepts of powerlessness, or despair, or eternity.

I am two. No, probably three. I sit beside my mother on the piano bench, watching her pretty, manicured fingers spread out over the keyboard as she plays the melody of the song. My father is standing behind us, the deep resonance of his voice chilling through and through my small frame with each mournful phrase. He is plucking on the strings of his mandolin.

". . . . I am sitting by the river and a-weeping all the day," he is singing. "For she's gone from the old Kentucky shore." And then comes the chorus. "Oh, my poor Nellie Gray, they have taken you away. And I'll never see my darling anymore . . . ."

Why not? Where has she gone, this "Darling Nellie Gray?" I want to know. And my mother answers, wiping the tears from my cheeks with the cloth handkerchief she always carries with her. She's sold, darlin', sold away from the husband who loved her. Gone; gone forever. The hot tears run down my face so fast that her handkerchief can scarcely wipe them back. The agony of the as-yet-unrecognized cruel universe is there in my father's doleful baritone; in the strings of the mandolin and the sad words of the song; in the terrible, incomprehensible fate of my darling Nellie Gray.

How? How did it happen? Why, she was colored, darlin'. Colored people were sold. Like shoes, in the shoe store. Or loaves of bread at the grocer's. Or ice cream cones. Don't cry, sweetheart. It was a long time ago. Things like that don't happen any more.

But . . . . too terrible to accept. Too cruel, never to see your family, those beloved faces, ever again . . . . And the tears continue to flow until the song is done, because I have not yet learned that big girls, especially those with no brothers, do not cry.

Don't sing the second verse, Kenneth, my mother is pleading. Gwendie Lou takes it so hard!

*   *   *

26.

**"It's very simple. I just want folks to be peaceful with each,
other and understand each other and solve their problems
without killing each other"**
                    —Rev. Andrew J. Young, Negro Male
                    Later, Mayor of Atlanta, Georgia and
                    U. S. Ambassador to the United Nations
                    (From Gwen's W.T.L.B.)

"Don't ever forget for a moment, you white folks from up North! Down here, in Selma, y'all are 'white niggers'!"

The familiar words and voice jolted me back to the present. The Reverend Jim Bevall was standing behind the podium now, looking light-skinned and jocular in his Movement uniform of denim jeans and jacket, but this time wearing a Jewish *yarmulke* to cover much of his nearly bald head.

"Two white men from Ohio were arrested downtown by the Selma police just this afternoon," he announced. I looked over at Albert in the pew next to me, sitting at my left elbow. "They could have been the owners of our car, the borrowed one that brought us here from Montgomery?" I whispered. But my companion shook his head. He must know something I did not.

Rev. Bevall continued, "We've been doing everything we can to get them released, which is why we were so late starting here tonight. The two of them drove into the business district against all our instructions. You folks who drove here have got to realize these out-of-state tags on your cars are a dead giveaway!"

I want to go to heaven because my Maker calls me, not because one of you people sent me there! Had he told us that only this morning.? Hadn't those numbskulls listened?

"Don't even *walk* downtown!" the good reverend continued, his voice deadly serious. "They can pick you out by your clothes, your walk, your speech. Maybe even by the fact you haven't started yet on your summer tans!"

With one voice, we, the many whites in his audience, exploded into laughter. A lot of these people here, I remembered, had been here for days, maybe weeks. They had probably had time to get bored, waiting for marches to begin, and had begun to take chances. As for me, I'd wait to see downtown Selma until I walked through it tomorrow, on my way out of town. Why, I'd been half-asleep last night, and had scarcely noticed the famous bridge as we drove over it. Tomorrow, I'd have myself a good look!

Dr. King had hoped to be with us this evening, Rev. Bevall went on, but plane schedules had not permitted it. We could be sure that he would be here to walk with us tomorrow. We clapped wildly to let him know we understood and approved. We were disappointed, yes, not to see him up on the stage. But we weren't children. We could take it.

"Now, down to business. I'm supposed to be getting a check from a lady who's driving here from Northern California. Does anybody . . . . ? Wait a minute; here she is!" Rev. Bevall looked up into the balcony as a white woman's voice rang out, "Here I am! I've brought a check for $600!" and she stood up and waved a piece of paper—the check!—and named her Episcopal church in San Francisco as the donor. The entire assemblage burst into wild applause.

Then a Presbyterian stood up and said she had $150 from her church in Illinois. And not to be outdone, at least not by the Presbys, some Unitarians from a church in Connecticut stood up in a group and announced they were contributing a total of $200 they had been delegated to bring with them from their congregation.

Another voice issued forth from the balcony, from a male this time: "Here's $75 from a group of atheists from all over everywhere! We just this minute took up a collection!"

That brought down the house once again, and we laughed as we applauded the atheists until our palms stung.

"Wonderful!" cried Rev. Bevall, bounding across the wooden stage to the other side to collect this latest contribution which had been tossed down from above. "Is there by any chance another group of atheists?"

And that *really* broke us up! Everything everybody said from then on was considered to be hilarious, and drew loud bellows of laughter and prolonged clapping from the audience, especially if it meant more money for the Movement to pay the mammoth bills being incurred by the march. I stifled back the guilt that tried to accuse me of having no money to give, that tried to say to me, you big freeloader! This was all too much fun for that sort of mental flagellation. And then I remembered Jim Clemson's twenty dollars. What, I asked myself, could be more fitting? From a man who would have to wipe his hand off behind his back if he shook hands with a Negro?

In the midst of all this frivolity, a latecomer in a dark raincoat made his way into the pew just ahead of me, stepping over several people's laps to get there. Almost furtively the white stranger sank down into the one empty place available, which was directly in front of Albert and me. And leaning back, the man scooched his neck down hard into his coat collar. His hair was longish and in need of shampooing and was turning a little gray above the ears. The line of his jaw from behind and to the side was oddly familiar. I leaned forward in the pew for a sneak peak, and sat back again, satisfied I had guessed correctly.

Albert leaned toward me and lifted his eyebrows in question. Who's that, the eyebrows asked.

I whispered carefully into his right ear: "Gary Merrill!"

The rabbi lifted eyebrows once again above his glasses' frames and mouthed the word, "Who?"

"You know. The movie star! Bette Davis' ex! Her fourth." *Albert, don't you know anything?* my facial expression teased him. But he nodded now in recognition of the name.

I signaled a question to him with my eyes and pointed a finger. Should I let that cockroach continue up Gary Merrill's shoulder and into his hair? The roach seemed to have miraculously appeared from nowhere, but I told myself it must have been hiding in one of the cracks in the old pews. Not having time to wait for a reply to my question, I stretched forth the same finger and gently!—because the man obviously was hoping not to be recognized—I flicked the shiny brown insect to the floor.

Looking to my friend for approval, I lifted my foot. The impish gleam in Albert's eyes was asking me something. "Do you know what you do?" his eyes said. Suddenly remembering our Supreme Being discussion on the bus, I half-expected the rabbi to give me a Roman Catholic "te absolvo"—"I absolve you"—sign with his flattened palm, holding it. vertically in front of him the way the Pope does in the newsreels. But Albert sat there, waiting to see what *I* would do. Mr. Merrill moved not at all, absorbed as he was in what was going on at the front of the church and utterly oblivious to my proposed act of sacrilege.

I put my foot down flat beneath the pew and the roach skittered away. None of us had come to Selma to kill anything. Not so much as one despised and lowly insect. Wasn't that true reverence for life?

Now here came Dick Gregory, the famous black comedian! He stood up on the stage, behind the podium, making jokes, making us laugh. Back home I'd have to pay as much as five dollars to catch his act at a Philadelphia nightclub. If I ever went to Philadelphia nightclubs, that is. And I would have to buy my ticket well in advance. Yet here he was, this celebrity Negro, his considerable girth dominating the stage in Selma, Alabama as he made us all laugh over and over again, for free.

But it was a different kind of humor than the fun with the donations had been a few minutes earlier. His act in Brown's Chapel that night centered around and fed upon the grim reality of being black in the United States of America in the year 1965. For twenty minutes and more he kept us in stitches with his pointed sarcasm tempered with droll wit, and then he turned serious when we least expected it, and spoke to us of his "four little black kids" and their tarnished hopes for the future.

He brought up the subject of "all the light-skinned black folks you see running around America." They were the results, he said, of three centuries of "integration after dark" by the white folks. He talked of his own boyhood in Chicago, and of his beloved black mother who had given him more than an ample share of pride in his blackness. And he said how hard it had been for him as a child, never thinking of himself as inferior, to have to adjust to the cruel fact of racial discrimination.

"But we niggahs, we ain't gonna just accept no mo'! We gonna demand jus-*tice*!" Loud claps and whistles came from the audience. "We gonna demand that equal protection under the law to which we're entitled as citizens of America! As Dr. King has often pointed out, the law may not be able to make a man love me, but it should surely keep him from lynching me!'

"And on that subject of love . . . ." It was apparent he was bringing his act to a close. "They're always telling us you can't legislate love. That's what the Man tells us as an excuse for depriving us of our freedom. But they're 'legislating love' right now, in thirty-two states in this country!"

We, his listeners, all knew without explanation that he was referring to the miscegenation statutes forbidding racial intermarriage that were still on the law books of many states, with their ridiculously anachronistic definitions of a Negro as anyone having "any ascertainable trace" of black ancestry.

Dick Gregory received a thunderous ovation when he was finished. Had he come there tonight, I wondered, with Gary Merrill? Perhaps on a plane together from California? How many other famous show-business people were here? It had never once occurred to me to look around for them.

The Reverend Andrew Young, slight and inordinately handsome in his symbolic denim jacket and trousers, was introduced next by Jim Bevall. He stood up in front of the huge bare-bulb cross and gave us final instructions for the march next morning.

We would assemble at nine a. m. in front of this same building, Brown's Chapel. Since it would be Sunday, there would be a church service held inside before the march began at ten.

We should be sure to obey without question the instructions of the march marshalls, who would be easily recognizable by the yellow bands of material around their upper arms. We should stay together at all times for safety's sake and remain completely non-violent no matter what happened. *No matter what, happened!*

Lunches were being prepared at this very moment by Selma residents for all the marchers. Special vehicles would be coming by us at regular intervals along the march route bringing food, drinking water and medical supplies. Portable toilets were being rented from a company up North, he reported. This, after a Southern-based firm had flatly refused to provide service to us marchers for any amount of money.

We were to walk in orderly rows no more than eight persons across and stay strictly to the left two lanes of the highway. Everything that could possibly be done to assure our safety was being done. The day promised to be a good one, according to the weatherman. Our cause was right. We would surely prevail as we witnessed with our presence for justice. Together, he told us, we would overcome.

Reverend Young was calm and articulate in his instructions to us. His tone of voice and manner had a reassuring effect. It was the final touch we needed to an evening of emotional highs coming one upon the next with scarcely a breather in between. Obviously, in the hands of this organized, intelligent man, all our other needs, as well as our safety, were being planned for. The rest was up, I thought, "To Whom It May Concern."

We leapt to our feet after Andrew Young's charge to us was over. Crossing arms over our chests and joining hands with our neighbors on either side, we let "We Shall Overcome" at long last burst from our collective throats. The hundreds jammed together up in the balcony seemed almost physically united with those of us on the ground floor.

"We shall overco-o-ome,
"We shall overco-o-ome,
"We shall overcome someda-a-a-a-ay!
"Oh-h-h, deep in my heart, I do believe,
"We shall overcome some day!"

My eyesight blurred as I sang my lungs out with all the rest. Our combined voices were so loud, that it seemed certain all the insecure and apprehensive whites in the other part of Selma must be hearing us. I wished they could realize we meant them no harm. We only wanted what was right, what was fair, what was just!

"Black and white toge-ether,
"Black and white toge-ether,
"Black and white together no-o-o-o-ow . . . ."

Our hand-linked bodies swayed in unison from side to side. We were touching each other in spirit as well as in flesh. Americans all. Black and white. Theists and humanists, believers and non-believers. Males and females. Young and old. We had a right—nay, an obligation!—to be here. Didn't we? Yes, I was sure of it!

"Oh-h-h deep in my heart, I do believe,
"We shall overcome some day!"

My voice broke on the last line. Electrifying seconds of silence followed our song as the notes of the last refrain died away. Then the kindly voice of the old minister from Florida cut through the hushed stillness with a brief benediction. All too soon—before any of us was ready for it—the mass meeting before the march was over.

Albert and I pressed forward with scores of others to shake hands with the speakers. Shyly, I thanked Dick Gregory and commended Andrew Young before other eager hands could pull them away. I sought out Jim Bevall then, and handed him a twenty. The one my friend Jim had given me. He would wipe his hand behind his back after he shook a Negro's hand, he had shocked me by saying.

"From . . . ?" the reverend asked, his round face smiling his thanks at me.

I hesitated. It would not be honest to let him think it was my own "widow's mite."

"Not me. Just mark it down as an anonymous donation," I said. "From a friend."

* * *

27.

"... So when at times the mob is swayed
"To carry praise or blame too far,
"We may choose something like a star,
To stay our minds on, and be staid."
—Robert Frost, American poet
(From G.G.s Words To Live By)

Looking back over the passage of several years, it has become clear to me that the talented organizers of the Selma to Montgomery march for voting rights were masters of psychology in more ways than one. They rose with splendid *elan* to an occasion they had precipitated but had not originally foreseen. Recognizing opportunity when it dropped full-blown into their laps, however, they quickly realized that by the time the larger march made up of both whites and blacks was due to set out, the eyes of the civilized world would be focused upon that small city in Alabama. They wanted that attention, they needed that attention. And when it came, they made the most of it.

To the marchers themselves, those who flocked to Selma from all over the United States to place their warm bodies on the line, the organizers provided three essential ingredients. First of all, they gave us full stomachs. Secondly, they provided instructions on how to behave in a threatening situation. And thirdly and most important of all, they gave us the heart to stand up and be counted. Not as individuals, not any more. But as separate ions amalgamated into a single-minded molecule by bonds of altruistic steel. It would be configured in my mind as a unique entity, a marching band. A band for freedom and justice, led by none other than Martin Luther King as our leader. Our drum major, who would be at the head of the line.

He had said it often enough. "Just call me a drum major for justice."

*   *   *

Just when I was beginning to wonder what had happened to him, Rabbi Friedlander reappeared at my side. Politely, patiently, the way he did everything, he made a path through the crowd for the two of us and we went out the side door of Brown's Chapel.

A young, denim-clad, Negro field worker for SCLC hailed us just outside the door and asked if Albert had an extra *yarmulke* with him that he could buy. Apparently it had become the style in the civil rights movement for a guy to display a Hebrew skull cap on his head as a symbol of peace. But my rabbi had had to respond with a regretful shake of his head.

"Sorry, my friend," Albert said. "This is the only one I brought with me. But see me tomorrow and give me your name and address, and I'll mail you one when I get home." And the young man had gone off, apparently quite satisfied.

Good old Albert, to make such a generous offer! "How will he ever find you, Al?" I asked when we were out the door. "Don't you know that all you rabbis look alike?"

"Very funny, Gwen." But he had to smile. "Come on. I'll walk you home." *"Home!"*

By my wristwatch the time was after ten o'clock. The mass meeting had lasted all of three hours without a break in the excitement! We walked side by side through the star-lit chill toward the George Washington Carver Homes across Sylvan Street, both of us sober now, and saying little. I wondered if Albert had been mentally caught as I was, by the sudden awareness that the morrow was not far off. That twelve hours from now, we'd find out—if anything bad was going to happen.

Sure, the President had called out troops to protect us. But how did we know for certain that the hearts of the federalized National Guard would be in their assignment? Most of them would surely be young Southern white men, brought up in the Southern tradition of race superiority. The mass meeting, however, had accomplished its purpose. It had turned all of us civil rights types into crusaders united. It made no matter, actually, the over-hanging sense of possible danger we all shared. We would go tomorrow no matter what, we would march behind Dr. Martin Luther King, Jr. our drum major, and we would revel in the opportunity.

"That little service you and your friends gave was just perfect," I said, breaking the silence that lay between us. *You were just perfect too, Albert. I was so proud of you up there, so proud to know you, too! I only wish*

I had the guts to stand up in front of people and do and say such admirable things.

"The Passover Seder? Yes, Maurice did do a beautiful job," he said modestly. "But the entire meeting was beautiful! Fantastic! Didn't you think so?"

"I'll say! I never saw two hours go by so fast!" I replied.

"Three!" he corrected me. He stopped dead in his tracks. "Look up there, Gwen. Now I know where the song came from."

I bent my head back on the same angle with his and beheld the mighty firmament above us. It was almost a blur of brightly shining stars.

"Twinkle, Twinkle, Little Star?" I asked.

"No! 'Stars Fell On Alabama,'" he said, and he hummed the first couple of lines. He was two or three years older than I. Which was how he knew the song much better. "That sky means no rain tonight and a clear day tomorrow," Albert said. "The sun may even decide to come out!"

"Let's hope it does," I said. I wondered if he could possibly be thinking along the same track as I. Thinking that these same little lights falling on Alabama this night were probably also shining on my house in Merchantville, New Jersey. And on his apartment in New York City. Shining on all our beloveds.

I hadn't thought about Bill and the children once since this afternoon in Adelaide's apartment. It would be past eleven in New Jersey now, I reminded myself. Saturday evening. Julie would be sound asleep in her bed by now. The two boys would be getting dishes of ice cream from the freezer, and probably staying up to watch the Late Show with Bill. And Wendi? If all had gone well, she'd be . . . . right now! . . . . Still at that party with the kid who had stood her up a week ago. And if it hadn't gone the way she hoped . . . . well, there was nothing I could do about it from here.

I felt a stab of guilt that they hadn't crossed my mind even once in the past several hours. But almost joyfully I accepted the guilt. I was not in New Jersey. And Albert Friedlander was not in New York. We were here, the two of us, a thousand and more miles from home, and the Vernal Equinox must have already taken place all over everywhere without our having had to give it another thought.

In the morning the sun would shine and we, my rabbi friend and I, would walk together across the Edmond Pettus Bridge over the Alabama River and keep going. I was glad that five years ago, when I was on the verge of dying, I had made up my mind to live. To really live. Guilt was a small price to pay for being awarded a worthy life, wasn't it?

I said, "Do you ever worry, Albert, what people back home will say about your coming to Selma?"

He said, "No, not at all. Do you?"

"Yes. A little," I answered. "But I feel sorry for all of them back home that they couldn't come. Especially that they had to miss that amazing mass meeting!"

"So do I!" he said.

"Albert, I've wondered sometimes . . ." And this was an understatement if ever there was one. "Why do you suppose some people—take us, for instance, you and I—why do we care so much about things like justice and equality for people other than ourselves? When so many others, perfectly nice folks, don't seem concerned about it at all? Oh, I know; some of us, like you, have known discrimination first-hand. Hiding out in those attics in Berlin, and all. But what about the rest of us? Like Keene Stassen, who's probably led a charmed life? What about me, for that matter? And don't tell me it's because I'm a left-handed Libra!"

"I didn't know you were a Libra, Gwen," he said gravely. "And I don't think this is a matter of astrological signs. If I knew the answer to what makes some human beings willing to stand up and risk everything for a cause, and others, nothing, much less be able to even recognize an injustice when they see it? If I knew why, I'd sell it. I'd market my discovery to every politician, religious leader and demagogue I could find, and become a millionaire."

"Spoken like a . . . well, like a true Jew." I'd never uttered ethnic slurs in my life before. Of course, Albert would know, or he should, that I was being facetious, that I didn't mean those ugly words at all. The same way he seemed to understand everything else.

"Bigot!" my new, true friend tossed back at me. We laughed aloud, feeling delighted with each other's presence as we walked along. We were still aglow with crusaders' zeal. It was wonderful to be in the company of another white person who wasn't frightened and xenophobic, the way my friend Jim was. Or went along with everything just because I said things were so, like my husband Bill. And just think! There were hundreds more of them here in Selma tonight, white people who thought the same way we did!

"But look, Albert, it doesn't make sense. If it's environmental influences that shape people's convictions, then how explain me? I've got eight sisters, and while they're all kind, considerate, intelligent females, none of them get exercised about things like race prejudice the way I do. All nine of us have led the same protected and relatively prejudice-free lives. And if it's in our genes, instead . . . . same argument! Unless it really is because I'm the only left-handed Libra in my family . . . . "No, wait! Sister number eight is also left-handed . . . but she was born in May . . . ." I let my voice trail off.

We had crossed the street and now we stood where the curb should be, but there was no curb, simply the muddy dirt of the road blending in with the scrawny lawns of the George Washington Carver Homes where the Sims lived. We tipped our heads back and looked up at the stars again, awed by their magnificence. We were reluctant to let the evening go. I went on with my mental search, thinking aloud.

"Family background, maybe? Maybe my grandmother, who was from old pioneer stock that ended up in Missouri. Maybe she told me more stories about the past than she told to the others. Back in 1868, she told me, her family went by train from Pennsylvania to Kansas City, Missouri, then all the way down in a covered wagon to cross west into Kansas and stake out a homestead. Took them a week to cover one hundred and fifty miles, can you believe that? She was my mother's mother, born on that homestead, and once before she died she confided to Mother in great secrecy that there was an actual *Indian* in our family tree!"

Albert was still looking up into the sky, still listening as I rambled on.

"But of course I didn't know about that supposedly shameful fact, until just a few years ago. Missouri, where my mother was born, was half-slave and half-free, you may know, during the Civil War. So I must have had relatives who fought on both sides. Some were maybe even slave holders? No, I refuse to believe that! Somehow, I always felt that I sprang from New England abolitionist stock, and maybe some of me really did, since part of my father's side came from Vermont, I'm told. At any rate, I learned that I had two great-uncles who spent a year in Andersonville Prison in Georgia during the Civil War. When the War was over and the prisoners-of-war were freed, and the train carried them home to Pennsylvania, their father had to carry them off the train in his arms, they were so weak and wasted from hunger and overrun with lice. At least that's what my grandmother told me."

"Gwen," Albert said. "You don't have to convince me."

"Of what?" I said. "That my two great-uncles were in Andersonville Prison?"

"That you have a right to be here." And he patted my shoulder several times.

Taken off guard, I blurted out, "I know that! I know that very well! It's just that . . . Albert, I feel so guilty! For leaving Bill and the kids to fend for themselves. For having such a fabulous time here in Selma!" And I told him then, in a rush of words, how lucky he was to have a reason. Lots of reasons besides having been personally persecuted. He was a Jew, and everybody knew how badly Jews had been treated by the Nazis before and during the Second World War. Who could ever forget the Holocaust?

On top of that, he was a rabbi, a worshipper of God and a server of people. Best of all, he was a man, and men were expected to have causes and to sometimes stand up for them.

"And to make matters worse," I wailed, 'I'm not even one-hundred percent anything No one would even *want* to persecute me! I'm just plain old, Heinz-soup American; 52 different kinds. No pedigree. Just an old alley cat. Dutch and English and Scotch and Irish and god-only-knows what else."

"The Indian," Albert said. He truly had been listening as I prattled on! "Don't forget the Indian."

"Right. The Indian, of course. But except for him or her, I'm also a WASP. White Anglo-Saxon, and for most of my life, Protestant. I'm supposed to be the ideal American, without any genuine gripes. Did you ever think of that? How come I don't *feel* like an ideal one most of the time? Maybe it's because everyone's always trying to make us feel guilty!"

"Gwen, Gwen," said the rabbi, his slight accent gently touching my name, not once, but twice. "Just for tonight, stop trying to figure it all out, It's too much for both of us to understand. Let's just be glad we're here, all right?"

Had I amused him with my intensity? Bored him with my anguish? How was I to know? But just before we arrived at Adelaide's door, he gazed skyward again. "See those stars up there?" he asked me.

"I see them," I answered, perplexed. Wondering what he would say next.

"Each of those stars has a special place of its own. They don't question. They just are. Who knows for sure how they got there, or why? I think perhaps we, you and I and everyone else, should be like that too. We should ponder the eternal questions, of course. Continue to strive for a better understanding of self, show much concern for others. But in the end, accept ourselves. Just be, Gwen. With no apologies."

Rabbi-speak. No guilt, he meant.

"I take it, then, you have no doubts about the rightness of your being here, Albert? You feel no guilt? You have a wife and a child back home, depending upon you . . ."

"No, no guilt at all. Man is morally committed to action in the face of evil, I think. To do nothing when he *can* do something, when he *wants* to do something, is a denial of human responsibility. That's when man should feel guilty! That's when man is not being!"

There it was again. Man, man, man. What about woman? But of course, he hadn't intended to exclude me, he was merely making use of the generic term "man" used frequently in my collection of "Words To Live By." I loved him for that, and for his having felt the same sense of obligation that had overwhelmed me back at Brown's Chapel.

We walked on, going up the walk between Adelaide's building and the next one. I was glad he hadn't tried to laugh away my frustrations. But neither had he tried to hand me any nonsense about predestination, or about Supreme Beings who manipulate us lowly beings like puppets on a string. I longed to tell him about the promise I'd made to myself five years ago, when Julie was born and I came close to dying, so I could explain how, if I hadn't yet learned to *be, I* had at least begun to *do.* But I'd already shared with him enough. He hadn't come here to play counselor to a guilt-ridden housewife-student-secretary with a bit of a messiah complex.

We said goodnight on Adelaide's front stoop. "See you in the morning, Gwen."

"At breakfast?"

"I may see you there. But in front of Brown's Chapel, for sure, in case I don't wake up in time to eat. And don't worry; I won't forget your sleeping bag."

"I'm not worried. Sleep well if you can, Albert." Another night on a sleeping bag, on a hard basement floor, at his age of thirty-eight? Knowing what was coming in the morning; yet not knowing? Who was I kidding? Ah, there it was, the guilt again. Guilt that I had an actual bed to sleep in, and he did not.

"You too! Good night, my friend. Shalom," the rabbi said.

"Shalom, Albert." I watched him walk away along the dark dirt street, and hoped he was staying alert to potential danger, the way we had been instructed. I found Adelaide Sims waiting up for me inside, with a hot mug of coffee and the news of a brand-new bedmate.

*   *   *

28.

"When a woman insists upon equality, she relinquishes her
superiority,"
                              —Anatole France, writer
                         (Yuk! GG.'s Words *Not* To Live By)

Her name was Nancy Thomas*, and she was neither black, nor young.
Rather, she was a sturdy, white-lady minister in her early forties from
Berkeley, California. She had arrived too late to catch all but the last of the
mass meeting in Brown's Chapel, and she was disappointed about that, but
just as fired up as I was about the march scheduled for tomorrow.

She had caught the end of Dick Gregory and all of Andrew Young.
She had been the nice lady from California in the balcony who brought
with her the $500 check from her church! She had not driven all the way
across the country from California, as Rev. Bevall had been told, but had
flown in by plane. And she had joined wholeheartedly in the singing of
"We Shall Overcome" at the end of the meeting. Then, with no buddies
yet with whom she could socialize and philosophize at any length, she had
beaten me back to the George Washington Carver Homes and was already
at Adelaide's kitchen table, talking and drinking coffee. The youngest
children were all in bed, and there was no sign of the older ones.

I learned from Adelaide that Dorothy, the young girl with whom I had
shared the bed the night before, had moved to different quarters. She was
staying in the house of a Selma girl her own age whom she had met during
the day. I was happy for Dorothy and intrigued by my new bedmate.

After we had drunk our coffee, bade the household goodnight, and
climbed into the double bed in the back bedroom upstairs, Nancy told me
she was an ordained minister of the United Church of Christ. The idea of
spending the night with a clergywoman fascinated me, since I'd never so
much as spoken to one of her gender before. I told her it was like suddenly
coming upon a unicorn in my garden, as James Thurber had once done,
and she laughed uproariously and we were friends.

Lying flat on our backs and staring into the blackness of the bedroom
ceiling, Nancy and I talked long into the night. We discussed the Selma
situation and how happy we were to be here, and why we had come. And

then we went on to exchange confidences that under normal circumstances and in more familiar surroundings, we'd only dare reveal to close chums of long standing.

I told Nancy about nearly dying of childbed fever when Julie was born, and about wanting to leave my husband someday if I could get up the nerve. About not even wanting to get pregnant the last two times, but I had anyway, even when using a diaphragm. I told her I had fallen in love with those last two babies when I first laid eyes upon them, just as I had done with the first two, the planned ones.

She told me about the long struggle she, as a woman, had had to become ordained and how her husband had nearly left her because of it. She told me how she was scared silly every time she got behind a pulpit to preach a sermon. She told me she was equally scared she'd get pregnant and have a change-of-life baby and have to give up her church. And she said how she loved being addressed by her congregation as "Reverend Thomas." Our talking honestly to each other like this was all very therapeutic. Problem was, we were both much too mentally and emotionally, as well as hyped up on Adelaide's strong coffee, to go to sleep.

"I'm a hopeless night person anyway," Nancy confessed. "I won't want to rise from my bed until the last possible moment tomorrow morning."

"In that case, maybe we'd better go our separate ways before the march," I said. A long-time morning person myself, I was leery of being held back by someone who didn't want to get up. "But we'll watch for each other, Nancy; okay? It shouldn't be too difficult to spot someone in lines that are only eight people across, don't you think?"

"It depends, I guess, on how many people actually show up," my bedmate said. Does anyone know what to expect?" I liked the way she smelled in the dark, exuding the familiar, pleasant odor of cold cream. She had done nothing more than cream her face before jumping into bed. No fussing with hair, or dallying long in the bathroom. She was casual and flexible, like me.

I told Nancy no one I had yet met had even dared make a guess as to how many civil rights sympathizers would show up in the morning for the march with Dr. King. Only that I had heard that three churches had been needed for dinner this evening. But in case we missed each other, we had already exchanged addresses, intending to keep in touch afterward. (But knowing we probably wouldn't, with both of us so busy with family and jobs and a whole continent stretching out between the states where we lived.)

I passed on to Nancy directions for finding the Tabernacle Church where breakfast would be served, just in case she managed to get herself up in time to eat. So now I, of all people, had become a tour guide in Selma, Alabama!

"Better get something in your stomach, if you can," I opined, playing the role of mother hen again. "We never know where our next meal will be coming from, or when. Also, there may not be enough of those lunches they're preparing to go around to everyone." And mere minutes after that final observation, about two a. m. I guessed, the sound of Reverend Thomas's breathing changed and I knew she had fallen fast asleep.

I lay beside her, not moving a muscle but with the wheels of serious thought spinning, spinning in my brain. To begin with, I reconstructed the conversation I had had with the rabbi this evening about the subject of guilt. It was the first time I had ever allowed myself to say those words aloud: "I feel so guilty about . . . ." Ordinarily, back home, I managed to put on a devil-may-care attitude to everyone. Everyone, that is, except Jim Clemson. And even he didn't know the extent to which the interesting pursuits in which I had lately been engaged had stirred up within me feelings of self-reproach.

Reproach about one thing, first and foremost. I had always felt guilty about leaving my children with a housekeeper and going out to work. None of the other women in my neighborhood in Merchantville would even think of doing such a thing. I knew that Bill was the only husband in my neighborhood who would put up with it. Most men would be mortified if their wives took employment outside the home, unless they as a family were destitute. It just wasn't done.

I had in past years, felt great guilt about not wanting Scotty and Julie in the first place. Oh, but I had loved them so, after they were delivered! So those feelings of guilt had disappeared at the moments of their birth. Others arose to take their place, however. I had felt guilty about getting to go to the prestigious University of Pennsylvania while most of the other New Jersey women of my age and acquaintance who went back to college had to settle for Glassboro State Teachers College. I felt guilt about getting to go to college at all, when so many could not. Guilt about not keeping my house clean enough for when my in-laws dropped in for a visit, and my mother-in-law saw dust on my baseboards. Guilt about having a job I enjoyed, working part-time as Connie Richardson's secretary. (Whoever said you should enjoy your job?) Guilt about not reading often enough to my kids because my time with them was so limited. Guilt about wanting so badly I could almost taste it to go to Europe and see the historical places I had heard and read about, and especially to Italy, to try out my Italian and see some of the storied roads that led to Rome.

Guilt about wanting to leave Bill after our eighteen peaceful years together so I could see the wide world. Who, among those who knew me best, would believe that I was so discontented?

And now, I felt guilty about lying in a comfortable bed in Adelaide's friendly house, while Albert Friedlander, my dear friend by now, had to sleep on the hard floor of a church basement. The list of my guilts, that night in the dark, seemed to go on and on.

But one thing, at least, I was proud to be free of. I had never in my life felt one iota of guilt about what had been done to Negroes in America.

Often these days, as more and more liberal white Americans became concerned about the abrogated rights of their fellow black citizens, I had heard this theory advanced: that our concern must be because we, the white majority, felt guilty over the sins of our forefathers, those who were the instigators and perpetrators of Negro slavery and invidious sharecropping and Jim Crow segregation laws and restricted neighborhoods in Northern cities, and integration after dark and all the rest. Even that brave Dr. Vivian had put forth that nonsense as an accepted premise during his talk at First Baptist this morning.

To which I now said silently in my head, *That's baloney.*

I didn't know about everyone else, but I, for one, had never felt the slightest twinge of guilt over the South's "peculiar institution," or the North's version of it, either. I had felt anger, yes. Sorrow, certainly. Indignation. Disappointment. Disillusionment particularly, over the gap between my country's ideals and its practices. All of these in large doses, getting larger by the year. But not guilt. I'd felt guilty about everything else I could possibly think of, but never ever about that. While I had sorrowed deeply from my earliest days over the treatment of America's Negro population, it had never once occurred to me that it could be *my* fault!

Nosirree!

Discrimination against America's dark minorities was none of my doing, at least not that I could see, and certainly not knowingly. Nor would it have been, I hastened to assure myself, had I lived during the time slavery was a legally-sanctioned cancer eating away at my country's sworn principles. I knew now as an adult what I had already sensed as a child. That back in those days I would have had no say at all about the way my country was run, since I would not myself have had the right to vote, and my personal rights in a court of law would not have been much better than those of a Negro slave. As a woman, I too would have been legally a second-class citizen, right up to the year 1920 when Americans of my gender who attained the age of twenty-one finally got the vote.

Ten years before my birth.

No. If you wanted to place blame, I told myself there in Adelaide's bed, pondering the past, the institution and perpetuation of slavery, and all that came after as a way to keep the Negro down, was surely the white *male's* burden of shame. It was he who had long been hung up on the economic and sociologic power play; on the acquisition of land and the need for someone, other than himself, to work it. He had been hung up too on his legendary lust, as a group, for sex with non-white women—after he had convinced his own white wife that it was lady-like and high-class to be cold in bed. (Jim Clemson had once told me that in the United States Navy it was accepted as truth that if you wanted to change your luck, you went to bed with a black woman.)

Many white men had also been hung up on the sexual threat implicit in the sight of a black male's well-developed body (which he possessed because he had been permitted only manual labor and got lots of exercise.) And if your game was placing blame, it was the white male who was still running the total society for us all, in spite of his silly talk these days about women owning most of the wealth of the country and therefore having nothing to complain about. "Owning" was a far cry from "controlling."

No wonder Negroes referred to a dominant white male as simply "The Man."

But as a controlling entity, now that I thought about it, white men in America also had many redeeming qualities. For one thing, they apparently valued peace in their own homes when the pressure from their womenfolk was on. I had had the good fortune to be born nine years after the advent of women's suffrage in the United States, grudgingly granted American women by many of the ruling male elite. I had thus been "born free" at least, with all the trappings and the promises of freedom.

For another, the white male power structure, not totally comprehending what women had in mind to do with this new voting tool, had attempted to make up for past female inequities to some extent. I had received the same education as a white boy, right from the beginning, all except for the sewing and cooking classes mandatory for girls in place of shop and auto mechanics in the eighth grade at Woodbury Junior High in South Jersey.

And in high school I had had to take physical education classes, just as the boys did. Except that ours meant playing less strenuous sports. But, don't forget, you were automatically excluded from taking solid geometry and trigonometry in your senior year. No girl ever took that class, it was only for the boys. *And you never questioned that, did you?*

You shouldn't forget, I said to myself, the miracle of tampons, beginning in my teens, and later on, after marriage, birth control. (So I had had two pregnancy accidents while using a diaphragm? Who knew how many more babies I might have had, without it!) These last two simple "luxuries" were male-developed technological advances that had surely gone a long way toward fulfilling the promise of physical freedom for me. With an assist, when my babies came along, from an automatic washer and dryer in my own kitchen, along with, in due course, permanent press fabrics for clothing. These, and a slew of other white-man-made contrivances had undoubtedly freed my body, and much of my time. So I could come to Selma, Alabama, in order to walk out of town.

Lying there beside Nancy, listening to her slightly audible breathing, I counted scientific advances in my head instead of sheep. Surgical techniques and antibiotics had twice saved me from early oblivion, both times connected with my pregnancies. Appendicitis. Childbed fever. Indeed, by banishing the specter of death at an early age from the bearers of children, male scientists had made it possible for us to outlive our men folk on a regular basis.

Symbolically, the guys seemed to be saying to us of the opposite sex: "We're giving you a boost up the ladder, and more years in which to climb. We may grumble and complain when you seem to be climbing too fast, when you want to take too much away from us, too soon. But at least we are trying." All that remained was for them to realize we too were ready now, inspired by their profusion of lofty "words to live by." And that we might also be ready to contribute some fine thoughts of our own.

All that remained for me was the toughest challenge of all: To free my own soul. To a certain extent, I had done that, hadn't I? I had begun to make my own, albeit rather unpopular, decisions about my life, hadn't I? *"To do nothing when he can do something,"* Albert had said to me on our walk after the mass meeting. *"When he wants to do something but doesn't, that's a denial of human responsibility. That's when a man should feel guilty."* And a woman too? I should have asked.

But what did a woman owe her children? Her husband? Her crippled parent? Her young and fatherless sisters? Her sick cat? Her house? Her society? Herself?

Historically the nurturer, when a woman took anything for herself, when she grabbed up new opportunities that were now open to her and her sisters in large numbers, did she automatically in the process take from all those others who were an integral part of her world? More than any other time in history, an American woman could now pursue higher education, travel on her own, take on stimulating and financially rewarding work, participate in politics and other areas of community need or personal growth. But where did a woman who had been given "freedom"—but only recently had run to accept it, indeed was endeavoring to seize it with her whole being—where did she fit into the rubric of the total society? Especially when she had once been snatched back from almost certain death at the time of her Julie's birth, and her continuing existence on this earth she considered a bonus?

What did I owe now, would someone please tell me? And to whom? I honestly did not know.

For more than five years now I had been making a genuine, conscious effort to at least choose what I would feel guilty about. And with this one, this Selma business, I decided with a soft sigh into the darkness, I had reached a new pinnacle of satisfaction. So that no matter what happened to me out there tomorrow, nor afterward, when I got back home, I would know that it had all been worth it! I hoped my children would come to see that too. That I had done it for them.

Stretching to my full length in my side of the bed, I extended my arms out in both directions, like a figure lying on a horizontal crucifix. The fingers on my left hand just grazed the top of slumbering Nancy's head. My right arm hung into emptiness. I let myself sink down, down into the softness of the lumpy old mattress. I loved soft mattresses, almost as much as I loved summer. I had had a soft mattress to lie on that other time, five years ago, and I had lain just so, like this. But I was alone, that morning, in the middle of the bed I shared with Bill. My arms were out in what appeared to my husband to be helpless resignation. Feeling no pain, I was scarcely able to feel my own body but only the soft-soft-softness of the bed.

I tried to recreate those sensations now. That strange awareness five years ago of being more mind than body; the all-consuming knowledge that before long I was going to die. To die, before I had had a chance to live.

*   *   *

29.

"Live so that if annihilation awaits you, it will be an unjust fate."
—Leo Tolstoy, Russian novelist
(From G. G.s WTLB)

I am helpless but I am not resigned, I am resentful. It isn't fair. It is the day after my thirtieth birthday and I have not had sufficient minutes to live—not anywhere near thirty years worth. But the die of fate has apparently been cast and my number has come up. What can I do about it? And the silent answer comes back from the atmosphere: "Nothing. You can do nothing. It is part of the price you must pay for being a woman; a wife and a mother. Nothing more."

As a child I had sometimes contemplated the eventuality of the magic year of 2000, and wondered if I could possibly make it that far. I was born in September of 1929, the last month of the Roaring Twenties; one month before the Stock Market crashed, though I knew nothing about all that then nor for a long time to come. By the year 2000 I'd be, let's see, I'd be seventy-one! Could I really hang on that long? I had doubted it then, because the idea of ever being seventy-one was to me utterly inconceivable. Now, in September of 1959, I am certain I won't even make it into the nineteen sixties, a mere four months away.

I lie still in my bed this afternoon and feel life seeping out of me painlessly, in a warm flood of blood between my legs. I have been home from the hospital with my fourth child only two days, and nothing has gone right. From the beginning I have been listless and without energy, fighting a miserable head cold. To make matters worse, a dreadful odor as of rotten flesh has seemed to emanate from my body. I don't remember noticing that strange smell after the other three babies, I have been telling myself for the past two days. It is probably my imagination because of this stupid cold.

And now I have this fever. And now I am certain something is wrong, because I am hemorrhaging, and I have become too weak to care for my baby and the other three, and too weak to do anything about my weakness, as well. All I can do now is lie here and realize that "rotten" odor was a warning signal, and I have ignored it until it is too late, and now I am going to die.

Bill tries his best to take care of me. I am not accustomed to that, it has always seemed to be the other way around. That other time of catastrophe, when

I was three months pregnant with Kenny and developed acute appendicitis, Bill had actually left me and baby Wendy in the old Boy Scout cabin where we lived and gone off to work, fearful of his boss's anger if he didn't show up that morning. It was my mother, frightened by my constant retching, who had called the doctor, and had me sent to the hospital for the emergency surgery. Baby Kenny had, of course, been saved, taking ten months to get ready to emerge from my body instead of nine. And it had been difficult for me to forgive Bill for his negligence and lack of backbone.

Now, after this mess I am making in our bed, I can forgive him anything. He cleans me off again and again, using pads of old newspapers beneath old diapers beneath my hips, in a valiant attempt to absorb the blood from the huge clots that never seem to stop coming. He has phoned my doctor several times to report on my rise in temperature and on the fact that the bleeding has not yet slackened. He hasn't let me down this time. It is just that his efforts have not been good enough.

So I lie here, in September of 1959, arms thrown wide as if in supplication, but who is there to appeal to? I am staring at sunbeams pouring through yellow dacron curtains; telling myself there is no way I can beat this. I haven't the strength to call for deliverance. Nor do I know of any deliverer. I figure I can't last much longer, before my veins are drained of the last drop of red blood and my heart, unfed for too long, has stopped beating.

My mind stimulated by the column of sunbeams, resentment rushes back. I tell myself again that my impending death is not at all fair. I hadn't wanted this last baby; true. I can't deny it. I hadn't wanted Scotty, the one who came four years before that, for that matter. I'd followed the instructions on the diaphragm box to the letter—but still the third, and again the fourth, had come. The two unplanned-for ones had been added to the two planned ones we already had, after I'd decided that someday I would leave Bill.

But from first sight, I'd loved each of my four equally, fiercely; willing to kill, if necessary, to protect any one of them from harm. This new one, this sweet Julie, born only six days ago, I yearn to protect her most of all, because she is the littlest. All my life, I have felt most protective toward the littlest of human beings, the most helpless, the underdog. It had been easy for me to stick up for my younger sisters all the years of my childhood.

But now it is plain I will not be around from today on to give Julie a mother's love and care, and I am silently furious about that. Because no one else wants these chicks of mine, at least, not the way I do. Not even Bill, whom I'd had to talk into conceiving the first two. Bill's parents certainly wouldn't want to be bothered with them, engrossed as they were with his sister's two little girls. (Which is fine with me. I wouldn't want my four little ones to be imbued with my father-in-law's paranoid and racist attitudes.) My mother? Out of the question. A widow of fifty-two with Parkinson's Disease slowly paralyzing the muscles of her body, she still has two of her nine daughters to finish raising.

My husband will certainly not be able to handle the care of four children by himself. A challenge such as that will throw him completely. He'll have to marry again, and as soon as possible. And some woman I have never seen will have the joy of watching my Wendy and my Kenny and my Scotty and my new little Julie grow up. Or worse, she will consider them a burden and hate their very existence. It is maddening to contemplate such a possibility.

There is more, though, to my gripe against fate. I have been putting off my "real" living until the children grow up. I have wanted so much to see the world—or at the very least, to take an active part in it. But I threw that prospect away, at eighteen, to play the wife-and-mother role American society had most approved for the members of my sex. I did the relinquishing joyfully, without a backward glance. I considered the rewards to come would more than equal the opportunities I had waived.

Bat it hasn't worked out that way. Twelve years of repetitive domestic chores combined with lonely busy-work and incessant conversations held almost exclusively with children have dulled my brain, stifled my daring, frustrated my love of adventure by holding the prospect of it always just beyond my reach. Those conditions have made me feel an onlooker, an outsider, an unworthy aspirant to a sorority of thinkers, one to which I had never consciously been pledged.

Worst of all, they have given rise to substantial and unmitigated feelings of guilt in me because of the chronic resentment I have come to feel at being what I consider only half a person. Resentment of one's beloved children? How can that be? This is the sort of mental pain that cannot be excised as easily as an infected appendix.

For six or seven years, I have fought against its insidious encroachment. Once, six years ago, I joined the local little theater group for some sporadic adult company and got leads in two plays. Later I took piano lessons again, spending weeks and months trying to finger my way through the arpeggios of Chopin's "Revolutionary Etude," before acknowledging I would never be better at piano than just passing.

For a while, I even taught beginning piano students in their homes, as an assistant to my children's music teacher. I polished up my sewing skills. I learned to plant shrubs in the yard that would actually bloom in the spring. Long ago, at the age of twenty and with only one child to care for, I actually wrote a lengthy children's book on the subject of Europe's displaced persons, and nearly sold it to a publisher.

As a final pick-me-up over recent years, I have befriended a paranoid schizophrenic schoolteacher, and served as her unofficial psychiatrist. I was the person who rushed over to her house regularly to stop her from committing suicide. When she turned out to be a professed lesbian as well, I said "thanks, but no thanks," but redoubled my efforts to extend to her the hand of friendship. My efforts were never enough for Susan,* who had an insatiable need for the dependency role she had been cheated out of as a child.

And my continuing efforts to keep myself involved in a wide range of aesthetically-satisfying pursuits were not enough either. None of them held my attention for long. Either I mastered them, or they mastered me, and I moved on to something else. Recently I have begun to suspect that only an outside job—a chance to make a genuine, remunerated contribution to the serious business of holding society together—would fill the growing void in my soul and remedy the stunted growth of my mind.

The pleasures of family life, with children and routine and a peaceful refuge to which a loving father-and-husband could return? Or the world beyond my four walls, beckoning and busy and full of interesting situations and people? Why had I always had to pick one or the other? Why couldn't I have had them both? Other women did, I have read about them. I have known a couple of them personally. And now that I am lying here, bleeding to death, I have finally grasped that these choices didn't have to be mutually exclusive.

Why does it have to be too late?

Ill as I am, I tell myself that I am quite lucid and in control of my mental faculties, and I make myself a promise.

I swear to myself that if I do not die; if by some miracle, I get up from here and live; I will make matters different. I will live the remainder of my life the way I think it ought to be lived, with as little resort to hypocrisy as possible. I will try to hurt no one with deliberate intent. This above all, to mine ownself be true. And if I must feel guilty about it—well, let's face it: I'm probably always going to feel guilty about something, and at least it will be of my own choosing what to feel guilty about!

Of course! It is all so simple. Why didn't I think of it sooner? I'll choose my own guilt complexes! I'll never again let anyone else decide for me what they will be.

I am drifting now, into delirium. I hear baby cries that are not real. Hungry baby cries. I imagine I am Scarlett O'Hara when she came home to Tara after the burning of Atlanta. She had lifted a fist defiantly toward heaven, and she had sworn she would never be hungry again. Hadn't I seen Vivian Leigh do it at least six times over the years since 1939? Every time they brought it back to the Rialto Theater.

Bill tiptoes into the bedroom and spoils the illusion.

"The doctor wants to talk to you, honey," he says in a doleful tone of voice, and he holds the extension phone from the bed table up to my ear.

"Gwennie?" Dr. Rogers has known me since I was a little girl, and she refuses to believe, even after delivering me of four children, that I have grown up into a Gwen. "Gwennie, would you say this is worse than a monthly period?"

Tears begin to run down the sides of my hot face, into my hair. "Ten times worse," I sob. I've been trying to tell someone all day, Dr. Rogers. I'm hemorrhaging. Really bad."

Bill takes the receiver from my fingers and puts it to his own ear.

"Get your family doctor to come to the house and check on her," Dr. Rogers is ordering him, so loud and imperative I hear her words distinctly. "Do it now! He can get there sooner than I can. Tell him it's an emergency!"

Which is how it happens that it is Dr. Grant who comes from close by and takes one look at the mess beneath my blankets and strides to the telephone to call an ambulance.

"I'm not altogether certain," he tells Bill, "because it almost never happens these days. I've never seen a case personally. But Mr. Gain . . . . I think your wife's got childbed fever!"

Bill trailing anxiously behind, I am borne down the steps to the first floor on a stretcher by two muscular men in white coats. My three white-faced little children stare silently as I am carried past them and out the front door. I am taken outside into the cool air and lifted into an ambulance with an eerie red light winking overhead. I am taken to the isolation ward of Cooper Hospital in Camden, New Jersey. Antibiotics, administered without delay, kill the infection inside my body within a matter of hours and save my life.

The miracle. I have not had to die after all! I have been granted an extension by fate, or whatever, and by those clever scientists (all of them male and Caucasian?) who developed miracle drugs like penicillin. And I do not forget that oath I made in my agnostic, all-questioning Unitarian heart to "whom-it-may-concern."

Puerperal fever. (Childbed fever, by another, more graphic name). *Retained placenta that has become infected, Dr. Grant explains to me later. The killer of millions of newly delivered mothers, he tells me, back in the nineteenth century. But no one gets it any more, not in the present generation of mothers, anyhow. Not since new sterilization and hygiene techniques have been instituted in hospital delivery rooms.*

No one gets it, but me! Is there a message in that?

When Julie is four months old and I am safely into the nineteen sixties, I go out to work, telling myself I am resuming my search for adventure, and for challenge, and for real living again.

*   *   *

END OF PART SIX

PART SEVEN

WAITING TO GO

30.

"The woods are lovely, dark and deep,
"But I have promises to keep,
"And miles to go before I sleep,
"And miles to go before I sleep."
—Robert Frost, American Poet
(From G.G.'s WTLB)

A wintry chill still hung over Selma Sunday morning, the scheduled day of the long-awaited and much-debated march. And the sun had not lived up to the stars' promise of last night, after all. It was going to be not only cold, but with skies overcast.

Four hours after I had mesmerized myself to sleep in Adelaide Sims' double bed with memories of my brush with death after childbirth, I was once more wide awake. It was well past seven, I guessed by the intensity of the light streaming through the shade of the one window. There was nothing for it but to get up, and I did so as quietly as I had done it yesterday, so as not to awaken my new bedmate. The Reverend Nancy Thomas slept on, lying on her back with a serenely contented look on her face.

In the Sims' bathroom I pinned up my hair into my customary French twist as neatly as I could without a rear-view mirror, and got into my marching clothes (the same dress I'd worn yesterday, but my underclothes, at least, were fresh).

In the year 1965 pantyhose, another male invention that would contribute to the further liberation of the human female, were not yet widely utilized and I had none. Snapping my long girder-belt clips onto the hems of my nylon stockings, I again cursed my stupidity at bringing such a constricting outfit as dress and slip and stockings on an extended hike that might prove dangerous. I went on to silently curse the clothing makers for *their* stupidity at not finding some way to build pockets into women's dresses. (How could I have guessed then that a mere half-decade later, we American women would be wearing trousers with suit jackets almost as freely as men? And that a niggardly few of those matching trousers would indeed have *pockets?*)

I prepared my knapsack as compactly as possible for traveling. I almost threw into the bathroom wastebasket the large brown paper supermarket bag into which I had stowed my change of clean stockings and underwear. But at the last moment I decided not to part with it. My squirreling instincts said to me that I could never tell when I might need a makeshift container like that. I reminded myself that I should always think ahead and be prepared for anything. So I folded the paper bag and shoved it into the top of the knapsack and tied down the flap.

One decision at least I didn't have to make, because it had been taken out of my hands from the very beginning. I might have been tempted to stay with the Sims family here in Selma in order to find some way to help, in spite of the fact that I had no car, and was forbidden to march after today. That way, I could at least have been here for the big rally in Montgomery on Friday. Missing the final ceremony would be hard, like starting a project you weren't allowed to finish because of a stupid technicality. Since that charter bus was the only way I could afford to get back home, I had to be on it as it left Montgomery at eight o'clock tonight. But I managed to convinced myself it was all for the best. I had "promises" of my own to keep, made back in South Jersey and Philadelphia.

Tossing my toilet articles into my shoulder bag, I put on my black coat in a repeat of the previous morning. I took up my shoulder bag in one hand and my packed knapsack in the other. I closed the door to the room where the Rev. Thomas was still slumbering peacefully. As I tiptoed along the hall, I threw mental kisses toward the four unmoving angels in the big bed at the top of the stairs. Oscar and Willis and George and Claire. I said things to them mentally, as well.

Today we give you back your family's other bed. Today we also hope to give you back your rightful heritage as American citizens, the right to vote when you grow up. I will remember you kids, all of you. As long as the River flows.

I crept down to the first floor and caught a glimpse of the sleeping lump on the couch that was Adelaide Sims, knowing I was seeing her there for the last time. We had already exchanged our final farewells the evening before, promising to stay friends forever, and go on caring about each other the rest of our lives.

I had said to her, "Goodbye, Adelaide. I'll be leaving in the morning before you and the children are up. Once again—thanks so much for everything! You've been so wonderful to me! You made me feel so welcome!" We had embraced spontaneously, warmly, our cheeks for a moment pressed together.

"Don't thank me none, Miz Gains! I must say, I was honored to have you here!" Adelaide said.

"And tell your husband I said thanks! Especially for giving up his bed!" I said.

I had met Andrew Sims only briefly the evening before, just after the mass meeting and before Adelaide and Nancy and I had had our coffee together. A big, laconic Negro, the shy fellow had taken my proffered hand quite calmly and then gone off to the couch he had been assigned to in a friend's apartment for the duration of the protests.

"Yes, ma'am, I'll sure tell 'em," Adelaide had said in response to my message for her husband. Could I really expect her to break a habit of nearly twenty years' time in two short days? It would take longer than that for her to learn not to call me ma'am. How long? I had wondered. And in my imagination, Dr. King had answered back, in that way he had in his most stirring speeches, *Not long!*

"Say goodbye to the children for me, too." I had told her. "You've got wonderful kids, Adelaide. And tell Charlie I said good luck! I do hope he makes it to Atlanta this summer."

"'Night, Miz Gains. God bless you! I must say, I'll never forget you, long as I live. We never knew before this, the Selma colored people, we never knew there was any white folks cared what happened to us." Older white folks, she meant. Lots of young white males were involved in the Movement. Standing close, I had looked down at her thin figure, noticing for the first time the bulge showing just below her waist in the slightly tight cotton housedress she was wearing. Could she be pregnant? Yes; I was almost sure of it! No wonder she had hesitated when I had asked her about marching out. It could have been more than a job she had been worried about losing!

I said, "I'll write to you, Adelaide, I promise."

She said, "You write me, I'll sure write back."

"It wouldn't make any trouble for you to get mail from me?" I wanted to know. "With the post office people, I mean?"

"No! No!" Her strangely unsynchronized eyes had twinkled at the thought. "A lot of us has folks up North. We gets letters from 'em all the time," she said.

"And you really promise to write back?" I asked.

"You can count on it, Miz Gains!"

"And Adelaide . . . ." I had to give it one last try. "When you write, call me Gwen, okay? I'd sure like that!"

That conversation had taken place last night. This morning, no one else was around. As I took one last look around the empty kitchen, a fat brown cockroach scurried straight up the wall and disappeared into a large crack where ceiling and wall were joined. Good lord! Right up the walls! So brazen! I smiled a cynical farewell toward its point of exit. It was an even larger roach than the bold one running on movie star Gary Merrill's shoulder last evening.

These were Alabama roaches, all right. Bigger than their Florida cousins, the brown water bugs I'd come across now and then in my mother's house in St. Petersburg, Florida. Those were the gigantic kind you could never get permanently away from, no matter what you did to them, nor how clean you kept your house. The sad part about Adelaide 's friendly home was not so much the fact of the cockroach, but the fact of the crack.

I waved a last goodbye to the Sims' empty kitchen and went out the door, knapsack and shoulder bag slung over my shoulders.

Maybe someday in some way, Adelaide! Maybe what we are doing here today will help to change all that too! You never know what voting can do to change a community for the better . . . if together we vote in a leader who really cares about the poor. But even as I thought it, I was aware I was being naively optimistic. Negroes comprised only ten percent of our population. There was no possibility . . . .

Arriving at the Tabernacle Church for breakfast, I found the same organized confusion, the same rattling of utensils and barrage of good smells that had been amply in evidence there yesterday morning. But this time, there were more takers, many, many more! Lots of men and women, Negroes and whites, young and old. And many were already crowded around the long tables, their many-pitched voices blending into one monotone buzz of sound.

I downed my second free breakfast of grits and eggs, toast and coffee (not free, after all, I soothed myself, thanks to Jim Clemens $20 donation I had handed to Rev. Young.!). As soon as I finished, I moved quickly out of the way to make room for another prospective eater. By this time, the clamor in the church basement had grown almost to a din, with everyone seeming to have some deliberate purpose there but me.

Newcomers were arriving every minute, the sleep barely washed from their eyes. I sensed that many of them were my wide-awake and wildly-clapping buddies from the mass meeting at Brown's Chapel last evening. They looked more subdued now, but hungry, and plainly eager to eat before walking out that morning in earnest. I disposed of my eating utensils and dropped two of my own precious dollars into a can I hadn't noticed before. The same big black woman as yesterday morning flashed at me a toothy smile and called out, "Thank ya, honey!" I knew better than to ask if she needed help dishing out the grits. I could see through the open door that the kitchen was swarming with even more helpers than the last time.

As I started toward the front of the room to retrieve my knapsack from the coat hook I had left it on, I all but bumped into a group of four young men; two white, two black, with skimpily loaded duffel bags hanging loosely over their shoulders. They had apparently just succeeded in worming their way through the cheerful, already-fed crowd milling around the double entrance doors, talking. And once inside, they were easing their burdens onto the floor with satisfied grunts of pleasure at having at last reached their destination.

"*Peter!*" I cried out.

I couldn't believe it! I had almost instantly recognized my young seatmate from the bus. The freckled-faced twenty-year-old with the alcoholic father and the unacceptable Negro college friends.

"Gwen! It's you all right!!" the surprised young man said. We wrapped each other in bear hugs and exchanged quick updates, neither of us attempting to hide our general excitement at impending events, as well as our thrill at running into each other again, like two long-lost cousins. Or like in a scene I pictured, from a 1940's combat movie, where two buddies meet unexpectedly at the front just before a major battle.

My bus companions had all spent Friday night in the basement of that Montgomery church, Peter reported, with no pillows or blankets for any of them. At least the basement had been warm. Some of them had sat leaning against the walls all night, unable to sleep at all. Peter had at least had his duffel bag to use for a pillow. And then Saturday morning, yesterday, the travelers from my bus had taken a vote as to what the group should do that day. Demonstrate in downtown Montgomery and help to pack the jails, as many others were deliberately doing that weekend? Or stick to their original purpose of canvassing the Negro neighborhoods on behalf of the voter registration drive?

"I was the only one who voted to get arrested," Peter said with a gesture of disgust. "Can you believe it, Gwen?"

"Oh, Peter! Not you too!" I threw up both hands in mock horror. "What am I going to do with you? You didn't come down here to get arrested, you came to help!"

"But the SNICK people in Montgomery told us that was one way we could help," he insisted. He had left the group in the church basement and had gone with a SNICK man into center city and taken part in a lengthy demonstration. But to their disappointment, the police had passed them over, possibly because all the jails and holding areas were already full.

Peter had met these two new black guys at the demonstration. And after all the excitement was over, the two Negro youths had taken the two white students, Peter and Nick, the other youth, home to their houses for the night. The four of them had borrowed camping gear from another guy early this morning, Peter reported. And they had taken the SNICK-operated private-car "shuttle service" into Selma. They had only just arrived, and were famished.

The other three boys, two black and one white, as unshaven and uncombed as Peter, stood back shyly, listening to us exchange our information. As for Peter, it seemed to bother my young friend not at all that he had acquired an older woman in dress and French twist for a buddy.

"You talked me into this, Gwen," he said with the boyish laugh of a Hollywood infantryman (Van Johnson, perhaps?) volunteering to be first over the top. "And here I am, in Selma, and isn't it great we'll both be makin' the walk after all?" Was I mistaken, or had Peter's New York speech already begun to acquire a Southern black accent?

"Don't blame *me* for bringing you here, Peter!" I retorted. But I had laughed back at him. I was still caught up in my Walter Mitty military illusion of the two of us about to embark on a dangerous mission together. I noticed Peter's special blue windbreaker jacket had already lost some of its sheen.

"Well, if *you* can march at your age, Gwen, I certainly can too!" he said.

What did he mean by that? That I was frailer than he because I was a woman? Or older, and therefore automatically weaker than the strapping young "bruiser" that he thought himself to be? Or did he simply mean that I was setting for him an inspiring example?

"I'll watch for you, Pete," I said. "I'll probably be going with my buddy the rabbi. You remember him from the bus, don't you?"

"Sure I do! Nice guy!" It had been only a little longer than a day, after all. But it seemed like a week since I had last seen the people from my bus. "I'll watch for you, too!" Peter said. His three friends' stomachs were growling from hunger pangs. Patting their abdomens, they had gone to line up in the ever-lengthening cafeteria line.

"Even if we miss one another, we'll meet in the bus on the way back home and swap stories," I said. I noticed there was a two-inch slit in one of Peter's jacket sleeves, just below the elbow. And the string he once used to draw in the waist of his jacket was missing.

"Nope. 'Fraid not." Peter shook his head, a shock of his unruly blond hair falling into his eyes. "I'm staying down South for awhile. I'm going to stay and try to help until this business is over. Gwen—I never realized how bad it is down here."

Keene Stassen, he said, had given him a twenty dollar refund on his return trip bus ticket, and that ought to last him for awhile. He thumped my arm with one gentle fist. "Gotta go eat. I think I'll even try some of those grits I keep hearin' about. I'm in missionary trainin' now, you know." He grinned at our private joke, the one I had told him about my brother-in-law who had wanted to become a missionary in the Philippines and had forced himself to learn to eat everything. "But y'all take care today, ya hear?" Peter instructed me. "And don't y'all do anything crazy, Gwen."

Just like that! He was staying. He was going to make his supportive mother be sick with worry. *But don't y'all do anything crazy.* (Jim Clemson had said something like that. *"Don't do dumb things, Gwen,"* he had said when I'd told him goodbye. Was that only last Thursday?) Craziness, I guessed, was all a matter of perspective. Peter was staying. With no thought to bed, or TV, or where his next meal was going to come from when his twenty ran out, he was staying. The Lord—or more likely Martin Luther King's organization, the Southern Christian Leadership Conference—would provide.

"Peter," I grabbed at his sleeve before he could walk away. "Your mother will be terribly worried."

"I know. I'll get in touch with her."

"When?" It was really none of my business what my young friend did or didn't do.

"Soon!" So she'd get no phone call until tomorrow, Monday, his one word said. And maybe not even then. I figured she'd be terrified until she found out where her son was. "I have to do this. See you around, pal," and without warning he planted a damp kiss on the side of my nose and left to go join his companions waiting at the serving counter, saving him a place. He got safely away from me before the lecture he feared about his mother was coming.

I stood beside the coat hooks a minute, watching him walk away. This could be my own son Kenneth, six years or so years hence, saying to me, "Mom, someone has to go, so I have to do this," about some wild-eyed crusade of his own. For one brief moment, I envied Peter his youth and his freedom from home responsibilities and his evident lack of self-reproach. Not to mention his "consider the lilies of the field; how they grow, they toil not, neither do they spin" philosophy. And then I remembered that Peter had no home where he felt he was welcome just now. And that we—he and I and all these others still jamming this church basement in order to be fed before marching—were really here to help change things as best we could. This, so my Kenny and his peers would no longer have this one particular kettle of fish to fry when they grew up, or even worry about.

Something told me I'd never see my optimistic young friend again. But I should memorize him well for when I got back home. Because the way I had just momentarily viewed Peter was definitely the way those people who populated my small world back home were going to regard *me*. Hadn't Jim Clemson tried to warn me? "Guileless. Irresponsible. Duped. Self-centered. Inconsiderate. A kook and a bad mother." Because none of them would be able to see and understand . . . . any better than Jim could.

And I should make myself accept too that we shouldn't try to solve all the evils of the world, we older idealists. We should leave a few causes for the younger ones coming along after us to deal with. Kenny, now only twelve going on thirteen, might say to me someday, Mom, please understand that I have to do this. And regardless of what it was, I would have to understand.

But good grief! My *own* mother! I had forgotten that my own mother was out there somewhere, at the other end of a telephone line. Seeing and talking to Peter so unexpectedly had caused images of my older son to break through my defenses, and these in turn had reminded me of another relationship I had nearly overlooked. My mother!

∗ ∗ ∗

<h1 style="text-align:center">31.</h1>

"Let your heart feel for the affliction and distress of everyone."

—George Washington,
first president of the United States
(From GG.'s WTLB)

Suppose something did happen to me out there today, after all? I ought to at least say goodbye to my mother, let her know why I had taken so drastic a course of action as to come here. So if anything did happen—though of course nothing would!—she could explain it to all the others in my large extended family.

Eight-thirty now. Nine-thirty, Florida time. Maybe it was not too late yet! I could still catch her before she and my two youngest sisters began their marathon day of Sunday School, Church service, roast beef and potatoes dinner back at the house, followed this evening by something at the Baptist Church called Training Union, and then Church again.

Turning around, I found my way to the Tabernacle Church office just off the dining hall and made my arrangements with the old black man seated as sentry outside the door. I was perfectly welcome to use the phone, he said, as long as I called collect.

Hurriedly, because there wasn't much time before the family left for Sunday School, I asked the long-distance operator to ring my mother's number in St. Petersburg, Florida. "I'm calling collect. Please tell her it's her daughter." *Calling collect from your daughter.* I chuckled to myself. She had nine daughters, only two of them still living at home. *Will you accept the charges?*

I waited impatiently until I heard a familiar voice say, in bewilderment, "Why yes, operator, I'll accept the charges." She hadn't yet been picked up for Sunday School!

"Why, Gwen, it's you!!" she said. It never failed to astound me that she could instantly pick my voice out of all seven of her daughters who had left the nest. I had tested her many times with only that one word "Mother?" long-distance, when she came back on the phone, and she had never once missed. Now I could see her in my mind's eye standing in her Sunday dress beside her kitchen window, outside of which a lush papaya tree was growing. Her two dark chestnut braids would be coiled neatly around her head after my sister Lynn had braided them afresh, and fastened in place with hair pins. Her right hand, crippled by Parkinson's Disease, would be shaking more uncontrollably than it normally did. Because she sensed from the collect call from me that something was out of the ordinary. Something distressing.

"Where *are* you, dear?" she wanted to know.

Almost jubilantly I said, "I'm in Selma, Mother!" No need to tell her Selma Where. I knew she'd know where. She kept up with the news on the color television set that we, her older married children, had recently chipped i n and bought for her. She must certainly have been following the civil rights developments of the past several weeks. Was there anyone left in America who didn't know by now where Selma was?

I came right to the point. "I'm here for the march. I'm calling before we start out because—well, because I wanted to thank you, Mother, for sending me here."

"What do you mean, *I* sent you? I did no such thing!" *Don't blame me, Peter,* I had told him, *for bringing you here!* Too late, I realized I had made a mistake. She didn't get it. She didn't get that all through my growing up years, she and Dad had taught me to be brave, to be strong, and to be concerned about the less fortunate. But if the Good Lord hadn't sent me to Selma, she wouldn't want to hear about anyone else.

And then, after a long pause, came the question I had least expected from her.

"But dear," she said, "Haven't they got what they wanted?"

She meant the Voting Rights Bill, of course, introduced into Congress by President Johnson four days ago. She didn't yet understand all the ramifications of that bill. That even if it passed, it might be no good. That it needed federal registrars to implement it, for one thing. And who would sign up to do that job?

Her accusatory question—"Haven't they got what they wanted?"—still hung in the silence, long-distance. What had I expected from her anyhow?

Instant understanding? Approval? A medal, perhaps? "No, Mother. *We* haven't got what *we* want. Listen, I've got to go now. Someone else is here waiting for the phone. We'll be starting out very shortly, Mother, and I think it's going to be perfectly safe. The President has called out the troops. But I guess you know about that." Surely *everybody in the entire country must know about that, by now.*

"Yes," she said. "I do." There was an unfamiliar coldness in her voice. Or was it worry?

"Wish me luck anyhow! Sorry to call you collect . . . . !"

"Dear—I'll pray for you."

For what? For my safety? Or for my sins? Once, not too many years ago, she had refused to sit at a banquet in St. Pete because a Negro woman she did not even know had been turned away at the door because of her race. Where had she gone, my indignant, altruistic mother?

I said, "Okay, Mother," and promising to phone her again as soon as I was able, I sent my love to the "Little Kids," as we Big Kids called Dory, sixteen, and Ellyn, eleven, the two little sisters still at home. I hung up and gathered up my little blue notebook and my shoulder bag. I thanked the old man for the use of the telephone, retrieved my knapsack from the coat hooks in the dining hall, and went out into the cold world where I could better face the facts.

Jeez, that was an idiotic thing for me to do!

It had been completely unfair of me to expect understanding from my mother at a time like this. Especially taking her by surprise as I had done. Especially since she had lived in the South for the past decade and was surely getting opinions from people who were biased in the other direction. And who knew what she was seeing on *her* television news every night?

There would be no more calls. Not to anyone else. Bill and the children would surely be watching on television, staying at home that Sunday morning to root for me, their personal entry in the race. It was enough to know that.

But . . . . why hadn't my mother understood what I meant? She should have grasped instantly the import of my message; understood that I was giving her credit for all the cherished ideals I had learned on her lap or at her knee: a worship of democratic principles; compassion for the weak; empathy and tolerance toward others and the courage of my own convictions. Dad may have stimulated my mind to the theoretical and the intellectual, but Mother had certainly taught me by her example to be altruistically involved in life. Hadn't she? Of course she had!

Her tone of voice over the telephone just now had seemed to convey quite a different message to me. A message of horrified disapproval, even condemnation. What I regarded as devotion to democratic principles? Seen by her now, perhaps, as flouting the established order she had taught me to love and respect when we lived up North.

My compassion for the weak? This might now be seen by her as molly-coddling people who only wanted to make trouble for the society they lived in. My desire to demonstrate my concern for the woes of a down-trodden minority? No doubt, to her, a grave irresponsibility toward my husband and children. In her eyes, my "courage" was not bravery at all, but foolhardiness. Her tone had said, in no uncertain terms: "Don't you dare blame me because you're there!"

She had probably long since forgotten taking me into the synagogue in Woodbury one Friday evening when I was nine. It was one of the very few times I had had her all to myself. It was on the spur of the moment when we were merely walking by, on our way home from a shopping trip up town. Maybe she had only taken me into such a place because of the hauntingly beautiful chanting of the cantor that had come wafting forth through the open door that November night in 1938. Perhaps she had not taken me in there, after all, because she had wanted me to learn tolerance of other faiths, or sympathy for people who were being pushed around.

We had sat down in a back row of chairs, my mother and I, and listened to more of the mysterious chanting in an unfamiliar language. And then the rabbi stood up behind the dais on the raised platform. He spoke of Jews being sent off to concentration camps in Europe. Of shops owned by Jews being broken into by the shattering of their plate glass windows and all the goods inside stolen or destroyed. This was done, the rabbi intoned, by some horrible men in Germany called Nazis, led by an evil man called Hitler. The date of the attacks was ever-after called Krystallnacht, Crystal Night in German; so named because of all the shattered glass store windows, lying in the streets all over Germany. At the age of nine, I was ignorant of all that.

After the service, as we attempted to slip out the side door unnoticed, we had been borne away without protest by some of the congregants to another part of the building, the basement. There we had helped ourselves to cheese and sausage sandwiches and other delicious foods I had never tasted before. Mother kept saying to the people who came up to shake her hand, "I'm sorry, I'm just so sorry."

And I remember Mother saying in reply to various questioners, after she introduced us, "No; We're not Jewish. My husband's name of Simon is Dutch, and we're Baptists."

I did not yet know about what, nor did I realize she had gone into the temple because of what had happened in Germany. But that Friday evening I had come to realize that Jews were not just cross and suspicious shopkeepers up on Broad Street in Woodbury, but could also be kind and friendly and able to laugh in the face of adversity. The women, too.

Even if my mother had not realized the effect of that experience on my perception of the world, could she possibly have forgotten the American Legion oratorical contest she had virtually pushed me into entering during my freshman year of high school when I was only thirteen? But I saw it all now; it must have been for the speaking practice, the prestige of coming in second behind my big sister Jackie, who was a senior and had won the contest. It had not been, I saw now, because of what I would learn about the Constitution and the Bill of Rights. Whereas I fell in love with both of those documents, being most impressed with their revolutionary ideas of democracy, and the protection of minorities against the will of the majorities.

And there was that time when Tootsie, the little colored girl from one of the run-down houses whose backyard touched ours, had come over to bring a message from her aunt who did our ironing. That time, Tootsie had come into our kitchen at my mother's urging and suddenly burst into tears and told us her mama was sick and her head itched so bad she could hardly stand it!

My mother had washed Tootsie's hair with her own hands, her strong fingers that were only partially crippled back then, working the white lather into the black snarls. And then rinsing, rinsing. A grateful Tootsie's head was bent face down under the faucet in our kitchen sink. Had that not been an act of caring extended by one human being to another weaker and less fortunate? Or had it been, rather, the brand of compassion you show to a dog who is frantically scratching at fleas?

And there was Rydie, of course. Unity's daughter who was the last, best hope of her very large Negro family. We had always known that Rydie was supposed to be a nurse when she grew up. Unity had decreed it would be so, and we had all believed. But Rydie had graduated from high school two years after me, and no one in her family had known how to go about sending her off to nursing school. And the guidance counselor at school hadn't done a thing to help. Because Rydie was black, and back then, in 1948, black girls weren't accepted into to all-white nursing schools. At least, they didn't in our little corner of South Jersey.

So September had come, as I recalled much later. And Mother had asked Unity one fine day how Rydie was enjoying nursing school. Whereupon Unity had burst into tears, only the second time any of us had ever seen her do it.

"Mrs. Simon, we jest didn't know how to go about it!" she had confessed after a great deal of gentle prodding. So my mother had spent hours on the phone that morning, and made umpteen local, then long-distance phone calls. She had finally gotten Rydie accepted into a nursing school in Harlem, New York City, ninety miles away, and with a full scholarship besides.

Then it developed there was not enough money for Rydie's bus fare to New York. Even that hadn't phased my mother. She had marched into my ill father's den where he lay listening to his classical music, and had emerged a short time later with a check in her hand for one hundred dollars. And Rydie went off on the bus the next day to Harlem, joining other Negro girls for nurse's training.

She had gone through nursing school in short order. And then somehow she had found the means to go through medical school in Philadephia. And only a few years ago I'd driven to Philly from my home in New Jersey, to attend Rydie's church wedding to a wealthy car dealer from Jamaica with a fancy French name. I had gone as my mother's ambassador, followed shortly thereafter by my attendance at Rydie's graduation from Women's Medical College in Philadelphia. And now Dr. Mariah Dubeque* was a practicing pediatrician with two children of her own; and wouldn't her mother Unity be proud if she hadn't had to die before the happy ending?

So why could *my* mother not now be proud of me? She'd given me Unity and Rydie and the Jewish temple and Tootsie and the Bill of Rights, and first but not least, My Darling Nellie Gray when I was three. I'd accepted them all unquestioningly, gathering them to me with an open mind and heart. How could I have guessed I'd read her message wrong?

Listen here, Mother, I scolded her inwardly as I stomped off in the direction of Brown's Chapel for what I hoped and assumed would be the last time. *I didn't read you wrong all those times. You really did send me here, goddammit, whether you like it or not!*

*   *   *

32.

"Liberty is not in any form of government. It is in the heart of a free man. He carries it with him everywhere."
—Rousseau, French writer
(From G.G.'s WTLB)

We early birds shivered a long time on the grounds in front of Brown's Chapel that Sunday morning, waiting for that still scary civil rights march to begin. Even though the sun emerged timidly through a curtain of gray about ten o'clock, as prayed for or as hoped for, depending upon your own particular belief system, the chill persisted.

March recruits had begun to gather from nine a. m. on. The first-comers were generally the white out-of-staters like me. I was one of those not yet attuned to the reality that Southern civil rights marches, unlike Northern business meetings, had no possibility of starting anything near on time. At least, that is what we began to suspect as we waited there, shivering in the chill air, not knowing what the hold-up was.

I had shown up early, as I had planned, lest I miss any preliminaries and in order to find myself a good vantage point. And find one, I did! As the crowd thickened, I climbed up and took a seat on one of the concrete abutments that jutted out on either side of the cement steps stretching across half the width of Brown's Chapel. Plopping down beside me the bulging knapsack bearing my dirty clothing and other supplies, I swung my legs over the edge of the abutment facing the steps. From my perch I surveyed the incoming crowd, pooh-poohing the memory of my mother-in-law's voice admonishing me: "Don't you know your children will catch cold if you let them sit their little bottoms down on cold concrete?"

From this spot, I noted, pleased with myself for having thought so far ahead, I would be able to see plainly all that would transpire on the steps beside me, as well as keep an eye peeled for the rabbi and my borrowed sleeping bag. Already someone had placed a microphone on a slim metal stand about halfway up the steps and toward the middle, where a speaker would not be in shadow. I assumed it was there for Dr. King's use before the march.

One by one, and two by two and group by group, marchers of all types continued to filter in to the wide space in front of the Chapel. Until by the appointed hour of ten o'clock, when the march was actually scheduled to begin, their numbers had mounted into the hundreds and the gathering was still growing! It was a marvel to observe from my higher vantage spot on the abutment.

I was surprised to note that a great many of the people arriving were conservatively dressed and middle-aged, many with graying hair. Far more men were coming than women. There were many more whites, at first, than blacks. The men were in all-weather tan coats or nicely cleaned-and-pressed jackets, or wore suits and ties with sweaters underneath. Many of the men, both whites and blacks, wore dark suits and clerical collars.

Many of the white women came clothed in their Sunday dresses and knee-length cloth coats, carrying colorful purses. Some wore matching shoes, I noted, that had high heels and were not at all ideal for walking long distances. Well-dressed Negro couples were scattered here and there, too. Their outfits with matching accessories were every bit as fashionable as those on their white counterparts. And in addition, a few of them actually wore their fancy dress-up hats! Dark brown felt fedoras were on the Negro men, fake-flowered Easter creations on their women. Watching the first marchers arrive, I felt shabby and out of season in my full-length black winter coat.

But then the younger element, male and female, began to straggle in, their various sleepy faces a testament to every possible shade of skin tone, from cameo pink through ebony black. Far more casually and comfortably dressed than I was, they came, their blue-jeaned numbers vastly overwhelming their nicely dressed elders. And male and female, they were also less carefully coifed, with straggly uncombed hair to their shoulders on the boys, or unwashed pony tails hanging down the girls' backs. Standard foot wear for both sexes were the worn leather sandals on their feet, and the girls' faces were completely unadorned. Many of the young wore faded jackets over T-shirts that bore messages across the front that couldn't be read. (But their wearers were not, I noted with a maternal shiver of sympathy, as warmly clothed as they should have been.)

Those young men, both black and white, who were most closely tied to the SCLC Civil Rights Movement were easily recognizable in their blue denim overalls and matching jackets, with many of them wearing black *yarmulkes* on their heads.

I saw no girls who were similarly attired.

Some of the younger Negro men who gathered there in front of Brown's Chapel that morning carried on their backs knapsacks like mine, or juggled small children on their shoulders. Some of their women had lunch bags, or carried purses that were stuffed full of some kind of provisions. Dozens of people, the optimists in the crowd as well as the ones who didn't want to be recognized, had worn sunglasses. A few of the more outspoken or foresighted marchers had put together homemade picket signs that bore defiant messages along the lines of, "One Man, One Vote!" or "Justice Now!" Some boasted the name of a particular church up North, painted on a wide banner that several people could carry in front of them as they walked. Everyone seemed cheerful if somewhat subdued, as the crowd milled around, waiting. Waiting.

Soon other participants, much younger than I, began to join me on my abutment, crowding ever closer but staying on their feet, squeezing me in from behind and both sides. I could see there would be, for me, no more sitting down. Alarmed at this new development, I stood up beside the challengers to stake out my own small piece of territory.

Just as I did this, a chunky, middle-aged television cameraman clambered up beside all of us, pushing his own way in. He proceeded to set up a tripod for his camera, passing wires back to his crew who had parked their work truck marked "NBC" close-by on the edge of the street. We pressed back out of his way as best we could under the circumstances of our precarious perch and watched him with mute interest. When all seemed in readiness to suit him, he left his tripod set in place, and ordered us not to dare bump into it or jostle it in any way. And jumping off, he disappeared into the crowd.

Another hour passed, and by eleven a. m. the crowd had swollen into what had to be in the thousands. They had succeeded in covering all of the steps above, below and beside the waiting microphone. The old and cracked asphalt road that ran parallel to the front steps of the church had been obliterated by the onlookers, who were now spilling out into some of the adjacent yards around the Chapel.

From where I stood, I could easily make out the rooftops of the George Washington Carver Homes that fronted onto Sylvan Street. The roofs were already dotted with a few enterprising black youngsters who had found a good place, they had apparently decided, from which to watch these historic proceedings.

The crowd, growing ever larger and without guidance, began to get restless. Someone, I couldn't see who, started up the singing then. "Woke up this mornin' with my mi-i-i-nd—Sta-a-ayed on freedom!" A few other voices from all over supported him in the song, and almost immediately, hundreds of voices joined in. Next we did "This little light of mine," with all its appropriate verses. And then we did a dress rehearsal of "We Shall Overcome." Hearts leaping, we rendered the spine-tingling messages of the night before. But chilled as we were, and as yet without leadership, the singing died out after the first enthusiastic go-'round. From that point on we simply waited, recognizing our vocal chords had limitations in the cold morning air.

At one point, before the crowd had become too thick for me to attempt it, I asked someone to hold my spot on the abutment. For a few minutes I walked around the perimeter of the gathering to keep the circulation going in my legs. And during that venture, I fell into conversation with a Negro couple who stood beneath one of the church windows on the side wall. They were leaning their backs against the maroon bricks and seemed not at all anxious. A handsome man and an attractive woman, looking to be about my age of thirty-five, they were well dressed in their Sunday best. From their speech as we talked, I could tell they were also well educated.

They were both teachers in a Selma elementary school, they told me in answer to one of my questions. There were all black children in that school, of course, they said. We talked about SCLC's voter registration campaign in the town of Selma and this new and exciting turn of events that had occurred over the past two weeks. Selma was not a town but a city of over 25,000, the wife corrected me. Dallas County, of which Selma was the county seat, was over fifty percent black. And yet only a few dozen Negro residents had ever been allowed to even register to vote, much less would actually have dared to go to the polls.

I told them I was surprised to learn that any had.

"Oh, yes. They have to have their token Negroes on the rolls so they can say they don't discriminate," the wife said.

"You? I would think that you two could, if anybody could!" I said, appalled.

They both chuckled bitterly. "Not us!" one of them said.

"But you're both college graduates . . . . ?"

"What's that got to do with it?" The husband said. They had gone together to the County Courthouse in Selma a year ago, to try to register so they could vote for president of the United States in November. And the white registrar had leered at them and then asked them the one question he said they needed to answer to his satisfaction to quality for the vote. The question? He had asked them, "How many bubbles are there in a bar of soap?"

"What did you tell him?" I asked, incredulous.

"What could we say?" and he shrugged. They had stood silent, in shock, before the registrar, he told me. They had at least expected some kind of citizenship question on which the man would almost certainly flunk them, because he would say he didn't like their interpretations. And the wife calmly told me how that white registrar had laughed in their faces and said, "So you thought you were ready to start votin', did you? Well, you failed the test." And he had pointed out to them without words or further discussion the way to the door.

Now this handsome black husband who was a teacher of many of Selma's young said to me, "You know, for so long they've made us feel, against all reason, that as a race we didn't deserve it. The vote, I mean. But we know better now. *This* man . . . ." and he gestured toward the waiting microphone, "he has convinced us we're as deserving as anyone! Maybe more so."

He meant Martin Luther King, of course.

I smiled and nodded in approval of his remarks. I said, "He's very persuasive, all right! That's why *I'm* here!" I told them I had to get back to my place on the abutment before I lost it. "Could I ask you a favor? Could I leave this here with you?" and I indicated the bulky knapsack containing nearly all my earthly possessions at that moment. Until my current little walk, it had been dangling by both straps about my knees, getting in everyone's way after I stood up to keep from being suffocated or pushed off by the newcomers crowding onto my treasured space on the abutment.

"Sure thing!" and the two teachers assured me they would be happy to lean the knapsack against the wall by their feet, and keep a close eye on it. I would retrieve it, I told them, when the marching began.

Back on my abutment again, standing above the majority of the crowd gathering on the steps and the ground below, I continued to be haunted by the two teachers' story as bits of our conversation kept coming back to me. *How many bubbles in a bar of soap? So you thought you were ready to start votin', did you? You flunked and there's the door.* He hadn't said that last, but had pointed them toward the exit.

How terrible it must be to have grown to adulthood absorbing American ideals, only to find yourself put in a position of such helpless humiliation and defeat! The emotional toll, the utter frustration, the bitterness—it could be almost as bad, I decided, as an out-and-out physical attack on one's person. Maybe worse. Because how could you fight a nebulous insult such as that? Especially if you'd been brain-washed all your life, as these two teachers had admitted to being, to believe you weren't worthy?

If Martin Luther King had done nothing else for Southern Negroes—and he had already done plenty—he was giving them a new sense of worthiness. His campaigns were helping these older Negroes to acquire a good self-image that should have been theirs all along. I had seen it in Adelaide Sims. I had concluded that some sort of mental metamorphosis must have been in process in her family for a long time before I came on the scene. And now these two teachers, along with many of the parents of Selma's Negro children, were shaping the attitudes of the young ones still coming up. Because they now knew they were deserving . . . .

I already knew about the internalizing of concepts like inferiority, didn't I? It had once happened to me. I had been all of fifteen-and-a-half before I had occasion to confront an adult's frank view of my own supposed limitations. My own right to the franchise lay a long six years away. I had been not one bit concerned, that spring day in 1945, about my right to vote. I was free, and the United States was free, and the whole world was almost free. I was living in New Jersey, a basically tolerant, segregation-free state, I had always assumed while growing up. I would be twenty-one in 1952, and the vote would be out there waiting for me to claim it when the time came.

What I had wanted more than anything else that day as I was ending my junior year of high school, was not to play softball with five nasty boys on a vacant lot in my neighborhood when I was nine. No, I had set my sights much higher since that head-splitting day. I had reached out for what I saw as the really big prize. What I had hoped for that day more than anything in the world was to be able to play my flute in the Woodbury High School marching band.

*   *   *

33.

"If a man does not keep pace with his companions, perhaps it is because he hears a different drummer. Let him step to the music he hears, however measured or far away."
                —Henry David Thoreau, American writer
                                        (From my WTLB)

Mr. Rafferty,* the principal of Woodbury High School, was short and small, yet powerfully built, with a grizzled face, ears too large for his head, and *the jaunty walk of a fighting cock. He had once been a star on the high school's football team, and now he was back as principal, and had been serving in that capacity for many years. By that day before Memorial Day in 1945, when school was just two weeks short of closing for the summer, Mr. Rafferty had long since gotten the knack of dealing with the adolescent kids placed in his charge to be educated.*

To his credit he took no stuff, we students all knew, from anyone. Not even from the guys who were over six feet tall and the current stars on the football team. Behind his back, the boys at school called him "Jiggs," after a character in a newspaper comic strip of the times. To his face, they all but saluted him. Most of the girls merely quaked in their white bobby socks when he rushed by them by in the corridors, tracking down wayward boys.

But I had been lucky. My good grades and proper deportment had endeared me, I thought, to this enigmatic personality behind his desk in front of me. I had been a favorite of his since my freshman year. Besides that I had two older sisters who had been outstanding students at Woodbury high; one, for academic excellence, the other, for cuteness and friendly personality. Surely my request would seem a simple one to grant, if I approached him respectfully and laid out my case in a logical manner.

He looked up from his desk with a pleasant flash of teeth across his usually stern features as I walked into his office. "Well, Gwendolyn," he said, "What can I do for you?"

I had not yet learned the art of small talk. So I came right to the point. "I came to see you because—well, because I'd like to be in the marching band next year, Mr. Rafferty," I said.

He stared at me, nonplussed. (It was the same reaction, I guess in retrospect, as that of Sigmund Freud when he uttered those infamous words claiming total confoundment: "Woman! What does she want?" A rhetorical question, on Mr. Freud's part; requiring no answer because there was none, not at that date in history at least.)

With me standing there on the other side of his desk looking down at him expectantly, Jiggs had to say something. "Well, Gwendolyn, you're going to be in the concert band next year, are you not?"

I nodded. "Yes, you know I am, and thank you. But—" How best to explain it? I had rehearsed it so many times in my head, but now all the fine, proud words were gone. The Woodbury High School marching band, historically all male, needed more members, since some of our best instrumentalists had dropped out during the previous four years to go to war and would almost certainly not be coming back. In desperation, the band director Mr. Chance had a month ago petitioned the principal, who petitioned the superintendent, who petitioned the Board of Education, which, in its infinite wisdom, had decided to let girl students perform in the concert band for the first time ever, come September.

The concert band would always be up on stage, the reasoning went; up where the fact of girls in skirts would not be overly obvious to the audience and thus detract attention from the music and the aesthetics. I would have to supply my own medium-blue, knee-cap-length skirt to go with the uniform jacket Mr. Chance had already issued to me. No hats would be necessary, he told the handful of us females who played woodwinds and brass in the orchestra, since we would always be indoors and up on stage when we played with the band and would never be marching.

At first I was ecstatic when that School Board decision was handed down. I had already practiced several times this month with the concert band. I would be a senior next year, due to graduate in May of 1946. Germany had surrendered to the Allies in Europe two months ago. Only the war in the Pacific was continuing to be fought. And it looked as though that might end by my graduation date a year from now. (With the dropping of the two atomic bombs on Japan two months later, in August of 1945, the war in the Pacific would be over much sooner than anyone dared dream.)

But the high school drop-outs who had answered their country's call were gone forever. One had been killed in action. The others were too mature now, too involved in the business of adult living to care about coming back to little old Woodbury High School, the place of their adolescent imprisonment, much less rejoining its marching band.

Football season would be starting in September, come hell or high water (or atomic energy) and the marching band had to be ready. To my delight, I had noticed that it was stretched more than a little thin. Surely Mr. Rafferty had noticed its pathetic appearance during the V-E Day parade down Broad Street last month, on the eighth day of May?

The addition of eight, perhaps ten, of the girls from the orchestra and concert band would fill out the ranks of the marching band, and give it more depth and volume. The flute section alone, next fall, would be constituted of only one person when the boys were marching around at halftime in their blue and gold uniforms. And that lone flutist would be a senior who could not play the instrument, I was convinced, any better than I. It would not be just for my own pleasure, to be able to march with the band. It was my duty to help save it!

"I really do like being in the concert band." I said. Trite statement. I liked it so much I wanted to add, that I was here asking for more. The orchestra, with which I had played for three years now, had given me Tchaikovsky, Wagner, Rimsky-Korsakov, and a few other pieces of classical music. They had made me, by means of my fingers rippling up and down the padded keys on my silver flute, a devotee for life.

I had listened to the composers' compositions often enough, the magnificent sounds pouring forth from my father's bedroom radio on Sunday afternoons. But to actually play their works was to claim them as friends, those dead composers. It was to appreciate their genius and their music forever.

My appetite having been whetted by this awareness, I desired still more. I wanted to say, Mr. Rafferty, what I really want is John Philip Sousa. Practicing with the concert band had given me only a taste of him. "Stars And Stripes Forever." "Washington Post March." "High School Cadets." One of those three, usually, would end an evening's stage performance after all the heavier numbers had been performed. But that wouldn't be quite the same.

I longed to say, I play as well as Dan Biddle,* Mr. Rafferty. Why do I have to have a—dared I utter the word aloud?—a penis to be allowed to march in the band? Envisioning the dreadful word spelled out in my brain, I felt my face turning red with shame. Suppose he had read my thoughts?

But if he had, my principal gave no sign. We each waited for the other to continue.

So I found voice to say, with false bravado: "Concert band won't even start up until football season is over. I—we girls—we want to practice marching right now, and be ready!"

Silently my inner self was pleading, Please listen to me, Mr. Rafferty, won't you try to understand? I want to wear the entire band uniform and put on that blue military-style cap with the gold braid that the fellows here in school get to wear! I want to get out on the field with them, in the mud and the cold and the wind and the heat, and toot my heart out! I want to lift my knees skyward and do left and right wheels and about-faces in time to the music's pulsations, and help spell out W H S in the middle of the field at halftime.

And if by some miracle our football team wins the South Jersey regional championship this fall, I want to march down Broad Street here in Woodbury, playing the flute obligato to "Stars And Stripes Forever!" You know the part I mean; where the swell music of the flutes stepping high and fast above the melody makes your heart almost stop with joy! I want to march straight past the County Court House with the police stopping traffic at the intersection of Broad and Delaware Streets, after those rare and glorious games when our football team beats the almost invincible schools like Paulsboro and Collingswood.

But listen: I've got only one season left to do it in!

I would turn sixteen in September, and go on to graduate from Woodbury High the following May. Now I was fulfilling an early birthday promise I had made to myself. It was too late to help celebrate the end of the War with Germany three weeks ago. But maybe by next May, Japan would give up too! And surely other, smaller victories lay ahead of the marching band, as well. And I wanted to go all the way with Sousa. I felt certain he had never intended for his music to be played by a bunch of high school students sitting down in wooden folding chairs in front of rickety old music stands that had to be shared with two or more players.

"Hm-m-m. So you want to join the marching band, do you?" Jiggs ruminated a moment in silence, pulling at his jowly chin, leaning back in his chair with the front legs dangerously far off the floor, the way the teachers never permitted us to do. My heart leaped inside my chest. He was going to find a way! A way to do it gracefully, so as not to offend those grim-faced men on the School Board. I was so glad we were friends, he and I, and that I had been brave enough to express to him my heart's desire.

"Well, Miss Simon, I'm afraid you can't." While he had phrased his response with a personal "you," it was plain he meant, "you females."

And I had the audacity to ask in a meek little voice, "Why not?"

He sat his chair legs flat at my timid question and drummed his fingers on the desk top, on a pile of papers with some drawings of football formations, I saw, on top.

"How would it look, Gwendolyn, now I ask you—how would it look, having girls' skirts and bare legs mixed in with the blue trousers of the fellows? And all that long hair flying around your heads, along with it?" And then, without waiting, he answered his own question: "I'll tell you how it would look, young lady—it would look completely inappropriate. To put it to you bluntly, it would ruin the band."

Inappropriate? Ruin the band? What was he talking about? We girls could pin up our hair under the caps, Mr. Rafferty, so we'd look like boys! And we could—we could wear the necessary blue trousers! Did you ever think of that?

As if he had read my mind, the principal said next, "No, no! They couldn't wear trousers, which would call attention to their figures in an unseemly manner. The idea of our girls running around in trousers in public would upset the School Board no end."

I had no words to reply to that. Apparently to make such a suggestion, even in that avant guard year of 1945, was to utter a form of blasphemy. Or what was worse, an obscenity. Woodbury High School girls, wearing trousers and strutting around in the public eye? We could wear them at home for play after school, around our own homes, and on Saturdays—"slacks," they were called in those circumstances—and most of us bobby-soxer girls owned a pair. But never, with official sanction, were we to wear them in school or at a public performance! Breasts could be hidden under heavy uniform jackets, but hips would always out.

"So what can we do?" He continued to stare up at me, the hint of a smile touching the corners of his mouth. Was he teasing me? Or did he truly expect an answer? And if he did, could I really seriously consider suggesting to my principal that we flout a social convention of such long standing that it was almost a sacred tenet? Girls, nice girls in a nice town and a nice school like ours—in fact, in all the institutions of learning in South Jersey that I knew of—simply did not wear trousers in school, much less in public. It wouldn't be nice. That made sense, didn't it? And to let us play in skirts with our bare legs exposed would ruin the Band's appearance even more. In the face of such indisputable logic, what, really, could any of us do?

Here it was again; the message I had gotten when I was nine and stopped to watch boys playing softball in a vacant lot. Girls weren't supposed to play, or even look like they wanted to play. They were only to be spectators, to watch for a minute or two, and then move on. But this time instead of hurt bewilderment and honest indignation, I was filled with self-loathing for even having challenged such a valid concept as this.

In my quest for what I had considered right and fair, which was to play my flute in the high school marching band, I had spoken all of five brief sentences and had my entire self-image changed temporarily by the man in charge. I stood there for a few seconds, hot-faced with shame. Not because of my cowardice, but because I had been thinking right in front of the principal about penises or the lack thereof.

And what about the prospect of girls wearing trousers which would outline their hips in a Board-sanctioned public event? How could I have entertained such thoughts when I had been brought up to be a lady? I managed to stammer some sort of agreement with Mr. Rafferty's "So what can we do?" and all but scurried from his presence. No one had to point out to me where the door to his office was.

* * *

34.

"I shall pass through this world but once. If, therefore, there be any kindness I can show, or any good thing I can do, let me do it now; let me not defer it nor neglect it, for I shall not pass this way again."

—De Grellet (?)
(From my WTLB)

Past eleven, I noted by my watch. The march was late beginning. The sun had still not come out from behind a solid curtain of gray, and the air was still uncomfortably cold. I managed to hold my own while squeezed onto my crowded perch three feet above the bulk of the crowd in front of Brown's Chapel. With one hand I grasped the belt of a young white boy beside me, and he in turn clutched at a friend's arm to keep us both from being dislodged. In spite of our discomfort, the eight of us standing on the abutment kept scrupulously away from the NBC tripod and camera that had somehow been set up on our vantage point beside us.

There came no wave nor call of recognition from Nancy or Peter or anyone else who looked familiar. No sign yet either of Dr. King, our leader, or of Albert Friedlander, my rabbi friend. I was beginning to be concerned about him. He still had my borrowed sleeping bag, true. But more than that, I had become very accustomed to his company.

Anxiously I searched for a black *yarmulke* atop that bespectacled, and almost cherubic face. Could he have overslept? On the hard basement floor of this very church, with all the racket going on outside? *Not likely, Gwen!* Could he be still at breakfast? *Over, hours ago!* He didn't have a watch with him, remember? *Plenty of time pieces around.* Had he perhaps decided that he'd rather make the march with his fellow rabbis? There were a good number of them here. Could he be worried what they'd think about his being with me, a woman and a gentile, so much of the time?

He *promised we'd march together. He said so, just last night. There were no reservations in the way he said it.* But wait a minute. Had he really said that? He said he'd see me in the morning, and bring the sleeping bag, and I had just assumed . . . . (I had made that other assumption, the one with Keene about the bus. I had assumed I would be going to Alabama with a bus full of students bound for Selma, and I had been wrong!) Albert had better get here soon, at any rate, or we'd never find each other in this mob of people, even to tell each other good luck. I'd never been among so many people standing together in one place! Nor so many faces I'd never laid eyes upon before this!

Safety in numbers, my mother had said so many times in my childhood. And it was true. But thinking all this, and about not being with my special friend Albert, I was pinched with a sense of loneliness. I started thinking about home. My children. My job at Penn. The pages of Italian that were to be translated by me for Tuesday morning class . . .

Eleven-thirty now. The choir in which I sang at the Unitarian Church of Cherry Hill would be getting ready to go into its anthem just about now. What would they choose? Would they sing my favorite Robert Frost poem set to music, the one about the star? *O, star, the fairest one in sight* . . . .

Suddenly—Albert? Yes; there he was! And right where I had least expected him to be: halfway up the steps, just to the right of the waiting microphone which was now almost buried in the sea of heads that bobbed before me. All I could see was Albert's face and head, but that was enough. A curl of dark hair had escaped onto his forehead, while sunlight bounced off the thick lenses of his glasses. Gleefully I flapped my free arm to get his attention, but Albert had spotted me at the same instant and yippee! he looked equally pleased to find me.

It was impossible now for either one of us to try to join the other through that jam-up of pressing bodies. So we contented ourselves with smiling at each other now and then and nodding our heads in a kind of secret agreement that matters were going exactly as planned. My anxiety for his whereabouts thus put to rest, I resigned myself to the spirit of brotherly-and-sisterly love that had apparently gripped the entire crowd. Otherwise, people would certainly have rebelled before this at the long wait.

The NBC cameraman joined us on the abutment a few minutes later. He began pushing and jabbing his way into position, knocking two white youths off altogether, scowling and grumbling his disapproval of the rest of us as he lowered onto the waiting tripod the heavy camera handed up to him by one of his crewmen. Burly, scowling, and super-Caucasian, he had come to us complete with earphones, and these appeared to be giving him information we spectators were not privy to. He took a phone from one ear. Bending over his camera, he adjusted the lens, trying for the best view of the spot on the steps where the microphone had last been seen.

"He's coming now." He said it matter-of-factly, his crisp Northern accent announcing without further debate that he was completely in charge of our position. And that he was well aware that *we* were well aware who the "he" was that he referred to.

"You people will have to get off and give me more room," he snarled. And when no one responded to his command by moving so much as a muscle except to turn our faces expectantly toward the direction of downtown, he growled, "Get out of my way! How can I operate a camera like this?"

I considered appealing to the man's reason and sense of fair play. I considered telling him we had come early in order to get a good place, up there on that chilly slab of concrete, and therefore, and quite naturally, we didn't want to give it up. We had no intention, I thought of telling him, of sinking ignominiously into the masses below us when none of them in the yard or on the steps in front of us had been waiting as long as we had. But I could see by the expression on the cameraman's ruddy face that it would do no good to try to reason with him. Instead, at my suggestion since I was the closest to him, we all eight shifted around again on our concrete island, affable strangers crowding ever closer to each other to make more room for this one disagreeable human being.

All to no avail. Nothing we did to help made him happy. He continued to grumble beneath his breath and play with his camera adjustments, punctuating his frustration with an occasional angry outburst directed at me, as the nearest: "I got to have more room! Can't some of you get down?"

I clung desperately to my lifeline, the white boy's belt, fearful I'd be shoved off the edge by a sudden jostle. Should I try another tack by making an evangelical-style witness to the fellow? Try to explain how much it meant to all of us to be up there, in the manner of Matthew the tax collector who had climbed a tree for a good look at Jesus? No. Such an analogy would smack of religious fanaticism to this obvious skeptic of the "miracle" of Martin Luther King. I had learned from personal experience that one man's food was another man's poison, or something like that.

Nor would this guy want to hear about how at that particular moment, we all loved one another so hard it hurt. Nor would he accept a suggestion from me that he, the one sour note in our symphony of peace and justice this morning, should try to get himself right with the world? Not knowing what to reply to his pejoratives, I said nothing, and made no answer back. But none of the six of us remaining there got down.

The widespread swelling of voices from all over made me look once again toward the street. A car had managed to work its way along it through the crowds, and had pulled up near the huge tree that shadowed the other side of Brown's Chapel's front yard. Car doors were opening, and figures were being helped out by march marshalls wearing the yellow armbands we had been told about yesterday at the mass meeting. The crowd began to part and fall back, making a temporary aisle for several Negro men to pass through.

And yes! I could see him now! At least a small piece of him, but enough to recognize Martin Luther King, Jr. Baptist minister! 1964 Nobel Peace Prize winner! Pricker of the consciences of American liberals!

He was barely visible, moving forward behind two of the marshalls. Following close behind were the bobbing heads of several other persons, most of them white. Patiently the heads of the new arrivals made their way up the steps of Brown's Chapel through the path made by the excited mass of volunteer crusaders. Until at last the men stood in a close cluster around the now invisible microphone.

Even from my raised observation point, I could see little of Dr. King because of the hordes of people packed tightly together on every step. But I had been immediately struck by one thing: he was not very tall. Attired in what appeared to be dark suit, white shirt and tie, he was a much shorter person, and more slightly built, than I had conceptualized from the many pictures on television and in magazines and newspapers over the past eight or nine years. He was, in fact, nearly dwarfed by some of the taller but just as conservatively dressed dignitaries who flanked him.

Dr. King turned his head, smiling, to acknowledge the presence of several people he knew from the crowd, and to exchange a few words of greeting inaudible to us on the abutment. I liked the idea of his shortness. It made it even easier now, to identify with him. But I did wish I could see him better . . . .

"Damn! How can I see through you people?" It was that cameraman again, peering into his eyepiece right beside me. He let out another muttered exclamation of disgust, but this time directed it at the spectators who stood between him and his subject. "Move over! Move over!" he hissed in an undertone, waving his arms wildly at their backs and heads.

But no one of them noticed, nor cared.

All attention was focused upon the group closest to the microphone, and in particular, upon what little they could see of the famous brown face with the neat black mustache he let grow on his upper lip. There were the wide nostrils, the full lips and wide mouth, the small ears folded back tight beneath short-cropped wiry-black hair. There were the oriental traces about his cheeks and eyes. Dr. King had written in one of his books that there was an American Indian in his family tree—just as rumor had it by way of my maternal grandmother that there had also been one in mine! And there was that serious, almost sorrowful, almost oriental, countenance I had seen so often on the television news each evening.

The crowd sensed that their leader would shortly begin to speak, and the buzzing voices faded in anticipation. "Goddamn!" groaned the cameraman in a half-whisper, clapping one flattened palm to his forehead in frustration. "This guy's always too short!"

A little to the right of the microphone still stood Albert Friedlander, his black-capped head further away from me than Dr. King's. Since that automatically faced him in my direction, I caught his eye and he beamed at me in ecstatic glee. The broad smile and the smug set of his chin said it all.

Here we are, Gwen Gain! Right here where we have all along hoped and planned to be. And isn't it good, more than good, isn't it great to be alive, and great to be here at this fantastic party!

Across the human bridge of heads between him and me, I nodded my concurrence.

"I still can't get this guy! What's the matter with you people?" The insolent cameraman again. I had almost forgotten him. He was making one last attempt to command obedience from us, and from the people in front of us. He was bent over with his eye glued to his eyepiece, jolting me back to the realities of his frustrating situation. His words were more audible now as he demanded in my direction, "Don't you know this guy needs us? He wouldn't be anything without us! Now get out of the way!"

This guy, sir? He has a name! One of the best!

A few members of the crowd, those standing on the steps closest to us, looked around, confused by the cameraman's angry words, not understanding them, not even certain whence they had come. Then, satisfied of their unimportance, the eager faces turned back toward the man at the microphone. There was a flurry of motion there, caused by several of Dr. King's aides attempting to adjust the microphone's height.

To myself, I conceded that the unhappy soul beside me had a point. Dr. King and his Southern Christian Leadership Conference colleagues did indeed need the news media, particularly television. They needed every bit of coverage they could find in order to carry their demands for justice and equality far and wide. This fellow from the National Broadcasting Company was attempting to perform a difficult task in a trying position. What matter that he was the typical Northern bigot, as long as he did his job?

Why, my own family might be tuned in to his channel, NBC, right this very minute, looking for news of the march! Moreover, I was chagrined to be standing directly beside him. Suppose someone, hearing his punctuated complaints, assumed he was making threats against Dr. King. With the two of us standing so close together, I could be found guilty by association!

But most important of all: this man beside me was a threat to the state of high morale reigning over the crowd, a state of mind carefully built up to its present peak over such a short period of time. Now that our own man was here at last to lead us, we were all high on *agape,* brotherly love. All of us gathered here loved everybody else.

At that moment, I even loved him, this NBC rotten apple who was spoiling the mood for me and everyone around me with his surliness. Something had to be done to help him, and quickly.

I said to the cameraman, "Suppose we ask 'em to switch? Swap some of the tallies for some of the shorties?"

Without waiting for a reply, or even needing one, I went into action. Stooping down and hanging on for dear life to the sneakered heel instead of the belt of the kid next to me, I used gentle pokes on the shoulders of the people directly in front of me to get their attention, and whispered suggestions for them to pass toward the standees in front of them. With appropriate grimaces, the waving of my arm and jerking of my thumb at those further forward who looked back at me, I got quite a few nods of approval with only one shake of refusal. In seconds I had managed to create a nearly clear path for the eye of the camera as the taller onlookers on the steps obligingly changed places with their shorter neighbors.

I got no expression of gratitude from the NBC cameraman.

"That guy!" he ordered me, flailing both arms about. "You've got to get that big one out of there!"

I stood up. Catching Albert's eye once more, I gestured frantically with my free hand toward the camera on the tripod, then to the one giant head still blocking our full view of Dr. King behind the microphone. This I followed with a series of descending stair-step motions, with my palm held flat in front of my face along with the mouthed word, Down!"

Rabbi Friedlander was quick to catch my point. Raising one of his own arms high, he pointed to the offending head, the one facing innocently in his and Martin Luther King's direction, and motioned plainly to it to get down. Bewildered, the tall black man looked around, discerned the problem, and complied at once by bending his knees and dropping himself lower—just as all voices fell completely silent and Martin Luther King poised for an instant behind the magic silver cylinder, preparing to open his mouth and speak to the multitude. And maybe, I told myself happily, to the world.

The cameraman found himself with an unblocked avenue straight to his target.

"There!" My not-altogether-unkind murmur was for his ears only. "Get your pictures now, Mister. But will you please for heaven's sake stop being so rude!"

*   *   *

END OF PART SEVEN

PART EIGHT

THE WALK OUT

35.

"Let us have faith that right makes might; and in that faith
let us, to the end, dare to do our duty as we understand it."
—Abraham Lincoln
(One of GG.'s chief heroes)

Dr. King's message to us before the march lacked much of his customary flair for eloquent oratory. He kept it brief, as if he were constantly aware the sun was already at its zenith and we still had those eleven miles to cover before darkness fell around six. It felt as if he had decided there was insufficient time, really, for the careful building of phrase upon phrase before reaching and delivering at last the magnificent emotional climax to a speech. It was the skill he had over the years mastered so well, and you knew it was coming. Or maybe not? Maybe he was conserving as much energy as possible for the long hike ahead.

In those stentorian tones that suddenly seemed anomalous to one with so small a frame, he spoke to us of what he called "creative dissatisfaction," and of what he believed to be the "redemptive power of unmerited suffering." On a sudden impulse, I took from my shoulder bag my ballpoint pen and my little blue notebook. I felt a friendly invisible hand pushing on my waist from behind so I could brace my elbow against the wall and write without falling. As I scratched out the shorthand characters of his sentences on blank pages in my little blue notebook, Dr. King took the time to make another point.

"Resistance and nonviolence are not in themselves good. There is another element in our struggle that makes our resistance and nonviolence truly meaningful. That element is reconciliation. Our ultimate end must be the creation of the beloved community. The tactics of nonviolence without the spirit of nonviolence could become a new kind of violence!"

As I lifted my head from the page for a quick moment, I beheld at the other end of the Chapel front steps a Negro father in faded work clothes standing on the abutment opposite to mine. He was lifting his tiny son to his shoulder so the child could better see with his own eyes the head of the famous personage, the peaceful man who stood there speaking in the midst of the crowd on the steps. So the child could remember this special day all his life, long after the rest of us, I thought philosophically, are dead and gone.

High praise came next from Dr. King for President Johnson's speech to Congress the previous Monday, in which the president had outlined his proposed voting rights legislation. "He spoke out of his heart. Never before has a president of our nation spoken more passionately, more eloquently, more unequivocally and more sincerely of the cause of civil rights," Dr. King said.

I had always marveled at this man's ability to blend so fittingly the emotional delivery of the Southern evangelical minister with the logical conclusions and rhetoric of the Northern university graduate's trained mind. But today his deep baritone voice seemed a little on the tired side. Today too he got none of the verbal reinforcement from his listeners that he usually got when addressing Southern, largely black, congregations. The "that's right!" and the "yes, Lord!" punctuating each sentence as it ended, were always there, in a church, delivered unabashedly by a select few of his more elderly parishioners.

Judging by the looks of us gathered here this morning, we were predominantly white; Northern white. We considered ourselves too disciplined to resort to vocal chorusing. We were too inhibited, too staid, to help our soloist out except by applauding with our hands. As he spoke of what we were about to do, the measured, drawn-out cadences that were part of his charisma, I noted, were occasionally there: "We're on the move, *now*! Nothing can *stop us now*!" But always and unfailingly, there was the one attribute I secretly admired most of all about this man of destiny as he spoke to us: his perfect grammar and flawless syntax.

Dr. King was nearing the end of his speech, and his voice became suddenly stronger, his words more robust, emphasized as they were in all the right places. "We go today in *peace* and love, *no guns* in our hands! Our powerful weapons are the *voices,* the *feet,* and the *bodies* of dedicated, united people! Living *witnesses,* moving without rest toward a just goal! Greater tyrants than Southern *segregationists* have been subdued and defeated by *this* form of struggle!" How many times has he had to utter these self-same lyrics, I wondered. Yet he does it so well.

And he further suggested that the march from Selma to Montgomery could well turn out to be as important an event in American history as Gandhi's salt-march to the sea in March of 1930 was, in the history of India. And hearing this supposition, I was reminded of my own mental analogy made the day before in Adelaide Sims' peaceful apartment; the one comparing Selma to Gettysburg. *Suppose we, Martin Luther King and I, turn out to be right?*

"This is *America's* cause! We are standing together to make it *clear*—that we are determined—to make *brotherhood*—a reality for *all* men! We are *tired* of waiting! We have waited three hundred and forty-five *years* for freedom—and the day is at hand! *Now* is the time to make Alabama—the heart of *Dixie*—a place of good will!"

As I scribbled, I got a lump in my throat and tears in my eyes. *Aren't I lucky to have learned Gregg shorthand so well?*

And then he compared what we were about to do with the flight of the children of Israel through the parted waters of the Red Sea and on to the Promised Land. And then he told us, and he was all Southern evangelist now:

So walk together, children, don't you get *weary!* And it will lead *you*—to the Promised Land!"

His speech was now over without a doubt. As I thrust notebook and pen back into my shoulder bag and prepared for action, the waiting crowd went wild. We clapped long and hard, those of us who had the use of two hands. And then, apparently following Dr. King's example though I could not see further down his body than his head, the great mass of blacks and whites gathered before Brown's Chapel and covering the road on either side as far as I could see, responded. They crossed their arms over their stomachs in the tradition of the civil rights movement, borrowed from some fundamentalist religious custom, I had been told. They joined hands with their neighbors, ready with similarly crossed arms on either side, so that lengthy, integrated lines were formed spontaneously all over the area.

Swaying slowly from side to side in undulating waves of opposing motion, we rendered "We Shall Overcome" with all the zeal and determination of the mass meeting held inside this same building last evening. From my raised position on the concrete abutment I joined in, trying to sing loud enough for both myself and the busy cameraman. The difference in our delivery this time was that we poured our hearts out not merely for our own jubilation. Not even for the benefit oft the ever-present eyes and ears of the television equipment we knew would be all around us this morning. We sang, this time, for our leader. So he would know without any doubt that we stood staunchly behind him; that we intended to march into the gates of Hell itself, if necessary, to prove our commitment to his cause.

Last night's hundreds of voices had become today's thousands, ringing out in awesome unison over the humble houses and schools and stores of Selma's Negro Compound. More tears welled up in adult eyes as we sang. How could we hold them back as we stood face-to-face with this courageous and highly principled human being upon the steps of Brown's Chapel? Not a kleenex nor a fist was raised to wipe the tears away. To do so before the end of the song would be to break not only the physical bond but also the spiritual one.

I had felt this peculiar surging in my throat many times before. During a burst of patriotism, while watching the American flag go by during a parade. Singing "America The Beautiful" at a church service. Listening to the words at the base of the Statue of Liberty, set to music. "Send me your poor, your tired, oppressed, your hungry masses yearning to breathe free . . . !"

I knew as I sang that this was the mark of the True Believer, this choking up with joy at the sight or sound of some particularly cherished shibboleth. Like the salivating of Pavlov's dogs at the ring of their food bell. But I had never cared, when it came to my much-loved democracy; and I didn't care now. Even the morosely silent cameraman at my elbow could not dismay me for long.

"Oh-h, deep in my heart,
"I do believe . . . . !"
"We shall overcome some day!"

A low voice cut through the hush that followed the last fading notes of the song. "Why'd you stop singing? You all get seasick?" It was the NBC cameraman, still insolent, still refusing to give up his insults.

I burst out laughing almost in his face, a tiny explosion of mirth far back in my throat. "I gotta tell you, you really are the only rude person I've met since I left home three days ago," I said to the bent-over cameraman beside me. I shook my head in disbelief, but I was now not the least bit angry. Instead, I felt sorry for him.

Someone came forward from the melange of people on the steps as soon as the song was over. The man draped Hawaiian leis of fresh flowers around the necks of Dr. King and several of his colleagues, none of whom I recognized but who were obviously prominent figures of some sort in their own right. Most of the five or six men who received the garlands were white, and therefore, I deduced, were from somewhere up North. One old gentleman, salt-and-pepper-bewhiskered and no taller than Martin Luther King, stood next to him. He wore a *yarmulke* like Albert's and was obviously also a rabbi.

Upon orders from one of Dr. King's lieutenants, the mass exodus gathered below the steps and on the steps began moving as if one from the churchyard to the appointed spot further down Sylvan Street where other march marshalls with yellow armbands were waiting. We were to form up there, behind a rope strung between two barrels. We were to line up, row upon row, eight marchers to each line, as quickly as possible, until everyone had found a niche. Only then would we be able to begin the march.

At the request of newspaper photographers, Dr. King and his colleagues remained behind near the microphone to pose for group shots. The flashbulbs of thirsty cameras sparked in the hazy air like fireflies. As the steps began to be cleared off of the ordinary participants, who were hurrying now to get in line, I looked over and observed that Albert Friedlander had lingered behind with the dignitaries. To my astonishment, someone had put a lei around *his* neck, as well! In vain I sought to catch his eye in order to signal to him, "Let's go!" But he neither glanced my way nor appeared to have any intention of hurrying.

My abutment companions for the speech having also departed, the NBC cameraman and I had been left alone on our perch. His responsibility was over for now. He began to ready his equipment for moving on.

"Well?" I said sarcastically, feeling that a comment of some kind was in order. "You got your pictures, didn't you? Maybe you guys need *us,* too!" Could I actually have said that? To a stranger, and with such derisiveness?

Scarcely looking in my direction as he folded his tripod, he took me off guard by mumbling a few words of appreciation. "Yeah, Thanks. You were a great little assistant. Wish I had you with me on my next assignment."

"That's okay. You know, we civil rights advocates are not so bad."

I hadn't meant to sound as harsh as it came out, however. It was just that a residue of the disciple's fervor still burned in my heart from the song we had just sung, and this fellow here was as good a place as any to start practicing reconciliation. I thrust out my arm to indicate the famous black figure still standing on the steps, being photographed shaking hands with each of the Northerners. Including Albert!

I said, "In case you don't know, 'this guy,' as you call him, has a name. And not just a first one, but a middle and last one too. He's Martin Luther King." I said it deliberately, calmly, in no rush to get through. "*Doctor* Martin Luther King. *Junior.* Please try not to forget it, and show him some respect."

"I know his name." Indignation was printed upon his pudgy face as he turned to face me. "Why do you think I'm here?"

"Gotta go. Been nice knowing you." Jumping down from the abutment without waiting for further response, I went to retrieve my knapsack where my two schoolteacher friends had left it leaning against the bricks of Brown's Chapel. Earlier they had signaled their intention to wait for me there, but I had been able to discern from above that the lines behind the barrels were already several dozen rows deep. It would have been unfair to have held these two up while I waited to see what the rabbi's plans were, so I had thanked them with a wave, and motioned to them to go ahead without me.

Down from my perch now, I looked again toward the Chapel steps wistfully, wondering just what I should do now. And there was that impossible Albert, the flowers still around his neck, gesticulating at me from halfway up the steps. His mouthed one-word message was as plain to me as mine had previously been to him:

"Wait!"

Alternating between hope and despair, I dutifully bucked the flow of the crowd hurrying past me in the other direction. I finally reached the relative isolation of the ancient shade tree that grew in the front yard at the far right corner of the maroon-brick Chapel. Unconcerned with any problems of mine, the massive trunk of the tree soared far upward, spreading its green-sprouted limbs in especially lofty disdain above all the confusion. I stood there, wondering what was going to happen to me next.

The Reverend Nancy Thomas, my bedmate from last night, came scurrying past me, pausing only long enough to tell me she was going ahead with some people she had met on the Chapel steps while waiting for Dr. King to appear.

"I saw you standing up there, Gwen, big as life, directing traffic!" she said, still overcome with enthusiasm. "Listen—we're so anxious to get started. You really don't mind if we don't wait?" Her newer friends were jiggling impatiently at her sides, worried about being too far back in the lines. And to think, I had been worried that *she* would hold *me* back!

"Of course not," I replied. "We'll surely run into each other on the road, Nancy. Good luck!" And she was gone.

Peter appeared in front of me next. Peter, my young friend from the bus and the breakfast church, whom I had sensed this morning I would never see again. *So much for my intuitions!*

"Aren't you coming, Gwen? You can go with us!" Peter called out, stopping short in front of me. "We'll take turns carrying your gear for you, won't we, fellows?" Even this morning he had not been so animated, so brimming over with excitement.

"Thank you, thank you, Pete!" I said. I patted his arm and urged him on. "You go ahead. I have to wait for the rabbi. I'll watch for you on the road!" He hugged me quickly. And then he too was gone.

So much for most friendships, here in this unlikely Shangri-la, I thought. An instantaneous bonding of hearts, and at the same time, necessarily casual affairs. For the most part, these faces belonged only to this world, not to the one I would return to. I told myself I should not try to hang on, not to any of them. I had to settle for remembering these Selma acquaintances as long as I lived.

Though of course, you have to accept it: as the years take their toll later on, you probably won't be able to recall their dear faces. And they, for their part, won't remember yours.

* * *

36.

"Don't you understand? These things (equal rights) take time! They can't be rushed!"
—Charles Paine,* brother-in-law
(Post-Selma Comments from one of the folks back home)

Once again, to my dismay, I stood waiting, this time with a nagging sense of something akin to annoyance. It was impossible to ever be fully annoyed with the likes of Albert Friedlander, however. And besides, what was the use? Whether I marched one hundred rows to the rear, or two hundred, the scenery would all be the same. He'd surely be coming along any minute; and weren't lots and lots of march recruits still pouring past me?

The flashbulbs on the steps continued to pop. The featured players of the drama chatted congenially with one another all the while, pretending to ignore the cameras for some media-imposed group shots. Meanwhile, the sea of prospective foot-soldiers continued its tidal current unabated. Individuals, or couples, or whole families with parents and several young children, were all hastening briskly toward the rear to my left, looking to find places in the ever-lengthening line. Their still-glowing faces as they surged past me were intent upon their mission of at last getting this happening underway.

I began telling myself that the stream of live bodies could not continue passing by me in these numbers forever. If Albert didn't come soon, then both of us would have to be walking at the very end. And that wasn't fair! To be in Selma so long ahead of time, since early yesterday, and now, to be left for last? To have to walk back past that multitude of eager hundreds, many of them late-comers, before my friend and I could hope to find ourselves a place! Worse, being at the tail end also meant being sitting ducks for any redneck crazies who wanted to harass our heels. Let someone with more courage than I bring up the rear!

But the longer I felt sorry for myself, the more unconcerned the conglomeration of dignitaries on the top of the steps seemed to be about the fact that the start of our long walk was at hand. At least we all hoped, and many prayed, that the line of eight across would be long. I had assumed that Dr. King, during his unusually short speech, had been acutely aware of the lateness of the hour and the need to get going. But newspaper reporters were swarming up the steps, now that the picture-taking was over and the still cameras gone. They were asking questions I couldn't hear, putting them to Dr. King and another Negro man standing beside him and some of the white Northerners. The dignitaries all stood in a close cluster, unsmiling, looking patiently solemn in their black all-weather coats and the incongruous leis around their necks. Even Albert in his black suit jacket was being interviewed by a reporter. I had to hand it to him, the man had—what was that Hebrew word I had heard often lately? *Chutzpah!*

Sighing in resignation, I lowered my knapsack to the ground and hunched my shoulders against the cold shade under the tree. I did not want to go on without Albert, my rabbi friend, so why fight it? It would simply be no fun without him. So we'd be in the last row of the march; what of it? *The soldiers will be there, remember? The federalized National Guard.*

Besides, since I'd seen Albert last, he might have decided to try for a plane back to New York tonight, so he could go back home with his fellow rabbis. Maybe he had already managed to get a reservation, and that is what had made him so late this morning. In that event, he'd have to get the sleeping bag back to me sometime today. There would be no other opportunity. And if I lost sight of him now, in this mob, I had a feeling I'd never find him again. And where was the borrowed sleeping bag, anyway? Albert Friedlander standing up there, talking freely with both hands to a reporter, certainly didn't have it with him, not that I could see.

I became aware just then of a large trash can standing not far from the trunk of the tree, its contents overflowing. Some unknown dispenser of *manna*, I noticed all at once, had placed a giant-sized package of supermarket doughnuts, with only a couple of them removed from under the cellophane, on the very top of the trash. I consulted my watch. Almost noon. It had already been four hours since I'd eaten breakfast.

I remembered my cautionary comment to Nancy Thomas last night about being sure to eat breakfast before the march. And here it was, almost lunchtime, and all I had with me in the way of provisions was the can of Metrecal Powder my husband Bill had put into my knapsack. Heaven only knew when I, and Albert too, would eat again—and my rule was to always think ahead. Trusting to Providence, as my rabbi friend had an understandable penchant for doing, should never be carried too far. I, the down-to-earth agnostic, would have to look out for us both.

Hoping no one was noticing—I told myself that surely everyone's attention was directed elsewhere—I whipped out and unfolded the brown paper bag I had decided to store in my knapsack that morning. I picked up the package of doughnuts and deposited it hurriedly in the bottom of my paper bag. What's this? More goodies! An unopened package of sandwich cookies reposed on the trash can beneath where the doughnuts had been, and without a moment's hesitation or look around, I added them to my cache. *When I think of all the times I've scolded my poor little Scotty for being a trash-picker!*

Provisions clutched to my bosom, I looked over to see that the dignitaries, all of them and Albert with them, were at last ready to begin their descent of the steps. Martin Luther King was flanked by two of the visiting white men, the one with the gray facial whiskers and *yarmulke*, and another in fedora hat and sunglasses and who I saw now was not white, but an extremely light-skinned Negro. Three more white faces, all male, and two black ones, a man and a woman, were pressing up close behind them. The black man, I recognized now, was Ralph Abernathy, Dr. King's second-in-command. He wore an olive-drab Army jacket and a matching cap with ear flaps snapped up. Albert Friedlander brought up the rear, his own black cap topping a face that seemed on the verge of an enormous grin. The face was signaling a message to me. What was it? Was it . . . ?

Get ready!

The entire group of nine plunged forward off the steps into the rolling TV cameras, and then was steered forward by two yellow-banded marshalls. But not to the left, not as I would have expected, in the direction of the barrels indicating the front of the march line waiting in the middle of Sylvan Street. To the right, instead, straight past where I stood waiting beneath the branches of the arching tree! Sensing something big was about to happen, I grabbed up my knapsack just as Albert, walking in the end of the third row, whipped out one hand, seized my wrist in a hard grip, and pulled me into line beside him.

"Look like you're somebody!" he hissed out of the side of his mouth, and seeing my arms were loaded, he dropped my wrist to seize the knapsack. My sleeping bag, tightly rolled and tied, swung from his other hand along with his shaving kit.

Somebody important, he meant.

"I don't know how!" I moaned back, *sotto voce*. I honestly didn't think I did. But wait! I'd acted in all those amateur plays back home, hadn't I? I ought to be up to a simple challenge like this. My legs obeying mechanically, I took a place beside the rabbi, one that had magically opened there for me.

Why should I be so surprised? Hadn't this man easily maneuvered me to a seat at the front of the bus when we first met? But this? This was special privilege! Completely undeserved, at least on my part. Unmerited rewards would more than cancel out the redemptive power of unmerited suffering, I felt almost certain of that. But then a little voice within me, the one I thought of as my Scarlett O'Hara voice, said, *"Why don't you just shut up, Gwennie, and walk!"*

Much as I loved being there in one of the front rows of the Selma march, however, it really wasn't fair. I had done nothing to deserve it.

Brought to a halt by the monitors in the middle of the street a hundred yards or so ahead of the rank and file, we were quickly joined by twenty or thirty Negroes who had been held in a group on the sidelines, waiting for just this development. Just as quickly, the combined group was organized by marshall leaders Jim Bevall and Andy Young into several rows of eight and brought up behind us. Miracle of miracles, I now found myself in the third row four places in from the left, in the same position held by Martin Luther King in the front row! No one questioned my presence there, nor lifted so much as an eyebrow. Of course! They all assumed I was with Albert, who waited beside me in the fourth place from the end! I was gradually realizing that Rabbi Friedlander must be more of a "somebody" than I had dreamed.

An enormously tall youth in ragged overalls and an ebony skin took his place to the left of me. With his rough clothes and kinky, untrimmed hair he looked like a "nobody" too, and I felt more at ease and less of a hypocrite. Positioned just in front of me, his at least six-feet of height blocking Dr. King from my view, was one of the white Northerners, a garland of what looked like the same white frangipani flowers encircling his neck. A slim and distinguished-looking black woman in her thirties or forties, also be-flowered, waited to his immediate right. Albert Friedlander stood to my right, my knapsack straps already fastened to his shoulders. At his instructions while we waited, I moved behind him and hastily stowed his shaving kit and the paper grocery bag containing my food finds inside the top of the knapsack. I tied the tightly rolled-up sleeping bag on below.

"We'll take turns carrying it, I promise," Albert assured me when I protested his bearing all the burden. "But Gwen, it's important that we have both hands free." To defend ourselves? But no, Rev. Bevall had told us, and he had been very emphatic about that, "Don't, whatever happens to you, throw up your hands!"

On either side of us and to the rear, we could see and hear the march marshalls. They were bringing up the already-formed lines of ordinary citizens behind us into place at our rear, exhorting them forward with the repeated order: "Eight across! No more than eight to a row! Move it up quickly, please!" Eagerly those rows upon rows of others who had been waiting so patiently for so long came forward, and the two pieces of the plan were joined together now, and ready to step off.

Catching glimpses between the shoulders of the people lined up in front of me, I saw that a special car with a large TV camera attached to its rear had moved into position several yards in front of the first row of dignitaries. CBS this time! To the left of this, on the edge of the shabby asphalt paving, an Alabama State Patrol car waited in silence, blue light glowing motionless on its roof, and the two ominous words "State Trooper" printed in big letters across the grey lid of its trunk. The following eyes of the trooper standing beside it gave no clue as to what he was thinking.

*   *   *

<h1 style="text-align:center">37.</h1>

"Live pure, speak true, right the wrong, follow the King—else wherefore born?"

—Alfred Lord Tennyson
(From my Words To Live By)

And then, in a matter of only seconds it seemed after the long delay, some signal must have been given by the marshalls. Because the marchers in the two front rows stepped off, walking gracefully, shoulder-to-shoulder, with no need for words. The eight in our third row were right behind them; others closing ranks close behind us. Down Sylvan, the street that ran in front of both Brown's Chapel and the George Washington Carver Homes, we went. Up to and through a traffic signal no one was paying any attention to, least of all the two uniformed policemen who stood in the middle of the street waving us on, looking eager to get rid of us. Patrol cars blocked off empty Selma Avenue on each side of us as we crossed the intersection. Heartened by these hints of official concurrence and citizen disinterest, our orderly lines of marchers stepped more resolutely now, one person neatly behind the one ahead, the participants calling quietly, gleefully to one another on all sides. All of us happy to be at last on our way, no matter what lay ahead.

Every few rows a marshall wearing the identifying yellow armband strode confidently outside the main body of the march. Moving forward, falling back; ever watchful of his charges, wary of any unusual circumstance that might signal trouble. Strong, muscular young men, some of them white but most of them black. All of them seemed to be veterans of the civil rights movement. Many were graduates, I had learned, of the lunch-counter sit-ins and the Freedom Rides of the late fifties and early sixties.

If any of us were accosted or attacked, we had been told by Rev. Andrew Young at the mass meeting last night, march marshalls would be there instantly to assist us. The marshall nearest me, the young black man in the green knit cap stationed just outside the front row, looked to be at least seven feet tall, with huge biceps on his upper arms. The very sight of him in his denim trousers and flannel shirt made me feel instantly secure.

The TV camera on the special car ahead of us stared down from above us as we walked. The driver was obviously pacing his vehicle to stay a consistent distance a few yards ahead of the first row. Behind that dark round eye, I thought, lay perhaps my family: my husband and my children. Maybe my relatives, a few of them, and a few of my friends. Perhaps fellow students and co-workers at the University of Pennsylvania. Edna, my housekeeper and friend? I hoped so. Members of the Human Relations Conference back home, surely. A lot of people would be leaving church at this hour. Or simply wouldn't be interested. My friend Jim Clemson would of course not be watching, I could count on that. His mother, an unadulterated racist, would never stand for it.

"We don't need people who want to show off and get on CBS television," Rev.Bevall had said to us yesterday. I cringed, remembering, and ducked my head behind the tall figure just in front of me, the white man wearing one of the colorful leis around his neck.

Down the two blocks remaining to get out of Selma's Negro Compound we walked in our orderly lines. And then we came to a stop at another traffic signal, the intersection of Sylvan and Water, according to the crossed street signs. And there we came to a stop and waited. It seemed obvious we were about to penetrate the "white" section of town. Better-kept store fronts stood on either side. A couple of white onlookers had turned up for the first time, standing on the corner to stare at us.

Somewhere here, I knew, a barricade had stood until late Friday night, holding back those previous marchers of the two weeks before; marking the point beyond which Alabama power and justice had said they could not go. But the barricade had been removed by federal court order.

Since the beginning, the eight men in the front row, Dr. King, Rev. Abernathy, and the six others I did not recognize, had walked with elbows linked as a symbol of unity. And now, sensing that a change of some magnitude was about to occur, those in the second row behind them reached out and grasped the hands of their fellows on either side. Our row of eight followed suit. The gesture must have swept backward through the ranks. In my mind's eye I could picture those many thousands of clasped palms behind me. Was this the reason Albert Friedlander had insisted our hands should be unencumbered? Not to defend ourselves, not at all. Non-violence techniques, I knew by now, would not permit that.

Nor even to protect our bodies from harm if we fell. Rather, so that all of us could face the anger and hostility of white Selma in a state of spiritual and physical community. Had ever an army this large gone forth thus in all the history of mankind? Holding hands?

To clasp my friend Albert's left hand in my right one seemed somehow as natural to me as breathing. But stealing a peek to my left, I was chagrined to see that my left hand looked dwarfed and sickly white and somehow incongruous in the large and ebony-brown grip of the Negro boy on the other side of me. Close ahead, beneath one arm of the tall man waiting directly in front of me, I could sometimes spot Martin Luther King's suited elbows. Since his forearms were linked around the elbows of the man on either side, it was all I could see of him. He was not very big, this Nobel Peace Prize winner, I was reminded once again.

Nor were the two Northerners who flanked him to his left. Their own small statures, along with Ralph Abernathy's middle-sized bulk to his right, afforded our leader no great amount of bodily protection. I pictured Dr. King as he must appear in the lens of that television camera out in front of us: fragile and innocuous in the dark suit with the delicate pink-and-white blossoms strung around his neck and hanging across his chest. He must come across to watchers as very vulnerable to attack, as well. What must he be thinking at this moment, in the vanguard of this wave of committed but relatively untrained men and women of both races?

Could he see himself as the amasser of a mindless human machine from which there was now absolutely no retreat? A marked man, centered in a bull's eye of frangipani blossoms; about to be swept along to his death by the machine's inexorable inertia? How could he help but be frightened? Over the past eight or nine years, while I had been living my safe suburban life, he had been threatened and punched and thrown in jails and stabbed with scissors and his house had been bombed and his phone had been tapped. And this latest of Martin Luther King's ventures had brought some sections of the South to a fever pitch of hatred, much of it aimed at him as personally responsible for lighting the flames of discontent, and continuing to stoke the fire.

Someone ought to shoot that man! My father-in-law, back in Woodbury, New Jersey had cried out a few months ago. We, my four children and I, were in his living room, watching Dr. King briefly explain his theories of non-violence on a TV news broadcast. "*If you say things like that in front of my kids, we'll never come back here again,*" I said to Bill's father. I had never spoken up to him before, but this was too much.

Out here today, I found it too horrifying to consider further the possibility of someone's making an attempt on Dr. King's life. And even more horrifying a matter to contemplate with me walking only two rows behind him and in the exact same file. A gunshot might miss . . .

I made myself concentrate hard instead on the two hands I was holding. Albert's, on my right: the hand of my friend, warm and reassuring, palm pressed unreservedly against mine as if it were molded there. A Jewish hand, this; a great deal like my own in both size and appearance.

In contrast, on my left, the Negro boy's hand, big and dark-skinned and rough with callouses, the lank fingers sweating and seeming to swallow up my own pitiful pinky-beige ones in their grasp. He had taken my hand and was holding it the way I remembered young lovers of puberty age did: with our fingers intertwined. Was he embarrassed, as I was, by the contact?

I shot the boy's face a look where it towered above me and shyly he looked back. It was an open face, and among the blackest I'd ever seen. A face completely lacking in sophistication. Was he a farm boy, perhaps? From somewhere outside Selma? He lacked the obvious vitality and self-confidence of Adelaide's town-reared teenagers. Was he scared at what he was doing here? He, along with Martin Luther King, had every reason to be. He had probably lived in this area all his life and knew nothing else. Could he have ever even so much as touched the hand of a white woman before? Did it concern this gangling lad in the long-legged overalls that white Alabama, out there on Water Avenue, would surely notice his physical contact with me, and take offense? (Or, since I was plainly a "white nigger", maybe I didn't count!)

I didn't even know this boy's name. How stupid, how thoughtless of me not to have asked when I had the opportunity. It was as if he didn't have one. I was as guilty as all those others I had criticized. In my mind, he must have been a "nobody," so I hadn't asked, and now it was too late. No one was saying anything as we all poised expectantly, waiting for some invisible authority to start us moving once more, around the corner and onto Water Street.

Buried in that press of waiting bodies, my eyes were drawn again toward my left hand, linked so strangely with the brown one. By turning my gaze surreptitiously to one side, I could study them, and observe my own five fingernails stark and pink against the knuckles of his right hand. "Black and white together," we had all espoused loudly in song over the past two days, and here it was, right here. The physical reality. The hint of the phenomenon most whites claimed was their biggest fear. This, in spite of all the living evidences, as Dick Gregory had pointed out last evening, of "integration after dark." For all I knew, this de facto integration was feared by many black parents as well: the physical thing, male-and-female skin-on-skin, black-and-white-together, with all the sexual overtones and genetic innuendoes implied by the sight of it.

In seconds now we would be walking down one of the main streets of Selma, Alabama, this nameless black boy and I, holding hands for all the world to see if it wanted to. And there was nothing in the least bit sexual about it. We would be doing it because—well, because it was our right, wasn't it? Because we needed to. It would help us to get through the fear, wouldn't it? And it didn't feel bad, really. Not bad at all.

I'd wipe off my hand. That was what my engineer friend Jim Clemson had said to me only three days ago. *Sure, I'd shake hands with him, but then I'd have to put my hand behind my back and wipe it off.* Suddenly reminded of that, and of the boy's hand clasping mine, and of what Unity had once taught me about the truth of skin color, I wanted to laugh out loud into the pregnant silence.

I was twelve in 1942. A World War had begun the previous December, expanding my child's vistas far beyond my wildest imaginings. I was scrubbing the kitchen floor that morning in place of Unity, who usually did it; and she was looking on, supervising but not nagging. She had taken my baby sister Lynnie's freshly laundered diapers off the outside line. She was folding the white cotton rectangles into thirds and stacking them onto the kitchen table and spreading them neatly into place with her lighter brown palms. As I dipped the scrub brush again and again into the bucket of suds and sloshed water around, Unity and I held another of our philosophical conversations about race.

This time it was about discrimination in the United States Navy, and the related perpetuation of poverty among Negroes back home. Though those were not the words we used. I was only twelve, remember? And something in my voice as I more than once said "colored people" (the term I had been supplied at a much earlier age by my Missouri-bred parents) must have given Unity the impression I thought myself to be superior. Though I truly hadn't meant to sound that way.

"Come here, Gwennie. I want to show you something." Her brown face is screwed up with disapproval. Mystified by the sternness in her command, I get up from my hands and knees and slowly obey. She has never, to my recollection, been angry at me before. What had I done?

"See there, girl!"

Reaching out, she grasps my damp hand and plunks it down on the pile of chloroxed and sun-dried diapers, placing her own fingers on my wrist to hold it there. "These di-pers is white. White, you aint!"

Why, she's right! My hand seems a dingy-pink intruder atop the whiteness of those diapers. On the other hand, Unity's dark brown skin color, the fingers like polished walnut on top and tipped by pearly-tan nails, makes an exciting color contrast.

I see that. I want only to make amends for any hurt I have unwittingly caused my friend.

"But if I'm not white," I come back at her, trying desperately to understand her exact meaning, "what color am I?"

"You be colored! Same as us!" She was absolutely right. Why had I never noticed it before? That I was colored too? I look at the two hands again, hers and mine, where they repose against the pile of clean baby diapers. I am certainly not white! Unity draws her hand away, a sign that I am free to go.

"Okay. So I shouldn't say 'colored' any more. And I won't. But what should I say, Unity? When we talk about—the problem, I mean?" Surely she didn't mean we should stop talking about—the problem. "Should I be saying "nee-groes'?"

Back came the answer, without hesitation. "Nig-goes is what we be, Gwennie. Not nee-groes, mind you. That bees stuck-up. We be Nig-groes."

Unity hadn't lived to the turbulent nineteen-sixties, to see her people turn "black and beautiful;" nor to see her little friend Gwennie on CBS-TV marching behind Martin Luther King. She, along with my Republican, fair-minded father, had died in the quiet and uncaring fifties. She suffered a stroke about the same time as he did, when I was twenty-five. I had gone to visit her on her little farm in Swedesboro eight miles away, and had found her lying partially paralyzed on a rusty bedstead in a room with the paint peeling from yellowed walls. The real shocker, however, was that the four legs of the bed stood on a dirt floor. *A dirt floor! When she had scrubbed so much linoleum in the houses of white women!*

She had died soon after my visit. But she had left me indelible memories, she had made gifts to me of privileged glimpses, now and then, into one noble Nig-gro's heart. And especially the memory of that work-worn colored hand, pressing with loving forcefulness onto my soft, young, ignorant, also-colored one.

*   *   *

38.

"Yes, if you want to, say that I was a drum major. Say that I was a drum major for justice. Say that I was a drum major for peace. Say that I was a drum major for righteousness . . . . ! just want to leave a committed life behind."

—Martin Luther King, Jr.
(GG's Words To Live By)

We were still waiting for the signal from the SCLC marshalls to take up the march again.

"What's your name?" I asked in a hoarse undertone, out of the side of my mouth. I had to know. As a salute to Unity who had taught me everything I knew about skin color, this boy could stay beside me no longer without being identified.

He looked down at me, startled. He mumbled something, between fleshy lips that scarcely moved.

"What's your *name*?" A half-whisper this time, hoping my voice would not carry beyond his ears to the others waiting all around and thereby spoil the mood.

"James." he mumbled. Or I thought that's what he said. James who? But it made no matter.

"Hi, James. I'm Gwen."

And then all of a sudden Albert squeezed my hand hard as if to say, Hang on, girl, here we go, and the two lines in front of us started up again. Right wheel onto Water Avenue in a sweeping arc, one behind another in orderly rows. None of us worried about staying in step but most did automatically; not so much marching as stepping rapidly along. Chins up; every eye looking forward now and trying to stay pinned on the back and shoulders of the marcher just ahead. We were hushed and sober; not exactly fearful, but wary.

Halfway around the corner, I grabbed a quick look to my right and back down the street we had just left. Expecting to spot the last row of marchers, I had to gasp at what I saw.

"Albert! James! There's no end in sight!" I lost a step and had to skip once to get back into rhythm with my two companions. "They're still coming, from 'way back up Sylvan Street! It must be a mile long, at least!"

Taking my hyperbole at face value, the rabbi nodded his head once in my direction, eyes glinting behind his glasses in a message of supreme satisfaction. I knew him well enough by now to know the nod of his head meant *"Good!"*

The Selma police had halted traffic completely in this part of the business district to let us go by. It must be just about noon, time for churches to be letting out, I figured. But because my hands were still being clasped by Albert and James, I was unable to look at my watch for confirmation. We stepped firmly along, straight down the middle of Water Street now, toward the business district of the city. A couple of white men in business suits stood at curbside taking our pictures with snapshot cameras. So later, I assumed, they could pick out familiar Negroes. Or worse, Adelaide Sims had told us. So they could carry out their threats to dismiss people from jobs after all this was over. Walking faster now. Closed stores and empty offices went past in a blur of bricks and concrete and glass and siding, all of which combined to make up what seemed to me a Southern version of the commercial blocks of Woodbury, the town where I grew up in New Jersey. Business establishments there were also closed on Sunday because of the so-called "Blue Laws."

White citizens of Selma had not turned out in strength, at least not yet. More were in evidence, however. Some in their dress-up clothes paused on the sidewalk to watch us go by. They were standing there casually, so as not to lend dignity to the occasion. As if they had found themselves there at this time and place quite by coincidence.

Why had I expected to see large numbers of them lined up as if for a parade? I felt a twinge of disappointment at their small numbers—a feeling quickly replaced by relief as I caught the expression of naked hatred on the faces of a middle-aged man and woman sitting atop the hood of their late-model car parked at curbside. I faced my own eyes forward again, feeling real apprehension for the first time since I had come here, and brought my step into closer synchronization with Albert Friedlander's and the boy James' feet, whose hands I still held.

My uneasiness was quickly replaced by poignant regret. How sad there was no music to see us off, keep us in step, bolster our courage! A little Sousa would have been perfect just now. After all these years, I was finally getting to march. And there was no Sousa, nor anything else, to step to.

Silently I hummed the chorus in my head from "Stars And Stripes Forever" and included, equally silent, the silly ditty from my childhood that went with the chorus: *Be kind to your web-footed friends, for a duck may be somebody's mother. Remember your friends in the swamp, where the weather is always damp . . . .* But the melody and the mood didn't fit the pace, not for this kind of walk. It was too absurd for the occasion, I analyzed to myself, and altogether too martial. We needed something much more—well, elevating.

Wouldn't you know, Gwen Gain, that when your big chance finally came to be in a marching band, it would be this way? No music. No instruments. But a marching band, nonetheless.

I guessed that the uniformed troopers leading us down Water Avenue in their highway patrol cars were doing this particular job under protest. Not the way the police had always done it back in Woodbury at the victory parades along Broad Street when I was a child, with all of those Northern cops obviously getting a vicarious thrill out of the fact that the high school football team had made good again. And the crowds of onlookers here? They were certainly not pleased that we'd beaten them, fair and square, with that federal court order, and had a right now to celebrate.

They, the white citizens of Selma, were our opponents, and they certainly had not intended for us to win. For that matter, where were the crowds? Darting my eyes to left and right without moving my head the slightest, I was unable to pick out more than a dozen persons on the sidewalks, and most of those were playing their own game, pretending to ignore us. At least they were not being openly hostile. Maybe the truly vicious ones were waiting for us further along, in the very center of town . . . . ?

Only the muffled clomp of thousands of shoe soles hitting the worn concrete roadbed almost simultaneously seemed to announce our coming. No lights flashed; no sirens wailed. A murmur went up along the line of march, side to side, row upon row, like whisper-down-the-lane. Albert passed to me the word he had received from someone on his right. "To the left, just up ahead," he murmured to me. "It's Sheriff Clark!"

I snatched one quick, sidelong glimpse as we went by the man who had ordered the brutal attack of the horsemen, followed up with tear gas, on the Negro marchers two weeks earlier. Hatless and out of uniform, he stood well back from the curb and in front of a doorway, hands deep in his pockets as he watched lumbering past him the black-and-white behemoth he had helped create.

I knew that face well. I had seen him up close several times on my television screen back home. Most memorable had been the time he had pushed the Reverend Dr. C.T. Vivian down the court house steps. Today his rough features were blank, but the stance, certainly not that of a proud general reviewing the troops, reflected his temporary defeat. In that one glimpse, however, I had been able to determine that he was still wearing his large and infamous "Never" button in plain view. ("Over my dead body," he had once said to reporters about the possibility of Selma Negroes getting the vote.)

"Hey, lady!" Was he addressing me, that young white man peering into our front ranks from the curb's edge, running a few steps along with us, a leer twisting his mouth as he yelled directly at me, "Hey, lady, you remember to bring your diaphragm?"

His scouring eyes had been offended by the sight of a white woman hand-in-hand with a black male. He must have found in me the perfect target at whom to hurl what was to him the ultimate insult. *Ewww, how gross!* A diaphragm was the one item I'd never considered bringing with me! Not only that, but for the past three days I'd not so much as entertained one conscious erotic thought! I tore my eyes away, embarrassed for my companions, and was separated from the young white man forever by the two firm hands on either side of me, pulling me onward. We kept going, kept slapping our soles to the ancient road bed, in rhythm with all the others. One, two, three blocks of Water Avenue were behind us now. And everything was quiet.

No, wait! Music, after all! At the curb in front of a block of closed stores, a record-player had been set on a wooden chair and turned up to top volume. We could see that a long extension cord had permitted it's owner to bring the player almost to curbside. I recognized the scratchy strains of the music long before our line came abreast of the white conveyor of the message, who was defiantly standing there to guard and attend his rudimentary audio equipment.

> "Pack up all my cares and woe,
> "Here I go, Singing low.
> "Bye, "bye, blackbird . . . . !"

Good grief! Not Sousa and my swamp ducks! A guy singing to blackbirds, instead!

> "Where somebody waits for me,
> "Sugar's sweet, so is she.
> "Bye, bye, blackbird!"

Not your standard march music, and not particularly elevating, I told myself with a chuckle, but better than nothing. And this was indeed a new day, wasn't it? Scads of the people behind me were doubtless stepping to different drummers, hearing different tunes.

> "No one here can love or understand me.
> "Oh, what hard luck stories they all hand me!"

Okay, okay, so we get the message. You're kind of pathetic yourself, if you could only take a good look at yourselves . . . .
The dancing melody with the derogatory insinuations faded behind us into the distance, but the words lingered on in my memory, long after the sound was gone:

> "Make my bed and light the light.
> "I'll arrive, late tonight.
> "Blackbird, bye, bye!"

So good riddance to you, too, buddy! But someday I'll come back to Selma. To see how you, the other half, lives under freedom for everyone. When you people have been freed from the need to keep your boots on the necks of black people, once enslaved by your ancestors . . . .
We were there now! Two more blocks safely traversed, and we had arrived at Broad Street, the main thoroughfare of Selma. Pausing briefly; we ignored another spasmodic traffic signal and wheeled our lines left onto Broad behind the television news car. Vehicular traffic was blocked behind two more grey state patrol cars with Confederate flags painted on their side doors. Half a block away from us beckoned the Edmond Pettus Bridge, its shiny grey steel girders looming in two sturdy side-by-side arches into the air. Big Jim Orange, our tall front-row marshall guarding our left, whooped out softly, "Halleluia!"

My peripheral vision told me that many more onlookers were there, waiting at the intersection as we swung around the corner. Silent, sullen faces standing in clusters, watching us, staring straight at us, resenting us. All of those faces were white. Several more were sitting on the hoods of their parked cars. What was written in those faces? I wondered. Hatred? Pity? Or resignation?

Exactly one hundred years ago, in April of 1865 as the Civil War was ending, a Northern army had overrun this town and captured its strategic munitions factory. My history book at Penn had touched upon it briefly.

Doubtless that army had passed along this same street! Sure, we Yankees were back again. Some of us were probably descendents of those Union soldiers who came here before. But we came this time without guns and in peace, asking not for the spoils of war, but only for justice. Couldn't at least some of these hostile people understand that?

And so we walked out of the city of Selma, without any sort of verbal communication with our adversaries. Not a syllable nor sound had been heard since we started, except for that one blatantly mean Blackbird recording, Jim Orange's "halleluia," and our own footfalls. We walked a sizeable distance behind one television news car and three state patrol cars. The staff of the Selma Times-Journal building, to our right just before the bridge ramp, came out to watch us pass by. What would the paper say about us afterward? That we were outside agitators, of course. But also communists? Law breakers? Of course. All the ugly euphemisms for uppity blacks and their white nigger friends.

I'll be back someday, you guys! Just you try and stop me! I'm an American citizen!

Our rows of eight had to be squeezed into the two left traffic lanes of Broad Street. We walked straight on toward the narrow bridge coming up ahead, our only link with the Jefferson Davis Highway to Montgomery. This bridge was the one route, for miles, across the Alabama River, the river named Shame River by the Negroes, because of the inconsolable grief of the mythical Indian mother.

Not far from the other side of the bridge lay the spot beyond which the March 7th march of Selma Negroes had been forbidden to continue, the place where they had been brutally struck to the ground by billy-clubs, and tear-gassed, and trampled on by white policemen on horseback.

Would that be the perfect spot, I wondered with an inner thrill of fear, for a bunch of misguided, red-necked Leonidases to guard their pass? Leonidas, the Spartan king, and his two hundred ninety-nine hand-picked warriors, had held off the evil Persians at the pass at Thermopoli for days, way-back—when in four-hundred-something B.C. They had fought until every one of them, he and all his brave men, had been betrayed and had perished by the Persian sword.

Chiseled into a rock by the pass today was the message Leonidas had sent home. *"Go tell the Spartans, stranger passing by, that here, obedient to their laws, we lie."* *Our* laws, this time. The laws of the United States, backed up by the most splendid Constitution ever written. Even if it had indeed left out not only the Negro slaves when it was first approved by the thirteen states, but the women of both races as well. *Funny, the things you think about when . . .*

Where, oh, where were those federalized National Guard troops President Johnson had promised to send to Selma to guard us?

Squeezed into a single lane of the roadbed now, the left one, we marchers felt a slight slope heading directly upward beneath our feet. Still linked to each other's elbows or clutching each other's hands, we were shoulder pressed close to shoulder now. Once we were on the roadbed of the bridge, it rose in a sharp incline, blocking our view completely of what lay beyond. I could have seen nothing anyhow. Thanks to the narrowness of the bridge or the faintness of their hearts, the marchers in the two front rows had closed ranks even tighter and had blended into one solid wall of heads and backs and arms. Only big Jim Orange stood out to one side above the human wall, his dark-knit-capped head putting me in mind of a medieval watchtower, looking out for all of us.

I looked up high. "Edmond Pettus Bridge. Vertical clearance 14 ft. 10 in." a sign proclaimed in large letters on the overhead girder. The bridge was familiar to us all. We had seen it in technicolor many times on the television news. I only wished I were tall enough to reach up and touch that familiar gray structure as we passed beneath. The way I sometimes wished I could reach up and pluck the full moon from out of the sky on a clear summer's evening.

My ears were supersensitive now, because my eyes were almost useless, surrounded as they were by heads and shoulders and linking arms and clutching hands. My ears picked up the swish of denim and gabardine and nylon as thousands of garbed legs stepped forward in time, bearing their owners inexorably on. Soles continued to slap rhythmically on concrete, the soft sound of each footfall combining to produce one blended roar of walking feet. The TV camera's eye seemed to be floating in air at the rear of the vehicle just ahead. While I could not often see it, I had no doubt it was there. I was glad it was there. I felt safer with it there.

Left foot, right foot, left foot again, right foot again. Slap slap, slap slap. Toward the crest of the bridge, the two exaggeratedly tall girders of grey steel were loping side-by-side overhead of us. "Shame River" was now a slim and murky ribbon beneath our feet. The "point man" for my position, walking only two rows in advance of me, was our self-proclaimed drum major, none other than Dr. Martin Luther King!

All at once I felt euphoric, and no longer fearful. I no longer felt anxious as to what lay on the other side. This business of being in a marching band was far more wonderful than I had ever imagined it could be. Here I was at last, Gwennie Simon from Woodbury High School, and I was a welcome participant in the scattered "flute section." All these hundreds of other women back there behind me, black and pink and all shades in between, all of us were playing flute out here today! Our treble instruments—our female voices—were silent for now, just as all the male voices—representing the trumpets and the drums and the tubas—were silent. We females were indicating by our very presence our desire to participate in this, our country's great symphony of justice. How could that be an unladylike thing to do?

And I was glad I had decided after all to wear a dress. There should be no mistaking my gender, nor where I stood on this issue of voting rights for all Americans. I was a woman, and I had a part to play here—not in a game, after all, but in a symphony.

And justice, not Sousa, was our song. *"Here we go, singing low . . . ."*

Over the crest of the bridge's roadbed we in the first few rows moved forward as with one giant step. And look! Look down there! On the road below awaiting us, nothing menacing was visible! Our hands still joined with those of our neighbors, our courage gradually being restored, we began to spread our lines out to left and right once more. Our silent symphony, we seemed to be saying by our presence, was not only loud and clear. It was brave and it was just. We were producing an *Eroica*. Who would dare to strike us down, or tear-gas us, and put a stop to our music? *Blackbirds, bye, bye!*

But no one—and we could see clearly now between the dignitaries in the front row who were walking further apart and going downhill off the bridge and gathering momentum—no one was waiting down there meaning to do us harm. We saw only a motionless strung-out line of young men wearing United States Army combat uniforms on their muscular frames, and when we got close enough to see, peach fuzz on their chins. Spaced at regular intervals several yards apart, they stood at attention along the wide medial strip of the now four-lane highway that stretched out before us. All of them were standing at attention, facing left toward the two lanes of Highway 80 upon which we had been ordered by Federal Circuit Court Judge Johnson to do our marching. Young white men in identical tans, frozen into identical statues with rifles held pointing straight up and close to their chests, the silent sentinels waited. In their helmets and combat boots, they made quite a meticulous display in contrast to the ragtag, unarmed, bi-racial and bi-gender marching band they had been sent to watch over.

Each soldier's gaze, as we swept by in front of him, was focused straight ahead. Each youthful expression bore the same noncommittal emptiness as Sheriff Clark's. Several of them were Negroes, maintaining somehow the same empty look in their eyes. What were those men thinking as they stood there? They had to be on our side, but so were all the white troops, we were well aware, and that made all the difference. They had no choice but to be. Lyndon Johnson had sent them there and they were, after all, our President's men.

Large numbers of marchers were streaming across the bridge behind us now. Still eight to a row, row after row after row after row, we were going strong, completely unopposed, into more open country. To our right, business establishments, with deep set-backs and. spaced further apart than in town, were spotted along the highway. There were new and used car dealers. Restaurants. Gas stations. All the customary accouterments of a busy commercial artery. A service road ran along the right side of the highway, keeping the buildings, as well as a score of white curiosity-seekers on that side, still further at bay. But there were no uniformed State troopers in gas masks holding billy-clubs. There were no deputies on horseback. There were no white mobs with sticks and bricks or guns or hand grenades. If danger lurked here, it was carefully hidden.

Turning my head without breaking stride, my eyes met Albert Friedlander's and we grinned broadly at each other. We squeezed each other's hands in triumph. I turned my head to look the other way and the boy James looked into my eyes and smiled, and I squeezed his hand as well. We've done it, I wanted to shout. By golly, the three of us, the rabbi, the Negro boy and I, the white agnostic, together we have done it!

The sun was finally out, but the white citizens of Alabama, for the most part, were not. And the world, I could see beyond the gas pumps and the used car lots skimming past my view at either end of my row, was turning green. I wanted to shout something to my fellow marchers all around me, but I couldn't remember what it was. I wanted to jump up and down on this road that is also called the Jefferson Davis Highway, named for the president of the long-gone Confederate States of America, and make a fool of myself.

I had a wild desire to twirl about on my toes like my five-year-old Julie would have done if she had accomplished something, to her, so completely wonderful. And more than that: I wanted to dance a few steps and clap my hands together in a frenzy of relieved delight. But I still held tightly the hands of my two stalwart marching companions. I couldn't let either one of them go, not quite yet. Because something else had happened. Something quite miraculous, if I could only remember what it was . . . !

And then, by golly, I had it!

"*Hey, you guys!*" I cried out, finding my outside voice that had for a few brief minutes of stress and apprehension been stifled. "*Guess what! It's March 21st, did you think of that? It's the first day of spring!*"

*   *   *

END OF PART EIGHT

PART NINE

FOLLOWING THE KING

39.

"... . Facing the rising sun
"Of our new day begun,
"Let us march on
'Til victory is won."

"... . Shadowed beneath thy hand,
"May we forever stand,
"True to our God,
"True to our Native Land."

—Lines from "Lift Ev'ry Voice And Sing"
(Official anthem of the NAACP)

Thousands of us civil rights crusaders were heading safely into the countryside of Dallas County. We were headed on our way east, through the heart of the Alabama Black Belt, bound for Montgomery, once called the Cradle of the Confederacy. Furthermore, each step was taking many of us in the general direction of home. And so far as we in the first few rows of the march knew, no one had been hurt, nor even confronted with hostility. We had no way of knowing what lay behind us, however, nor how many supporters of SCLC were actually there.

The news media reported later that our line of marchers, eight persons across and hundreds of rows long, stretched behind our front-row leaders for a half-mile. That it comprised anywhere from three thousand to ten thousand souls, depending upon whether the reporter who had done the estimating was from the North, and wanted to astound his readers; or from the South, and wanted to comfort them.

One of the marchers, they all reported, was a one-legged white man from Minnesota, walking on crutches. They said that the sun was out but not-too-brightly overhead, and that the troops were also out, just as President Johnson had promised. They said that a sizable number of white Alabamans drove their cars slowly along the two right-hand lanes of U.S. Highway 8O (converted for the occasion into two lanes of opposing traffic), just to get a close-up look at what "that communist-inspired Nigra preacher from Atlanta" had wrought. The media said that there were no incidents of any kind that first day. Which only goes to show you what little those newspapers and TV stations actually comprehended.

As soon as the vanguard of the march was safely over the Edmond Pettus Bridge and into the wider-open spaces, slogging easily down the lefthand two lanes of U.S. 8O, passing the strategically placed toy soldiers sent to look after us, we dropped hands and an atmosphere of restrained festivity took over. The mood was rapidly transmitted back from one row to the next, like "whispering-down-the-lane" but without the need for actual words this time. The mood said, It's okay now! We're going to be okay! Let's laugh, and be happy! But not too happy, so as not to offend.

James abruptly muttered goodbye in my direction and disappeared into the bowels of the march behind us, before I could question him further about himself, or find out where he had come from. The Negro woman next to the end of our row moved in next to me to take his place. Without further ado, she introduced herself to me and to Albert on the other side of me. About my age, she was wearing bright red lipstick and a new hairset with large straightened curls. She was nearly bursting with something she wanted to tell us.

"I'm Marie Bailey," she said, leaning forward so she could get a look at Albert too. "And that boy who was here is James Whittington. It was somewheres here comin' up . . . that's right! Just here, it was!" and she indicated an ordinary-looking spot off the shoulder of the road, where a custard stand stood in the background. "This is where me and that

James was both knocked down and trampled on, two weeks ago! And now we're goin' to Montgomery again, and this time, ain't nobody goin' to stop us!"

In a state of high excitement, Marie described to us how she had been run down that day by a sheriff's volunteer deputy on horseback. Knocked to the ground with his bull-whip, she had fallen under the horse's hoofs and been stepped on twice. The man had screamed at her that she was under arrest. He had looked down from his saddle to where she lay bruised and bleeding on the prickly grass and had ordered her to "Git up, nigger! Git up and help me with these other niggers!" and when she hadn't, when she couldn't do more than crawl, he had hit her with his bull-whip once again.

Listening to her story, the contemptuous voice from my tenth year rang in my head. *"Hey, girl!" I feel the rock the boy threw smashing into my forehead. I remember the blood, running down my cheek and off my chin onto my black flute case. I feet the disbelief, the humiliation, the helplessness. Is he going to hit me again? And why did he do it in the first place? I had done nothing, said nothing to make him want to hurt me. I had only wanted to watch.*

Marie Bailey went on to explain that the group of Negroes who had been given places of honor in the first few rows back in Selma before we set out, had all been residents of the city, or of the surrounding county, who had been injured or jailed or both on that infamous Sunday. Except for the one old man, now walking in the front row next to Rev. Abernathy. That old man, in his eighties, was the grandfather of Jimmie Lee Jackson, the Negro youth who had been beaten to death during the voter registration demonstration in Marion last month. The old man was marching in place of Jimmie Lee, she said.

Ms. Bailey was jubilant as she told us all these things. Implicit in her voice and manner was personal triumph over previous defeat, and gratitude to those who had made the triumph possible. And I was reminded again that I had not earned my own place in that third row. I should have at least attempted to get better acquainted with James. I should have asked him to tell me his story before he melted away.

Something else for me to feel guilty about.

It was getting warmer now. And as we walked and talked, all of us began to relax somewhat our customary self-discipline and to breathe more freely, fighting back the temptation at times to cavort outside our lines like young lambs supposedly did in the fresh spring air. What stopped us was an awareness that the large and all-encompassing electronic eye was still out there in front of us on the CBS-TV truck, still poised to catch some kind of nasty diversion like that other time two weeks ago. The camera was eager for anything the least bit out of the ordinary that it could preserve for posterity—or at the very least, to amuse or horrify its hungry-for-news audience. But the two rows of dark-clad shoulders between me and the TV camera nearly shut it from view, and in time I almost forgot the eye was there.

At first, unable to grasp the ease with which the whole business had been pulled off, we marchers had paid careful attention to our marching style. Now we let ourselves get increasingly out of step. More and more marchers fell out of rank and out of file, and we began calling out to each other, and laughing, and getting further acquainted with our fellows in the line in front of us, and in the line in back of us, and it wasn't long before the neat, straight arrow that had traversed the bridge in such short and dignified order had become an attenuated caterpillar, bulging here and there, pushing on this side or that. But none of our marshalls seemed to be concerned about it. Not as long as we kept moving; ever moving toward the east.

It would be more open country from here on. As we passed Bill's Flea Market on our left, lots of stony white faces appeared on our right. We heard some jeering and cat-calling, but no matter. Now Jane's Trailer Park was on the right. And again after a mile or two further on the right, we saw the heavy gates and the guard house for Craig Air Force Base. But only one lone sentry in uniform stood there.

Occasionally now, we passed solemn and silent clusters of black faces, Negroes grouped on the lefthand side of the highway to watch us go by. They looked to be poor sharecroppers and their families. What could they be thinking? Could they possibly be thinking, *What are these madmen up to now, to make our lives even more difficult than they already are?*

I had seen that same haunted look before, issuing from many pairs of Negro eyes. But where? And when? Yes! It was long ago, right after the great Detroit race riot in the summer of 1943! Quite by coincidence I had been there when it happened; a thirteen-year-old visitor for several weeks in the home of Italian-American friends.

Because it was the middle of the Big War in 1943, no one was supposed to air complaints, no matter how legitimate. Especially "not the coloreds, who are getting too pushy everywhere you turn!" It was unpatriotic of them, white people said, didn't they know we were all in this war together?

There had been some kind of altercation over whites getting all the good-paying jobs in war plants around Detroit, and Negroes, not. In a fury at being left out, Negroes had turned over cars, started fires, even broken into stores. In the resulting official police actions to put down the riot, thirty-four people, mostly blacks, had been killed, and a thousand more injured.

Rosina, the mother of the household where I was visiting, needed to go downtown the morning after the three-day riot had been quelled by the police and the Michigan National Guard. She needed to pick up her eyeglasses from the repair shop on Woodward Avenue, so she could read well again. But her husband Ben said no, she could not go, it would be too dangerous. There was nothing to fear, I had said to Ben with thirteen-year-old self-assurance. I have lots of Negro friends back home, I told him. And I had duly offered to escort Rosina on the trolley downtown to pick up her glasses and come back again. I would look after her, I said. Failing to grasp the fact that *she* would be the one taking care of *me*.

We had ridden in a streetcar that morning, past overturned burnt-out cars and the shattered glass of store-front windows. And I had seen that same look in the eyes of black faces then. The City of Detroit finally under marshall law, Negroes had been allowed to stand around in groups of no more than three at a time, and they did so, talking together on the sidewalks. Many had stared wordlessly at me as I sat on the long bench in the streetcar, staring back out at them through the window glass. Their look had said to me: "We're beaten. So what are you madmen going to do to us now, to make our lives even more miserable?" I was only thirteen. But my heart had been wrenched, and I had felt only pity for them and their paltry, fruitless, and thoroughly destructive efforts to make their misery known.

But maybe it wasn't that way this time. Surely this time, as they watched the throngs of humankind passing by unopposed, those Alabama Negro eyes were saying, *"Oh, Lord, they done won! All these black folks and these white folks done got together and done won for sure, and things is gonna be better from now on!"* And later, when a group of the Negro by-standers applauded and waved an American flag in our direction, I was certain I had read them right.

What was it Adelaide Sims had said to me in her kitchen when I left her? "We never knew there was any white folks . . . . that cared what happened to us."

* * *

40.

"That was a communist plot you took part in!"
—GG's brother-in-law
(Post-Selma Comments from one of the folks back home)

A handful of black children were playing on a railroad track that had appeared on our left side out of nowhere. Their bodies were struck motionless in various postures of surprise and wonder at the unexpected sight of thousands of human beings, both white and black, taking a Sunday stroll together down their highway. I knew that in years to come, this would be one of the indelible pictures that would be inked upon my memory of that Alabama day. As I hoped it would be on the children's.

Also captured forever would be the image of that sparkling-new, yellow brick rancher just outside the city of Selma, built well back from the highway in a comfortable nest of shade trees and shrubs. Standing before it, as close to the despised rabble as they dare to come, are the rancher's two unsmiling white occupants—a man and a woman—holding between them a large, hand-lettered sign which says "COMMUNISTS AND WHITE TRASH GO HOME!" This, to the obvious delight of their several small children, looking on with permanent smirks from the safety of much further back.

Still scenes of the Selma March for Voting Rights, two frozen pictures that will stay with me forever.

Now that we could all relax, Rabbi Friedlander began proudly introducing me to some of the people who made up the second row of marchers just in front of us. He seemed to know most of them already. The tall, attractive Negro woman whose distinctive appearance I had noted earlier, walking in the second row, in the same file as Albert? She was Constance Baker Motley, he said, the Borough Mayor of Manhattan.

The white man directly ahead of me, behind whose broad shoulders I had considered myself sheltered from both sight and harm? He was New

York City's Commissioner For Human Rights. The two other men walking beside him, were there from New York's municipal government. They all turned around in turn and shook my hand and Albert's. And all the while everyone kept walking.

"That man to Dr. King's immediate left," Albert murmured in my ear, "is Dr. Ralph Bunche, Under-Secretary General to the United Nations." Ralph Bunche, the light-skinned Negro I had at first taken for a white man, was the first "man of color" anywhere in the world to win the Nobel Peace Prize. That had been fifteen years ago, back in 1950, I had remembered. Because I had connected the date with the year my first child Wendy was born. A brand new mother at the time of the ceremony in Stockholm, Sweden, I had followed the news reports on my parents ten-inch black-and-white television. Dr. Bunche had won the honor, the media reported, for his skill as a negotiator for the United Nations in helping to end the Arab-Israeli conflict the year before.

"And there, on the other side of Dr. Bunche," Albert said, "is my good friend and colleague, Dr. Abraham Heschel. He's a professor at Jewish Theological Seminary in New York, Gwen. Also, he is very highly respected worldwide as a theologian and philosopher." So that explained the funny little man with the Santa Claus whiskers! And it partially explained too why Albert Friedlander, his much younger protege, had also been treated like a visiting celebrity.

As we kept moving along the paved highway, we marchers were still swapping places in line, exchanging names and impressions, meeting new acquaintances. As Constance Motley moved to walk elsewhere, Albert and I suddenly found ourselves in the second row! Trying not to tread upon Martin Luther King's heels, I twice managed to step upon Ralph Bunche's instead, but he only looked around miserably to see what had happened and then assured me it was quite all right.

The City Commissioner for Human Rights, now walking to the left of me where James had once been, told me in a confidential voice that the U.N.'s Under-Secretary General had been ill with a fever of 101 degrees that morning. But he had insisted upon flying down from New York to march anyway. And on the strength of that fairly reliable information, I made a superhuman effort to stay clear of poor Dr. Bunche's heels as well.

The sun, trying hard, had at last come out in full force. We were beginning to notice the results of its heightened effort. All around me as the walk continued, the warm-blooded among us were removing their coats. A slight breeze caressed our faces from above. We felt utterly safe from danger, with those National Guard troops spotted every now and again along the medial strip. And we felt ravenously hungry, since it was well past lunch time and we had been on the go for more than an hour.

All at once I remembered my food cache. Dipping into the brown paper bag after first retrieving it from the pack on Albert's back, I pulled out sugared doughnuts one by one without breaking stride. I passed them around to the entreating hands reaching out to me from both sides and in front, until all the doughnuts were gone. And then I broke open the package of chocolate-and-vanilla sandwich cookies and distributed them as well.

The Commissioner for Human Rights, and the Borough Mayor of Manhattan, and their two co-workers from up North, and Marie Bailey, the Selma woman who had tried unsuccessfully to walk to Montgomery two Sundays ago because she wanted to vote—all these people welcomed my offerings with grateful thanks, as did a group who were now right behind us bearing a banner proclaiming "Hawaii Knows Integration Works." They had flown in from the islands just this morning, they told me. They had brought the leis of frangipani blossoms with them on the plane and had presented them to some of the dignitaries. Including one to my friend Albert!

My rabbi was enjoying the first doughnut I handed him. "These are good! Where did you get them?" he asked innocently enough.

I sidled closer to his ear. "I found them. In the trash can under the tree by the church, while I was waiting for you. Someone deposited them there," I muttered in a low voice.

He choked on his second bite. "Please, Gwen—don't tell that to anyone!"

"Don't worry, I won't! It'll be our little secret," and I couldn't help letting out a little chuckle.

I ate a doughnut myself, and Albert had two, and they tasted fine. And then we both had cookies. When one of the former recipients reached his hand over for more, I obliged him. Someone commented that my supply seemed never-ending.

I had not grown up in a Baptist Sunday School for nothing. "These are the fishes and the loaves, that's why!" I announced to anyone within sound of my voice. A number of religious leaders of both races and several faiths were walking in those front rows. They would understand, and maybe even appreciate, my "blasphemous" metaphor. They had no need to know of the suspiciously agnostic status of the thirty-five-year-old New Jersey housewife who proffered it. Everyone around me smiled and kept on chewing, none of us ever breaking stride.

And then I had another, even more brilliant idea. Pleased with my own cleverness, I threw all caution to the winds and skipped forward between Martin Luther King and Ralph Bunche. Walking backward in a clumsy skip-hop, uncaring about the black eye of the camera which was already some distance away by this time, I announced brazenly to the entire front line that "these are civil rights cookies—black and white together!" Everybody laughed. And kept right on walking. After assuring the marchers in the front row that we'd already eaten our share, I doled out to them the remainder of the cookies. To Dr. Ralph Abernathy. To the nun walking beside him. To Jimmie Lee Jackson's grandfather.

Dr. King's eyes met mine for only an instant when I got to him. Then he smiled and said "Yes, thank you," as I handed him two of my special cookies. It was the same sort of fleeting smile and the same grave thank you he had used from behind the podium in Stockholm the previous summer. That was where he had accepted the Peace Prize from the Nobel Committee for his role in the nonviolence movement for Negro civil rights. This one time, however, out on that Alabama road in the sunshine, the smile and the words were for me alone.

Years later, made much less naïve by events than I was then, I have to wonder if the incident in any way frightened or alarmed him. After all, he had once been stabbed in the chest by an emotionally ill Negro woman, a stranger, coming from out of nowhere without warning at one of his book signings, and wounding him with a pair of scissors. I prefer to think I provided for him a welcome distraction from the underlying seriousness of the day's events. At any rate, he cheerfully accepted two civil rights cookies from my hand, and while I still pranced backwards before him, he popped one into his mouth and chewed it with gusto. Dr. Bunche declined a cookie with a weak but friendly wave of refusal. But Dr. Heschel took my last three, and thanked me heartily.

Wadding up the empty paper sack with the empty boxes inside, I mentally thanked it for being useful and managed to shove it into the pocket of my coat. I ducked back into my place in the second row beside Albert. I had been out front doing my backward jig only a minute or two at the most, but it had been long enough for me to come to a necessary conclusion.

This time my gift of sustenance had truly been the "widow's mite." I had made a contribution, however small, to the success of our venture.

And in doing so, maybe I had finally earned the right to be where I was now, walking eastward in the second row of the Selma March for Voting Rights and Justice.

*   *   *

<h1 style="text-align:center">41.</h1>

"If we can buy a ticket on a fast jet to freedom, then we'll go by plane; if we can't fly, we'll take the train; if we can't take the train, we'll go in car pools; if we can't go in car pools, we'll run; if we can't run, we'll walk; if we can't walk, we'll drag; if we can't drag, we'll crawl; if we can't crawl, we'll inch along like a little inch-worm. But we're going to be free, by and by!"

—The Rev. Wyatt Tee Walker, SCLC Executive Director
(from G G's Words To Live By)

All in all, the first day of the march went superbly well. Probably far smoother than either organizers or participants had a right to expect.

Army trucks bearing soldiers to a further point up ahead of us rumbled slowly along on the far right side of the highway from time to time. In the beginning, they passed cars bearing Alabama license plates, even slower moving, going in the inner right lane in the direction of Selma. The white occupants of the cars craned their necks for a longer view of Dr. King and the others in the front row. Bumper to bumper they sometimes appeared, in spite of their governor's appeal to them to stay at home that day. And now I felt like we were not only in a parade, but we were seeing one, too.

One especially slow-moving car was draped with a banner which read simply: "Martin Luther Coon." Another declared, "I Hate Niggers." And one particularly intrepid soul dared to park on the left shoulder of the highway, where no cars were supposed to be, in order to sit on his hood and glare at us threateningly. Four white boys looking to be in their early teens hiked single-file along the railroad ties that ran behind him, yelling obscenities at us but keeping their distance. We grinned over at them, and some of us waved.

And there were of course the amateur photographers. Two different ones, with a short interval between. Sitting boldly on their car hoods, they were taking motion pictures for evidence this time, not just snapshots.

We whites smiled especially for them, too, and some of our younger companions called out, "Cheese!"

And then, as mysteriously as it had come, that parade of hostile viewers was gone. And we thousands of "niggers" and "nigger-lovers" were left out there in the spring air, almost alone. We had occasion to halt the line of march only once throughout the entire day; just long enough for the half-mile-long line of participants to throw themselves down on the sloping side of the highway and eat the bagged sandwiches passed out to us by the busy march marshalls. Prepared by the Negro housewives of Selma the day before, the food had been brought out to us in especially designated cars.

Albert and I sat on the slope of a grassy knoll beside Dr. Bunche, passing him slices of an orange left over from breakfast that Albert had thought to bring along in his coat pocket. Now I peeled it just for the sick man, who felt too ill, he told us, to eat anything else. I felt his forehead with a sticky but practiced hand.

"You're quite right! You're burning up with fever, you really shouldn't be out here in this parade!" I said. But I knew before I said it what his answer would be.

"I have to be," Dr. Bunche said.

And I could understand that. "You ought to at least let the medical truck give you some aspirin or something, don't you think? To bring down the fever?" I said.

Dr. King sat nearby, laughing happily and exchanging jokes and hugs with Andrew Young's two little girls who had been brought up by their parents to meet him. They had quickly conquered their awe enough to be at ease with him, something we older ones never quite managed.

Dr. Heschel sat close at Dr. King's elbow, looking on with open approval and hungrily eating his own sandwich. He did not at all resemble a jovial Santa Claus, I saw now. Rather he appeared to be wraith-like, almost ethereal behind the mist of nearly white hair encircling his head and ears and falling down from his chin upon his chest. He was a prestigious Jewish scholar and philosopher, Albert had told me when we were earlier introduced. But he seemed not at all egotistical; rather, he was quiet and unassuming.

The march marshalls dared not let us dally long, since we, and all those coming along behind us, still had much ground to cover before nightfall. Big Jim Orange soon cajoled us to our feet and got the first lines moving on once more, and the others behind us were quick to follow suit, like rows of fallen dominoes setting themselves on end again.

Ralph Bunche sweetly ignored my advice that he ask for aspirin. He was probably an expert at ignoring unsolicited advice from people far more sure of their opinions than I was. He looked to me to be sicker than ever. But he resumed his position without complaint, up there in the front line beside Martin Luther King. Albert and I slipped in behind them, into our customary spots. The weather, once chilly, had turned pleasantly warm, so I was able to at last pull my dark scarf off my head and stuff it into the knapsack my rabbi was still carrying on his back.

Telling Albert where I was going, I dropped back alone for a few minutes to use the portable toilet facilities, which were brought forward by truck and set up on the medial strip from time to time. By now, they were well-used and rather pungent. The doors to all nine of the stalls were marked "Men", but an obliging young marshall stood guard just outside the ones reserved for the women and girls.

Afterward, I stood watching from the edge of the medial strip for a few minutes as the thousands of marchers streamed past in front of me. It seemed obvious to me that they did indeed number in the thousands. There seemed to be nothing in any way conformist or structured, however, about the human beings who had come in answer to Dr. King's invitation to march with him out of Selma. I scanned their faces and clothing as I watched a representative portion of them go by. There seemed to be no one characteristic I could discern that all of America's civil rights crusaders shared in common. Except for the fact that none bore arms, and all were plodding resolutely up hill and down dale, toward the east. Toward Montgomery, the capital of Alabama.

"Motley" is the best word I can find to describe the over-all effect of that unusual gathering of human beings. By far the majority of them were males—men and teen-aged boys of both races. But large clusters of women and girls and a few children were present too. In all sizes and heights and ages and colors the marchers came. By their appearance, they seemed to be from different economic and cultural backgrounds, but all of them were jumbled nicely together here in one comically casual mass of humanity.

No one tried to be in step with anyone else now. Most of the marchers still chattered happily, some occasionally laughing aloud or joining a few others in song. Some greeted me with a wave or a smile if they noticed me standing there, searching their faces for someone I knew. Others, some of the more subdued, less sturdy souls, simply trudged along, eyes forward and jaws set in weary determination as they planted one foot in front of the other in endless sequence.

There was a liberal sprinkling of canteens and thermoses and lunch bags, a few sleeping bags, and knapsacks on the order of mine, and an occasional small American or United Nations flag fluttered in the breeze. A smattering of banners and signs were borne past me. The signs displayed a variety of messages. "We Demand An End to Police Brutality" and "We Demand Equal Voting Rights." "Cincinnati." And "Philadelphia." Even a banner that announced, to my utter surprise, "Mississippi." A Southern state that seemed to me to be utterly racist.

All manner and style and color of parade dress lent visual excitement to the mix. Walking past me here and there were lots of nuns and priests in their distinctive white collars and bibs and black clerical garb. All of the nuns wore their special black-and-white headdresses, but some were sporting the new knee-length black skirts recently approved by the Vatican.

Ebullient young black men in faded blue jeans and wearing Jewish *yarmulkes* ("freedom caps" was how the Movement now referred to them, I recalled). Mature white men in dark suits and tasteful ties, their London Fogs now draped over one arm because the day was becoming quite warm for people on foot. Besides the *yarmulkes*, a wide variety of headgear went past as I stood there on the medial strip, trying to take it all in. Yellow construction helmets, calico bandannas; one football helmet; an Army cap of World War II vintage.

The older women, particularly the black ones, were in good dresses, and sometimes Easter hats. The younger Negro women wore trousers but with their hair well in place. A wild collection of hair colors and styles, among both the males and the females, topped the peaks and valleys formed by the heads of the marchers, whose heights never seemed to match that of the persons accompanying them.

The line of march stretched forward and backward in both directions as far as my eye could see. In vain did I search for a sign of Peter, my young friend from the bus; or Nancy, the lady minister from Berkeley; or Dorothy, my bed-buddy from the first night; or James, the boy whose hand I had held; or Charlie, Adelaide's Sims' oldest son; or someone, anyone, I even faintly recognized. And I realized it was hopeless to search amongst all these thousands. It would only be by accident if I saw any of them again. But how could we ever have guessed? That so many marchers would come?

And then, suddenly, here they came past me: Maria and Lela, my two acquaintances from dinner last evening before the mass meeting! They were smiling broadly and waving madly at me, and Maria no longer looked sick, or angry at all white people. She must have gotten over her case of "pneumonia" rather quickly, I said to myself. I smiled just as broadly and waved just as heartily back at them.

Next, I slipped into a gap in a line I selected at random. I wanted the novel experience of being completely surrounded by strangers, all bent on the same nondescript destination. We were heading to an empty cow pasture just across the border in Lowndes County, eleven miles from Brown's Chapel. It was there I would have to find a way to get back to my charter bus.

Working my way in a matter of minutes over to the left margin of a row, I studied the scenery as it went by. The land was much hillier here, in contrast to the gentle slopes where we had stopped to eat lunch. And the highway, once straight, had begun perceptively to wind around and through small hills. Almost everywhere the countryside had turned a timid green, except for an orange-rust field here and there that ran off into the distance, still sprinkled with the stalks of dead plants that could have once yielded cotton. Houses were few and far between, barely visible from the highway and most looking like shanties. A faded and skimpy look seemed to touch everything, right down to the Spanish moss clinging half-heartedly to the branches of a few tired-looking trees. Even the occasional group of grazing cows looked thin and underfed.

The medial strip, which had been quite narrow and flat on the Selma side of the Edmond Pettus Bridge, had been gradually widened into two generous slopes with a drainage ditch in the middle. I noticed that it, like the unkempt berm on my left, had been poorly tended. Hardy survivors from the previous autumn, dried stalks that had once probably been white Queen Anne's lace or yellow black-eyed Susans, jutted up on either side of the four-lane highway. Further back from the road, the pale limbs of mimosa trees were still struggling to bud.

The roadbed beneath my feet was faded too, its brownish-grey surface worn down and patched with big splotches of newer but almost equally faded concrete. In contrast to Georgia, with its stunning red dirt, the entire area looked as if it had been washed out by a surfeit of bleach. I remembered learning in a high school history class that Alabama was one of the two poorest states in the United States, with its neighbor Mississippi being the worst. It probably still was, and I felt bad about that. In fact, except for racial crises like this one, Alabama's only claim to fame, as far as I was concerned, was being first on the roll calls of the states, at both the Democrats and the Republicans Presidential Nominating Conventions. And that was only because of alphabetical circumstance. In memory, I could hear one of those scrupulously booming voices now, calling out over a loud-speaker in the same-pitch monotone: "*Al-a-bam-a!*". And the invariably pompous reply comes back from someone in their delegation, "Al-a-bam-a, proud state of (whatever; whoever; whenever), casts all its votes (every last, white-racist one of them!) "nay!"

Thickets and woodsy patches bounded our route now, interspersed by wide expanses of the orange-rust fields not yet cultivated for spring planting. In one fallow field a white man stood watching us from not too many yards away, his arms folded across his chest. He wore riding jodphurs and coat; and nearby just up ahead he had tethered a muscular white stallion to an oval Coca-Cola sign lodged between two posts pounded into the ground. This fellow would have been a plantation owner one hundred years ago, I imagined to myself. Had he lived through the 1860s, I imagined, he would have been watching emancipated "darkies" walking down this same road, a dirt one back then at the end of the Civil War, heading east toward what they had been led to believe was freedom.

Next to me, a white woman intruded into my reverie with a squeal of fright.

"Look!" and she pointed with trembling finger to the horse in the field. Apparently frightened by the strange, once-in-a-lifetime sight we presented, the white stallion had reared up in terror and had pulled the thick posts to which he was tethered completely out of the ground. Bolting, he began to run in ever-widening circles through the field, the red Coca-Cola sign on the two uprooted four-by-fours held tight against his flank by the reins. The earth-covered wooden points projecting straight out in front of him made him look like some sort of primitive battering ram.

Now the ever-more terrified beast broke out of his circle and thundered in our direction.

My section of marchers, now obviously the most threatened ones, stood frozen in place in our rows, all of us staring at the deadly weapon pointed like a double arrow at each of our hearts. The pounding hoofs, however, were still some distance away when we came to our senses. Emitting soft shrieks of fright or shouts of "look out!," we broke rank with one accord and scattered in every direction, pushing into the marchers in front or into the marchers behind, each reacting instinctively on his or her own, without any thought to the others. Just as the fear-maddened creature veered off his course and galloped back out into the field, trying to make good his own escape. His owner, galvanized at last into action, chased frantically after him, up and over a rise until both were lost from sight.

The dozen or so of us who had panicked and run had given some nervous giggles and gasps of relief while we regained our outward composure. We had immediately gotten our lines formed up again and had gone on. Pulses still pounding with the sudden surge of adrenalin that had raced through our bodies, we had walked a little faster for a few seconds to catch up to where we should be. We were ashamed that we had been stampeded so quickly without waiting to assess how immediate the danger was.

It was plain to see that that brief training in non-violence behavior at First Baptist Church only yesterday had not prepared me, or any of us passive resistance novices, for dealing with the threat of injury from an unexpected source. Tear gas, billy-clubs, foot kicks, mounted horses, arrests and jail—all manner of official forms of verbal and physical abuse, had been covered yesterday by our instructors. But how could they possibly prepare us for the capriciousness of nature, animal or human, on the rampage?

I slipped out of line immediately after the incident and eventually caught up again with the front lines of the march and my more familiar traveling companions. Albert Friedlander greeted me with his big smile, happy to see me again. "Good! I'm glad you're back! Would you care to take your turn with this now?"

But while he was trying to transfer the straps of the knapsack from his shoulders to mine without the two of us having to break step or fall out of line, a husky Negro boy from just behind us came up and insisted upon carrying the entire contraption for a few miles. The burden that had bent the rabbi's medium frame ever lower seemed a mere gnat on our benefactor's back.

Then Albert said, as if I had just arrived late at a cocktail party, "There's someone back here, Gwen, I know you'll want to meet." And he introduced me to, and left me with, a rangy and rough-featured man walking field position a couple of rows back. Mr. Charles Evers, by name, he was, and I already knew the last name well. I walked along a few minutes beside Mr. Evers, talking to him about his hopes to improve conditions for black folks in Alabama, and thus I had been spared for awhile from further thoughts of the white stallion.

I made no mention either of Charles Evers' murdered brother Medgar, the NAACP Field Secretary who had been shot to death from ambush a year ago in front of his own house in Mississippi. I wished for the nerve to tell this dark-skinned, brooding man how I'd cried and cried when his brother was shot. But lest I come across as an emotional, do-gooder white woman who didn't really know the score, I stayed quiet about that, and we went on talking of impersonal matters.

Afterward, when I had caught up to Albert once again, he too a hard look at me and broke into laughter. He said, "You should see your face, Gwen Gain-without-an-e-or an-s-on—the-end! Your face is a bright pink all over from the sun!"

And I had retorted, "Pink is fine, lad! Your own nose is redder than those cute posies you were wearing around your neck when I left you!" The wilted leis had been discarded by now, by all those who had worn them. Thinking about that white stallion again, I told Albert the story. I told him about it briefly, in a few words, as if it were of little importance.

*   *   *

42.

"One hour of life, crowded to the full with glorious action, and filled with noble risks, is worth whole years of those mean observances of paltry decorum, in which men steal through existence, like sluggish waters through a marsh, without honor or observation."

—Sir Walter Scott, English writer
(GG's Words To Live By)

The eleven miles between Selma and the first campsite were covered on foot that Sunday in less than six hours, with an additional fifteen minutes or so for the tail of the caterpillar to catch up to its front. Albert and I had finished our walk in what we agreed was fine fettle, stepping almost literally on the heels of Dr. King and Dr. Bunche and Dr. Heschel and Rev. Abernathy and Jimmie Lee Jackson's grandfather and the nun.

The sun, which had unmistakably done its part in helping us along, was still a few degrees above the horizon behind us. This was the furthest by far that I had ever walked in one stretch in my whole life, and I was proud of myself, but feeling sun-burnt and hot on my cheeks and forehead.

A roadside sign told us that we had left Dallas County and entered Lowndes County only minutes before, after which the four lanes had narrowed once again to two. And then we spotted the four brown tents, set up in advance on the Steele Farm's vacant pasture, on the right side of U.S. Highway 8O. I had learned from someone enroute that Lowndes County was eighty percent black. Yet not one Negro was on its voter registration list! I surmised that the courageous owners of the Steele Farm could only be black.

The campsite was needed, we had been told at the mass meeting the night before, for the use of the three hundred already-selected marchers who were to continue on toward Montgomery the next day. These were the ones who would be making the longer hike scheduled to last still another four days until Thursday evening.

All the rest of us had been asked for our understanding and cooperation. We were to please absent ourselves from the area as soon as possible after our arrival at the Steele Farm, Rev. Young had pleaded when he spoke to us last evening. A fleet of private cars was being organized to make continuous journeys back and forth between the campsite and Selma, for those who would need to go there. Albert and I already knew that we had a bus to catch, but that we would have to go back to Selma in order to get a ride all the way to Montgomery. And that, we were beginning to grasp, could present a problem.

The front rows of marchers came abreast of the campsite at last, to where helmeted National Guardsmen waited to hold back the few Alabama cars still in evidence on the highway. In a final symbolic gesture, Albert Friedlander and I clasped hands. Following our leaders, we swung right and crossed the medial strip, which was flat here, and walked across the two righthand lanes of the highway and up a rutted dirt road into the cow pasture, a large portion of which was covered with what seemed dozens of parked cars, along with an equal number of piles of cattle dung. And it was here, as if at some mysterious signal, that the rows of marchers at last dissolved into their individual components and disappeared around the tent walls of brown canvas, some of us being directed here, some being escorted there.

There was to be no ending ceremony to the first day's march, nor did anyone expect one. But without further ado, all the front row marchers were gone, whisked away for protocol reasons, or security reasons. Still hand-in-hand, speechless and momentarily confused, Albert and I went alone into the largest tent—the mess tent, it turned out, and almost large enough to hold a circus—and sank wearily to the ground inside. Only then could we let each other go. Our legs had suddenly turned to rubber. Our Northern white faces, shut too long indoors by winter, were already much changed in color, we knew without having to see them for ourselves. Our cheeks were beginning to feel quite tender from the combined effects of sun and breeze. Immediately we were inundated by a flood of tired marchers arriving just behind us.

Albert did not permit himself to rest more than a few minutes before making his move. "Wait here until I come back," he told me, struggling to his feet. "I've got to find Dr. Heschel before he gets away. He'll be leaving shortly to catch his plane, and he told me there might be room for us in the car to Montgomery. Don't go anywhere!"

"Don't worry, I won't." I nodded wearily and wordlessly, no longer surprised by Albert's connections. I watched him make his way with quiet persistence through the tangle of tired bodies now strewn all over the pasture ground beneath the canvas, with still more marchers constantly arriving. The familiar *yarmulke,* set firmly upon the head of wavy black hair, disappeared from sight around the side flap of the tent. Did he think I would go anywhere? I had no intention of getting up and going anywhere, not until he came for me. If it meant I had to sit there and be smothered to death by arriving marchers, swarming relentlessly into the mess tent like ants to their anthill. Nearly seven hours of walking upright on my unexercised, inadequate frame had been quite enough!

Wedging my knapsack behind my hips for a backrest, I stretched forth my throbbing legs as far as I could without getting them sat upon or stepped upon, and reflected upon the day's events. I had to accept the revelation that I wasn't all that ready to be a martyr after all. For a few brief moments of my life, albeit running backwards, I had been out in front. It had been glorious, but it had been quite enough. And I was convinced of it now—I really only wanted to continue to "play flute." Let M. L. King, Jr. be the leader of the band!

But shivering inside beneath my deepening sunburn, I faced up to the truth of what had shaken me. It was not the realization in retrospect that while walking backward I could have been shot in the back by some hidden sniper out to get Martin Luther King. Nor even the possibility that a telescopic camera lens might have picked up and beamed my cookie antics to an unsympathetic watching world. Instead, it had been that ridiculous, completely unexpected incident with the horse that had thrown me.

I went over it in my mind, step by step. I reviewed the initial shock, the paralyzing fear, as the white stallion with the "spears" galloped toward me, followed instantly after by the reflex action of getting myself away from imminent danger any way I could. I had been physically and emotionally shaken by the experience for a long time afterward.

And now I sat stiff and aching and hot-faced on the prickly ground under this crowded, suffocating canvas tent, and chastised myself for the hundredth time for not having stood my ground a few seconds longer when the horse had charged. And I was growing ever more aware of the constraints of that garter belt squeezing at my mid-section and thighs. In short order I began to wonder what, for heaven's sake, had happened to Albert? Didn't he realize we had to hurry and get out of here? That it was already past six o'clock, and our bus would be leaving Montgomery for home in a mere two hours? I was certain that I knew him well enough by now to know he would not desert me. I had to stay calm, and be patient.

Yesiree; that one frightening incident with the horse had certainly been an eye-opener for me. I really was not as brave nor as mentally prepared for possible martyrdom as I had once considered myself to be. Nor had any of my marching companions been, for that matter, so it had not been just I who had been found wanting. Psyched up though we all still were by our presence in the march, we hadn't been able to turn and stand our ground in order to ascertain the danger of the galloping horse. We weren't able to wait long enough to see whether danger truly existed. Instead, we had scattered like leaves before the March breeze, mindlessly reacting to instinct, forgetting our training. It had been every person for himself or herself, and with never a thought to our fellows, or to the good of the group, or to the good of the Cause.

How was a stampeding horse so different, when you analyzed it, from an emotionally hyped-up and armed human being who stood "on the other side of the fence," a person unreasoningly fearful of a change in the long-established social order? Well, we had a long way to go, we ordinary folk, before we could be counted on to fully utilize Gandhian principles, much less stick together in a pinch. I wondered again if Dr. King had been constantly aware of our weakness throughout the afternoon. And if he had been aware, how awful for him, to be at the head of such an undisciplined collection of well-meaning novices and greenhorns. To not ever be sure of what they might be up to, or have been exposed to, back there behind you!

Mentally, I compared the situation to a man single-handedly escorting ten thousand Red Riding Hoods on a forest hike, knowing there might be hungry wolves all around but having no weapons with which to fight them off! And worse: not believing in using weapons, even if we had them. But he, Martin Luther King, had all those young marshalls close by to help him, I shouldn't forget. Those wonderful marshalls, some white, most black, who seemed to know just what they were doing.

Still no sign of Albert; so I went over those moments still further back of the cookie-sharing, trying to conjure up my feelings of exaltation as I danced out before that magnificent army for peaceful change. But those joyous sensations refused to come again. Instead, an entirely new thought, a horrifying thought, flashed across my brain.

Good lord, Gwen Gain! Do you realize what you might have done? Two Nobel Peace Prize winners and all those other church folks, and those Selma heroes, and the important government officials from New York City, and some from Hawaii as well! And you fed them food you picked off a trash can! Suppose it had been poisoned, and planted there . . . !

I guessed I'd had enough of rubbing elbows with the big guys. Yesiree; let Martin Luther King, Jr., be the leader of the band. Carry the baton. He was the exact same age as I, born in my year of 1929, that ridiculous year when the stock market crashed and instigated the disaster known as the Great Depression. But he was a male, and that made all the difference. I'd do what little I could to help, as long as it meant not having to stick my own fragile neck out too far. But my little female light was too dim to stand alone. Even back in "safe and tolerant" New Jersey.

A man would have thought about the possibility of poison. A man would have been suspicious. I was too utterly naïve, I now understood, to play in the big leagues.

Where, oh, where, was Albert?

What a big talker I had once been about commitment. Once, when I was sixteen, in that long-ago year just after World War II had ended, I had delivered the valedictory address at my high school graduation. I had actually stood up there on the auditorium stage at Woodbury High School, taken my place behind the podium in a rented white cap and robe, and given the prepared speech my father had helped me write. It was a speech about conscious choices and leadership in a world that had been given a second chance, and about the rightness of causes that benefited all of humanity. I had expressed those ideals, my own deeply held convictions, to a packed audience of parents and other relatives and friends, almost all of whom were white.

"To every man there openeth a high way and a low," I had begun my address in early June of 1946, quoting from my mother's liberal Baptist hymnal which often turned secular poems into hymns of inspiration. "And every man decideth the way his soul shall go."

I could hear behind me in the back row of bleachers on the stage some of the General Studies boys prying caps off of Coca-Cola bottles they had sneaked into the auditorium under their robes. I had already been warned they would do it; it was a school tradition. Although the tell-tale pops and hissing sounds distracted me as I spoke, I was yet relieved that these same kids, my classmates, had been spared the necessity of going off to fight for democracy around the world. My remarks had been directed toward ending war forever, not about improving race relations in America. It seemed that nobody had wanted to hear yet, in 1946, about improving race relations in America. My father and mother had talked me out of including it, and I had ultimately been convinced.

But okay, all that had happened back in the old, made-safe-for-democracy days when I was in my teens. Back then I still had the guts to get up before an audience and say stirring things, or anything that smacked of an opinion, without blushing scarlet. Back when I still hoped, and indeed, presumed, that the concept of that loaded word "man" included me.

But I saw it all now, very plainly. The thing I had always suspected deep inside, but could never accept. Those high-sounding pieces of rhetoric, like all those others I had copied into my little blue notebook—they were written *by* men, *for* men. Every last one of them. "To every *man* there openeth a high way and a low." "A *man's* reach should exceed his grasp, or what's a heaven for?" "What *men* believe is a function of what they are." And on and on and on. And finally, Rabbi Albert Friedlander's own splendid contribution: "*Man* is morally committed to action in the face of evil."

They, those high-minded men who spoke or wrote those words, truly, truly hadn't meant me. I was lucky, after all, that I was a woman and a mother! From now on, I was off the hook!

*   *   *

43.

"We Italians (Greeks, Poles) made it on our own. Why can't these people (Negroes) work hard and deserve their freedom too?"
      —Gina Alesandrini,* co-worker, U. of P,
            —Tony Nikolos,* mailman
      —Mary Ellen Alinsky,* neighbor
      (Post-Selma Comments etc . . . .)

Rabbi Friedlander came back for me as dusk was falling. He had found his colleagues and had made arrangements for our transportation with them as far as the 'Montgomery airport. From there, he had been told, he and I could take the airport limousine service, or perhaps a cab, to the Benmor to catch our charter bus.

I followed Albert outside the tent to where a car stood with engine running amidst the hordes of wilted marchers who had just completed their eleven miles. They now stood or sat about in the tent between piles of cow dung, not certain what to do or where to go. Only three hundred could stay, to continue on in the morning. The rest had to leave. I winced at thought of the effort and the hours that would be required for a few private cars to transport these thousands back to Selma and their homes, or their hostesses homes, or their own cars. But of course, once some got to their cars in Selma, they too could come back for others. If only I had driven our VW bus down. Think of the numbers it would have held!

There was nothing I could do about that now. Now I had to take what help was offered to me by others, and be grateful, and keep moving. I had to get myself out of the way.

I was eased quickly inside the back seat of the waiting sedan by several outstretched hands, and scarcely before I was aware of what was happening. There was no time to take a last look around at the first campsite, or find out what had happened to poor, ill Dr. Bunche, or send a message to Martin Luther King to thank him for having me, or even to say goodbye to anyone who might be listening and care to say goodbye back.

I found myself balancing on Albert's knobby knees in the back seat, my shoulder bag squeezed onto my lap. The other two parts of my traveling gear, the knapsack and the sleeping bag, were crammed in beside our four legs as the door was slammed shut. The trunk, someone said, was too full of suitcases and SCLC march supplies to add anything else.

Next to me, in the middle of the back seat, sat bewhiskered Abraham Heschel, looking none the worse for his hike in the Alabama sun. And beside him by the window was Maurice, the "Shavua Tov" rabbi from the mass meeting who spoke with the Long Island accent, the man who had met Albert and me at the bus stop Friday night. Two other rabbis in black all-weather coats were in the front seat beside the driver. They did not seem to be the same men who had been in the back seat that night, along with the trade sheet reporter who had once been tortured. But I could not be certain and I was too embarrassed to ask.

A white kid who looked to be about twenty was driving the car. He explained to us as we pulled slowly away from the campsite and headed down the now-unguarded highway toward Montgomery, that he was always careful never to exceed the speed limit by a single mile per hour.

He said cheerfully, "They watch for us, you see. Al Lingo's guys on the State Highway Patrol. They know we're SNICK drivers by our northern license plates and our young age, and they look for any excuse to pull us over and give us a hard time and a ticket."

Maurice was worried. "We've got to catch that plane," he said. "Those are the only seats available until Tuesday." Day after tomorrow.

"We have plenty of time." Dr. Heschel spoke up with quiet authority. "Don't worry, young man; just you drive carefully." And from then on, Maurice kept his concern to himself, though we could all tell he was nervous. Just as I was beginning to be, thinking about our charter bus leaving at eight from Montgomery.

The two rabbis in the front discussed for awhile the miracle of modern flight. How amazing it was that two hours after take-off this evening, they'd be at Kennedy airport outside New York City, waiting for cabs that would possibly require another two hours to get them to their own homes. And they had left their homes to come here only this morning.

Albert and I sat silent. I was thinking about our eight o'clock deadline. Thinking also about the night-and-day-and-another night trip on the bus after that. If we made it, that is.

Cramped as I was, I could do little more than lean against the seat in front of me, trying not to squirm too much on Albert's knees. I stared straight ahead at the headlights of our car snaking along the sweeping curves of the dark highway, at least what little I could see of them between the head of the driver and the suspended rear-view mirror. Night had fully descended, and with it had come even greater uneasiness.

The young driver kept up a running commentary. He told us that he was from Rhode Island. "I've been down here helping with the voter registration project for the past six months, taking a leave-of-absence from college." he said. Straining my ears to hear him, I thought of Peter, who had decided to stay on a whim, and wondered how much help he could possibly be down here without a vehicle of his own. Jacob*, this fellow at the wheel, seemed so much more mature for his young age of twenty-one. Maybe the six months he had already put in had "weathered" him. One thing was for sure, he drove a large and expensive car.

Someone asked him why he had come South.

"I dunno," came the answer. "Guess I just wanted to see what the commies were really up to down here," and we all snickered appreciatively at his little joke.

"And you, young woman. What brought you here?"

I was the only female, young or otherwise, in the car. I realized with a start that Abraham Heschel was directing his question to me. When I turned to look at him where he sat close beside me, I could see he was attempting from beneath his bushy eyebrows to scan my face through the darkness. Though I could not see him well, I was nevertheless reminded of pictures I had seen of Albert Schweitzer, the great organist and humanitarian, living his Unitarian reverence for life in the jungles of equatorial Africa.

Legs still aching, cheeks and forehead beginning to smart from the sunburn, waist pinched and thighs sweating under my relentless garter belt, I had hoped to remain as inconspicuous as possible on this part of the trip. I wanted to just be left alone to direct what energy I had left to keeping as much of my weight as possible off Albert Friedlander's knees. My one-hundred-and-thirty-five pounds must surely seem to him double that. But I had to answer the deceptively innocent question coming from beneath Dr. Heschel's whiskers. Those piercing eyes through the darkness compelled me to. And the last thing I wanted was to appear rude or simple-minded so that Albert would be ashamed of me in front of all these smart and well educated men, his friends and colleagues.

You, young woman. What brought you here?

The question still hung in the air, while thoughts whirled in my weary brain. What could I answer that would not sound outright schmaltzy or even childish? Could I reply, even with earnest simplicity, that I thought I knew how it felt to be denied a basic right because of an irrelevant condition like the color of one's skin? No one had ever, that I could recall, denied me a basic right.

Oh, certainly; I'd been denied the opportunity to play flute in the Woodbury High School marching band, simply because I lacked the necessary anatomical equipment in one part of me, or possessed too much in the other, to be seen in public wearing a uniform jacket and trousers. But no, that was too trite an example to offer this distinguished scholar and theologian.

Nor would he truly be able to comprehend my unique frustrations as a female. I had long ago discovered that the most sympathetic of men were seldom able to grasp the connection between rights denied to Negroes and the state of *de facto* second-class citizenship in which women had long been kept. Women were not being kept down, as most men saw it, but cherished and protected. Why couldn't they be happy with that? most men wondered.

The problem that has no name.

What brought me here? If Dr. Heschel hoped I was going to say something pious like "God sent me," he had another think coming! I could say, pretentiously, that I was just working out one of my long-sublimated guilt complexes. In these days of psychoanalysis being considered respectable, that might suffice. That would sound sophisticated and not at all schmaltzy.

But then I remembered that all these men in the car with me, with the possible exception of the SNICK driver, were—Jews!

I said, "I'm here because of Anne Frank, I guess." Instantly I regretted my choice of words. When I said them out loud, they had sounded to me worse than schmaltzy. Like I was trying to make points with all these Jewish men of the cloth. Like I was apple-polishing the lot of them.

As if he had read my mind, Maurice guffawed derisively from his seat on the other side of Dr. Heschel. "No comparison!"

"But of course there is!" My burnt face and aching limbs were forgotten for the moment, and so was my resolve to take the easy way out from then on, to not get involved. Now that I had gone this far, it was vital that I make myself understood. "What I meant to say was, we can't . . . we can't let what happened to Anne Frank . . . happen here . . . . here in this country!"

"How so?" The nosy Maurice again, trying to rattle me.

"The murder of all those Jews in Europe by the Nazis . . . that happened, didn't it . . . because the German people didn't even try to say no . . . until it was already too late? And when an entire group of people are permitted no say in their own destiny . . . and no one else stands up and says no . . . ?" Why did I always talk much too fast, when I talked to men? Was it because I feared they would not listen to me, a woman, for very long? Because they had decided in advance I had nothing of any importance to say? It was like I always felt I had to hit with my quick sentences, then run. Or rather, shut up before I got shut off.

"I'd never read anything written by a woman," my brilliant father is telling me. "They don't have anything to say."

"When people are made scapegoats . . . and other people don't stand up to protest their mistreatment . . ." Was I blushing? How could I know? But my face must be already a bright shade of pink, and so hot even I couldn't tell a blush from a burn. And the inside of the car was dark, thank goodness. "I'd think you guys, of all people, could see that!" I snapped out, directing my annoyance past Dr. Heschel's head and shoulders to the rabbi Maurice. Of course they would all know what I meant: you Jews, of all people.

The comparison must have been unwelcome. I'd apparently offended them. Even my good friend Albert said nothing. Remembering his words about commitment to action in the face of evil, I had hoped he'd at least agree with my premise. But maybe he didn't, not when it came down to Jewish brass tacks, my comparing their plight with that of Negroes.

But then hadn't he had done just that, last night in Brown's Chapel!

"The German people!" scoffed Maurice. He leaned over in front of Dr. Heschel to get closer to me. "What could the German people have done against Hitler and his storm troopers, even if they'd wanted to. It was a different situation entirely!"

"They waited too long!" I said, telling myself to calm down. "That's all. They simply waited too long. Until it was too late. That's all." And I let my words trail off to silence.

I hoped he would drop it. I had held my own, up to now. The best I had done in a long time, debating an issue with a male other than my prejudiced friend Jim Clemson. Maybe the rest of these men in the car with me were being cautious, waiting to see what the great theologian beside me would say. But I was rapidly losing steam, and wanted to quit.

"You're quite right, my dear." Once again I was startled by Abraham Heschel's voice coming at me through the darkness. His words were directed straight at me. He gave my cheek one approving, fatherly pat and then withdrew his hand. "Maurice is just teasing you. Maurice, that's enough!" And now I saw that of course, Maurice had been doing just that and like a fool, I had fallen for it.

"Yes, my dear," said Dr. Heschel again. I could just make out that his flowing beard was bobbing up and down on his chest. "You're quite right about all that," Albert Schweitzer, I suddenly remembered from the photographs I had seen, had no beard, merely a bushy white mustache.

"Thank you," I said, relieved that the conversation had apparently been ended. I sank back still further onto Albert's legs, hoping I wasn't causing him too much pain. Dr. Heschel too seemed to want to slump down on the seat and remain quiet. I had no idea how old he was, but he looked to my thirty-five-year-old eyes to be quite ancient. And today he had walked eleven miles in the sun, with no chance to rest in between except for those few moments when we sat down with Dr. King and Dr. Bunche to eat the prepared lunches on a hillside.

[I would lay eyes upon him once again in my life, this kindly, venerable old man. He would give the eulogy at Martin Luther King's funeral services in Georgia, three years hence, and I would watch it all over the television through grief-swollen eyes. A few short years later, I would read in the papers that he too had died. But before that happened, he would visit Philadelphia, to speak to an all-male Conference being held in a synagogue, a Conference from which women were excluded. And I would send him a note saying welcome to Philadelphia and that I was a paid staff worker in fair housing now, and did he remember that he and I had conversed about Anne Frank on our way to the Montgomery airport after the Selma march? And he would write back and say of course he remembered me, and "you were quite right, my dear, about all that."]

When we arrived at the entrance to the modern Montgomery airport terminal, we passengers piled out quickly. All at once we were energized again. We bade farewell and god speed to Jacob, our SNICK driver, who had gotten us there with a few minutes to spare before the New York-bound flight would take off. Before he left, however, I pointed to the white card stuck onto his windshield from the inside that read, "Staff Worker, March on Montgomery."

"Maybe you ought to take that off of there for your ride back?" I suggested.

The young man chuckled, "Don't worry about me! Now that I'm alone, if I see anyone suspicious, I'll lose 'em!" The biggest threat, he had told us earlier, was not the state highway troopers, who only harrassed SNICK drivers and gave out tickets. It was the "night riders" from the Ku Klux Klan that he tried to stay clear of, he said. And then we watched him speed away with a determined lift of his chin behind the wheel.

While I waited inside the brightly-lit terminal with my luggage, Albert went to check at the ticket counter for a seat to New York.

"Just as I thought, filled up and nothing until tomorrow night. I'm stuck with the bus," he said, coming back to where I sat. But he sounded not in the least disgruntled. He and I parted with still more cordial goodbyes from the four other rabbis, whose plane was due to take off in fifteen minutes. Alone again, Albert and I we went in search of the next airport limousine headed for Montgomery.

*   *   *

44.

"Oh! Signore,
fa di me un istrumento della tua Pace.
Dove e odio, fa ch'io porti l'Amore.
Dove e offesa,ch'io porti il Perdono,
Dove e discordia, ch'io porti l'Unione . . . ,"
—S. Francesco di Assisi
(From my WTLB)

Now it was our turn to get panicky about being late. Now we got a good dose of how worry-wart Maurice must have felt. Surely Keene would not let the bus leave at eight o'clock without us, we told each other, company contract or no company contract. Surely she'd know we were on our way, and would convince the two drivers of that. But it was already well past seven-thirty, and we were still at the airport.

The two of us sat facing each other, shoulders rounded with fatigue, at the very back of the two long seats running lengthwise down the rear of the airport limousine. We hoped that in the gray shadows our tell-tale red faces would not be too apparent to the driver, nor to the other six passengers, all of them white businessmen types who had just gotten off planes and who climbed in the side doors one by one during the long wait at the terminal entrance. My knapsack and sleeping bag, further evidence of our recent annoying activities, were tucked inconspicuously beneath one of the seats. I told myself to stop worrying along those lines. Wouldn't it be "logical," I leaned across the aisle and whispered into Albert's ear, for everyone else here to assume that he and I, too, had just de-planed? But still I felt nervous. Suppose someone guessed where we had been, what we were doing . . .

Surely, surely our team leader Keene Stassen would hold the bus!

No one spoke to us or paid us particular heed as the limousine picked up speed and got onto U.S. 8O again, bound for Montgomery five or six miles away. The two men next to me smoked cigarettes and made my eyes smart along with my burnt cheeks and chin. Lights played over all our faces in eerie patterns as the limousine approached the city limits and got into the commercial district. Once, at a red light, Albert and I were pinioned in the glow from a restaurant sign. We stared at each other long and hard until Albert winked at me. The look and the wink said, "Don't worry. I'm starved, aren't you?" At least I think that's what it said.

And I could only muster the ghost of a rueful smile. It hurt my face to smile, and besides, I had no desire to call any attention to myself from anyone else. For a few minutes I pretended it was all still fun. I pretended to myself that we, Albert and I, were Huck Finn and his slave friend Jim again, this time trying to escape from the bounty-hunters who would take Jim away forever. I was Huck, who had long ago "lit out for the territory."

As we went into the section of Montgomery's big office buildings, we were holding our breaths. We wanted to shout "hurry!" while the other passengers were let off, two by two, at nice hotels. Then we were driving into the shabbier part of the city. The little stores and businesses were closed up tight because it was Sunday evening. We approached with mounting anxiety the street on which the Benmor was located.

It was now twenty minutes past eight!

But look! Look! There it sat, not a river raft, but our beautiful, familiar silver-gray bus with the blue trim and the running greyhound painted on its side, parked long and squat against the curb in front of the Benmor with its motor running.

"There they are!" said Albert, much relieved. "Our home away from home!"

"Good old, wonderful old Greyhound bus! Good old Keene! And Carl and Jeffrey! They didn't go off without us!" I declared.

Jeffrey was already behind the wheel, studying a map and looking impatient to be off. But alas, poor fellow! Because when we climbed out of the limousine and walked up to the open bus door, we expected to be greeted with remonstrations on the order of, "Where have you been?" and "Come on, get in, so we can get this show on the road!" from a chorus of voices. But we were amazed to find there was not a single passenger aboard!

Keene Stassen was inside the decrepit waiting room with only a handful of her young charges from the bus. She was kneeling beside one of the seats. Ever the efficient sohoolteacher, she checked our two names off her clipboard list before giving us so much as a word of greeting. And then she took another look, first at my face, then at Albert's. And grimacing in sympathy, she fished from her mammoth purse a large-sized jar of Noxzema.

"Hi, you guys," she said. "Welcome back. Look's like you both could use some of this."

"Thanks, Keene," said Albert, taking the jar from her hand. "You're wonderful. You think of everything."

"Not quite." She modestly made a face. "The drivers are getting up tight and all the kids aren't back. Go easy on that Noxzema. I have a feeling some of the others are going to need it too."

"The others? How so?" We waited for her to explain.

"Almost all of them went into Selma this morning so they could march out again with the rest of you."

"Hey, great!" I said, pleased for the ones who had told me they wanted to go too.

"I've learned from teaching Negro kids that even they can get sunburned." Keene said.

After telling us she'd managed to walk a few symbolic miles with the march herself during the late afternoon—someone had driven her there and back again—she returned to her business of implementing the return bus trip from her temporary "office" on one of the old plastic seats of the bus stop waiting room. She continued checking off names as people straggled in in small groups dropped off from car-pools. I was happy to see that we charter-bus passengers had the waiting room all to ourselves.

The rabbi and I proceeded to dip into Keene's Noxzema and smooth the unguent over our red faces until we resembled pale ghosts. Only my forehead, still eerily white under my protective bangs, had escaped the now-painful ravages of the Alabama sun. I was beginning to feel nauseated from hunger and sunburn, and the bad veins in both my calves throbbed harder than ever. There was nothing to put in our stomachs but bitter coffee from an erratic dispensing machine. The machine in charge of crackers swallowed our dimes with arrogant clicks and coughed nothing back in return.

Within the next hour all of the "kids" on Keene's list were finally accounted for. The white couple with the Peace Corps children were among them. The black professor. Bill and Tom, our two primary Snick leaders, too. And Wilma and Donna and their shy girlfriend. The confident young black woman with the dangling earrings who was doing a story on the proposed Alabama Freedom Democratic Party for her college newspaper—she got back, one of the last to make it. All these, and most of the rest, had indeed been transported by the SNICK-run shuttle-service of private cars to Selma for the march, and as Keene had predicted, most were badly in need of the benefit of her Noxzema jar, regardless of their skin color.

Peter and the blond-haired social worker from Harlem were the only ones of the original passengers not going back with us. The social worker had sent word to Keene that he'd just be fired anyway when he got back to New York City, for taking two days off without leave. He might as well stay with the SCLC people in Selma and try to make himself useful, he had told her. Keene had already signed up two one-way-paying customers to take the available seats.

I felt a new kinship with all the home-bound riders, familiar to me or not, because nearly all of us there had walked the same path that day, the eleven up-and-down miles along U.S. 80. We had all followed Dr. King in his quest for voting rights for the South's Negroes. We knew we would always be proud of that, regardless of what anyone else thought.

Keene's busload of Southern-civil-rights initiates assembled at last, we took our seats, wild to get going now that the time had actually come for it. Albert and I found places together four rows back on the right, and this time I insisted that he take the window seat to start. He sank into it without protest. Stomachs were growling on all sides, but everyone understood we'd have to find a place far down the road, far distant from Montgomery, before we, an integrated group of brown and red, would dare to stop for supper. Surely I'd have a gruesome case of indigestion by that time, I thought, pitying myself.

The bus actually pulled away from the Benmor a few minutes after nine-thirty, that twenty-first day of March. But not before a volatile young black man of about thirty got aboard and paced up and down the aisle numerous times, ranting as he delivered his evaluation of the day's big event above the noisy vibrations of the bus engine. I had no recollection of having seen him before and did not recognize who he was. His manner and sound of speaking seemed unaccented to me, and thus Northern, containing only a trace of a Southern drawl.

"Do you understand, you people from up North, the importance of what happened here today? Do you understand what really happened here in Alabama? It is vital you people grasp the significance of this historic day!" the young man barked out at us as he paced up and down the aisle. He could only be referring to the Selma march, I gathered from his message.

"We have won here today, with our feet and our determination, a great victory for humanity! The Movement has chipped away at the structure of an evil society, struck another blow at tyranny, and we have been privileged to play a part in that process. We have been living instruments of freedom, all of you people here, and all of us in the Movement who have been laboring so long under such abominable conditions . . . ."

He too must have walked with us. Was still walking, marching up and down the aisle of the bus, reliving our accomplishment in retrospect, unable as yet to calm himself; or perhaps not willing to. He made me think of the runner who goes full-speed over the finish line and deliberately runs a few more paces past the goal before coming to a stop.

After one of his passes by us, someone whispered across the aisle to my questioning expression that this was Jim Forman, a fact that made it easier for me to comprehend his inordinate excitement. James Forman, Albert and I had learned by this time, was the Co-Chairman of the Student Non-Violence Coordinating Committee. What we didn't know was whether he and the other Co-Chairman, a Negro named John Lewis, had settled their basic differences with the Southern Christian Leadership Conference, and with Dr. King himself, over the strategy governing the Selma campaign.

I remembered Tom Courtney's words to me on the way down: "Forman and Lewis think Dr. King is compromising the Movement when he honors an illegal injunction against the March On Montgomery. So SNICK has pulled out for now. They've decided to concentrate instead on their registration efforts in Montgomery."

Apparently, judging by James Forman's passionate ramblings, and by the fact that the young people from our bus had been sent in to Selma for the march, and by the fact that SNICK drivers were today being used for march transportation, the SNICK people had somewhat gotten over their mad. Or they had at least decided to be good sports and pitch in where they were needed and thus present a united front to the white world. Apparently, too, the others from the bus had already met Mr. Forman, and were familiar by this time with his flamboyant style. One by one, they were settling themselves back in their seats for sleep.

Surreptitiously so as not to be caught talking behind teacher's back, I hissed to Albert beside me, "So what if we did do all that? I'm so hungry I feel sick!"

The time for speeches was over for awhile. I wanted to start for home, with no more delays. I was hungry and exhausted; yearning simultaneously for food and for sleep. I missed my children all at once. I missed Bill too. He was like my fifth child, wasn't he? And I had left him one thousand miles away in New Jersey, with all that unaccustomed responsibility. I had been crazy, at thirty-five and with my bad varicose veins and nervous stomach and dust-and-pollen allergies, to come here in the first place.

It seemed that ever since leaving my home for Alabama I had spent most of my time waiting. Waiting to go somewhere. Waiting for events to begin. Waiting for them to continue. Waiting for them to end. And all the time, I had been sitting or standing or walking behind and beside and in front of other people's heads and shoulders and backs and rear ends and arms, so that my vision was greatly curtailed and I could never see the whole picture, or know completely what was going on. It was always "apparently this, or could it be that?" Or someone was saying to me, "I guess it was because of this, that that happened. But I don't really know."

But then, apparently, it was always this way, this business of being part of an "historic event." Ninety-nine-and-nine-tenths of it, I now saw, was waiting. Waiting, and never being able to grasp the totality, like the blind men who had tried to describe an elephant to their blind king when they had each felt a different part of the strange animal's anatomy. Like waiting beforehand on ships, like those thousands of brave young Americans who had gone ashore on the beaches of Normandy in 1944. And because you couldn't see the whole picture, you never really understood anything that was transpiring. You could die without ever knowing that.

Being physically uncomfortable must be a part of helping to make history too. There was apparently no getting away from it, along with sometimes wishing you had stayed at home. Maybe it was that way with life's less significant achievements, as well. Like getting to wear your high school's uniform and playing a flute in a marching band. Maybe that wasn't always the fun and games I had imagined it to be.

My Wendi had joined her high school marching band last year, I reminded myself. She had used the very same flute I had played as a child. Not at the same school, of course. She had worn Merchantville High's colors, a kelly-green uniform of trousers and jacket, and a hat with a yellow tassel, and times had changed so much no one thought anything of it except that she "looked darling," something you'd never say about one of the boys.

But so many times during the football season she had complained to me, "Mom, I get freezing' cold on that field! And besides, playin' all the time, I never really get to watch the game!" To watch the players on the team, she meant. She didn't give a fig about the football. The worst part of it, she said, was the waiting. Always standing in your row and file, waiting. For something to begin. For someone to tell you what to do.

And I would say back to her something on the order of, "It's freezing, honey, not freezin'. And you don't understand what a privilege it is, to be able to march with your school band." And I would tell her again how it had been with me. How much I had hungered . . . .

But she definitely had a point, I saw now. Being a constant participant in life meant you could relish only one piece of the puzzle at a time. And there was something to be said for being a spectator, as long as you had a good seat. You could always get up and leave when you wanted to. And in the meantime, you got a good view of the field of action.

Abruptly, James Forman wound up his cathartic soliloquy. (I say soliloquy, because no one was listening to his voice now but himself; not really). And bidding us farewell, he swung himself down the steps of the bus. No one applauded or moved a finger to bid him goodbye, but I don't think he expected that. For one terrible moment, we feared he would say more from the bottom step, but the driver gunned the motor suggestively and Mr. Forman was soon gone, vanishing into the night. To go where? To do what? As far as any one of us knew, we were the only bus anywhere around for him to make a speech to. Why wasn't he one of the three hundred chosen marchers, still back at the first campsite? Was he, like us, feeling superfluous? Or had he come here to make certain we got safely on our way? How could we ever know?

He was undoubtedly a very smart and a very fine young man, one who had committed his life to our cause. Once he was gone I was sorry I had not listened closer, and shown more patience; or at least sat upright and made him think I was listening. "Patience is the companion of wisdom," St. Augustine had sagely said, and several hundred years later I had duly noted that in my little blue notebook. Tomorrow I would get the notebook out of my shoulder bag and add a postscript of my own. *"Participators in life need more patience than wisdom.—G.* Gain."

From her front-seat command post, Keene Stassen now signaled Jeffrey the driver that he too could leave. We bumped and growled our way out into the dingy, dimly lit street and I thought I was going to throw up from the odor of stale cigarette smoke and diesel fumes. I had finally discarded that brown paper bag with the crumbs of the civil rights cookies, and therefore had nothing left to be sick into. What could I do? Vomit into my lap? I would die, if I did!

But I was spared that particular embarrassment. Once the bus lights were out, the rabbi offered me is left shoulder in a business-like manner. Gratefully settling my head upon the comforting fabric of his suit jacket, I forgot about my burnt, smeared face and my pinched and upset stomach and my bum legs and how hungry I was, and went soundly, securely to sleep. My last waking awareness was that it had been years since anyone in my life had realized that Superwomen sometimes needed a shoulder to lean on.

*   *   *

END OF PART NINE

PART TEN

THE ROAD HOME

45.

"That's none of our business, down there. There's plenty that
needs to be done right here in Philadelphia."
—Constance Richardson, Director,
Continuing Education for Women,
University of Pennsylvania.
(Post-Selma Comments, etc, etc, ...)

The miles toward home slid quickly away beneath the wheels of the bus,
all that night and into the next day. Treasuring the successful outcome
of our venture, having gone, and done, and survived, and more than
that: having helped make a needed point, however personally small, to a
watching world—knowing these things made it easy for all of us passengers
to finally relax. Our lives were now in the hands of Carl and Jeffrey, our
two competent Greyhound drivers, who were as usual taking turns every
few hours with scarcely a notice to anyone.

Emotionally and physically exhausted riders of the winds of change, we
passengers were able to sleep away an hour or two at a time during the rest
of the night, sitting up in our seats, and doze fitfully by day. We were happy
to leave our fates exclusively to the skills of those two gray-headed bus
drivers and young Keene Stassen. The three of them decided, sometimes
after brief consultation with the two SNICK primary leaders, Tom and
Bill, when it was time to make a restroom stop or a food stop or a gas stop,
and preferably all those in combination.

With the cutting off of the bus motor, all we now docile followers would rouse ourselves as if on signal and lurch wordlessly from the bus in a groggy daze to line up at still another roadside counter for a sandwich and milk or coffee, gulped down as quickly as possible in order to get back on the bus and resume sleep.

As each stop, the twenty-or-so women in our party would invariably have to wait in a restroom line as well, since there were never enough toilets in the Ladies Rooms. Keene and Wilma and Donna and I would hold each other's purses or shoulder bags and stand in front of stall doors for one another when the locks invariably failed to work. Keene cracked once that we women should make better toilet facilities for females our next big cause, to which the nearly two dozens of us muttered our unanimous concurrence.

Once all of us passengers, male and female, were back on the bus and moving again, some of us were now more awake. With our physical needs relieved for awhile, we would engage for an hour or two in subdued conversation with our seat companions before one by one dropping off once more into light sleep. Occasionally some uninhibited soul would attempt to start up a Movement song or do a little public jollying, but it never lasted for long. No matter; the undercurrent of this new cameraderie was all the moral support any of us needed.

Twenty-six hours to home—to my own New Jersey Turnpike stop, at least. More time together in one stretch than most friends get over a lifetime, and Albert Friedlander and I made the most of it. When both of us were awake, we talked and we talked. Even in our restless sleep we sensed the other was there, caring as only two friends can care, and we luxuriated in the privilege of respectful touch. Sometimes Albert would lounge with his head propped against the juncture of window and seat, while I curled up sideways, my back against his arm. Other times we would both sit facing forward, leaning against each other's heads in perfect balance. And sleep. And sleep. Or yet again, he would put an arm around my neck for a change of position and rest his head on top of mine.

The bus was dark, and none of the others would have thought it strange anyhow. We were a man and a woman, and it was so much more pleasant a way to ride than the awkward way we had come. My legs, once recovered from the long hike, had ceased throbbing now that I could shift them somewhat freely about. And my body must have numbed itself to the torments of the garter belt, which no longer was trying to make its presence constantly known. Instead, it seemed to have annexed itself comfortably to my skin.

Our shared adventure had lowered other bars between the rabbi and me. We spoke often, during those intermittent wake-up times, of our personal emotions, not those of the past few days, but long before. We described to each other some of our innermost feelings, particularly those involving our deep love for our children, and talked candidly of our hopes for them of a better world.

I told Albert of little things: of Kenny's excruciating shyness, and his passion for doing research papers and making inventories of everything, including his Hallowe'en and Easter candy. I told Albert of Scotty's elfin, trash-picking ways and his desire to own his own personal flying machine. Of Julie's love affair with cats and her mother, me. Of Wendi's success in teaching herself to play guitar when the piano lessons we had paid for had been a pathetic failure.

Albert told me about his little Ariel, how she was just beginning to talk and loved being carried around by the hour on his shoulders, her tiny legs around his neck, her fingernails pinching his cheeks. My cast of characters was much bigger than his, but he didn't seem to mind.

Mention of those little ones we had up to now tried to exclude from conscious memory brought Albert at length to confide to me a carefully preserved secret. Evelyn, his adored young wife, might be pregnant for the second time. I was the first to be entrusted with this unconfirmed suspicion, he impressed upon me. Except, of course, for the two of them. Neither of their families, nor even the doctor, knew it yet.

"We've been hoping for a long time," he said. "We decided it must be true, only the day before I left."

"And that's why Evelyn couldn't come with you?" I suddenly guessed.

"Yes. She had some trouble, the first pregnancy. We could have found someone to keep Ariel, but it just didn't seem like good sense." Good sense. There it was again. But Evelyn, and Adelaide, they both had had good reason for using good sense. Albert went on to express to me the self-doubt he felt concerning his relationship with his wife, his apprehension that he might be too old for her. She was so young and alive and talented. He was thirteen years older than she, and someday, he said, when he was fifty or so—she might find herself bored with him.

I did my best to reassure him that kind of age gap was nothing to worry about; that I had happily married friends who were twenty years apart, and the wife was nearly forty to the husband's sixty. And I dared to share with him my own deep and somewhat darker secret. The resolve that someday, probably a hundred years hence, I said, I was going to cease the hypocrisy of my present life and get up sufficient courage to leave my husband. And Bill was only three years older than I, I told him.

As I had known would be the case, Albert was not a bit shocked. Even when I told him Bill didn't beat me, or drink alcohol, or run around with other women. What held me back was not so much our economic situation, I told the rabbi, though that was difficult. It was knowing how hurt Bill would be to lose both me and his children.

"So you see, Al, age has very little to do with how a relationship works out. Bill's a nice guy, and all that. Very conscientious about his job. We get along fine, and we're friends."

But I wanted more from my life, I told him. Much more. I wanted mental stimulation of some sort from the person I lived with. I wanted travel and adventures, large and small. I longed to share a variety of free but precious pleasures with a man in a home where the monster television was only a shade in the background and not the dominant force in the whole family's daily schedule. My growing-up years in a big family had spoiled me, I guessed, elaborating. No television was around until I was fully grown, and we children listened to very little radio. But oh, there were so many other things to think about and do. The things my parents had exposed me to: Music. Poetry. Plays. Games. Ideas. "Sometimes, I wonder," and I was puzzling over it out loud, "if I expect too much of marriage."

"No, I don't think so, Gwen," Albert said. Once again we were sitting up straight, leaning our heads against our headrests, our mouths talking into the air above us. "Evelyn and I have a good relationship. She has her music, and I have my writing, but we enjoy doing so many things together. We travel a lot. We make a trip to England once a year to visit her family. We hardly ever turn on the TV. But *we* talk to each other, constantly, about so much. In fact . . ." And here he paused, turning his head to stare out the bus window for a few seconds before continuing. "Before Evelyn, I never guessed how wonderful life could be. And I think maybe . . . maybe I should take her back to England to live. She'd like that."

Albert and I had thus offered, and accepted, these confidences without so much as a murmur of surprise, or any words of lecture. Yet we each were flattered by the evident ease with which the other made confession. We had begun to suspect by now that we were not revealing certain vulnerabilities to total strangers upon whom we'd never set eyes again, as was surely the case with the friends we had left behind in Selma.

A tentative and hopeful "who knows?" had crept into our conversation. Our trust in each other acknowledged that we could indeed meet again someday and for that reason it was important to be as honest as possible with each other. We could admit to having personal doubts and frustrations without fear the other would use them against us. This was no time for playing games, we suspected. Not if we meant to be permanent, through-thick-or-thin buddies forever.

Sometimes we were temporarily talked out. That was when we read in silence, sharing a newspaper purchased from a dispensing box at one of our stops. Albert, poor man, would have to hold the print six inches from his eyeglasses in order to make out the words. But he would manage to consume an entire column of material in half the time it took me.

Other times, as the hours toward home went by, we chatted with Donna and Wilma, who occupied the two seats in front of us. Donna was capable of sitting on her knees an hour at a time, leaning over the seatback to talk. Blessed with an abundance of energy and an obviously high I.Q., she would tell us jokes and ask us questions and get us involved in word games, her merry eyes alternately piercing mine and the rabbi's. At last wearying of these simple pursuits as a way to pass the time, she would loll over the back rest and gaze through the tinted glass of the window for miles, lost in her own thoughts and providing me in the seat behind her ample opportunity to study her smooth brown features. She was a bright and beautiful young girl of sixteen. I envied her the years that lay ahead for her, as well as the choices she would get a chance to make.

"Since you're an only child, Donna," I asked her once, "did you have any trouble getting your parents to sign permission for you to come on this trip?" I was thinking of my own daughter Wendi, who had wanted so badly to come with me.

"Nope. No trouble at all. They think I'm very responsible for my age." Donna giggled, but otherwise made no attempt to refute the general impression she figured her parents had of her. "They think it's important for smart black people with advantages to help the ones of our race who aren't as lucky."

Never forget, Gwennie, that superior intellect carries with it the obligation of social responsibility . . . The Baptist pastor of my childhood in Woodbury, with whom I'd fallen in love at the age of nine.

In contrast to Donna, her friend Wilma was too old, at twenty-four, to need parental consent. She was considerably more reserved than the bubbling Donna, and much less optimistic about her own future along with the future of all of America's Negroes. She told Albert and me of her growing disillusionment with democracy. How she had been, in her teens, idealistic like Donna. But then it had finally dawned on her in her early twenties that there was nothing she could do to change things, either for herself or for her race as a whole.

"I've got a decent job in New York," Wilma said. "I'm secretary to a couple of white stockbrokers and the salary is good. The job is okay, and it doesn't pay to rock the boat. Even when I see and hear things at the office that aren't fair to blacks." She had observed with a calloused and uncaring attitude the growing civil rights movement in the South, keeping it always at a safe distance emotionally. And then—the NCSM (Northern Christian Student Movement) had sent out a call for volunteers to go to Montgomery to help with the voting rights drive.

"I guess it was waiting there in me, all the time. The hope, I mean. I hadn't really killed it, it was just asleep. So when this opportunity came along, I said to myself, "Wilma, what concerns blacks down there, concerns me too. Maybe this time, girl, you can stop being a coward and do some good. So I asked for four days of vacation to do this. The other girls in the office, the white ones, thought I was crazy. They told me so. They just couldn't understand."

"I know," I said, "It would have been that way for me too, if I'd told anyone there before I left my job. But it had to be something spectacular like Selma to get me to make a move of this magnitude." And Albert had included himself in with several nods of his head that I knew by now meant, "Good. The same for me too."

The bus stopped in North Carolina for lunch that afternoon. The driver and Keene had sought out and found "a classy little eating establishment" in the country, somewhat off the beaten path. This was to be a special treat after all the dingy lunch counters and truck stops set right beside the highway.

"General Sherman Inn" proclaimed the black-and-white colonial-style sign at the entrance to the curved driveway. A name which brooked well for us, we figured, since General Sherman had been a famous Union soldier during the Civil War, the one who had taken his troops "from Atlanta to the Sea." Maybe today's restaurant proprietor was from up North, too.

And it was a known fact too, was it not, that North Carolina was the most liberal of all the states of the deep South when it came to racial concerns? We told ourselves all these things as we drifted up the walk in racially and sexually integrated clusters of people.

"Oh, baby," announced one of our young black students, describing his food fantasy aloud so all of us could hear, "I'm gettin' chitlin's and collard greens and maybe some corn bread . . . ."

"Not in this place, you won't," jeered his white friend, just as loud. "This place is gonna be strictly fried children and biscuits. None of that there soul food for me!"

"Steak, for me!" sighed the girl behind them, chomping her lips together in blissful anticipation. "I'm having a decent meal for a change!"

But as it turned out, all three of them were wrong. The management must have seen us dismounting from the bus before it pulled away to gas up. And they refused to admit us! Apparently they concluded that a racially mixed group of passengers getting off a Greyhound bus marked "Charter" and not on a regular route could be up to no good. Because some frightened or angry person had closed and locked the front door and drawn the drapes over the glass of the door as we came up the walk from the parking lot. The all-white clientele sitting at tables just inside the windows on either side of the door pretended not to see us. But they looked decidedly uncomfortable as they sat there.

Tom Courtney, our black Snick co-leader, pushed his knit cap to the back of his head and knocked politely while the rest of us stood back, looking on. The door was opened a crack from within and a white woman's face peered out at us from behind the edge of the drawn drapes.

"The restaurant is closed just now," she called out. "For clean up," she added hastily.

"But what about all those people in there?" Tom called back at her, again as politely as he was able under the circumstances. By that time, all of us had reached Tom's side in one large cluster.

"Oh, we just closed five minutes ago," the woman said. "From twelve 'til two!"

I whispered to Keene standing beside me, "How can someone who drawls so sweetly lie so brazenly?" and Keene grinned back in agreement. The restaurant door went shut again.

Just then another woman, well-dressed and obviously a customer, came around the building from the rear on a side walk and headed in a hurry toward the modestly full parking lot. Bill Morris, our white Snick co-leader, hailed her with a courteous "Ma'am?"

"The owner died a couple of hours ago, so they're closing the restaurant," she called over to us in a shaky voice, in her nervousness almost dropping her pocketbook to the ground. In seconds she was in her car and speeding away down the drive.

We stood for a moment on the stoop, the forty-and-more of us looking at one another, undecided about what we, a non-violent passive resistance group with hunger pangs, should do. Then Tom raised his brown hands delicately like a church choir director and began, in a confident tenor that belied his customary low tones, a parody of one of our favorite civil rights refrains. "Waiting for our dinner," he sang, turning toward us and pretending to direct the music with his arms, "we shall not be moved!" Catching on instantly and too hungry to capitulate gracefully to this restaurant's obdurate act of what we felt was rank discrimination, we all joined in, singing and clapping as loud as we could to the silent front door.

> ". . . Waiting for our dinner, we shall not be moved!
> "Waiting for our dinner, we shall not be moved!
> "Oh, yes, Lord!"

Bill Morris supplied the words to the second verse.

"Notifying the Attorney General, we shall not be moved!" he sang out, which took some doing to get all the syllables in. But we all joined eagerly in the next line of the refrain.

By the end of that verse, a note on a scrap of white paper emerged inch by inch through the crack under the door up to Tom Courtney's feet. Our black leader stooped over and picked it up.

"If you are not gone in five minutes," he read to us what was printed on the paper in large, succinct letters, "we will notify the police."

Chuckling but chastened, still hungry but unwilling to argue further, we turned and strolled back down the walk, being careful not to run. The two drivers had taken our steel chariot to a filling station across the road, intending to join us in the dining room afterward. Now the bus sat waiting for us to get in, the apprehensive relief driver Carl already in his driver's seat with the motor running.

Carl had already told us at a previous rest stop how frightened he was of the Ku Klux Klan. "Especially since as everyone knows, they're in cahoots with the cops down here!" he had said. They had given him trouble before, on his regular Greyhound runs through the South.

Only this morning, during his last turn at the wheel, the bus had nearly been struck head-on by a truck on the highway. The truck had missed

and had instead side-swiped a car directly behind us. Not hesitating an
instant, Carl had stepped on the gas. He was aware, he said, that some of
our passengers in the rear had witnessed the accident. They had called out
for him to stop.

"I'm getting out of here," he reported that he had said bluntly to himself,
"We can't afford a run-in with the police with a busload like this!" His eyes
said that to us now through the open door of the bus, as he anxiously
waited for us to board.

While we were lined up to get back on the bus, Albert said, "Obviously
this place has not yet heard of the Civil Rights Act of 1964." Passed by
Congress and signed into law by President Johnson, the 1964 Civil Rights
Act prohibited discrimination in public restaurants and motels, and in
employment.

"Don't worry, they will," said Tom, "We'll be saving them for next time."

Young Donna, the bright child from New York City's Science High
School, was the most indignant of all at our treatment. I had never seen
her get upset before. "Who do they think they are?" she kept asking, of no
one in particular. She had hopped aboard before anyone else and now she
was peering out at me from her window seat, her face a thunderstorm of
anger.

A young male Negro student I did not know reached up from outside
and traced with one finger the sarcastic word "FREEDOM" on Donna's
dusty window glass. Suddenly grinning broadly, Donna indicated with her
own thumb and forefinger that the O in FREEDOM was a bull's eye, and
she pretended to shoot me through it. I cringed in mock pain and then,
grinning back at the girl, I jumped up the two steep steps into the bus.

I was remembering something, all of a sudden, that I had said to Edna,
my housekeeper—had it been only four days ago? *Who would want to shoot
a defenseless woman?* In her hurt and anger at those white women behind
the restaurant door, maybe Donna secretly felt that way about me. *But no,
it couldn't be!*

Discourtesy and mistrust and a threat of police action could not dispel
our good spirits for long, however. None of us had a serious objection to
leaving The General Sherman Restaurant, either. We'd find another place,
further up the road, Keene assured us, an establishment that would be
only too happy to take our money and give us a meal. Some place where
we could sit close around tables without raising the eyebrows of waiters or
clientele. A place where we could joke about this latest proof that the new
day that was dawning in America had not yet fully arrived.

46.

"I still believe that at heart, people are basically good."
—Anne Frank (age 15)
(From G G.'s WTLB)

"Here they all are, Albert. Just so you'll know I wasn't kidding. That's Jackie and Jocie and Liz and me. Alice and Lynnie, Kathy, Dory and Ellyn." I passed over to him the photograph I had taken out of my shoulder bag, the picture of my eight sisters and my mother and me, the one that I always carried with me.

"And this must be Ellyn," said Albert, pointing to the small child Jackie held in her arms in the photograph.

"Yep, that's Ellyn. She's eleven now, but back then, in 1955 when our father died, she was only a year and a half. This photo was taken at my father's funeral. It was the only time in our lives all nine of us sisters were all together in one place."

"Why so?" Albert sounded as if he truly wanted to know.

"Well, three of us older ones were married before Dory and Ellyn were even born. And we sisters have lived all over the country, everybody except me. I'm the only one who stayed stuck in little ol' New Jersey."

I stared for a minute at the lineup of girls and young women in the old wallet-sized picture before I put it away. We were stair-stepped in height from the oldest to the youngest, except for baby Ellyn being held by Jackie, and Jocie being so much shorter than the rest of us grown sisters.

"They're one of the neatest things that ever happened to me," I said. "It's hard to accept that they've gone out of my life forever, Albert. By forever, I mean that I hardly ever get to see any of them anymore. The U.S. is a big country," I added. And then I remembered that my dear friend Albert would soon be gone forever, as well. Only seven or so more hours to go.

We had stopped at a modest roadside truck stop in Virginia for our late-lunch meal of hamburgers and potato chips all around. All, that is, except for Albert, the Reform Jew, who ordered a steak sandwich with the explanation to the rest of us at the table that the ground beef from which the hamburgers were made might contain pork.

We had been made more than welcome by the truck stop staff and waitresses, no questions asked. There had even been enough toilet stalls in the ladies' room, with sufficient toilet paper for everyone's needs, and stall doors that actually locked! Our platters had come decorated with tiny American flags on toothpicks, and we had all stashed them carefully away as souvenirs.

More than satisfied by our meal—indeed, feeling "stuffed to the gills"—we had re-boarded the bus in a state of lethargic contentment once more. Jeffrey, the head driver, had taken the wheel again. He drove so many hours that we came to think of him as the Marathon Man. Yet we trusted him with our lives all the way.

Back in our two seats, Albert and I had at last felt ready to do a postmortem of our portion of the march. Earlier it had been a topic we were not yet willing, by joint agreement, to touch upon. It had been as if our emotions regarding it were still too close to the surface for us to air them here, in these prosaic surroundings. But now we made up for our previous reticence.

Each of us admitted to the other the pinnacle of excitement we had reached while walking over the Edmond Pettus Bridge this morning. We admitted the extreme inner exultation at having at last found an appropriate outlet for the frustrations we had felt for years over the hypocrisy of our country's racial policies. So what if we had been instruments of Martin Luther King's clever stratagems for justice; what of it? We had loved being a part of it—and maybe it would even bear fruit and get for us all a decent, workable 1965 Voting Rights Act in Congress.

I told Albert of my own aspirations to do something even more socially useful than marching, if and when I ever got through college. I told him how I longed to participate someday in the decision-making processes of running our nation and our world, even if on an infinitesimal scale. Albert told me about his efforts as Jewish chaplain at Columbia University to make students think, and face up to their future responsibilities as leaders; to recognize their moral obligation to help create a world where a person would no longer be judged by the color of his skin but, as Martin Luther King had expressed it during the March on Washington in 1963, "by the content of his character." Albert had moderated panel discussions on this theme at Columbia University. He had brought prominent speakers in to help students of all faiths, and those of no faith at all but with a sense of decency and fair play, to become more aware.

We wondered aloud together how matters were going for Dr. King and the two hundred and ninety-nine other chosen ones, who would at this very moment on Monday afternoon, be on the second lap of the long walk to Montgomery if things were taking place as planned. We spoke of how lucky the two of us had been to have gotten so close to the front of the march out of Selma; to have actually walked our eleven historic miles in that distinguished company of so many famous people. And then we two felt sorry for ourselves because we couldn't go back down on Friday, to join in the big, tumultuous finale in front of the State House in Montgomery. It would be bigger, much bigger, everyone in the newspapers seemed to agree, than the numbers who had gathered in Selma for the walk out.

Musing over the events of the past four days, Albert said to me, "Maybe someday soon the white South will be able to realize that we have only been trying to help free all of us—us, as well as them—from ourselves."

I learned a good deal more about Rabbi Friedlander on the way home. First of all, that he preferred the use of his full first name. I had, in our many conversations, sometimes called him "Al."

"It's probably too late for me to totally drop the nickname," I said, thinking of Adelaide Sims and her never-ending ma'am's. "I've already fallen into the 'Al' habit. But I'll try, really try, to make the change. But for heaven's sake, Al, why didn't you tell me sooner?" And that made him laugh.

Second of all, I asked if he'd seen the play *The Deputy*. And I learned to my surprise and delight that he'd served as the English interpreter for Rolf Hochhuth, the German author of the play, when he had come to America from Germany on a recent visit. Having lots of time, we discussed the play itself at length.

The plot of the play *The Deputy* depicts the silent role of Pope Pius XII in the tragic fate of thousands of Rome's Jews at the hands of the Nazi Gestapo toward the end of World War II. Together Albert and I mulled over the play's accusation that the Pope could have saved the lives of most of them if he had been willing to use his influence with Hitler. As it happened, I had seen a production of the drama only months before—Bill and I had gone to see it together. Now I could not get over the fact that my friend here beside me actually knew the author!

I turned my head in time to catch the trace of a smile on the rabbi's lips. "Why are you looking so pleased?" I demanded. "That darned play was a real tragedy! It left me terribly depressed for a few days afterward."

"Oh, it's not the play, Gwen, I was just thinking about something else." he said.

"About what? Come on, do tell me!" I begged him.

You'll think I'm dropping names again," he said. I had teased him several times already about his being acquainted with many important people. I had even begun to suspect he might be rather an "important" person in his own right. But at my urging, he went on to confess that he was a close personal friend of Anne Frank's father Otto. In fact, he had known him for many years.

"No kidding, Albert. Really? How I'd love to meet him!"

"He's quite elderly now. And something of a recluse. But when you finally get to go to Europe, Gwen—if you like, I'll give you a letter of introduction."

"He'll probably be dead by then. But I accept!" I had already told Albert twice that I'd never been across the Atlantic Ocean, but had said how I was dying to go. The Anne Frank house in Amsterdam was certainly one place I never intended to miss, if I ever got there, and now—! Secretly, I knew it would never come to pass, my crossing the ocean. But it was fun to pretend.

"But Albert, if you know Otto Frank . . . . ? When Dr. Heschel asked me that question in the car and I answered . . . that I came to Selma because of his daughter, was that okay?"

"What you said was good. Better than good, it was perfect. The rest of us only kept quiet to see how you would handle Maurice. He loves to debate people."

"Bait them, you mean, that rat!" But I was happy. And I was pleased that Albert was proud of me. My answer was perfect, he had said.

We talked about Anne Frank for awhile longer. He told me more about his long friendship with her father. I told him that Anne and Dr. King and I were born in the same year. And then I described for Albert the first conscious memory of my life, the one about Darling Nellie Gray when I was three. How I had wept, sitting there at my mother's side and listening to my father sing. And the tears inside me had seemed never to have left since that day.

I told Albert how Anne's diary, which I read when I was eighteen, had brought the tears gushing forth again and had left me in a terrible state of depression for at least a month afterward. No one in my family had seen my tears, nor had I talked to any of them about the mental devastation I was suffering through. The evils of World War II had already left its permanent mark upon my soul. But there was no one to tell that to, either.

The rabbi and I seldom needed to look directly at each other as we exchanged these confidences. We lay for hours with our heads against the backrests, staring into space, talking in low monotones so no one else could hear what we said, or be bothered by our voices.

"She'd be thirty-five, Anne Frank would, if she'd lived," I said softly. "My age. The same age as Martin Luther King."

Something had begun to nag at me with a gnawing intensity. Until finally I had to let it out.

"Albert, do you realize what I'm going to get when I get home? Certainly not anyone's Annual Brotherhood Award. I can't explain to just anyone about My Darling Nellie Gray, and tragic Anne Frank. Lots of people are going to insinuate that I'm a terrible mother, or a communist, or both. Or just plain crazy, the way her white co-workers had told Wilma she was. Only more so, because I'm the wrong race to go on civil rights marches. Or the worst thing to be of all: a white woman consorting with black males, not minding her own business. In plain words, a slut!"

He was quiet for awhile, apparently digesting what I had just said. And just when I had begun to suspect he'd fallen asleep, he spoke.

"It's true, my friend, you won't be given any medals for going to Selma. This sort of thing isn't what folks back home have in mind for a medal winner . . ."

"But? I sense there's one of your 'buts' coming."

"But I think perhaps you want something else. I think you feel you must be punished for having fun on this trip."

"Punished!" Well, what ought I to have expected? I'd been feeding him all my frustrations since I'd first met him. Why should I be surprised that he, a trained counselor of people's minds and hearts and souls, was beginning to psychoanalyze me?

"You're right about the fun, of course," I said. "As my little Julie would put it, it's been 'the most funnest thing' of my entire life! When I had the chance I should have said, thanks, Martin Luther King, for inviting me to your big bash. For letting me be a 'white nigger' for two fantastic days. For letting me help. But you know as well as I do, Albert, that no one else is going to comprehend that. All anyone else is going to see is how 'dangerous' it all was!"

"The most dangerous missions, combined with the most challenging aspects of living, seem to be often the 'most funnest'. It's that element of danger that adds the spice, don't you think?" my rabbi said.

So he had felt this too, along with all the other emotions we had shared. The thrill of possibly being in mortal jeopardy, so necessary a part of standing up to a power greater than yourself. The glorious joy of laughing

in the teeth of the gods, saying I dare you to come and get me . . . ! Albert
Friedlander had felt it too!

"And so much of modern life in our country is aimed at trying to
eliminate all danger," Albert was continuing his analysis. "Which
incidentally also does away with a lot of the fun."

"You're certainly right about that," I replied. I thought of watching
young Peter as he walked away from me in the Tabernacle Church this
morning in Selma. How I had reminded myself that we grown-ups should
leave some challenges, some dangers, for the younger ones coming along
to have fun with.

"But what about me?" I said.

"You?" Albert said.

"I'm a woman!" I said.

"So you told me before," he chuckled. "Does that really make it so
different?"

"Doesn't it?" In a couple of hours darkness would be falling once again
outside the bus. So I wouldn't be able to see Albert's sweet face as well as I
was able to now. I told myself I had better look at him while I still could,
and memorize his features. I might need that in days to come.

"Only if you let it," he was saying. "I think you too have a right to
pursue the dangers of life if you want to, as well as its pleasures. Even more
important, to enjoy them without feeling you ought to be punished in
some way."

He would have brought his own wife along, he had said to me on
our way to Selma. He would have brought Evelyn, and be with her now,
instead of with me, if she hadn't been pregnant.

"Does it say all that in the First Amendment?" My question was
half-sarcastic.

"No," he said soberly. "It's in the Declaration of Independence, if I
remember correctly. It's something known as 'the pursuit of happiness,' I
believe."

"Thanks, Albert." I had recognized it too, those words in the
Declaration. I had believed them, internalized them, acted upon them
before this. Hadn't I? But the guilt had always been there. I thought of
telling him how I had once come to practical terms with the guilt. How I
had nearly died of childbed fever after Julie was born. And how that brief
flirt with the grim reaper had made me accept the fact I'd always have guilt
complexes about something or other, so they might as well be the ones I
could be happiest with. The ones I chose.

But the details were too gory, even to tell this gentle man, even to tell a chaplain surely familiar with illness and death on a grand scale. Besides, he might think I had made the whole thing up, the same way I had greeted the story the New York reporter told us about getting cigarette burns all over his body in the Birmingham jail. I had told Albert later that I thought the man was exaggerating. About being totally naked like that, and no longer having a belly button.

No one, but no one, got childbed fever these days. Hadn't my doctor told me so?

*   *   *

47.

"Why would all you white people have deliberately placed yourselves in such a losing position? When someone wins, someone else loses. And for the blacks to win such a victory in the South meant that all whites, everywhere, had to lose something. You were commendable, you white people who went to Selma, but—well, stupid."
—Karen Cartwright,* Negro college student, age 27
(Post-Selma comments from one of the folks back home)

Darkness was falling once again. My head nestled firmly in the crook of Rabbi Friedlander's shoulder so it couldn't wobble, I pretended to be sleeping. Actually, I was thinking over all the matters he and I had talked about during the past twenty-four hours on the bus. About our feelings of exaltation while participating in the march. About the surprise of Albert's knowing Rolf Hochhuth and Otto Frank and probably scads of other well known people he hadn't gotten around to mentioning yet. Last but not least, the right of us American women to participate in the dangers of a life committed to freedom and equality.

I'd never been exposed to much danger before, other than the perils of childbed fever after Julie was born and an appendectomy while pregnant for Ken. And just normally riding around in an automobile, of course, the way all Americans did.

Sure, my parents had had a boat when we sisters were growing up, but the most dangerous thing about it was that the bilge leaked so much that it had to be pumped out a couple of times a day to keep the Circe from sinking. Now that I thought about it, those summer weekends spent on that old wooden Chris-Craft cabin cruiser on the Chesapeake Bay must have accounted for my being so adventurous from an early age. That, and the fact that my father had a bad heart and no sons. We girls had had to get involved in everything on the boat, except for the balky motor, which was Dad's responsibility. We were the ever-obedient, unquestioning crew.

We did some daring deeds, no doubt about it, while Mother stayed in the cabin below so she wouldn't have to witness them. Things like swimming underneath the hull from one side to the other in sixty feet of water, just for sport. Jumping into water up to our waists and pushing the boat off of sandbars in swift currents. Circling around bell buoys in dense fogs on the Delaware River. Diving to locate the diaper buckets that accidentally got dropped over the side when one of my younger sisters was an infant. We had been brave in a fun sort of way, I guessed looking back. Courageous, without ever realizing it.

No, that's wrong. We had known it, but it had been an accepted fact of life. I had felt no guilt about anything back then. Nor had I known that doing brave things was supposed to stop when I grew up. I had thought, naively enough, that it was a desirable course of action to be brave and daring and true for as long as one lived.

It didn't make any sense. No sense at all that I could feel so free to tell perfect strangers of my agnostic religious views. I was well aware that most of the people in my daily life would rather hear me profess to being a prostitute than an atheist, who was someone they invariably considered a "murderer" of their particular concept of a Supreme Invisible Being.

And yet why did I now feel so blasphemous at the idea of admitting to someone back home that I'd had a fantastic time on a "dangerous" civil rights demonstration? What was more, that I had participated in it with that very expectation!

But that had been only one of my motives. Human beings always had more than one motivation for anything they did, everybody should know that. So I had gone looking for adventure, danger even. And I had gone expecting to have fun. I had sincerely wanted to help make for my four kids a country that was more honest that the one into which I had been born. But that hadn't been the biggest motivation, either.

The really big motivation was because I cared. Cared about them, the underdogs. The Negroes. Why be ashamed that I cared? I cared about me, too. But could I ever really admit this last to unsympathetic ears? That my desire for my own freedom, as well as for theirs, the underdogs, had goaded me into it? That I had wanted to stand up for a change and be counted? I could never explain it; not to anyone else's satisfaction. I had to snicker silently to myself, recalling how I had tried to explain all this to my five-year-old Julie last week, before I left home. But I hadn't yet known how to put it all into words.

Who did I know back home of even ten times five, who would approve of even one of my several motives? Ed Lane, the minister of the Unitarian Church of Cherry Hill, where I was a member of the congregation? Mr.McLoud, my American Government teacher at Penn, who had taught me more about the Bill of Rights than anyone else, especially about the First Amendment? Our friend Fred Clever, from the Human Relations Council, whose nice son had loaned me his knapsack and sleeping bag? Connie Richardson, my boss in the Continuing Education For Women Program at the University of Pennsylvania?

I hoped so. But I could count them all on the fingers of one hand, leaving out a thumb. And only one of the four of them was a woman.

Even my supportive husband Bill would have talked to a lot of others by this time about what I had done, and where I had gone, and he too would be having his doubts because he was so easily influenced. And Jim Clemson, the educated engineer in South Jersey? A hopeless case, if ever there was one. Albert was right that I would never get a medal, I wasn't the type to be presented a medal. There were not going to *be* any medals, none of any kind.

And why should there be? I demanded of myself as I leaned back into Albert's shoulder, thinking. I had only done my duty as I saw it. The duty of an American citizen who just happened to be female. And who happened also to have more insight into and empathy regarding this particular problem than most other white people I knew. *Sono americana.* (Not even with a capital "a". Those Italians were clever about not strewing capital letters around willy-nilly, the way the Germans did.) Just an ordinary fact of life, my American citizenship; but a tremendous responsibility at the same time. My only reward should be the sense of supreme satisfaction I was already getting out of having gone, and done, and survived to go home again.

But I had to get my story together, remember? Instead of continuing to congratulate myself, I should concentrate on deciding exactly what posture I should present to my friends, and my relatives, and my neighbors and school and church associates when I got back to South Jersey. And oh, my god, my in-laws!

I had to try to look at it from the viewpoints of each one of them. In the eyes of most of those folks back home, I supposed, my rushing off to follow the tune of a black Pied Piper had truly been a reckless, unforgiveable, *crazy* thing to do. Even, in the opinion of some of them including my in-laws, my act would be seen as traitorous to my race if not my country. So I would say to them, when the time came . . . .

What *would* I say? What *could* I say? How should I even begin it? I had better come up with something. Because before long I would be getting off this bus. And tomorrow, I would have to face the music. Alone, without Rabbi Friedlander to give me moral support.

At last I slept. Or rather, I daydreamed, half-asleep, unable to shake the warm torpor settling over me. Dappled sunlight flitted across my closed eyelids as we raced past immense stands of evergreen trees lining the highway in rural northern Virginia.

I see images before my face all of a sudden. The figures of my eight sisters and me, stair-stepped in a meadow full of white Queen Anne's lace and black-eyed Susans. I run closer to greet them, ecstatic that they are here with me, coming along with me.

Wait! No, not Jackie and Jocie and Lizzie and Alice and Lynnie and Kathy and Dory and Ellyn! Not those familiar beloved faces at all! Instead . . . . and I can see them better now, and they are—Gwen and Gwen and Gwen and Gwen and Gwen and Gwen and Gwen and Gwen and Gwen! Nine Gwens. Stair-stepped in a row in the meadow, but coming through the window into the bus uninvited . . . where all the seats are taken with none to spare.

The tallest and liveliest one, the one the closest to the end of the line, looks the most like me. French twist. Bright eyes behind bifocal glasses. A little plump. She is wearing my black coat with the fake fur collar, and she is carrying on a high pole an American flag, bigger than she is.

The next Gwen is in a nightgown, holding her legs tight together, her chin firmly set. The third Gwen carries a copy of the *Caine Mutiny* under her arm like it is some kind of life ring. She is wearing dungarees like my bus mate Donna's, and a man's flannel shirt, and she looks like a slob because her hair is uncombed. A sweet slob, nonetheless.

Next stands Gwen at twenty-four; dressed in her best dress to her calves and her recent Toni home permanent. Obligingly she is posing for the camera before going off to see Unity dying in the bedroom with the dirt floor. And there is another Gwen, a little shorter than the previous ones, a Baptist Gwennie Simon still and not yet a Gain, with a flute case under her arm and an apologetic look on her face. Indeed, she is blushing, thinking about boys having penises and she, not. She has on a gray flannel skirt and a lime-green sweater with push-up sleeves and she wears bobby-socks and the same Toni home permanent only with little straight ends sticking out in all the wrong places because she had no help.

Her little sister next, also Gwennie Simon, is beginning to shape up and have breasts. She is clutching a return ticket for the train trip from Detroit to Philadelphia. She has gone, and seen, and not forgotten. She will never forget, she tells me without words, those black faces and those hurt eyes after the riots.

And here comes Gwennie at twelve, chubby and boasting two long braids like Judy Garland in *The Wizard Of Oz*. A stack of white diapers is held tight beneath her chin, and she is carrying a scrub bucket in her pinky-beige, and decidedly not white, fingers. The nine-year-old Gwennie is last in the sister lineup. Lean and lithe, with her mousy-brown hair bobbed just below the tips of her ears, and blood is running down her forehead, dripping off her chin onto the flute case she is carrying, but she won't make a motion to wipe the blood away. Oh, no. She had not wanted to play baseball with the boys, why hadn't they seen that? She had only wanted to watch.

The baby is there, of course: Gwendie Lou. She is in the arms of the oldest Gwen, her mother now, and tears are streaming down her doeskin cheeks instead of blood, and the big Gwen is trying to console her in pantomime. The big Gwen's lips are mouthing silently, *We won't sing it any more! Please don't cry! Won't you smile now, for the camera? I promise you, we're not going to sing any more about Darling Nellie Grey!*

The baby Gwendie Lou has two little wisps of pigtails thrusting out from the sides of her head, and you wouldn't think a creature this small understands anything at all about the cares and injustices of the world. She looks into the eye of the camera, straight at me. And she *is* me. And—and—and she disappears, wafted away into the mist outside the window of my bus.

Jolted wide awake, I knew now exactly what I was going to do. My visit to Selma, Alabama had been, for me, another personal high-water mark, another new beginning, a new day. I'd been lucky. Unlike James Reeb, that other Unitarian struck down so mercilessly by another white man wielding a four-by-four on a main street in Selma, I had lived to go back home. I'd had no attacks from anyone, not even verbally (except of course from that young man who screamed at me about bringing my diaphragm to the march), nor even an allergy attack from the foreign spring pollens.

I'd had no indigestion after all, from the inadequate meals at odd hours and the long waits in between. The Southern sun had not killed me, either, but merely kissed me, and if I didn't peel, I'd have that early tan Jim Bevall had said we Northerners would be starting on today. My second-class legs had endured, they had taken me as far as it was necessary for me to go. I hadn't even come close to seeing the inside of a jail! But more than all of that, something good had jelled inside of me and I could visualize at last an attainable goal.

First, I'd get out of college as soon as possible. I had four full semesters of classes to go. No more fooling around with a part-time job and part-time course work, both at the same time. I'd quit the secretarial job with Connie. The schedule of doing both at the same time had threatened to break me anyway.

Julie would be going into first grade in September, and I'd be free from baby-sitting expenses for the first time in five years. I could arrange my class hours so that I could be home when she got there, instead of having to pay Edna. I'd apply for a scholarship. Penn still owed me something, didn't they, for the one I gave up at sixteen? If nothing came of that, I'd borrow the money somewhere. Finish at Penn in two more years instead of four and get a paying job in some area of social service or race relations or civil rights.

I'd be a leader for a change, not a follower anymore. And I'd help to change things even further. There was still such a long way to go, and plenty to do to fix what was wrong with my country. Messages, the show business impresario George S. Kaufman was reputed to have said, are for Western Union. But my Unitarian philosophy also said, messages should be lived, not merely shouted from the rooftops.

Together we'd do it. There were lots of us, coming out from backstage, just waiting in the wings to go on. Hadn't the march on Montgomery demonstrated that? Black and white together, male and female. President Johnson, with his Great Society, was playing a role, backed up by all of us non-violence direct action troops; our only weapons the Bill of Rights and the Declaration of Independence and a sublime faith in the principles of American democracy.

I'd let my little light shine wherever it could, this altruistic part of me. So what if I was a woman, with no power, physical or political or economic or even social; so what? I still had a good brain, didn't I? And courage? And the selfish part—the part of me that had once yearned to wear a blue-and-gold uniform and play my flute in a marching band—perhaps its need for fulfillment would be answered in the process.

"*Volere e potere,*" the great Italian painter and sculptor Michelangelo had said four hundred years ago. "To want is to be able." Yes. I'd have to choose my college major in the next month and now I knew that it had to be American Civilization, the study of all aspects of the United States of America. I'd take as many political science and race relations courses as possible. And that research paper I had to write for my American Government class? Dick Gregory had handed me the perfect topic from the platform of Brown's Chapel. I would do a comparison of the anti-miscegenation laws in those thirty-two states in the Union that were still determined to "legislate love."

If I were to accomplish all these marvelous goals, I would have to conquer a couple of remaining fears. I'd have to get over that silly hang-up about standing up and speaking my mind to a roomful of strangers. I'd force myself to start doing it; and do it so much I'd have to get over my silly discombobulating. I'd do it so often that someday I could, if I had to, get up behind the podium at the House of Representatives and address a Joint Session of Congress. And someday—did I dare hope? I'd even get up the courage to tell my kind husband Bill that I wanted to leave him.

*   *   *

48.

"Ships that pass in the night, and speak each other in passing,
"Only a signal shown, And a distant voice in the darkness.
"So on the ocean of life we pass and speak one another.
"Only a look and a voice, then darkness again, and a silence."
    —Henry Wadsworth Longfellow, American Poet
    (From GG.'s Words To Live By)

The wrench of the final goodbyes took place late Monday night, after an evening of relentless pushing at high speeds through the darkness with Jeffrey and Carl, our two skillful bus drivers, taking turns. Parting from the others, from Keene Stassen and Tom Courtney and Bill Morris and Wilma and Donna and all the other comrades whose faces had become cosily familiar, was an inevitable part of the drama's last act, and this time I began it while there was still plenty of time.

The entire busload stayed wide awake after our supper stop. People were talking quietly, even across the aisle, or reading Richmond newspaper accounts of the second day's march toward Montgomery (going well so far without incident, the Southern paper reported). Or people having cigarettes and debating what time the bus would arrive back at the campus of Columbia University in New York City and how they would get to their homes from there.

I exchanged addresses with a few of those around me whom I had gotten to know best, and since most of us were students, we wished one another good luck in our academic careers. I made my way up to the front and gave Keene the forty dollars I still owed her for my fare, thanked her for her calm and caring efficiency, and told her I'd love to see her in New York someday, maybe the next time I got up there to visit my aunt.

No one said much of a personal nature, or betrayed by so much as a whimper that an extraordinary experience was coming to an end. But I sensed that deep down inside, we all knew it, and while celebrating aloud the march and the friendships we had made, we kept the mourning inside ourselves.

It was during our last restroom visit, at a Howard Johnson Restaurant just before Washington, D.C., that Keene Stassen and I exchanged our formal goodbyes. We had gone in with the other women to do what we could for our straggly hair-dos and dirty faces, and out of necessity as well as for old times' sake, she and I had awaited our turn together in front of the toilet stalls. Last in line, the two of us had the room to ourselves for a few minutes, and in that interval we discovered we had a mutual acquaintance. One of her girlfriends in New York had introduced a family friend of mine to his future wife, whom I had also recently met. Her friend and my friend currently worked for the same publishing company in New York City!

"Eleanor* graduated from the University of Pennsylvania," Keene said. "She was an American Civ major."

Heart pounding in recognition, I said, "That's what mine is! At least it's going to be, as soon as I get back to school and declare my major!"

"Hey, it's certainly a small world, to use a trite phrase," Keene said.

"You know it!" I said in happy agreement. I looked at her typical middle-America face being liberally doused with soap and water from a dripping paper towel. I reached over to hold the spigot open for her while she rinsed. And I couldn't help thinking, "*But for a couple of political quirks of fate, this young woman might have spent her growing-up years in the White House. Our country could have done a lot worse.*

"Keene?" I finally summoned the nerve to ask the question that had been gnawing at me since last Friday. "I've been wondering about you. All the rest of us here know what it's like to have to struggle for a living, or we've watched our parents do it. But you—your father, a prominent attorney and potential presidential candidate, big on the political scene and all that. You must have grown up in the midst of affluence, and taken it all for granted. What made you come to care so much? About the 'little people' of this world?"

Maybe she, this "different" one, could give me a clue to the mystery of myself. I had grown up privileged, although certainly not rich. And yet I wept for those less fortunate.

Keene seemed to find my question hilarious but she dried her face on another towel before she answered. She was not at all offended. "I guess we really weren't so affluent that I got spoiled, Gwen. My father isn't rich, but he's always been a crusader. Sure, I'm a crusader too, although a quieter one. But I'm certainly not affluent! I'm a schoolteacher, for crying out loud!"

"You're not much help to me then, in trying to figure it all out," I sighed. Is it nature, or is it nurture, that makes some people care strongly about matters like this—racial discrimination, I mean—and others not?" We walked out of the restroom, side by side, to get back on the bus. We strode along like two comrades returning from the front.

Before boarding, I stopped long enough to buy from a stand a copy of the Washington Post newspaper. And there we were, in a big picture splashed across half the front page. Thousands of us "no-good communist interlopers" were shown swarming like soldier ants in an unending line over the Edmond Pettus Bridge. It was the high point of Our Big Moment, and for me it was the chance I'd gotten to play my flute—testify by my female presence—in Martin Luther King's marching band!

Just say that I was a drum major for justice . . . . He had voiced it many times.

All of us from the bus but Keene were there in that newspaper photograph, though you couldn't pick us out as individuals. She, the quiet and humble crusader, had joined us too late to make the walk over the Bridge. For much of yesterday she had been doing the job for which she had volunteered. Alone. Knocking on the doors of black folks in Montgomery

GWEN SIMON GAIN

to find out if they would have the courage to vote if and when the time came.

There was one last flurry of excitement around eight o'clock when we drove straight across the center of Washington, D.C. on the throughway and beheld, ablaze with lights in the distance, some famous landmarks. Most of the young students on the bus had never seen them before, except on television. The Lincoln and Washington Memorials, the Capitol building, the Pentagon. Donna, the youngest and still hopelessly idealistic in spite of the experience at the General Sherman Inn, sat spellbound, ooh-ing and ah-ing and asking "Look, look, what's that over there?" and anyone around her who knew Washington well enough would supply the answer.

And then these mighty symbols of white power and majesty had disappeared behind us and we were driving through Negro neighborhoods of our capital city and bound for Baltimore. And one by one, the younger passengers switched off their reading lights and dropped off to sleep. So that long before the time we reached the Delaware Memorial Bridge over the River to the New Jersey Turnpike, the bus was dark and still once again.

Albert and I sat unmoving, not speaking; but I knew he was awake. I couldn't help wondering what he was thinking. If he could be feeling the way I was feeling.

I felt no qualms of conscience about my love for this gentle and perceptive rabbi. My love for him was genderless. It was the way one *should* feel about the person with whom one has just shared most bravely and endearingly one of the greatest adventures of one's life. And just as there had been no definable beginning to our mutual affection—how could we ever, in after years, put a finger on exactly when it had happened?—so there would be no ending.

Parting would not end it. The unspoken satisfaction lay in knowing we had played it straight throughout. We were a man and a woman who had sat beside each other during these long hours of riding, baring our hearts and souls as only two human beings can who have gone through potential danger side by side. Lending each other a shoulder now and then for much-needed sleep. And we had come to love each other as separate and asexual entities, without pain, without promise, without future. Without regret either, and without much future longing.

For one split heartbeat of infinity, my life's voyage, and that of Albert Friedlander, had crossed. We had needed and loved each other these past four days as two human beings thrown together by fate, both of us unusually mindful for a little while of the glory of involvement. Together we had put our pinkish-tan complexions on the line, and in doing so, had helped to change the world, we hoped, one small fraction for the better. And now, and soon, we would be moving on, no longer together, but apart. Like two ships that pass in the night.

But oh, God, Or Jehovah, or Whom-it may concern. Couldn't you have given us, Albert and me, just a little more time together?

"Albert?" His name still sounded peculiar to my ear, but pleasant to pronounce. And definitely, as he had intimated, more dignified than "Al" for one of the rabbinate.

"Yes, Gwen?" Plain "Gwen" always became a special sound when he said it, affectionately but with precision. We sat with eyes staring straight ahead, as when we had walked together side by side out of Selma. Only dark seatbacks to focus our eyes upon now, in place of dignitaries' heads and elbows. We no longer touched our arms together, or our shoulders. Touching was over. We were Huck Finn and slave friend Jim again, sharing a raft down the Mississippi River.

"In just one more hour—I'll be getting off this bus," I said.

"I know. The bus will seem empty, Gwen, when you are gone," he said.

He felt it too, then! He did! The specter of an impending loss that must not be mourned. I sighed, a prolonged gathering and releasing from the depths of my being. No regret. There must be no regret. "I'll never forget you., A l b e r t."

"Nor I, you." And then, sensing I needed something more to ease my sadness, he said, "Do you know that bit from Tennyson's *Ulysses*? About parting from a friend?"

"No. How does it go?" I had to force myself to sound interested. I didn't want any more words-to-live-by. Not any more; they would hurt too much.

"I can't remember the exact wording," Albert said. "But it goes something like this: "I am a part of everyone I have met. And everyone I have met has become a part of me.""

Ulysses, the wanderer king, who had gone far from home to wage war against Troy, and then had taken ten long years to get back to his kingdom in Greece and his wife, in order to tell about it.

"Hey! That's a really lovely thought!" I said. And I meant it.

"I give it to you, Gwen. As a special present from me. You gave me one first, remember?"

"I remember. I'll bet you thought I was loony." Yes, I had quoted to him Thomas Hardy's sacrilegious bit about God: "*Has some Vast Imbecility, mighty to build and blend, yet impotent to tend, framed us in jest and left us here to Hazardry?*" Had that conversation taken place only last Friday, when we had first become friends?

"I thought you were wonderful," Albert said. And he said it like he meant it.

He had hooked me on words-to-live-by again! I took my little blue notebook and my pen from my shoulder bag resting between us. I reached up high to switch on the reading light above my seat. And I wrote his present down so I'd never forget it. When the last moment came, it was going to be the only help I had.

"Don't forget, you're going to visit Evelyn and me in New York sometime soon," Albert reminded me.

"I won't forget." Accomplishing that would be almost as difficult to achieve, now that I thought about it, as my getting across the Atlantic Ocean to see the wonders of Europe someday.

"But don't wait too long," Albert said. They might really be going to move to England, I knew he meant. Teasing me, he added, "You ought to appreciate the chance to see Columbia, another Ivy League school!"

"Sure. Of course I will." *I am a part of everyone I have met.* This moisture in my eyes; these sniffles. Darn! Not portents of unavoidable sadness, not even an allergy attack. But a cold. A real-life, genuine, humdinger of a cold! I could feel it working its way into the back of my throat and into my nose. Well, up to now I'd gotten off easy, hadn't I? But I should have listened to that voice in my brain of my critical mother-in-law. I should never have sat myself down on that cold concrete abutment beside the steps of Brown's Chapel, wearing only a skirt.

Hypocrite! Who are you trying to kid? Just two ordinary human beings, you say?

And swallowing back the increasing phlegm in my throat and wishing for a handkerchief or a Kleenex to wipe my runny nose, I had to be honest with myself. Of course we had done it, we had relished making our walk, first and foremost, as male and female. Not as Jew and Gentile, believer and unbeliever. Not as student and chaplain; housewife and breadwinner. Not even as a father and a mother, nor as Huck Finn and Jim. Not as *americana* and a*mericano* either, not primarily.

We had made the walk together as a man and a woman, the complementary sources of life, holding hands for one brief moment in time. Aware of that state of emotional symbiosis, we had never acted upon it. Not wanting to act upon it, because to do so under such circumstances would have been to defile it.

No physical arousal had been stimulated by any of our touching—the hands clasped on the road out of Selma, the closeness of our sleeping on the long bus ride back—because none was needed, nor even desired. Even had we been so inclined, even had there been ample opportunity, no indication of sexual awareness on the part of either one of us would have been tolerated. It would have been against the unspoken morality code of our partnership.

But this much I knew: When my rabbi and I had walked side-by-side out of Selma behind Martin Luther King, holding hands, we had done it first and foremost, no question about it, as a man and a woman. *It was true!*

Nearly one a.m. Tuesday morning, Eastern Standard Time, by my wristwatch. The bus drew to a wheezing stop in the parking lot of the Howard Johnson restaurant that was situated just before Exit 4 of the New Jersey Turnpike. Three of us were getting off there. John, a young black man who worked in a "Freedom Center," as he called it, in the North Philadelphia ghetto, was planning to hitch a ride home from the Turnpike stop. After Keene had whispered to me during the supper break that John was ill and that she was worried about him, I had offered to ask my husband if we could drop him off at the bus terminal in Camden, whence it would be an easy ride for him over the Ben Franklin Bridge to Philadelphia.

That is, if any buses were still running that late at night. It would be a mere twenty minutes out of our way, like taking the long route from the Turnpike to Merchantville. When I explained this to John, he had accepted my offer with a weak expression of gratitude and the request that his new friend Cass, who also lived in Philadelphia, be allowed to come with us too.

I'd have to keep my fingers crossed that my husband wouldn't mind the extra driving time. He'd be up anyway, not overly tired, probably watching the late movie as he often did even when I was there. He would be sitting in the living room recliner, listening now for the phone to ring and thinking it was getting awfully late.

The bus door swung open under Carl our relief driver's hand. John and Cass stumbled down the steps, followed by Rabbi Friedlander carrying my knapsack and sleeping bag. Setting both items on the ground, he stood waiting for me to follow. I buttoned my black coat around me against the unwelcome blast of cold air. Continuing the short distance up the aisle for the last time, I said a final goodbye to Keene and the two drivers.

Donna roused herself enough to rush forward and throw her arms around my neck.

"You've been—so wonderful!" she said into my ear.

"Love ya, Donna. Study hard. *Be* someone," I said. "Do it for me."

"I will!"

Then I turned and looked down the aisle toward the back of the bus and raised my arm in a final salute to the silent, shadowy rows containing my marching companions.

"So long, you guys," I called softly, so as not to awaken the sleepers. And I found I could say it, to all of them, with no shame: "It's been fun!"

In response to my goodbye, a lone male voice started up a line of song in a mellow tenor, softly but clear. It was Tom Courtney, our "choir director" from the stoop of the General Sherman Inn.

"So long, it's been good to know you . . . . !" A farewell blessing, issuing forth from the farthest recesses of the bus.

And a chorus of youthful voices, half-awake and barely euphonious, picked up the refrain from all around.

> ". . . . So long, it's been good to know you!
> "So long, it's been good to know you,
> "We're sorry you're going away!"

Not a freedom song for a change, but a friendship song. The many faces in the kaleidoscope of skin colors were scarcely visible, but no matter. I knew where most of them were sitting. *And everyone I've ever met has become a part of me.*

Using both hands to blow to them one communal kiss of appreciation, I turned and hopped down the two high steps to the ground. One thing was certain: this was not the place to let myself be emotional, not here. A. parking lot was too public, and I could scarcely breathe anyway from this darned cold that was fast taking hold of me.

Albert Friedlander took my shoulders with both hands and drew me forward in a tight embrace. He kissed first one of my cheeks, then the other, European style. I hoped he wouldn't catch any cold germs to remember me by. I pulled away and we looked into each other's eyes for fleeting seconds. I tried frantically in the dim glow of the arc lights overhead to memorize his beloved features: half-Semitic, half-angelic. The curl on the forehead, the magnified eyes through the thick glasses. Why hadn't I brought along a camera? Why hadn't I . . . . ?

Come on, Gwen Gain without an e or an es or an s on the end. Don't start falling in love with rabbis. Only unstable people do transference things like that.

"*Shalom*, my dear friend," my rabbi said.

"*Shalom*, Albert." My words were hoarse and rasping, becoming ever weaker in volume because of this darned cold. "*Shavua Tov!*" I managed to choke out. *Good week, Albert. Good year. Good forever. As long as the River flows. You—a part of me.*

He nodded, his eyes saying, "Good!" in that enthusiastic way he had. *I'm pleased you remembered the Hebrew farewell from the Passover Seder,* his eyes said. And the edges of his mouth turned up to give me that bright, eye-crinkling smile. Was that the glint of a tear behind those thick-lensed and protective glasses? "Shavua Tov, Gwen. Shavua Tov." It was his own farewell benediction.

And then he was gone, my half-blind, clear-sighted friend. He leapt back onto the bus and ducked out of the way as Jeffrey, our chief driver, tipped his hat to me in farewell and whipped shut the heavy door.

Gone. I waved until the bus too had disappeared, headed off the side ramp into the flow of late night traffic on the Turnpike, headed north toward New York City, another three hours away.

Dropping my arm at last, I turned to find that Cass and sick John had carried my gear, along with their own gym bags, inside the restaurant. And it hit me that through these entire four days, I'd had to carry my own things for a sum total of no more ten minutes. And I'd never once had to ask.

Feet dragging with fatigue, I followed the two Negro men into the bright lights of the lobby where no crying was allowed. I felt John's forehead with the same well-trained mother's palm that only the day before—could it be true?—had checked Under-Secretary General of the United Nations Ralph Bunche's brow for fever, and fed "civil rights" cookies to Nobel Peace Prize Winner Martin Luther King.

I told Cass yes, his friend definitely had a fever, a rather high one. And then sniffling because my nose had at last begun to run, I left them both to go in search of a phone booth. Because everything was all over now, and it was time to come back home.

*   *   *

49.

"I stand before the tribunal of my own mind."
—Gordon Kahn, Blacklisted Hollywood screen writer
during the McCarthy era of the 1950s
(From Gwen Gain's "Words To Live By)

But endings seldom come that easily. And still again, for the hundredth time, it seemed, I was waiting.

It would take my husband Bill twenty minutes or so, I calculated, to get to this point on the Turnpike, even if he had turned off the TV and left the house as soon as he hung up, as he had promised me he would do. I sat on a padded circular bench in the lobby of the Howard Johnson between sleepy Cass and his sick friend John, who simply hunched there, an uncommunicative bundle of misery.

I went over in my mind the conversation I had just had with my husband.

He had answered excitedly on the first ring. "Gwen! I was just beginning to worry! Where are you?"

"I'm back, honey. I'm at the Ho-Jo just south of Exit 4. We just got here."

"I'll be right there! I was just watching the Late Show for something to do," he said. But he usually watched it anyway.

"How are the kids, Bill?"

"Fine. Just fine. They stayed awake as long as they could, hoping you'd get here. Wendi got sick . . ."

"*Sick?*" Horror of horrors. One of my kids was sick, and I was not there! *Wouldn't you know this would happen!*

"It was strep throat. She came down with it the morning after you left. I knew you'd want me to take her to the doctor so I did, Saturday morning. He gave her a shot of penicillin. It fixed her up by this morning, and today she went back to school," he went on, a certain pride in his voice about his accomplishment.

So my eldest had missed the big Saturday night party, after all! She'd missed Selma too. But maybe she had also missed being stood up by the Glamour Boy of Merchantville High School. Not a bad track record of misses, for one teenaged girl's weekend.

Bill was saying, "Your boss wasn't too happy, Gwen, about your taking time off on such short notice."

"She wasn't?"

"And listen, I might as well tell you this now . . . ."

"What? Tell me what?" A warning signal had sounded in my brain. Had Connie fired me? But it wasn't what I thought.

"It's my Dad. He was mad enough to have a stroke when he heard where you'd gone. We were really worried about him. And my mother said, 'I'm not going to take care of her children if she gets herself killed down there.'"

"That's a riot!" I spat out. Why was Bill picking such a time to tell me that? "Did you watch the television? Surely you could see it was perfectly safe!" And then I had calmed myself, ashamed of my outburst. After all, Bill hadn't chosen his parents. And Bill himself sounded fine, chipper, cheerful. And that was all that mattered. "Oh, well, what did you expect them to do?" I had quipped, my voice artificially cheery to hide my fatigue and my sadness. "Give me a medal?"

"Your voice sounds funny, are you all right?" Bill asked. And I thought, you'd sound funny too if you had just said goodbye forever to one of the best friends you'd ever had. I told him I had caught a cold, that was all. Soon after, we had hung up, and I had totally forgotten to ask him about John and Cass.

It was chilly in the busy lobby with the door constantly opening and closing on travelers in both directions, and I worried about John in his thin trousers and baseball jacket. I pictured the affront the three of us must be to the sensibilities of many of the restaurant's clientele passing through.

Look at that thirty-ish white woman in her black coat with fur collar and super-rosy complexion, wiping at her dripping nose with a wad of toilet paper and sitting between these two scowling and roughly clad young Negroes at one o'clock in the morning on the New Jersey Turnpike. Scandalous!

Ordinarily, I would have had to fight back the urge to laugh out loud at the image we were presenting to the outside world, but I was too wrapped up in my own physical discomfort to appreciate the humor of the situation.

My exhilaration at all that I had done and had decided to do from now on was beginning to fade, right along with the unusual flush on my cheeks and chin. The plan I had so clearly delineated in my mind on the bus was also disappearing. The new fatigue creeping over my body was bringing with it a psychological let-down as well as a growing distress in my throat and nose.

I felt light-headed. My equilibrium was off again too, from the many hours of bus riding. If I shut my eyes, I saw evergreen trees and telephone poles rushing past me in endless array. Worst of all, the garter belt into which I had been molded for the past nearly two days straight had become suddenly an iron chastity belt, threatening to cut off my breath, as well as my will.

I thought of Dorothy's pink hair-curlers that first night in the double bed in Selma. I had regarded them as instruments of torture and had congratulated myself on being above all that. I was a fine one to talk, I could see that plainly now. I was feeling thoroughly miserable. I'd have—let's see, only five hours of sleep at the most before the next busy day, a Tuesday, began. And feeling tired, and wretched from this fresh cold, I'd have to talk to the children in the morning, answer all their questions about my trip, and find out what had transpired with them during my absence.

There would be Wendi's strep throat, of course, and possibly Scotty's final choice of birthday present to hear about, and Julie would probably not let go of my neck for at least ten minutes (I'd have to allow extra time for that). And I'd have to make it a point to ask Kenny if he'd finished his research paper on the Lenni-Lenapi Indians. He'd be too proud to mention it otherwise.

Bill would want to talk to me too. Maybe all five of them would try to talk to me at one time. They sometimes did that, and I'd have to say, "Wait a minute! Let's coordinate this chorus! One, two, three, go!" And they'd all burst out laughing and realize I could listen effectively to only one of them at a time.

None of my own school work was done for tomorrow—no, today! Would Professor Orvieto want to hear that my five pages of Italian translation weren't touched because the book had been too heavy to take on a civil rights march? Connie Richardson, my boss? Well, she would have to be faced in mid-morning, right after my Italian class. And Bill had already made it clear her response to my precipitous crusade had been less than favorable.

My sister Jocie, having received the shocking news from my mother of my whereabouts, would be phoning sometime during early evening with a cryptic comment all her own. But Jim Clemson, my unsympathetic friend? He'd wait a day or two before phoning me at work to see if I were still alive, thereby registering by his silence his disapproval.

The children might in all innocence have run to the neighbors with news of my doings for the past four days. That is, unless Bill had thought to caution them not to. And my appalled and prejudiced in-laws? No; I would not think about them, there was no law that said I had to think about them, not right now . . . .

At Cass's urging, John went into the men's room to lie down on the sofa there. Cass got paper cups of hot coffee from the drinks counter for himself and me. The two of us sat facing the front doors where we could see Bill the minute he drove up in the VW van.

I sipped at my black-and-light, unable to taste it, staring at the gift shop built into the corner. It was closed now so it was impossible for me to buy nasal spray or an inhaler even if they carried them. But its display window advertised a jumble of gaudy trinkets. Stuffed animals and cheap gold medallions on chains and keepsake China plates. Junk, all junk. Worthless glitter to waste money on. I was glad it was closed. I had brought my children something you couldn't buy in a Howard Johnson. High hopes for a more just country for them to grow up in.

But it was going to be rough, all right; coming back home. There surely were not going to be any medals. *Face that, Gwennie, old girl. No medals at all.* But hadn't I asked for this? Weren't the excoriations and the blame presently to be heaped verbally upon my head the price I had to pay? In the past four short days I had broken about ten of society's unwritten rules. In the eyes of most people I knew, I had sinned. Even that One-God-At-The-Most had apparently seen fit to inflict this infectious plague, this miserable cold, upon me . . . .

Wait one minute. Fiddle-dee-dee. If Albert had been right in implying I unconsciously yearned to be punished, then how far was I going to carry this thing? If I thought I had done good, then I had. Who better to judge that than I? I, and those other eight Gwens who I had thought were gone from my daily life forever like my eight sisters. The vision I had had on the bus, half-asleep, half-awake, of all the selves I had once been, came rushing back to me. They had been well pleased, all nine of those Gwens. They thought I had done a good thing, a wonderful thing. They had been with me all along, suspended in time in my subconscious memory, and they were here now, and we had done the wonderful thing all nine of us together. *Every one I have been in the past is a part of me too.*

And it hadn't been crazy, goddammit, to do what we did. Our response to Dr, King's plea had been the logical culmination of a lifetime of being sensitized to this one big injustice, each of us Gwens at a different stage of our emotional development. The big insanity, the really ultimate insanity, I saw now, would have been for us, my bus friends and companions and fellow marchers, not to have gone. All the signposts had been pointing us toward Alabama in March of 1965 for as long as any of Gwens could remember. To have resisted those mental proddings would have been sacrilege, for a simple cockroach-worshipper like the final, grown-up Gwen had turned out to be.

To have resisted would have been to tamper with the natural forces of the universe. With Him, or Her, or It, or Whatever. To have resisted that personal call to arms would truly have been the act of a crazy person. Something like the ending in Dickens' *A Tale Of Two Cities*. *A far, far saner thing we'd done, we nine Gwens, than any we had ever done.*

His coffee finished and no sign yet of Bill or the VW, Cass decided he was ready to be sociable. And not wishing to appear rude, I went along. He told me his real name was Casimiro and he was a surgeon from Angola, in Africa, taking special training at a Philadelphia hospital. I stared at him, amazed. We had, all of us, stopped being curious about last names long ago. Last names belonged to that other world we had been long away from. For a year or so, it seemed.

Yet here he was, this dark-skinned young man with the intense manner and the impeccable, British-accented speech. In some hospital operating room not too far away from my town in South Jersey, he was known respectfully as Dr. So-and-so. Once again, I had let external appearances—in this case, the worn and casual clothing, the brooding facial expression—lead me to a wrong conclusion.

Not only that: I had presumed to inform him, a doctor, about the state of his friend John's illness! (The same way I had given my well-read rabbi a formal lesson in Unitarian religious beliefs.) Cass had been in the United States only about a year, he said, and he would be returning soon to his own country. With him had come his wife and their two little children, all of whom were waiting for him now in Philadelphia. Their stay in this country, Cass said, had truly been an eye-opener.

"There really is no United States of America, you know," the doctor tried to convince me. "Your fifty states are not in any way united. That's just a figment of all your imaginations." I knew he was referring to our country's racial situation and what had been happening in the South. His was an interesting point-of-view, even if it made little sense to a native-born American in 1965.

"I know you'd like to think that, Cass," I said. "It's difficult for a foreigner to comprehend our federal system, to know why actions aren't taken so many times, when it seems obvious to so many of us that they should be. And I don't blame you for being critical of America. I am myself, quite often." But I went on to assure him that we are as a nation united, at least we are in what we say we stand for. I told him that was the one thing that gave me hope.

"Maybe we didn't include everybody in the dream, 'way back in the beginning. Maybe a lot of Americans still don't. But progress has been made . . ."

"Progress!" Cass blurted out disdainfully.

"Yes, progress. Much too slowly, I grant you. But every once in a while a moment comes along, like this one in Selma did, and a courageous person steps forward to lead us. That is when a lot of people suddenly realize it's time to get together and give democracy another shove in the right direction."

Why was I attempting to proselytize like this, when I felt so lousy? When I knew it would do no good? When half the time in moments of doubt, I didn't believe these things I was saying myself?

As if he read my mind, Cass was nodding his head in agreement. "It's not democracy that's at fault," he said. "It's the white race. It's made all this mess." With that, he looked straight into my eyes, his own filled with something like pity. "How can you bear to belong to it? Feeling the way you do?"

I could tell him I had indeed been ashamed of that fact once or twice. I could tell him how "bleached" and faded-out I had sometimes felt among those rich brown skin tones in Selma, Alabama. How filled with rancor I had been at sight of that lovely brick home on the Jefferson Davis Highway, its ugly white occupants holding the nasty sign out front, teaching their children to be bigots. But I wasn't going to let this young man win that easily.

"Somehow I always assumed people were pretty much the same, regardless of color. You, a doctor, would know better than I about that, I should think."

"I'm not going to sit here and argue with you," Cass said, shrugging. "What does it matter anyway? I spent the first part of my life loving the white race as hard as I could, but it didn't change anything. And then I spent years hating the white race as hard as I could, and that was no help either. And then one day I realized love and hate really have nothing to do with it. It's simply a matter of justice and dignity," he wound up.

I could buy that, I told him. That one thing he and I could definitely agree upon, if not much else. But there would be no point in my trying to explain that to other people who didn't share my basis for comprehension, I said to Cass. How could you hope to explain sanity to an insane world; much less concepts like justice and dignity to folks who believed those commodities were reserved, like those restroom signs I had seen ten years ago in South Carolina, 'for whites only." It would be as futile as trying to tell an Eskimo living at the North Pole about the warmth and loveliness of Florida.

We won't even try, will we, you eight girls from my past? We'll just play dumb. And you, Gwen-number-nine, you'll smile your inscrutable smile and never let them know if they are getting to us.

I now felt certain that I too was running a fever. Maybe I'd dare to put off going back to work for another day. Cass was sulking, his back turned to me. I certainly wasn't going to ask *him,* doctor or no doctor, to feel *my* head!

I would keep a secret account over the next days and weeks of what everyone said to me about my going to Selma. I'd collect the best ones in here, in my precious blue notebook. And someday when I had become a little gray-haired old lady in a wheelchair, with only a cat for company, I'd call each of those people up, wherever in the world they were, and I'd say, "Yah, yah, I told you so!"

History would vindicate me—us. I had no doubt of that.

And I wasn't going to let anyone make me feel guilty, either. Not about this one big happening, at least; not any more. I had only myself to answer to, remember? Only to the tribunal of my own mind. To all those past Gwens but to no one else, no sirree! And this time we had taken a vote and we had chosen to have no guilt complex at all.

"It's about time!" and here came my Scarlett O'Hara wraith again, up from the depths of my congested chest, shaking her imaginary fist to the imaginary sky, swearing that I was never going to feel guilty again. I was going to *be,* not just do. It would be mind over matter.

Easy to say, jeered my normal little inside voice. *But you'll never get away with it. Wait until you turn the last page of this adventure! And even if you succeed in pulling it off this time, I will make you feel guilty about not feeling guilty! Did you ever think of that?*

How you do go on, Rhett Butler! And Scarlett made me get up from the bench and go inside the ladies' room for more toilet paper to wipe off my drippy nose, and while we were in there she said I might as well get out of that ridiculous garter belt and be comfortable. So I did, stuffing it and the two nylon stockings into my shoulder bag beside the blue notebook and my toothbrush and what passed for make-up, and the wallet that still contained $16.32 of our advance grocery money.

I told myself I had made a splendid head start on getting ready for bed. Tying up my shoelaces once more, I went to rejoin Cass and my other belongings in the lobby. My nose, at least for the moment, was clear enough to breathe through, and my thighs and stomach and legs now felt cool and, unencumbered.

"When will they realize . . . ?" It was my rabbi's voice in my ears, this time. *"When will they realize we have also been trying to free all of us from ourselves?"*

Maybe that was the principle thing that had happened to me, while I had been away. Maybe the really important reward of my journey of two thousand miles was that I had somehow acquired the impetus to live my life as I saw fit, with a clear conscience. Maybe, in my miniscule efforts to free those others, I had managed somewhere along the road to free myself.

You . . . just . . . wait! Wait until your mother-in-law confronts you with that insipid little smile of hers and says, "Didn't you think about your children and your husband, before you did a dangerous thing like that?" And wait until your father-in-law makes a point of turning down his hearing aid in front of you so he doesn't have to listen to anything you have to say at all. And speaking of realizing, don't you realize, you sanctimonious fool . . . . It was my little inside voice again, not quite ready yet to stop scolding me and shut up for the night. *Don't you realize that you will never again be considered a respectable woman?*

What do I care about that? shouted dumb-mute Scarlett O'Hara by way of a loud sneeze. The noise made sullen Dr.Cass, slumped on the padded bench beside me, jump in pained surprise. And another sneeze, right after the first, and yet again. *What do I care about that, as long as I know that I'm the sane one!*

And then my husband Bill Gain was there to pick us up. Turning to look through the glass window behind us, we saw the red VW van pull up to the front entrance of the Howard Johnson. Cass got John from the men's room and led him to the bench where I was waiting. I slung my shoulder bag over my right shoulder.

And then, when I went to put the knapsack strap over my left shoulder and pick up the sleeping bag, Cass said, with a smile of gratitude, "Let me," and took them from my hands to carry them out for me. It was his way of apologizing, I knew, for the mean things he had said to me about America, and about white people in general. We stood up as straight and tall as we could and went out of the Howard Johnson like the Three Musketeers, I slogging along in the middle between the two young black men.

Bill was relieved and amorously happy to see me. He was full of little stories about our children, so that neither I nor the two men in the back seat had to talk much. And we were driving Cass and John all the way to their homes in North Philadelphia instead of dropping them off at the bus stop in Camden. And I was too weary and too feverish to care anymore what anyone thought, or to ponder further what it was going to be like, coming back.

*   *   *

END OF PART TEN

THE END

EPILOGUE

From THE PHILADELPHIA INQUIRER, Saturday Morning, March 27, 1965:

FOUR KLANSMEN HELD IN AMBUSH KILLING
$50,000 Bail Each Set For Suspects In Slaying Of Woman

Lowndesboro, Ala., March 26 (AP).—'FBI agents arrested four Ku Klux Klansmen from the Birmingham area Friday on charges of conspiracy in the highway ambush slaying of a vivacious [white] civil rights worker near Big Swamp on Highway 8O.

President Johnson announced the arrests in Washington and immediately declared he was stepping up his personal war against the Klan.

The four Klan members were charged under a Federal statute with violating the civil rights of Mrs. Viola Gregg Liuzzo, 39 from Detroit, wife of a union official and mother of five. She was shot in the head as she drove along a dark, lonely stretch of U.S. 80 between Montgomery and Selma, Ala., on Thursday night [March 25th].

The President said he was calling for special legislation to root out the Klan, which he termed "a society of hooded bigots."

The announcement of the arrests came 16-1/2 hours after Mrs. Liuzzo, who grew up in the South, slumped over dead while returning to Montgomery after ferrying a group of civil rights marchers back to Selma. She was en route to the state capital to pick up another group. In the car with Mrs. Liuzzo, who was singing a civil rights song at the time of her death, was an as-yet-unidentified 19-year-old black youth, a resident of Selma. By pretending to play dead the youth was able to fool the attackers, and once they had left the scene he quickly flagged down a passing car for help.

GWEN SIMON GAIN

Arrested were Eugene Thomas, 43, and William Orville Eaton, 41, both of Bessemer; Gary Thomas Rowe, 31, of Birmingham, and Collie Leroy Wilkins, Jr., 21, of Fairfield, Ala.

Bond for Thomas, Baton and Wilkins was fixed at $50,000 each at a brief hearing before U. S. Commissioner Louise O. Carlton at Birmingham. The three remained in jail. Authorities there said they did not know where Rowe is being held.*

Acting on direct orders from the President, scores of FBI agents plunged into the investigation that led to the arrests. The agents were in the Selma-Montgomery area because of racial troubles stemming from a Negro voter drive.

The charges against the four—conspiracy to violate the civil rights of the slain woman—are the same charges under an 1870 law that have failed to stand up in two other widely publicized cases, the nightrider slaying of Washington educator and Army officer Lemuel Penn in north Georgia last July, and the slaying of three civil rights workers in Mississippi last June.

*Author's Note: Gary Thomas Rowe was later revealed to be an informer for the FBI and was chief prosecution witness at the trials that followed the murder of Mrs. Liuzzo.

*   *   *

George Washington Carver Homes, Selma, Alabama
March 28, 1965

Dear Mrs. Gain, (Adelaide had got it right, she really had!)
    It was so nice to hear from you, and I must say that I didn't have very much to offer you, but the little bit that I did, please do not think of that. This has been the best part of my life. I only regret one thing, I couldn't have done more for you than I did. You was so sweet, and the children has talked about you ever since you left. So I can see that you played a big part in my home as well as you played in the Movement.
    I must say that I miss you so very much and I do hope that if you ever come to Selma again please come to me. My doors and my heart is open to you and the rest. Even if some of your

friends should decide to come, please send them to me. They are welcome from the bottom of my heart.

Oh, by the way, I went to Montgomery for the big show [last Thursday]. And you wouldn't believe when I say I came barefoot—because the mud tore up my shoes! But that isn't going to stop me. I guess I will get the chance to go and get me some shoes (smile).

I guess you have seen and heard of what happened since you left. It really has upset all us here, and the most of all, the boy who was in the car with her lives almost in my back door, and we don't know where or what happened to him. But all we can do is hope and pray that we shall overcome some day.

I would like to ask this of you as you know we can't buy any clothes. If there is some used clothes that you can get if you will let me know you can send C.O.D. and I will pay the cost. I have some [children] barefoot, and some of the other colored people here too. This will be a big thing for us.

Give to your family my family's love and please come to Selma again but come to me.

Very truly yours,
Adelaide

*   *   *

October 23, 1965
The Editor
Philadelphia Evening Bulletin
Philadelphia, Pennsylvania

Dear Sir:

White Alabama has spoken out for Collie Leroy Wilkins. I would speak for Mrs. Viola Liuzzo, the victim of his ignoble act. I feel well qualified to do this. I too was in Selma, Alabama, last March. I too rode over that lonely fifty-four-mile stretch of highway where they permit American citizens to be murdered with impunity.

"I, too, am a mother. I have four young children, and I went to Selma as much for them as for anyone. My husband

and I are white Anglo-Saxon Protestants; members of a Human Relations Conference in the county where we live, and therefore familiar with some of the awesome problems that face Negroes in Northern communities.

"To the twelve Southern jurymen whose own peculiar sense of duty compelled them to give Collie Leroy Wilkins back to the world, I would say: "We people who work for human rights do not regard you as inferior, except in your behavior. We know your attitudes were instilled in you when you were too young to grasp what equality was all about, and that you learned your lessons well. With the fact of this we can sympathize, for we too learned lessons while very young, and learned them thoroughly. We learned them every time we saluted our flag, sang our national anthem, read our Declaration of Independence. We learned them when we went to school with children of all shades and religious persuasions and considered those children equals.

"Had you jurymen served justice in Lowndes County this time, we would have been tempted to say, Perhaps those people down there are capable of managing their own affairs, after all. You have shown us you are not. So for every Viola Liuzzo, Medgar Evers, James Reeb and Jimmie Lee Jackson you encourage your fellows to kill, ten of us will rise to take their places. And not just in the picket lines and demonstrations, but in the courts and schools of law, the churches, the universities, the legislatures, the private homes of future Presidents—anywhere there are United States citizens who eschew violence but believe in liberty and justice for all.

"I would speak thus for Viola Liuzzo, my sister marcher in Selma, as I feel certain she would have spoken for me."

Sincerely yours,
Gwen S. Gain
Merchantville, New Jersey

"That broad who got killed down there—she had it coming to her."

—Anonymous male phone caller
(Post-Selma comment from one of the folks back home)

UPDATE

**"What men believe is a function of what they are. And what
they are is, in part, what has happened to them."**
**—William Golding, author,
and writer for Holiday magazine**

The Voting Rights Bill was passed by Congress soon after the Selma March and signed into law by President Johnson on August 7, 1965, five months after the successful first-day-of-spring March on Montgomery. The Act provided for the monitoring by special agents from the federal Justice Department of the registration and voting practices of ten Southern states.

Viola Liuzzo's murder was never properly avenged, because the four KKK members who were responsible for it were never convicted in a state court. They were, however, found guilty in a suit brought by the federal government, which charged them with the crime of violating Mrs. Liuzzo's civil rights. Three were sent to prison for terms of ( ) years. The fourth man, Gary Thomas Rowe, turned out to be a government informer against the Klan. As for me, I turned out to be quite naïve in my opinion that "no one would want to shoot a white woman."

Dr. Martin Luther King, Jr. was assassinated on April 4, 1968, shot to death on the balcony of the Lorraine Motel in Memphis, Tennessee. Rioting broke out that same evening in many cities across the United States, as angry Negroes vented their rage. The likes of this brave and dedicated man has never been seen again, though many have tried to fill his shoes.

For the two years after the Selma march, I attended the University of Pennsylvania as a full-time student, graduating in May of 1967 with a major in American Civilization and a minor in Black Studies. That fall, on the first Monday in October, I began a paid staff job as Fair Housing Field Representative for Southern New Jersey. (My employment began the first Monday of October, 1967,the same day that Thurgood Marshall, the first Negro ever to be appointed to the Supreme Court of the United States, began his Associate Justice term for life.)

I held that position for the next four years, working with a small group of volunteers, both blacks and whites. Together we were able to break down many barriers of housing discrimination in South Jersey. Among our successes: We were instrumental in having the first real estate license revoked in the nation. We got the first financial award for emotional pain and suffering on the part of a victim. And we were successful in bringing about the opening of a branch office in Camden of the New Jersey Division On Civil Rights.

Rabbi Albert Friedlander and his family did indeed move to England, where he became a Jewish Chaplain at Westminster Synagogue in London. He and I corresponded several times over the years and then fell out of touch. He had his publisher send me two of his books, however. The one we discussed with each other on the bus ride home from Selma was entitled *Never Trust A God Over Thirty.* It was a compilation of essays by several educators and philosophers, postulating as to what the role of chaplains should be in dealing with activist students at American universities. Rabbi Friedlander died in England in the spring of 2005, fifty years after our glorious walk together in Alabama.

Emotionally drained by national and international events occurring in 1968 and 1969, and weary of pretending all was well at home, I left my husband Bill Gain in the summer of 1970, taking ten-year-old Julie to live with me. I married again in 1981 to Robert Smith, a college budget administrator. With Jim Crow laws long gone from the South, and with warm weather and year-round ocean sailing beckoning, Bob and I moved to Florida in 1978, where we both worked at the University of Miami. After retirement we moved to the Orlando area. My husband died in 1999, leaving me widowed and once again into writing.

Since the changes instigated by the passage of the Voting Rights Act of 1965, many blacks have found visible places in every area of American society, including that of President of the United States. Martin Luther King's birthday of January 15 is now celebrated as a national holiday in every state. And I have lived long enough to hear America's "Negroes" now customarily referred to as "African-Americans," a title which I greatly cherish and admire.

*   *   *